でる順
パス単

文部科学省後援
英検 1 級

旺文社

英検とは

　文部科学省後援　実用英語技能検定（通称：英検）は，1963年に第1回試験が実施されて以来，社会教育的な役割という発足当初からの目的と日本社会の国際化が進展するに伴い，英語の四技能「読む・聞く・話す・書く」を総合的に測定する全国規模の試験としてその社会的評価はますます高まっております。

　2011年7月，文部科学省が発表した「国際共通語としての英語力向上のための5つの提言と具体的施策」の中では，中学卒業段階での英語力を英検3級程度以上，高校卒業段階で準2級から2級程度以上を目標とすると明言しており，指導する英語教師も準1級程度以上の英語力を要すると謳っております。

　このように英検の資格はいつの時代も日本人の英語力を測るスケールとして活用されており，大学入試や高校入試での優遇や英語科目の単位として認定する学校が年々増えております。

　また，海外においても英検資格が認知され始め，現在，アメリカやオーストラリアなど多くの大学で留学要件として認められております。

　受験者の皆さんは自己の英語能力の評価基準として，また国際化時代を生きる"国際人"たり得る資格として，さらには生涯学習の目標として大いに英検にチャレンジしてください。

試験概要

(1) 実施機関
　　試験を実施しているのは，公益財団法人　日本英語検定協会です。ホームページ http://www.eiken.or.jp/ では，試験に関する情報・優遇校一覧などを公開しています。

(2) 試験日程
　　試験は年3回行われます（二次試験は3級以上）。
　　第1回検定：一次試験 ― 6月／二次試験 ― 7月
　　第2回検定：一次試験 ― 10月／二次試験 ― 11月
　　第3回検定：一次試験 ― 1月／二次試験 ― 2月

はじめに

本書は英検合格を目指す皆さんが,「出題される可能性の高い単語を,効率よく覚えられる」ような単語集として,1998年に誕生した「英検Pass単熟語」の4訂版です。

今回の改訂では,以下の3つが本書の特長になります。

> ### 3つの特長
>
> #### ❶「でる順」で効果的に覚えられる!
> 過去5年間の最新の英検問題の分析に基づき,よく出題される見出し語を「でる順」に掲載しました。
>
> #### ❷ すべての見出し語に例文つき!
> それぞれの見出し語はすべて例文つきなので,それにより,例文の中で意味をイメージし,効果的に暗記することができます。また,同意語・類義語,英英定義,用例なども多く掲載されています。
>
> #### ❸ 単語暗記のサポートつき!
> 「難しい単語はなかなか覚えられない」「効果的に単語を覚える方法は?」といった皆さんの不安を解消するために,英検1級の指導者,合格者の方から単語学習法についてお話をうかがいました。本書を始める前に読んで,参考にしましょう。

本書での単語学習が皆さんの英検合格につながることを心より願っています。

最後に,本書の刊行にあたり多大なご協力をいただきました,日米英語学院講師 柴山かつの先生,早稲田大学教授 Adrian Pinnington先生に深く感謝の意を表します。

もくじ

本書の利用法 …………………………… 6
音声ダウンロードについて ……………… 8

教えて！ みんなの単語学習法 ……… 9

単語編

でる度 Ⓐ よくでる重要単語

動詞 ……………………………………… 26
名詞 ……………………………………… 74
形容詞・副詞 …………………………… 122
1分間 mini test ………………………… 168

でる度 Ⓑ 覚えておきたい単語

動詞 ……………………………………… 172
名詞 ……………………………………… 216
形容詞・副詞 …………………………… 268
1分間 mini test ………………………… 314

でる度 Ⓒ 力を伸ばす単語

動詞 ……………………………………… 318
名詞 ……………………………………… 362
形容詞・副詞 …………………………… 412
1分間 mini test ………………………… 460

熟語編

熟語300 ……………………………… 464

さくいん ……………………………… 507

でちゃうくん
でちゃうくんは、「でる順」をコンセプトとする問題集に登場する旺文社のキャラクターです。
本書の中でも、形がさまざまに変化していきます。『英検でる順合格問題集』(2011年刊行) で誕生しました。

編集：九内麻妃, 山田弘美
編集協力：株式会社シー・レップス, 有限会社ファイアウィード 成澤恒人,
　　　　　Sarah Matsumoto, 金子典子
本文デザイン：伊藤幸恵　　イラスト：三木謙次
装丁デザイン：及川真咲デザイン事務所 (浅海新菜)
録音：有限会社スタジオ ユニバーサル
ナレーション：Greg Dale, 瀬乃加奈子

本書の利用法

単語編

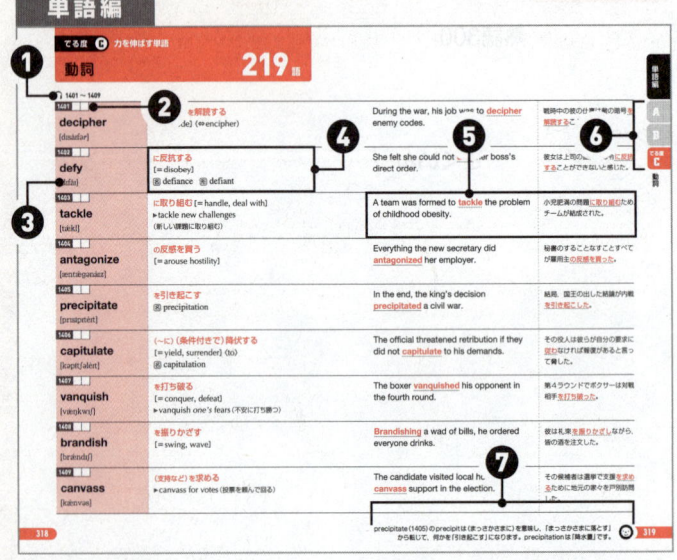

❶ **音声ダウンロードファイル**：表示の見出し語番号が1つのファイルになっています。（詳しい内容はp.8を参照してください）

❷ **チェック欄**：チェックして繰り返し学習しましょう。

❸ **発音記号**：発音記号は原則として『オーレックス英和辞典』（旺文社）に準拠しています。

❹ **語義その他**：見出し語の語義のほかに，同意語・類義語や英英定義（＝），反意語（⇔），派生語，用例（▶）などを掲載しています。（動詞の訳に「を」「に」などがあれば他動詞，なければ自動詞です）

❺ **例文と訳**：見出し語を使った例文とその訳です。

❻ **でる度**：英検問題のデータ分析に基づき「でる度A, B, C」のランクに分けて掲載しています。

❼ **でちゃうくん**：でちゃうくんが見出し語のちょっとした豆知識を教えてくれます。

本書は，英検1級に出題されやすい単語や熟語などを短期間で効率的に学べるように構成されています。このページで使い方を確認してから，学習を進めましょう。

本書についている赤セルシートをページの上に載せると，赤で印刷されている部分が隠れるので，覚えるのに効果的です。

熟語編

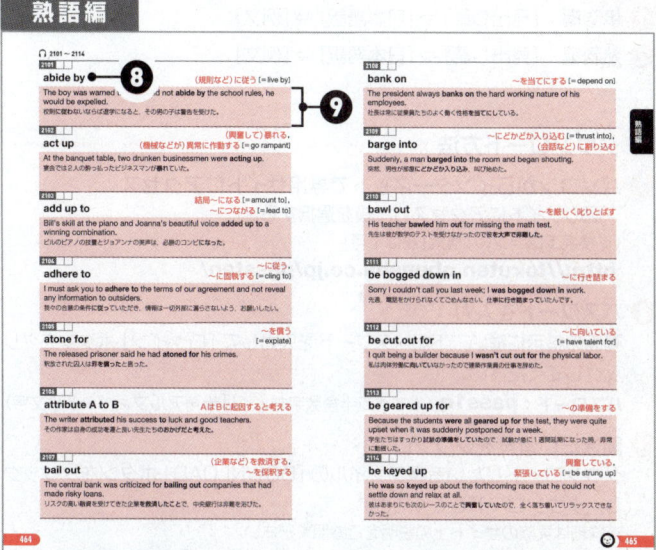

❽ 熟語：英検1級の短文語句空所補充問題でよく出題されるものを取り上げています。

❾ 例文：用法を理解できるように，すべての見出しの熟語に例文を掲載しています。

表記について

- 動 動詞　　名 名詞　　形 形容詞　　副 副詞
- ＝ 同意語・類義語や英英定義　　⇔ 反意語　　cf. 関連語
- ▶ 用例（見出し語に関連した用例）　　語源 見出し語に関する語源情報

音声ダウンロードについて

本書に掲載されている単語編・熟語編の以下の音声が無料でダウンロードできます。

🎧 内容

① 単語編：[見出し語] ⇒ [日本語訳] ⇒ [例文]
② 熟語編：[見出し語] ⇒ [日本語訳] ⇒ [例文]

🎧 ダウンロード方法

① **パソコンからインターネットで専用サイトにアクセス**
下記のサイトにアクセスし，級を選択する。
（※検索エンジンの「検索」欄は不可）
http://tokuten.obunsha.co.jp/passtan/

② **パスワードを入力**
画面の指示に従い，下記パスワードを入力して「ログイン」ボタンをクリックしてください。
パスワード：pass1q（※すべて半角数字もしくは半角アルファベット小文字）

③ **聞きたい音声をダウンロード**
ダウンロードしたい音声ファイルの「DOWNLOAD」ボタンをクリックし，ダウンロードしてください。
※詳細は実際のサイト上の説明をご参照ください。

④ **ファイルを解凍して，オーディオプレーヤーで再生**
音声ファイルはZIP形式にまとめられた形でダウンロードされます。解凍後，デジタルオーディオプレーヤーなどでご活用ください。
※デジタルオーディオプレーヤーへの音声ファイル転送方法は，各製品の取扱説明書やヘルプをご参照ください。

[注意]
- 音声はMP3ファイル形式となっています。音声の再生にはMP3を再生できる機器などが別途必要です。
- ご使用機器，音声再生ソフト等に関する技術的なご質問は，ハードメーカーもしくはソフトメーカーにお願いいたします。
- 本サービスは予告なく終了されることがあります。

教えて！ みんなの単語学習法

単語暗記のコツ，教えます！ 土屋雅稔 …… 10

1級合格者が教える！ 私の単語学習法 …… 18

1級対策指導者，1級合格者による単語学習法をまとめました。合格につながる語彙力がつくような，自分に合った効果的な学習法を探しましょう。

単語暗記のコツ，教えます！　土屋雅稔

英検1級を受験する上で語彙力に不安を感じている方も多いでしょう。長年多くの英検1級受験者の指導にあたり，また英語学習法に関する著書もおありの土屋雅稔先生に，英検1級の単語の特徴や学習法をうかがいました。

話したり書いたりするためではなく，読んだり聞いたりする時に大事な単語

英検1級の単語は，「ネイティブでも知らない難解な単語だ」という印象を持つ人が多いようです。そして，「そんな難しい単語は覚えても仕方がない」と感じて，学習意欲がわかない人も多いようです。

本書の読者の中にも，上記のように感じている人はいるのではないでしょうか？

しかし，英検1級の単語は，話したり書いたりする時に無理して使う必要はありませんが，**読んだり聞いたりといったインプットでは，頻繁に出会う単語**です。

このようなことは「百聞は一見にしかず」のような一面があります。実際に，『道は開ける』などのペーパーバックの一節の中でも，『英検1級 でる順パス単』の単語が当たり前のように使われているのがわかります。

『道は開ける』（*How to Stop Worrying and Start Living*）デール・カーネギー著　冒頭の一段落
―本書に掲載された単語　infested, scatter

『ハリー・ポッターと賢者の石』（*Harry Potter and the Philosopher's Stone*）J.K.ローリング著　冒頭の4ページ
―本書に掲載された単語　tantrum, huddle

『海辺のカフカ』（*Kafka on the Shore*）Philip Gabriel訳　冒頭の4ページ
―本書に掲載された単語　sluggish, scatter, ominous

『無実』（*The Innocent Man*）ジョン・グリシャム著　冒頭の4ページ

―本書に掲載された単語　corrode, cramp, faculty, stigma, affiliation, ordinance, periphery

英検1級の単語が冒頭から当たり前のように使われていることがわかると思います。英検1級の単語を学習していて、「こんな単語は見たことも聞いたこともないし、ネイティブも知らないのではないか？」と感じたら、その単語を Google で検索してみるのもよいでしょう。たいていの単語が数千万以上ものヒット数になりますから、「現実に使われているんだ」ということが実感できて、覚える意欲も高まるでしょう。

覚えにくい理由

英検1級の単語は、当たり前のように使われている単語だと言いましたが、そうはいっても私たち日本人が覚えるのは簡単なことではありません。例えば、次のような困難が予想されます。

- 新しい単語を覚える時に、似たような単語が既に頭にあるので、混同しやすく、暗記の負荷が高くなる。例えば、complement を覚えるにあたって、似たような compliment が既に頭にあるので、混同しやすくなる。
- 基本単語の時は有効だった覚え方（例文や語源や多読や音声の活用）が、語彙レベルが高くなると、有効ではないケースも出てくる。
- 英検1級の単語は覚えた後で、基本単語よりは出会う回数が少ないため、定期的な復習をしないと忘れてしまう。
- 覚えた単語が増えてくるにつれて、復習の負荷も高くなってくる。例えば復習して間違えた単語にマーキングしているうちに、ページ全体がマーキングだらけになってしまい、どの単語をマーキングしたのかわからなくなってしまう。

これらの対策については、次ページ以降で説明します。

📕 覚え方の基本

覚え方は，自分に適した方法を試行錯誤して見つけるのがいいと思いますが，参考までに，私の方法を紹介しておきます。

私は単語暗記を，**下準備，暗記，復習の3ステップ**に分けています。これは当たり前のことのはずなのですが，実際にはどれかを欠いたまま「自分は単語が覚えられない」と嘆いている人が多いものです。

❶ 下準備

未知の単語をピックアップする作業です。**単語集を先頭ページからチェックして，知らない単語にマーキング**します。未知の単語のピックアップが目的ですから，さっさと済ませてしまいましょう。数日で終わるはずです。

❷ 暗記

マーキングした単語を意識的に覚えていく作業です。この作業を省いたまま「覚えられない」と嘆く人が多いのですが，それでは覚えられないのは当然ですね。

簡単な基本単語であれば，未知語のマーキングや，単語集の音源を通勤時に聞き流すといったような，本来は下準備にすぎない作業だけでも，そこそこ覚えられることもあります。しかし，1級単語のような難しい単語になれば，下準備だけでは覚えるのは無理です。そこで，意識的に暗記する作業が必要になるのです。

覚え方はシンプルです。**英単語と訳語を「scatter 散り散りになる，scatter 散り散りになる」のように数回暗唱したあと，訳語を隠し，意味を思い出せるかチェックする**だけです。これの繰り返しです。

このような覚え方は非効率的・非人間的と頭ごなしに否定する人もいると思いますが，実際に試してみれば，それほど大変ではないことに気付くと思います。中には相性のよい単語もあって，数回の暗唱だけで覚えられるものもあるのです。暗唱するだけで覚えられる単語が存在するのですから，それらは時間をかけずに覚えてしまう方が合理的なのです。

一方で何回繰り返して暗唱しても覚えられない，相性の悪い単語もあります。そういう単語を覚える段階になって初めて，語源や例文や音声など，さまざまな手段を併用して覚えていけばいいのです。

　理想論にとらわれる人が多いようなので，繰り返し強調しておきますが，機械的な暗記で覚えられる単語は，機械的に覚えてしまうにこしたことはありません。その方が時間がかからないからです。機械的な暗記では覚えきれない相性の悪い単語のみ，時間のかかるほかの手段を併用していくのが，効率的と言えます。

　「機械的な暗記では，実際に使えない」と心配する人もいるかもしれませんが，1級の単語は，発信で使うのではなく，受信で使うのが目的です。まずはリーディングで意味がわかることが最優先です。余裕があれば，リスニングでも役立つように発音を覚えれば，当面の目標として十分でしょう。

❸ 復習

　復習の手順は，上記の暗記とほぼ同じです。**マーキングしてある単語を覚えているかチェック**していくだけです。忘れていたら，再度マーキングして暗唱を繰り返していきます。

　1級の単語は，覚えてしまった後であれば，多読をしていれば普通に出会う単語です。ただ，「普通に出会う」とはいえ，基本単語ほどには頻繁には出会いませんから，意識的に復習していないと忘れてしまいます。復習しないまま「覚えてもすぐに忘れてしまう！」と嘆く人も多いのですが，これも当たり前のことですね。

　以上が，私の考える単語の覚え方の基本手順です。

1級単語ならではの注意点

「1級を目指すからには，単に意味だけ覚えて満足するのではなく，細かい用法やニュアンスや副次的な意味までマスターするべきだ」のような理想論にとらわれる人が出てきます。しかしこれは，受験して合格した後，余裕がある人がやればいいでしょう。本書の読者の大半は，まずは英検1級に合格することが当面の目標のはずです。まずは，できることからやりましょう。初期の段階では，単語は，その代表的な意味を覚えていれば十分です。

過去問を見れば明らかですが，微妙なニュアンスの違いで正解を選ぶような問題は出題されません。どの問題にしても，選択肢は，意味が大幅に異なるのです。つまり，意味で正解を選ぶということです。したがって，**微妙なニュアンスの違いなど，当面は意識する必要がない**ということです。現実的な対応をしましょう。

技術的なヒント（復習とヒストリー機能のすすめ）

暗記が苦手だと感じている人は，新しく単語を覚えるよりも，覚えた単語の復習を優先するといいでしょう。例えば今まで1日のノルマが「5ページ新しく覚えて，5ページ復習する」だったら，これからは「2ページ新しく覚えて，8ページ復習する」のように変更してみるのです。負荷が軽いというのが直接の理由ですが，間接的な理由として，負荷が軽いのでスキマ時間にもマメに復習しやすく，単語学習を習慣化しやすくなることが挙げられます。

ただし，復習の方が負荷が軽いとはいっても，誰にでも覚えにくい相性の悪い単語はあるものです。そして復習を繰り返していると，何度も間違えてマーキングすることになるので，ページ全体が徐々にマーキングだらけになってしまい，見づらくなってきます。そこで人によっては，別途に単語カードやノートを作成したりとさまざまな工夫をするのですが，ただでさえ単語を覚えるのに時間がかかっているのに，別途でカードやノートを作成していては，時間がいくらあっても足りません。そこで私は，**電子**

辞書の「ヒストリー機能」を活用することをおすすめします。

　電子辞書の「ヒストリー機能」というのは、メーカーによっては「履歴機能」とも呼んでいます。携帯電話の履歴機能のように、一度引いた単語の履歴が表示される機能です。使い勝手は、電子版の単語カードといったイメージです。紙の単語カードと比較して、以下のようなメリットがあります。

- 自動的に作成されるので手間がかからない
- 単語の並べ替えが簡単
- 写し間違いが皆無
- 例文も語源も発音記号も参照可能
- 携帯性が抜群

　特に「自動的に作成される」というのが最大のメリットです。相性の悪い単語に出会ったら、その単語を電子辞書で引くだけなのです。それだけで電子辞書に"自家製の単語カード"が作成されています。お使いの電子辞書の「ヒストリーボタン」を押してみれば、使い方はすぐにマスターできると思います。関心のある方は、拙著『中上級者がぶつかる壁を破る英語学習最強プログラム』(ベレ出版)を参照してください。

📖 精神論的なヒント（思いこみを捨てることと，甘えを捨てること）

単語学習には，さまざまな「〜するべき」といった意見があります。

「例文で覚えるべきだ」

「コロケーションで覚えるべきだ」

「語源で覚えるべきだ」

「書いて覚えるべきだ」

「耳から覚えるべきだ」

しかし例文やコロケーションごと覚えようとすれば，暗記する量が増えますから負荷が高くなります。それに，もし発信に使うのであれば例文やコロケーションごと覚えるのは効果的ですが，1級の単語は，発信ではなく受信で使えるようになるのが目標です。

語源で覚えようとしても，すべての単語に覚えやすい語源があるわけではありません。

書いて覚えようとすると，時間がかかるのはもちろん，いつでもどこでも気軽に学習できなくなります。

耳から覚えようとしても，英語の音を正確に識別できていない段階では無理があります。たとえば/s/と/th/が聞き分けできない人は，sinとthinを聴いて覚えようとしても無理があるでしょう。

要は，どんな覚え方であれ，絶対的に正しいというものはなく，一長一短があるのです。

前ページでも説明しましたが，**単語は機械的に覚えられるものは覚えてしまい，それでも覚えにくい相性の悪い単語に限定して，前述のような方法を併用するのがよい**のです。本書のような羅列型の単語集も，食わず嫌いする人もいるかと思いますが，最初の機械的に覚えてしまう段階では，シンプルに暗唱して覚えていくための手段として，とても優れているのです。

さまざまな「〜するべき」だという理想論にとらわれている人は，それで首尾よく学習できていれば問題ないのですが，もし壁に当たっている場合は，そのような思いこみを捨ててみるのもよいと思います。

もう1つ、私が捨てた方がよいと思うものに、甘えの姿勢があります。例えば、単語集によって「覚えさせてもらう」ことを期待していて、「こちらから覚えよう」という姿勢に欠ける人です。このような人たちは、単語集を漠然と眺めたり、付属音声を聴いたりといった、負荷の軽い下準備ばかりして、暗記の作業を省略しがちです。

また、「1級にチャレンジするのだから、これまでの準1級や2級よりは、負荷が高くなる」という当たり前のことを認識しないまま、今までと同じ心づもりでいる人も要注意です。たとえてみれば、今まで近所のハイキングを楽しんでいた人が、富士山にチャレンジしようという時に、今までと同じ心づもりでいるようなものです。挫折するのは目に見えています。

逆にいうと、**英検1級の単語は、「負荷が高くなる」ということを覚悟していれば、意外とアッサリ克服できることも多い**のです。再び富士山にたとえるならば、しっかり覚悟をきめて準備しておけば、誰でも登れる山だというのに似ていると思います。

皆さんが英検1級という登山に成功されることを願っています。

土屋雅稔（つちや　まさとし）
千葉県船橋市で「エクセレンスイングリッシュスクール」を主宰。英検1級、TOEIC990、国連英検特A級合格。30歳で英語学習を開始し、34歳から英検などの資格試験指導を始める。著書に『〈具体的・効率的〉英語学習最強プログラム』『中上級者がぶつかる壁を破る英語学習最強プログラム』『今度こそ必ずモノにする英語習得プランニングノート』（ベレ出版）などがある。

1級合格者が教える！ 私の単語学習法

それでは，今度は英検1級に合格した人たちが，実際にどのように単語学習を進めてきたのかをさぐってみましょう。3人の方にお話をうかがいました。単語の学習法，暗記法は人それぞれです。ほかの人がどのような方法で暗記しているかを知り，あなた自身に合った一番効果的な方法を見つけましょう！

Sさん　30代，会社員

英検1級合格までの対策学習期間と受験回数は？

対策期間：24か月
受験回数：6回

書店で見てPass単熟語を購入。購入の決め手は，持ち運びに便利なサイズで通勤時に勉強しやすそう，また赤シートがついていることでした。試験には5回落ちていますが，1回目に落ちた直後に購入しました。

そのほかの英語学習の状況についてお聞かせください。

英検の試験対策の問題集を購入し，問題を解くことはもちろんですが，それと同時にさまざまなことを実践していました。例えば，NHKの語学ラジオ番組（「入門ビジネス英語」と「実践ビジネス英語」）は毎日録音して最低1回，時間があれば4回ほど繰り返し聞いていました。ただ聞き流すだけでなく，テープを止めて何度も音読もしました。また，週1回英会話教室に通うことで「英語を話す」アウトプットも欠かしませんでした。

その他，毎日出勤前にBBCのニュース番組も欠かさずチェックするようにしました。朝出かける準備をしながらですので，そんなに集中して聞けませんでしたが。常に英語に触れ，英語を話す，また英語で情報を聞き取るという習慣を生活の中で実践する工夫をしていたと思います。

Pass単熟語を使ってどのように勉強しましたか？

　平日は毎日通勤の電車の中と寝る前に勉強。週末には自宅でじっくり時間をかけて暗記しました。

●平日（通勤時・寝る前）

　朝の通勤時に，プラットホームで電車を待つ時間，電車に乗る時間（合計片道15分程度）で，始めは1ページ目から順番に読んでいましたが，しだいにその日パッと開けたページから読むようになりました。大体片道で2, 3ページぐらいです。寝る前はベッドの中で何か読まないと眠れないので「どうせ何か読むなら勉強になるものを」と思い，Pass単熟語を読んだり，その日の気分で参考書や好きな海外アーティストのブログをプリントアウトしたものなどを読んでいました（10～30分程度）。

●週末（自宅で）

　まず，赤シートを使って単語の意味がわかるかチェックしていきます。覚えていない単語には印をつけます。何度も繰り返し，印がたくさんついた単語については，その例文を3, 4回ずつ音読したり，さらにその単語を含む例文を作ったりしました。私は，1次試験の英作文と2次試験・面接対策のためにテーマ（教育・犯罪・健康・家庭・労働など）を決めて作文を書いていたのですが，その中で単語を意図的に使ったりして何度も「意識して使う・触れる」ことで暗記するようにしていました。

★つづりが似ていて紛らわしい単語はノートにまとめて書きだす！

- sporadic と spontaneous（なぜかよく混同します）
- impetus と impulse（意味も似ていますが）
- solidarity と solitude（意味は逆ですが）

　ある単語から別の単語を連想することがよくあるのですが，その時にそれぞれの意味やつづりを自分の中で整理するためにノートに書きだします。意味を混同しやすい，見分けにくい単語は，セットで意識して覚えると印象に残りやすくなります。

 Hさん 40代, 会社員

英検1級合格までの対策学習期間と受験回数は?

対策期間:2か月
受験回数:1回

英検のほかの級の受験対策でもPass単熟語を使用しており, 以前から本のことを知っていたため購入。音声も活用して学習したいと考えていました。

そのほかの英語学習の状況についてお聞かせください。

日常的には映画, 海外のテレビシリーズを見たり, CNN, BBCを見てとにかく多聴しました。また, 映画を見ながら字幕なしでディクテーションしてみたり, ニュースを見ながらシャドーイングしたりしていました。

英検以外にも, 常に資格試験(TOEICなど)受験に挑戦し, 対策の勉強などを継続的にしていました。

Pass単熟語を使ってどのように勉強しましたか？

　Pass単熟語に掲載されている単語を中心に，通勤時，自宅で毎日勉強していました。単語集のみの勉強で終わるのではなく，最初に単語集で語義と例文をチェック→覚えられない単語，自信がない単語は辞書やサイトを活用→単語に関する情報を自分で集めて，覚えていきました。具体的には，以下のような方法です。

★覚えにくい単語，難しい単語は語源情報を利用

　単語集の中で自分が覚えにくい単語，難しいと思われる単語はすべてオンラインで利用できるサイトを利用し，語源情報を調べました。最初は，単語集に掲載されている語義や例文を暗記します。この中で，特に覚えにくい単語は，さらにオンラインの英英辞書も引き，意味やコロケーション，例文を確認しました。このようにして，なるべくいろいろな形でその単語に触れるようにしました。調べた内容はデータを保存し，プリントアウトして，常に持ち歩きました。

　それらの情報をもとに発音を聞く，音読，紙に繰り返して書いて覚える。電車の中，歩きながらでもどこでも時間があれば繰り返し見て，何度でも単語に接するのが一番だと思います。単語の学習は基本的にどれも同じ方法で勉強しました。

★多読を通して，何度も単語と出会う機会を作る。NewsweekやTIMEなどを読んだり，ペーパーバックを読むことを通して，覚えた単語の定着を図る！

　ペーパーバックを読む時に，1度目は楽しんで読み，2度目に読む時に，単語を調べてノートを作りました。単語だけ覚えるのではなく，文章や，覚えたいコロケーションで抜き出したりもしました。そして，そのノートを見て覚えるようにしました。ただ，1冊の本の知らない単語を全部調べようと思うと，本によっては，膨大な量になりかねないので，負担にならない程度に調べました。

Eさん　20代，大学生

英検1級合格までの対策学習期間と受験回数は？

対策期間：6か月
受験回数：1回

　Pass単熟語を購入したのは，それぞれの単語に例文がついており，単語の意味を覚えやすそうだと思ったため。また，単語が出題頻度ごとに分かれており，学習効率がよさそうだと感じたためです。

そのほかの英語学習の状況についてお聞かせください。

　通学時や授業の合間に，iTunes PodcastでBBC Newsなどの英語番組を聴いていました。また，大学の図書館に置いてあった英字新聞を読む習慣をつけて，リーディング力を高めました。対策書では，『DAILY 30日間 英検1級 集中ゼミ』(旺文社)や『英検1級 予想問題ドリル』(旺文社)を用いて，1級の出題内容の把握に努めました。

Pass単熟語を使ってどのように勉強しましたか？

●知っている単語を省く作業から

まず，掲載されている単語のうち，すでに知っているものをチェックしました。チェックした単語はその後の学習過程から省くことで，知らない単語を覚えることに集中しました。

●例文で覚える

いろいろな方法で単語に触れると覚えやすいという話を聞いたことがあったので，目で見る（読む）以外にもさまざまな方法を試しました。具体的には，例文を紙に書き出したり，声に出して読み上げたりしました。また，前述したようにニュースや新聞を読んで，1級で出題されるような単語に触れる機会を増やすように心がけました。結果的に，単語の学習にはかなりの時間を割くことになりましたが，より多くの単語を体にしみ込ませることで，リーディング，リスニング，ライティングの総合的な力も効果的に伸ばすことができたと感じています。

●書いて覚える

裏紙など，気軽に使える紙を束ねたものを用意して，1枚に10個程度ずつ，左端に単語，右端に意味を書いていきます。書いてある単語をすべて覚えたら，その紙は捨ててしまい，次の紙に新しく単語と意味を書き出し，同じことを繰り返します。きれいなノートに書いて覚える方法は，文字をきれいに書こうとしてしまうなど単語を覚えることに集中できないので，どうでもいい紙を使いました。また，全部覚えたら捨てる，という点に達成感があるのでおすすめです。

●友人と覚える

授業の合間などに，同じ日に1級を受験する友人と単語クイズを出し合いました。単語学習は，黙々と暗記するなど孤独な作業になりがちなので，友人とゲーム感覚で問題を出し合うのはとてもよい気分転換になりました。

●時間を置いて確認する

　新しく覚えた単語については，一度覚えた後，1週間経ってもまだ覚えていたらチェックをつける，という方法で学習を進めていきました。だんだんとチェックのついていない単語を絞っていき，それらの単語のみに学習時間を割くようにしました。

でる度

単語編

よくでる重要単語 700

動詞 (233語) ······ 26
名詞 (239語) ······ 74
形容詞・副詞 (228語) ······ 122
1分間 mini test ······ 168

でる度Aは、1級でよく出題される単語を選びました。まず、ここに掲載されている700語を確実に覚えましょう。

	1周目	2周目
動	/	/
名	/	/
形・副	/	/

でる度 A よくでる重要単語

動詞 233語

0001 **thrive** [θraɪv]
成功する [= be successful, do well], 繁栄する [= prosper] (⇔ decline, wither)
形 thriving

0002 **grind** [graɪnd]
(コーヒー豆など)を挽く
形 grinding (過酷な)

0003 **confiscate** [kάː)nfɪskèɪt]
を没収する [= impound, seize]
名 confiscation

0004 **derive** [dɪráɪv]
(〜に)由来する, を(〜から)受け継ぐ 〈from〉
名 derivatives (金融派生商品)

0005 **detest** [dɪtést]
をひどく嫌う [= hate]

0006 **mock** [mɑ(ː)k]
(仕草)をまねる, をからかう [= ridicule, scoff at]
名 mockery (あざけり)

0007 **feign** [feɪn]
ふりをする [= pretend, fake, simulate]

0008 **elicit** [ɪlísət]
を(〜から)引き出す [= draw out] 〈from〉

0009 **apprehend** [æ̀prɪhénd]
を逮捕する [= arrest, capture], を理解する [= understand]
語源 ap(〜へ) + prehend(つかむ)

According to her letter, her business is **thriving** in Australia.	彼女の手紙によると，彼女の事業はオーストラリアで**成功して**いる。
She **ground** some fresh beans to make coffee.	彼女はコーヒーを入れるために，新鮮な豆**を挽いた**。
Any cellphone found on school premises was automatically **confiscated**.	学校の構内で見つかったすべての携帯電話は，自動的に**没収さ**れた。
Many English words are **derived** from Latin.	多くの英単語はラテン語に**由来する**。
Even though he **detested** broccoli, his wife often served it.	彼はブロッコリ**が大嫌いだった**が，彼の妻はそれをよく食事に出した。
The comedian made his name by **mocking** politicians and other powerful figures.	そのコメディアンは，政治家やほかの影響力のある人物の仕草**をまねる**ことで有名になった。
The students were bored but some tried to **feign** interest.	学生たちは退屈していたが，関心を持っている**ふりをし**ようとした者もいた。
They tried to **elicit** an answer from the little boy, but he refused to speak.	彼らは，その小さな男の子から答え**を引き出そ**うとしたが，男の子は話したがらなかった。
The spy was **apprehended** as he tried to leave the country.	そのスパイはその国から出国しようとした時に**逮捕さ**れた。

0010
commiserate [kəmízərèɪt]

(〜を)哀れむ
[= sympathize] 〈with〉
cf. misery(悲惨さ), miserable(惨めな)

0011
condone [kəndóun]

を許す
[= pardon, overlook, forgive]
▶condone an offense(違反を大目に見る)

0012
epitomize [ɪpítəmàɪz]

の典型である
[= embody]
图 epitome(典型, 権化)

0013 ✓
fluctuate [flʌ́ktʃuèɪt]

変動する, 上下する [= undulate]
图 fluctuation
語源 fluct(流れる) + ate

0014 ✓
forgo [fɔːrgóu]

をなしで済ませる [= do without],
を慎む

0015
frisk [frɪsk]

を(衣服の上からさわって)ボディーチェックする,
跳ね回る

0016
insulate [ínsəlèɪt]

を(〜から)隔離する [= isolate] 〈from〉
图 insulation(絶縁体)
語源 insula(島) + ate

0017
liquidate [líkwɪdèɪt]

を清算する [= settle the accounts of],
(会社など)を解散する
图 liquidation

0018
meander [miǽndər]

(川・道などが)曲がりくねる

0019
meddle [médl]

(〜に)干渉する
[= interfere] 〈in〉
▶meddle in internal affairs(内情に干渉する)

His family **commiserated** with him when he failed to get the job.	彼が仕事を手に入れられなかった時，家族は彼を哀れんだ。
One could **condone** his mistake, but not his arrogance.	彼のミスを許すことはできても，彼の傲慢さは許せない。
For many people, the band's music **epitomized** the spirit of the 1960s.	多くの人々にとって，そのバンドの音楽は，1960年代精神の典型であった。
The exchange rate between yen and dollars has **fluctuated** wildly all year.	円とドルの為替レートが一年中激しく変動した。
I agreed to **forgo** my bonus to help the company face its financial crisis.	私は会社が，その財政危機に対処するのを助けるため，ボーナスをなしで済ませることに同意した。
At the crime scene, police **frisked** each suspect to ensure that none of them had any concealed weapons.	犯行現場で，警官は容疑者1人1人のボディーチェックをして，誰も武器を隠し持っていないことを確かめた。
When living in a remote area of Alaska, I was completely **insulated** from the real world.	アラスカの辺ぴな所に住んでいた当時，私は実社会から完全に隔離されていた。
The company announced yesterday that it was going to **liquidate** its assets.	昨日，その会社は資産を清算すると発表した。
The view from this road is beautiful as it **meanders** through the mountains.	この道からの眺めは，山中を道が蛇行している様子が美しい。
The man advised his wife not to **meddle** in her friend's marriage.	男性は妻に，友達の結婚に干渉しないようにと忠告した。

---

liquidate (0017) は，liquid「液体」のイメージから資産や借金を洗い流す，つまり「を清算する」と覚えよう。

0020 ~ 0029

0020
pamper
[pǽmpər]

を(〜で)甘やかす
[= spoil] 〈with〉

0021
peruse
[pərúːz]

を熟読する
[= read something especially in a careful way]

0022
pique
[piːk]

を立腹させる [= offend],
を刺激する [= excite]

0023 ✓
plagiarize
[pléɪdʒəràɪz]

(他人の思想・作品など)を(〜から)盗用する
[= pirate] 〈from〉
图 plagiarism

0024
plummet
[plʌ́mɪt]

(真っすぐに)落ちる, 急落する
[= plunge, fall sharply] (⇔ skyrocket)
▶ Stock prices plummeted. (株価が急落した。)

0025
rehash
[riːhǽʃ]

を作り変える
[= put into a new idea without significant changes]

0026 ✓
implant
[ɪmplǽnt]

を(〜に)埋め込む [= insert],
(思想など)を(〜に)植えつける [= instill] 〈in〉
图 implant (インプラント)

0027
indoctrinate
[ɪndɑ́(ː)ktrɪnèɪt]

に教え込む
[= instruct, teach]
cf. doctrine (教義)

0028
inculcate
[ɪnkʌ́lkeɪt]

を(〜に)教え込む
[= instill] 〈into〉

0029
enlighten
[ɪnláɪtən]

に(〜について)教える〈on, about, as to〉,
を啓発する
語源 en (にする) + light (明るい) + en

She **pampered** her pet cat with expensive foods such as smoked salmon.	彼女は，自分のペットのネコにスモークサーモンのような高価な餌を与えて甘やかした。
Over breakfast, he **perused** a copy of the local newspaper.	朝食を食べながら，彼は地元の新聞1紙を熟読した。
Her persistent complaints began to **pique** many of her colleagues.	彼女がいつまでも文句を言っていたので，同僚の多くが腹を立て始めた。
The professor accused the student of **plagiarizing** an essay from the Internet.	教授は学生がインターネットから論文を盗用したことを非難した。
We stood on the shore and watched the sea gulls **plummet** toward the sea in search of fish.	私たちは海岸に立ち，カモメが魚を求めて海面に向かって真っすぐに降下するのを眺めた。
Critics said the comedian just **rehashed** old jokes for his new show.	評論家はそのコメディアンが新しいショー用に古いジョークを作り変えただけだと言った。
A tiny chip was **implanted** in the animal so that they could track it.	追跡できるように，その動物の体内には小さなチップが埋め込まれた。
Children in Catholic schools are **indoctrinated** in Catholic beliefs.	カトリックの学校の子どもたちはカトリックの信仰を教え込まれる。
The teacher **inculcated** patriotism into his students.	その先生は生徒たちに愛国心を教え込んだ。
I asked her to **enlighten** me as to what had happened during my absence.	私は留守中に何があったのか教えてほしいと彼女に頼んだ。

0030 implement
[ímpləmènt]

を実行する
[= carry out, execute]
名 implementation

0031 undergo
[ʌ̀ndərgóu]

(検査・治療)を受ける，
(試練・変化)を経験する
[= experience, go through]

0032 manipulate
[mənípjulèit]

を巧みに操る
[= control shrewdly]
名 manipulation

0033 address
[ədrés]

(問題)を取り上げる，
に対処する [= cope with, tackle]，
に話しかける [= speak to]

0034 fabricate
[fǽbrɪkèit]

を組み立てる，をでっち上げる
名 fabrication

0035 administer
[ədmínistər]

を運営する [= manage]，
を施行する [= implement]

0036 enact
[ɪnǽkt]

を制定する
[= ordain, decree]
名 enactment

0037 duplicate
[djúːplɪkèit]

を複製する
[= make an exact copy of]
語源 du (2つ) + pli (重なる) + ate

0038 orchestrate
[ɔ́ːrkɪstrèit]

を画策する
名 orchestra (オーケストラ)　形 orchestral

0039 inaugurate
[ɪnɔ́ːgjərèit]

を(正式に)開始する
名 inauguration　形 inaugural
▶ inaugurate a new policy (新政策を開始する)

The policy proved impossible to **implement** and so was abandoned.	その政策は実行するのが不可能だと判明したので、破棄された。
All new employees are required to **undergo** a medical examination.	新入社員全員が健康診断を受ける必要がある。
The new king was easily **manipulated** by his advisers into doing what they wanted.	新しい国王は側近たちにたやすく操作されて、側近たちの望むことをやらされた。
In his speech, he failed to **address** the criticisms that had been aimed at him.	演説の中で、彼は自分に向けられてきた批判を取り上げることができなかった。
The engineers had to **fabricate** a temporary, emergency bridge over the river.	技術者たちは、その川に架かる応急用の橋を組み立てねばならなかった。
The new literacy program will be **administered** by a group of NGOs.	読み書きを教える新たな講座が、NGO（非政府組織）団体によって運営される予定である。
In the 1960s President John F. Kennedy **enacted** a number of civil rights laws.	1960年代、ジョン・F・ケネディ大統領は、多数の公民権関連の法律を制定した。
We needed to **duplicate** the video so we could show it to several groups.	いくつかのグループに見せるために、我々はビデオを複製する必要があった。
The politician **orchestrated** a smear campaign against his rival.	その政治家は、ライバルに対する組織的な中傷を画策した。
The prime minister announced that he would **inaugurate** a new policy on education.	首相は教育に関する新政策を正式に開始すると発表した。

0040 persist
[pərsíst]

やり抜く，持続する，固執する
图 persistence 形 persistent 副 persistently
語源 per(完全に) + sist(立つ)

0041 enhance
[ɪnhǽns]

を高める [= heighten, augment]
图 enhancement

0042 invigorate
[ɪnvígərèɪt]

を元気づける
形 invigorating

0043 fortify
[fɔ́ːrtəfàɪ]

を(〜で)強化する〈with〉
图 fort(砦), fortification(要塞，防備の強化)

0044 expedite
[ékspədàɪt]

をはかどらせる，促進する
[= hasten, facilitate, speed up] (⇔ impede)
图 expedition(遠征，迅速)

0045 galvanize
[gǽlvənàɪz]

を活気づける [= stir, rouse],
を刺激する [= stimulate],
に電流を流す

0046 bolster
[bóʊlstər]

を強化する，
を支援する [= support]

0047 ✓ sustain
[səstéɪn]

を維持する [= uphold], に耐える [= withstand]
图 sustenance(食物)
語源 sus(下から) + tain(保つ)

0048 facilitate
[fəsílətèɪt]

を容易にする [= make easy],
を助長する [= assist]

0049 ✓ supplement
[sʌ́plɪmènt]

を補う [= complement],
に付録を付ける
形 supplementary(補足的な)

Despite numerous disappointments, the scientist **persisted** until he found a cure.	何度となく失望したにもかかわらず，その科学者は治療法を見つけるまで<u>やり抜いた</u>。
His recent novel will certainly **enhance** his literary reputation.	最近の小説のおかげで彼の文学的名声はきっと<u>高まる</u>だろう。
The early morning jog refreshed and **invigorated** her.	早朝のジョギングで，彼女はリフレッシュして<u>元気になった</u>。
Recently, it is customary to **fortify** milk with vitamin D.	最近では，ビタミンDで牛乳<u>の栄養価を高める</u>ことが普通になっている。
The company had to **expedite** the development of the new product to meet demand.	その会社は，需要に対処するために新製品の開発<u>をはかどらせる</u>必要があった。
The President's speech was intended to **galvanize** his public support.	大統領の演説は大衆の彼に対する支持<u>を活気づける</u>目的があった。
The government has recently taken steps to **bolster** market confidence.	政府は市場の信頼<u>を強化する</u>対策を最近講じた。
Many people barely get enough food to **sustain** their health.	健康<u>を維持する</u>のに必要な食物を手にするので精いっぱいの人も多い。
I recently found a new book that **facilitated** my grasp of quantum mechanics.	私は最近，量子力学に対する私の理解<u>を助けてくれる</u>新しい本を見つけた。
He **supplemented** his income from the university by writing articles.	彼は記事を書くことで大学から得る収入<u>を補った</u>。

最後に -ment がつく動詞として，supplement (0049) のほか，complement「を補足する」や implement「を実施する」のような単語があります。

0050
subsidize
[sʌ́bsɪdàɪz]

に補助金を与える
图 subsidy (補助金)

0051
amend
[əménd]

(法律など)を改正する, 修正する
[= revise, rectify]
图 amendment

0052
rectify
[réktɪfàɪ]

を修正する [= amend, redress]
图 rectification
語源 rect (まっすぐな) + fy

0053
endorse
[ɪndɔ́ːrs]

を推薦する, を承認する,
(手形など)に裏書きする
图 endorsement

0054
exhort
[ɪgzɔ́ːrt]

に熱心に勧める
[= urge, encourage]

0055
coerce
[kouə́ːrs]

に(〜を)強いる
[= force] 〈into〉
图 coercion

0056
implore
[ɪmplɔ́ːr]

に(〜するように)懇願する
[= beg, entreat] 〈to *do*〉

0057
instigate
[ínstɪgèɪt]

を推進する [= prompt],
を扇動する [= agitate]
图 instigation

0058 ✓
trigger
[trígər]

を誘発する
[= precipitate, set off]
图 trigger (引き金, 誘因)

0059
incite
[ɪnsáɪt]

を扇動する [= instigate, stir up],
を引き起こす [= provoke]

The company **subsidizes** my monthly rent.	会社は，私の毎月の家賃を補助している。
The law was **amended** to take into account new developments in biotechnology.	生物工学の新たな進展を配慮して，法律が改正された。
By the time the mistake was discovered, it was too late to **rectify** the official report.	誤りが発見された時点では，公式報告書を修正するには手遅れだった。
The tennis player agreed to **endorse** the company's products in return for a large fee.	そのテニスプレーヤーは，多額の謝礼と引き換えに，その会社の製品を勧めることに同意した。
The teacher **exhorted** the students to prepare for the final exam.	その教師は期末試験の準備をするよう生徒たちに熱心に勧めた。
The company was **coerced** into paying a higher tax rate by the corrupt government.	その会社は，さらに高い税率を支払うことを，腐敗した政府に強いられた。
The students **implored** the teachers to make the examination easier.	生徒たちは試験をもっと易しくしてくれるよう教師たちに懇願した。
The head of the hospital said he would **instigate** an investigation into the doctor's conduct.	院長はその医師の品行に関する調査を推進すると言った。
The economic turmoil in Southeast Asia may **trigger** chaos elsewhere.	東南アジアの経済混乱はほかの地域の混乱を誘発するかもしれない。
The leaders tried to **incite** the crowd to violence.	リーダーたちは暴力に訴えるよう群衆を扇動しようとした。

0060 ~ 0069

0060	**muster** [mʌ́stər]	を集める [= assemble]、を奮い起こす [= gather]
0061	**extol** [ɪkstóul]	を激賞する [= applaud, eulogize]
0062	**emulate** [émjulèɪt]	を見習う [= imitate]、と張り合う [= rival, vie with]　图 emulation
0063	**entice** [ɪntáɪs]	を引き寄せる [= tempt, allure]
0064	**dazzle** [dǽzl]	を幻惑する
0065 ✓	**sprout** [spraut]	発芽する [= bud, burgeon, germinate]　图 sprout (野菜などの芽)
0066	**burgeon** [bə́ːrdʒən]	急成長する、(植物が)芽を出す [= sprout]　形 burgeoning (急成長する)
0067	**detect** [dɪtékt]	を感知する [= perceive]、を発見する　图 detection (発見), detective (探偵, 刑事)　語源 de (分離) + tect (覆う)
0068	**debunk** [diːbʌ́ŋk]	を暴露する、の誤りを暴く [= disprove]
0069	**unravel** [ʌnrǽvəl]	(難問など)を解明する [= straighten out]、(もつれた糸など)をほどく

The General **mustered** all the forces for an early-morning attack.	将軍は早朝の攻撃に向けて全軍を集めた。
The most distinguished people at the conference **extolled** his contribution.	その会議にいた最も著名な人たちが彼の貢献を激賞した。
strive (v) (~しようと) 努力する (strove, striven) [to do] She strove to **emulate** her mother's example in her personal life.	彼女は私生活では母親の例を見習うよう頑張った。
Enticed by the air-conditioning, he entered the store.	エアコンに引き寄せられて彼はその店に入った。
Dazzled by the man's charm, the woman eventually agreed to a date.	女性はその男性の魅力に幻惑され、ついにデートに応じた。
Vegetable seeds begin to **sprout** in my garden in April.	私の菜園では、野菜の種は4月になると発芽し始める。
As the market for exotic spices **burgeoned**, the company made a fortune.	外国産香辛料の市場が急成長したので、その会社は一財産を築いた。
The machine could **detect** the slightest sign of a radiation leak.	その機械はごくわずかな放射能漏れの兆候さえも感知することができた。
One effect of science has been to **debunk** many traditional beliefs.	科学の効能の1つは多くの古説が間違っていることを証明することである。
Patient research has enabled doctors to **unravel** the cause of the disease.	忍耐強い研究の結果、医師たちはその病気の原因を解明することができた。

unravel (0069) の元の意味は「もつれた糸をほどく」ですが、そこから「(難問など) を解明する」という意味が生まれました。

0070 excavate
[ékskəvèit]

を発掘する [= dig up]
图 excavation
語源 ex(外に) + cave(穴) + ate

0071 recoup
[rikú:p]

(損失など)を取り戻す, に埋め合わせをする [= make up for]

0072 recuperate
[rikjú:pərèit]

(病気・損失)(から)回復する
[= recover] 〈from〉

0073 disseminate
[dɪsémɪnèit]

を普及させる [= spread, circulate, disperse]
图 dissemination

0074 prevail
[prɪvéɪl]

(〜を)圧倒する〈over〉, 普及する
形 prevailing(支配的な), prevalent(流行の)

0075 propagate
[prá(:)pəgèit]

を広める
[= disseminate]
图 propagation

0076 transmit
[trænsmít]

を(〜に)伝達する, を(〜に)感染させる〈to〉
图 transmission, transmitter
語源 trans(越えて) + mit(送る)

0077 garner
[gáːrnər]

を得る
[= gather]
▶ garner a lot of votes (多くの票を得る)

0078 garnish
[gáːrnɪʃ]

(料理)に(〜を)添える〈with〉, を装飾する

0079 infer
[ɪnfəːr]

を(〜から)察する [= deduce] 〈from〉
图 inference
語源 in(中に) + fer(運ぶ)

All work on the new building was stopped while archaeologists <u>excavated</u> the site.	考古学者たちが用地<u>を発掘する</u>間、新しいビル建設の作業はすべてストップした。
She took a holiday after the tournament to <u>recoup</u> her energy.	選手権大会終了後、彼女は気力<u>を取り戻す</u>ために休暇を取った。
It took the driver six months to <u>recuperate</u> from his accident.	その運転手が事故から<u>回復する</u>のに6か月かかった。
The first printing press allowed people to easily <u>disseminate</u> the written word.	印刷機が作られて初めて、人々は容易に書かれた言葉<u>を流布させる</u>ことができるようになった。
The school team finally <u>prevailed</u> over their rivals and won the championship.	その学校のチームはついにライバルたちを<u>圧倒し</u>、優勝を勝ち取った。
He suspected his colleague of <u>propagating</u> the idea that he was lazy.	彼は自分が怠惰であると同僚が<u>吹聴</u>しているのではないかと疑った。
During the war, the BBC often <u>transmitted</u> messages in code to agents overseas.	戦時中、BBC放送は海外の諜報部員たちにしばしば暗号文でメッセージ<u>を伝達した</u>。
In an attempt to <u>garner</u> support, the mayor held a town meeting.	その市長は支持<u>を得</u>ようとして市民集会を開いた。
The meat was <u>garnished</u> with fresh sprigs of parsley.	その肉には新鮮なパセリの小枝が<u>添え</u>られていた。
He <u>inferred</u> from the professor's remarks that he had failed the class.	彼は教授の発言から自分が単位を落としたこと<u>を察した</u>。

0080
surmise [sərmáɪz]

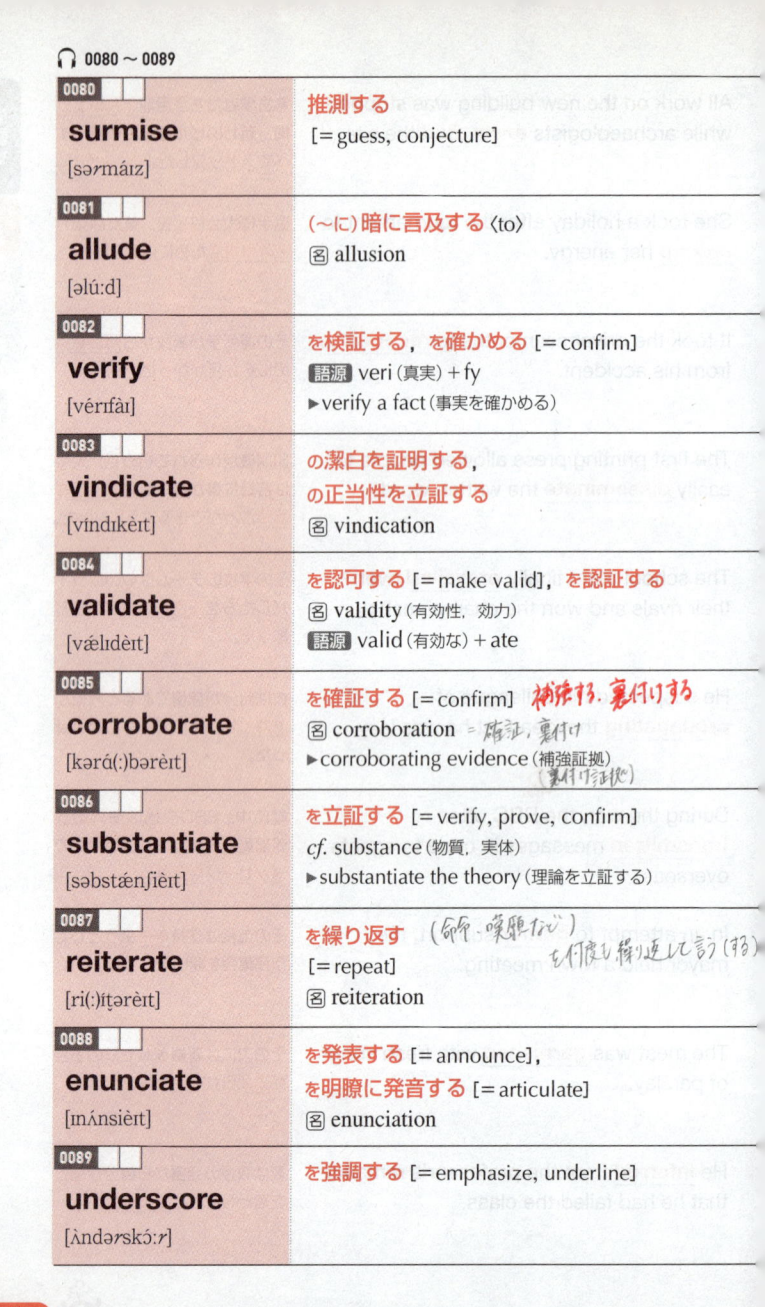

推測する
[= guess, conjecture]

0081
allude [əlúːd]

(〜に)暗に言及する ⟨to⟩
名 allusion

0082
verify [vérɪfàɪ]

を検証する，を確かめる [= confirm]
語源 veri(真実) + fy
▶ verify a fact(事実を確かめる)

0083
vindicate [víndɪkèɪt]

の潔白を証明する，
の正当性を立証する
名 vindication

0084
validate [vǽlɪdèɪt]

を認可する [= make valid]，を認証する
名 validity(有効性，効力)
語源 valid(有効な) + ate

0085
corroborate [kərά(ː)bərèɪt]

を確証する [= confirm]　補強する、裏付けする
名 corroboration = 確証、裏付け
▶ corroborating evidence(補強証拠) 　裏付け証拠

0086
substantiate [səbstǽnʃièɪt]

を立証する [= verify, prove, confirm]
cf. substance(物質，実体)
▶ substantiate the theory(理論を立証する)

0087
reiterate [ri(ː)ítərèɪt]

を繰り返す　(命・嘆願など)
[= repeat]　を何度も繰り返して言(する)
名 reiteration

0088
enunciate [ɪnʌ́nsièɪt]

を発表する [= announce]，
を明瞭に発音する [= articulate]
名 enunciation

0089
underscore [ʌ̀ndərskɔ́ːr]

を強調する [= emphasize, underline]

I **surmised** that I could do better by investing in real estate than in stocks.	株より不動産に投資した方が自分はうまくやれると私は推測した。
In his speech, the principal **alluded** to some famous lines from "King Lear."	校長はスピーチの中で、『リア王』の有名なせりふのいくつかに暗に言及した。
The journalist had failed to **verify** the facts before writing his article.	記者はその記事を書く前に事実を検証することができなかった。
After his acquittal, he claimed he had been completely **vindicated**.	無罪放免されて、彼は完全に潔白が証明されたと主張した。
The degrees given at the art school are **validated** by the University of Sussex.	美術学校発行の学位は、サセックス大学によって認可される。
The detective tried to **corroborate** the woman's accusations.	刑事はその女性の罪を確証しようとした。
He could not **substantiate** the allegations he made, and he lost the lawsuit.	彼は自らの申し立てを立証することができず、訴訟に敗れた。
The ambassador **reiterated** his nation's policy at the start of the meeting.	大使は会議の初めに自国の政策を繰り返し述べた。
My boss forcefully **enunciated** his policies to the employees.	私の上司は従業員に対し力強い調子で彼の方針を発表した。
The accident only **underscored** the poor condition of the machines.	その事故は機械の不調を強調したにすぎなかった。

0090
flaunt [flɔːnt]
を誇示する
[= show off (proudly), display ostentatiously]

0091
alleviate [əlíːvièit]
(苦痛など)を和らげる
[= assuage, soften, mitigate]

0092
allay [əléi]
を和らげる
[= alleviate, lessen]

0093
appease [əpíːz]
をなだめる
[= pacify, quiet]
名 appeasement

0094
defuse [diːfjúːz]
(爆弾など)から信管を除去する,
(危険)を取り除く,
(緊張)を和らげる

0095
mollify [má(ː)lɪfàɪ]
(怒りなど)を和らげる
[= assuage, pacify, appease]

0096
placate [pléɪkeɪt]
(怒り・敵意など)をなだめる
[= appease, conciliate, mollify]

0097
modulate [má(ː)dʒəlèɪt]
を調節する
[= vary the pitch of]
名 modulator (変調器)

0098
intervene [ìntərvíːn]
(〜を)調停する,
(〜を)仲裁する [= interpose] ⟨in⟩
語源 inter(間に) + vene(来る)

0099
curb [kəːrb]
を抑制する
[= control, restrain]
名 curb (抑制, 縁石)

People who like to **flaunt** their wealth are lacking in refinement.	富を誇示したがる人々は品に欠ける。
The medicine could not **alleviate** his pain.	その薬は彼の痛みを和らげることができなかった。
The government tried to **allay** public fears of a stock market crash.	政府は，株式市場の暴落をめぐる社会不安を和らげようとした。
The manager tried to **appease** the angry customer.	支配人は怒った客をなだめようとした。
Recently, many police forces have experts who can **defuse** bombs.	最近，多くの警察隊には爆弾から信管を除去できる専門家がいる。
Nothing I said could **mollify** the anger of the boss.	私が何を言っても，上司の怒りを和らげることはできなかった。
He tried to **placate** his angry girlfriend with a bunch of roses and a box of chocolates.	彼はバラの花束とチョコレートで怒ったガールフレンドをなだめようとした。
That singer's voice coach advised him to **modulate** his voice more when singing.	その歌手のボイストレーナーは，歌う時にはもっと声を調節するよう彼に助言した。
I asked my lawyer to **intervene** in the dispute.	私は弁護士に，その紛争を調停してくれるように依頼した。
The mayor announced that he intended to **curb** spending on the city's parks.	市長は市立公園への支出を抑制するつもりであると発表した。

0100 ~ 0109

#	単語	意味
0100	**oppress** [əprés]	を抑圧する，を虐げる 名 oppression 形 oppressive 語源 op(〜に対して) + press(押さえる)
0101	**subjugate** [sʌ́bdʒugèɪt]	を征服する [= subdue]，を隷属させる 名 subjugation
0102	**suppress** [səprés]	を鎮圧する，を抑圧する [= put down] 名 suppression 語源 sub(下に) + press(押さえる)
0103	**subvert** [səbvə́ːrt]	を覆す，を打倒する [= overthrow]
0104	**encroach** [ɪnkróʊtʃ]	(〜に)侵入する [= intrude, trespass] ⟨on⟩ 名 encroachment
0105	**deter** [dɪtə́ːr]	に(〜を)思いとどまらせる [= prevent] ⟨from⟩ 名 deterrent(戦争抑止力)
0106	**retard** [rɪtɑ́ːrd]	を遅らせる [= delay]， を妨げる [= impede, obstruct, hamper]
0107	**avert** [əvə́ːrt]	(視線・考えなど)を(〜から)そらす [= turn away] ⟨from⟩ 語源 a(離れて) + vert(向ける)
0108	**balk** [bɔːk]	(〜を)ためらう ⟨at⟩， を妨げる [= resist]
0109	**stifle** [stáɪfl]	を抑える [= repress, suppress, curb]， を窒息させる [= suffocate] ▶ stifle a yawn(あくびを抑える)

regime = 政体，政権

For years, the regime had **oppressed** the people, denying them their freedom.	何年にもわたって，その政府は人々に自由を与えないで，彼らを抑圧した。
Countries with power often **subjugated** weaker countries.	力のある国はしばしば弱い国を征服した。
The king immediately sent troops to **suppress** the rebellion.	国王は反乱軍を鎮圧するために軍隊を即時派遣した。
The opposition accused the government of **subverting** the democratic process.	野党は政府が民主的な手続きを覆したことを責めた。
The plane was shot down because it **encroached** on enemy territory.	その飛行機は敵の領土に侵入したので撃ち落とされた。
We could never **deter** him from a course of action that would destroy his career.	彼がキャリアを台無しにしてしまうような一連の行為を彼に思いとどまらせることが，我々にはできなかった。
Government red tape has **retarded** progress on economic reform.	政府の官僚的な形式主義は，経済改革の進行を遅らせてきた。
In her embarrassment, she **averted** her eyes from my gaze.	彼女は当惑のあまり，私の視線から目をそらした。
The ruthless businessman did not **balk** at lying to his competitors.	その無慈悲な実業家は競合相手に嘘をつくことをためらわなかった。
The robbers had to **stifle** the cries of the guard to avoid detection.	強盗たちは見破られないように，守衛の叫び声を抑える必要があった。

avert (0107)「視線をそらす」の意味に加えて，イメージで広げて覚えられそうなのが，averse (形)「嫌で，反対して」，aversion (名)「嫌悪感」の意味です。

0110 ~ 0119

0110
quell [kwel]

を抑える，を鎮める
[= soothe, suppress]

0111
quench [kwentʃ]

(渇き)を癒やす [= satisfy, relieve, slake],
(欲望)を抑える [= subdue, suppress]
▶ quench *one's* thirst (喉の渇きを癒す)

0112
curtail [kəːrtéɪl]

を切り詰める
[= shorten]
图 curtailment (短縮)

0113
diminish [dɪmínɪʃ]

を減らす [= reduce, lessen]
图 diminution

0114
eclipse [iklíps]

の影を薄くさせる [= surpass],
(ほかの天体)を食にする

0115
debase [dɪbéɪs]

(品位・評判)を落とす
[= demean]

0116
demean [dɪmíːn]

の品位を下げる
[= debase]
图 demeanor (振舞い, 態度)

0117
detract [dɪtrækt]

(〜を)損なう，減じる〈from〉
图 detraction (中傷)

0118
dwindle [dwíndl]

だんだん減少[縮小]する
[= shrink]

0119
deviate [díːvièɪt]

(〜から)逸脱する [= diverge] 〈from〉
图 deviation

He **quelled** his fear and dove into the river to rescue the boy.	彼は恐怖心を抑えて，少年を救助するために川へと飛び込んだ。
After hours in the hot sun, he drank several beers to **quench** his thirst.	暑い日なたに何時間もいた後，彼は渇きを癒やすためビールを数杯飲んだ。
We were forced to **curtail** our trip due to a family emergency.	家族に緊急事態が発生したため，私たちは旅行日程を切り詰めねばならなかった。
Most countries want to **diminish** their national debt.	たいていの国は自国の債務を減らそうと思っている。
The team's triumph was **eclipsed** by news of the prime minister's resignation.	首相辞任のニュースのためにチームの勝利の影が薄くなった。
The star **debased** his reputation by appearing in a series of cheap, sensational movies.	一連の安っぽいセンセーショナルな映画に出演したことで，そのスターは評判を落とした。
The feminist group complained that the advertisements **demeaned** women.	その広告は女性の品位を下げていると，フェミニストの集団は不満を述べた。
His latest book was a failure but did not **detract** much from his good reputation.	彼の最新作は失敗だったが，彼の名声をさほど損なうことはなかった。
The number of many species of whales is slowly beginning to **dwindle**.	多くのクジラ種の数が，ゆっくりと減少し始めている。
The soldiers were warned not to **deviate** from their instructions in any way.	兵士たちは，いかなる場合も指示から外れることのないように注意された。

0120 elude
[ɪlúːd]

をうまくかわす，から逃れる
[= evade]
形 elusive (理解しにくい，捕まえにくい)

0121 circumvent
[sə̀ːrkəmvént]

の抜け道を見つける，
を回避する [= avoid, eschew]

0122 plague
[pleɪg]

を (〜で) 絶えず苦しめる 〈with〉

0123 torment
[tɔːrmént] ← 37セント後ろ！

をひどく苦しめる [= afflict]，
を悩ます [= distress]
名 torment ← 37セント前！

0124 confound
[kənfáʊnd]

を混乱させる [= bewilder, perplex]，
を (〜と) 混同する 〈with〉

0125 stump
[stʌmp]

を困らせる [= puzzle]，遊説して回る
名 stump (切り株)
▶ be stumped for words (言葉につまる)

0126 dismiss
[dɪsmís]

を却下する [= reject]，を解雇する [= fire]
名 dismissal (放棄，解雇)
▶ be dismissed from one's job (解雇される)

0127 dissect
[dɪsékt]

を分析する [= analyze]，
を解剖する [= anatomize]
名 dissection (詳細な分析，解剖)

0128 refute
[rɪfjúːt]

を論破する [= disprove]
▶ refute a claim (主張に反駁する)

0129 rebuff
[rɪbʌ́f]

を拒絶する
[= reject]

Although I looked everywhere for my student, she **eluded** me.	学生をあちこち捜したが，彼女は私をうまくかわした。
He accused the company of trying to **circumvent** their earlier agreement.	以前の協定の抜け道を見つけようとしているとして，彼はその会社を非難した。
The department store was **plagued** with shoplifters, some of whom operated in gangs.	そのデパートは，中には集団でやって来る万引き犯たちに絶えず苦しめられていた。
The school bully delighted in **tormenting** the younger boys.	学校のいじめっ子は，年少の男の子たちをいじめて喜んでいた。
He **confounded** his enemies by coming up with a brilliant plan to save the company.	彼は会社を救う素晴らしいプランを案出して，敵対者たちを混乱させた。
Everybody in the class was **stumped** by the problem that the teacher had given them.	クラスのみんなが，先生の出した問題に困惑していた。
Jane was irritated when her boss casually **dismissed** her proposal.	ジェーンは，上司が彼女の提案を無頓着に却下した時，いらだった。
The philosopher carefully **dissected** the scientist's argument in order to disprove it.	哲学者はその科学者の論証が誤りであることを証明するために注意深く分析した。
The politician finally succeeded in **refuting** his enemies' accusations.	その政治家はついにライバルの非難を論破することに成功した。
She **rebuffed** all his advances, insisting she was not interested in him.	彼女は彼に興味がないと言い切って，すべての誘いを拒絶した。

re- には（後ろに・再び）以外に（逆らう）という意味があります。refute (0128) や rebuff (0129) のほか，refuse, reject などがイメージしやすいでしょう。

0130
rebuke
[rɪbjúːk]

を(〜のことで)叱責する
[= blame, berate, reprimand, reproach] ⟨for⟩

0131
denounce
[dɪnáʊns]

を公然と非難する
名 denouncement

0132
rebut
[rɪbʌ́t]

に反論する
[= refute, deny]
名 rebuttal (反駁)

0133
reprimand
[réprɪmæ̀nd]

を(〜のことで)叱責する
[= blame, rebuke, berate, reproach] ⟨for⟩

0134
berate
[bɪréɪt]

を(〜のことで)責め立てる
[= blame, rebuke, reprimand, reproach] ⟨for⟩

0135
lambaste
[læmbéɪst]

を厳しく非難する
[= berate, rebuke]

0136
seclude
[sɪklúːd]

を引きこもらせる [= isolate]
名 seclusion　語源 se (離れて) + clude (閉じる)
▶ seclude *oneself* in 〜 (〜に引きこもる)

0137
ostracize
[ά(ː)strəsàɪz]

を追放する [= banish from society],
を排斥する
名 ostracism

0138
purge
[pəːrdʒ]

から(〜を)追放する [= expunge] ⟨of⟩,
を清める [= cleanse]

0139
repatriate
[riːpéɪtrièɪt]

を本国に送還する
(⇔ expatriate を国外に追放する)

The police chief **rebuked** the two officers for their poor handling of the case.	警察署長は事件の処理がまずいとして2人の警官を叱責した。
The opposition **denounced** members of the government for corruption.	野党は汚職を理由として政府の閣僚たちを公然と非難した。
The lawyer successfully **rebutted** all the prosecutor's claims.	その弁護士は見事に検察官のすべての主張に反論した。
The school principal **reprimanded** the students for poor discipline.	校長は規律の低下を理由に生徒を叱責した。
He **berated** himself for having trusted a stranger with his money.	彼は見知らぬ人にお金を預けてしまったことで、自分自身を責めた。
The newspaper editorial **lambasted** the government for their poor economic policies.	新聞の社説は政府の拙劣な経済政策を厳しく非難した。
After the tragedy, the famous actress has **secluded** herself in her mansion.	悲劇の後、その有名な女優は自分の大邸宅に引きこもってしまった。
They were **ostracized** by the townspeople for breaking the law.	彼らは決まりを破ったことで、住民から追放された。
The mayor promised to **purge** the police of corrupt officers.	市長は、汚職警官を警察から追放すると約束した。
Many refugees were never **repatriated** after World War II.	多くの避難民が第二次大戦後本国に送還されなかった。

0140 ~ 0149

0140
repulse
[rɪpʌ́ls]

を撃退する，を拒絶する
名 repulsion
形 repulsive (不快な)

0141
rebel
[rɪbél]

(〜に) 反逆する
[= revolt] 〈against〉
名 rebellion 形 rebellious

0142
renege
[rɪníːg]

(約束などを) 破る
[= back out] 〈on〉

0143
renounce
[rɪnáʊns]

を放棄する [= abandon],
と関係を絶つ [= disown]
名 renunciation

0144
revel
[révəl] レベル

(〜を) 大いに楽しむ
[= delight] 〈in〉

0145
suspend
[səspénd]

を一時停止 [中止] にする [= intermit],
をつるす [= hang (up)]

0146
abort
[əbɔ́ːrt]

を中止する [= terminate] (⇔ continue)
名 abortion

0147
adjourn
[ədʒə́ːrn]

を休会 [閉会] する
[= postpone, temporarily suspend]
名 adjournment

0148
nullify
[nʌ́lɪfàɪ]

を無効にする [= annul, make void]
名 nullification
語源 null (ない) + fy

0149
revoke
[rɪvóʊk]

を取り消す
[= cancel, repeal, annul]
形 revocable

The soldiers did their best to **repulse** the enemy attack.	兵士たちは敵の攻撃を撃退するために全力を尽くした。
Finally, the army lost patience and **rebelled** against its own government.	最終的に軍は忍耐力を失い,自国政府に対して反逆した。
Suddenly, the bank **reneged** on its promise of a loan.	その銀行は突然,ローンの契約を取り消した。
At an early age the king **renounced** his throne and retreated into private life.	若い頃にその王は王位を放棄して,ひっそりと暮らした。
The actress **reveled** in all the publicity her divorce brought.	女優は自分の離婚がもたらしたすべての報道を大いに楽しんだ。
Before an agreement could be reached, the parties **suspended** negotiations.	合意に至る前に当事者たちは交渉を一時停止した。
Bad weather forced the explorers to **abort** the expedition.	悪天候のために探検家たちは遠征を中止することを余儀なくされた。
The judge **adjourned** the hearings for a long lunch break.	判事は審理を休会して,昼休みをゆっくり取ることにした。
They hoped to get a legal decision that would **nullify** the terms of the contract.	彼らは契約条件を無効にするような法的判断を望んでいた。
The judge **revoked** his driver's license after finding him guilty of drunk driving.	飲酒運転で有罪とわかった後,裁判官は彼の運転免許を取り消した。

suspenderは「ズボンのつりひも」なのでsuspend(0145)は「をつるす」と推測できます。
suspend negotiationsは「交渉をつるす」→「一時中断する」とイメージできるでしょう。

0150
thwart
[θwɔːrt]

(計画など)を阻止する、を挫折させる
[= foil, frustrate, baffle, prevent]

0151
disband
[dɪsbǽnd]

(軍隊・組織などが)解散する [= dissolve]
名 disbandment
語源 dis(～でない) + band(団結する)

0152
dislodge
[dɪslɑ́(ː)dʒ]

(敵)を退陣させる、を(～から)除去する [= remove] ⟨from⟩

0153
disperse
[dɪspə́ːrs]

分散する、を分散させる [= scatter]、(知識など)を広める
名 dispersal, dispersion

0154
eradicate
[ɪrǽdɪkèɪt]

を根絶する
[= exterminate, wipe out, root out]
名 eradication

0155
rout
[raʊt]

を完敗させる
[= defeat overwhelmingly]

0156
wreak
[riːk]

(破壊・損害)を引き起こす
▶ wreak havoc on ～ (～をめちゃめちゃに破壊する)

0157
contaminate
[kəntǽmɪnèɪt]

を汚染する
[= pollute]
名 contamination, contaminant (汚染物質)

0158
exacerbate
[ɪgzǽsərbèɪt]

を悪化させる [= aggravate]、をいらだたせる [= irritate]

0159
aggravate
[ǽgrəvèɪt]

を悪化させる
[= worsen]
名 aggravation

The FBI managed to **thwart** a terrorist plan to attack government buildings.	FBI は何とか，政府の建物を攻撃しようとするテロリストの計画を阻止することができた。
The rebel organization announced that they would **disband** and give up their weapons.	反乱軍は解隊して武器を捨てると宣言した。
They found it difficult to **dislodge** the enemy from their mountain fort.	彼らは，自陣の山の要塞から敵を退陣させることは困難だと悟った。
The demonstrators were ordered to **disperse** by the local police.	デモ参加者たちは解散するように地元警察に命じられた。
Smallpox was completely **eradicated** from the village.	天然痘はその村から根絶された。
The leader announced a great victory, saying that the army had completely **routed** the enemy.	当軍は完全に敵軍を敗走させたと言って，指揮官は大勝利を宣言した。
The storm **wreaked** havoc on the village, destroying a number of houses. *大損害，大惨事*	嵐は多数の家屋を倒壊させて村に大損害をもたらした。
After the accident, the water supply was **contaminated** with chemicals.	事故の後，上水道は化学物質で汚染されてしまった。
His mother's attempts to help simply **exacerbated** his problem.	母親が助けようと試みたが，彼の問題を単に悪化させただけだった。
The economic crisis was **aggravated** by a fall in the currency.	経済危機は通貨の下落で悪化した。

0160
abdicate
[ǽbdɪkèɪt]

(王位など)を退く [= resign]
(⇔ be enthroned)
名 abdication

0161
abscond
[əbská(:)nd]

逃亡する

0162
tamper
[tǽmpər]

(〜を)改ざんする 〈with〉

0163
juggle
[dʒʌ́gl]

を改ざんする
[= tamper with]
名 juggler (手品師, 詐欺師)

0164
cajole
[kədʒóʊl]

(人)を言いくるめる
[= coax, wheedle]

0165
defraud
[dɪfrɔ́:d]

(人)からだまし取る
[= swindle]

0166
swindle
[swíndl]

(人)から(〜を)だまし取る 〈out of〉
名 swindler (詐欺師)

0167
dupe
[djú:p]

をだます
[= deceive, cheat, trick, fool]
名 dupe (だまされやすい人, かも)

0168
mutter
[mʌ́tər]

つぶやく, ぶつぶつ不平を言う

0169
stammer
[stǽmər]

(〜を)口ごもりながら言う
[= stutter] 〈out〉

After the revolution, the king was forced to **abdicate** by the rebels.	革命の後，王様は反乱軍によって王位を退くことを強いられた。
The bank manager **absconded** with the money after his theft was revealed.	銀行の支店長は，自身の窃盗が発覚してからお金を持って姿をくらました。
The police were accused of having **tampered** with the evidence.	警察は証拠を改ざんしたとして告訴された。
The shareholder said the company was **juggling** its sales figures.	株主は会社が売上高を改ざんしていると言った。
When at first I refused to help, she began to **cajole** me in a sweet tone of voice.	最初助けることを拒絶したら，彼女は甘い声で私を言いくるめようとし始めた。
He was charged with **defrauding** the insurance company.	彼は保険会社から保険金をだまし取ったことで起訴された。
The old woman was **swindled** out of her fortune by a con artist.	その高齢の女性は，詐欺師に財産をだまし取られた。
Many members of the public were **duped** by the company's promise of quick profits.	すぐにもうかるというその会社の約束に，大衆の多くがだまされた。
His teacher told him to stop **muttering** and to speak more clearly.	ぼそぼそ言わずに，もっとはっきりしゃべりなさいと，先生は彼に言った。
The frightened little boy **stammered** out his name and then fell silent.	おびえていたその少年は名前を口ごもりながら言って，それから黙ってしまった。

ab-は「離れて」という接頭辞です。abdicate (0160) の「を退く」，abscond (0161) の「姿をくらます」がその例です。

0170 ~ 0179

#	見出し	意味
0170	**invoke** [ɪnvóuk]	(神の加護など)を祈願する, (法など)を発動する
0171	**crunch** [krʌntʃ]	をぼりぼりかむ 名 crunch (危機)
0172	**dawdle** [dɔ́:dl]	ぐずぐずする [= idle, waste time]
0173	**undermine** [ʌ̀ndərmáin]	を衰えさせる [= weaken], の下を掘る [= excavate beneath]
0174	**diagnose** [dàɪəgnóus]	を診断する, の原因を究明する 名 diagnosis
0175	**blur** [bləːr]	を不明瞭にさせる [= make vague] 形 blurry
0176	**squabble** [skwá(:)bl]	(~のことで)口げんかする [= brawl, quarrel, wrangle] ⟨over⟩
0177	**vie** [vaɪ]	(~を得ようと)競う [= compete] ⟨for⟩
0178	**bluff** [blʌf]	虚勢を張る [= pretend to be strong] ▶ bluff one's way (はったりで切り抜ける)
0179	**broach** [broutʃ]	(話題)を切り出す [= introduce, bring up]

60

In a moment of crisis, the man **invoked** the name of Buddha.	危機の瞬間，その男は仏陀の名を口にして祈った。
The children sat happily, **crunching** cookies and watching the TV.	子どもたちは楽しげに座って，クッキーをぼりぼりかみながらテレビを見ていた。
The principal scolded the students for **dawdling** in the school parking lot.	校長は，学生たちが構内の駐車場でぐずぐずしていたので叱責した。
The numerous contradictions in her argument **undermined** her main point.	彼女の論理には多くの矛盾があったので，要点が曖昧になった。
The doctors performed a series of tests but failed to **diagnose** her illness.	医師団は一連の検査を行ったが，彼女の病気を診断することができなかった。
The drizzling rain **blurred** my vision, making it dangerous to drive further. (霧雨が降る)	そぼ降る雨のため視界がぼやけて，それ以上車で進むのは危険となった。
When the children began to **squabble** over the dessert, their father lost his temper.	子どもたちがデザートのことで口げんかをし始めた時，父親はカッとなった。
These two students are **vying** for valedictory honors. (告別の，別れの)	この2人の学生が卒業生代表の座を競っている。
The intruder **bluffed** his way into the palace by pretending to be a guard. (侵入者)	侵入者は守衛のふりをして虚勢を張り宮殿へ入って行った。
At a certain point in the meeting, I **broached** the sensitive matter of etiquette.	会議の途中で，私は礼儀作法に関するデリケートな問題を切り出した。

#		
0180 **clench** [klentʃ]	を握り締める, (歯)をくいしばる ▶clench one's teeth (歯をくいしばる)	
0181 **perish** [périʃ]	死ぬ, 滅びる 形 perishable (腐りやすい, 滅びる運命にある) 語源 per (完全に) + i (it 行く) + sh	
0182 **ransack** [rǽnsæk]	(場所)を徹底的に捜す [= rummage], を略奪する [= plunder, rob]	
0183 **heave** [hi:v]	を (〜に) 投げる 〈at, onto〉	
0184 **wrench** [rentʃ]	をねじる [= twist], を捻挫する, を歪曲する [= distort] 名 wrench ((工具の) レンチ)	
0185 **beckon** [békən]	に (〜するように) 合図する 〈to do〉, をおびき寄せる [= attract, lure]	
0186 **deploy** [dɪplɔ́ɪ]	を配置する [= station], (軍隊)を展開させる	
0187 **detonate** [détənèɪt]	爆発する [= explode] 名 detonation	
0188 **dispatch** [dɪspǽtʃ]	を急送する, を急派する [= expedite]	
0189 **encompass** [ɪnkʌ́mpəs]	を囲む [= encircle], を含む	

He clenched his fist and punched the other man.	彼はこぶしを握り締め、もう1人の男を殴った。
The explorer said that he would reach the North Pole or perish in the attempt.	その探検家は、自分は北極にたどり着くか、挑戦の途中で死ぬか、どちらかだろうと言った。
The police completely ransacked his house in search of drugs.	警察は薬物を探して、彼の家中を徹底的に調べた。
The men heaved the old sofa onto the back of the truck.	男たちはトラックの荷台に古いソファーを投げ入れた。
The force of the accident wrenched his torso so forcefully that he broke his back.	事故の時、あまりにも強い力が彼の胴体をひねったので、彼は背骨を折った。
From the edge of the garden I saw her beckon him to follow her.	私は、彼女がついてくるように彼に手招きしているのを、庭の端から目撃した。
America responded to the threat by deploying aircraft carriers to the region.	アメリカは、その海域に航空母艦を配備することでその脅しに対応した。
Fortunately, the bomb failed to detonate and no one was hurt.	幸い、爆弾は爆発しなかったので負傷者は出なかった。
The company promises to dispatch all orders on the day that they are received.	発注されたその日にすべての注文品を急送すると、その会社は約束している。
The new housing development is starting to encompass the entire woodland.	新しい宅地開発は、その森全体を取り囲む形になり始めている。

0190
encrypt
[ɪnkrípt]

を暗号化する (⇔ decrypt を解読する)
图 encryption
語源 en (にする) + crypt (秘密)

0191
exonerate
[ɪgzá(:)nərèɪt]

を (〜から) 無罪とする 〈from, of〉
图 exoneration (免罪)

0192
fetter
[féṭər]

を拘束する
[= bind]

0193
gloat
[gloʊt]

ほくそ笑む,
さも満足そうに眺める

0194
haggle
[hǽgl]

値切る,言い争う

0195
alienate
[éɪliənèɪt]

を遠ざける [= estrange]
图 alienation　*cf.* alien (外国の)
語源 ali (ほかの) + en + ate

0196
shun
[ʃʌn]

を避ける
[= avoid, evade]

0197
dissuade
[dɪswéɪd]

に (〜を) 思いとどまらせる
[= discourage] (⇔ persuade) 〈from〉

0198
admonish
[ədmá(:)nɪʃ]

を (〜が理由で) 注意する
[= reprimand] 〈for〉
图 admonishment

0199
slam
[slæm]

をぴしゃりと閉める,
をたたきつける

The message was **encrypted** in a mysterious enemy code.	その伝達文は謎めいた敵の符号で暗号化されていた。
As a result of the trial, he was **exonerated** of all the charges.	裁判の結果、彼のすべての容疑は晴れた。
The new president soon found himself **fettered** by his campaign promises.	新大統領はすぐに自身が選挙の公約に拘束されていることに気付いた。
His enemies within the company **gloated** when he failed to win promotion.	彼が昇進できなかった時、社内のライバルたちはほくそ笑んだ。
Just when we thought we had reached an agreement, the other party began to **haggle**.	合意に達したと思ったら、相手側が値切り始めた。
Many voters were **alienated** due to the candidate's aggressive attacks on his opponent.	その候補者が行った対立候補への過剰な攻撃によって、多くの有権者が離反した。
Even after he was released from prison, he was **shunned** by his former friends.	彼は刑務所から出た後も、以前の友人たちに避けられた。
A social worker managed to **dissuade** the man from jumping to his death.	ソーシャルワーカーはその男性の飛び降り自殺をどうにか思いとどまらせることができた。
When the man **admonished** the teenagers for smoking, they just laughed.	男性が10代の若者たちに喫煙を注意した時、彼らは笑っただけだった。
He was so angry that he stood up and walked out, **slamming** the door behind him.	彼はとても腹が立っていたので、立ち上がって、後ろ手にドアをばたんと閉めて出て行った。

0200
squander
[skwá(:)ndər]

を浪費する
[= lavish, waste, spend extravagantly]

0201
subordinate
[səbɔ́ːrdənèit]

を(〜に)従属させる〈to〉
名形 subordinate (部下, 下位の, 二次的な)
語源 sub (下に) + ordin (順序) + ate

0202
succumb
[səkʌ́m]

(〜に)負ける
[= give in]〈to〉
語源 su (下に) + cumb (横たわる)

0203
tally
[tǽli]

(〜と)符合する〈with〉, 一致する、を表と照合する
を集計する
名 tally (勘定)

0204
teeter
[tíːtər]

ぐらつく, シーソーに乗る
▶ teeter on the edge [brink] of 〜
(〜の瀬戸際にいる)

0205
tout
[taut]

を押し売りする, hard sell
を(〜だと)褒めちぎる〈as〉

0206
traverse
[trəvə́ːrs]

を横断する
[= travel across]
▶ traverse a desert (砂漠を横断する)

0207
veer
[vɪər]

進路を変える, (政策などが)転換する
▶ veer off course (進路を外れる)

0208
veto
[víːtou]

(法案など)に拒否権を行使する
名 veto (拒否権)

0209
weather
[wéðər]

を切り抜ける
[= survive]

That young man is reported to have **squandered** his entire inheritance.	その若者は相続した全財産を浪費してしまったそうだ。
He said he would never **subordinate** his family life to his career.	家庭を仕事に従属させるつもりは全くないと，彼は言った。
The man finally **succumbed** to temptation and smoked a cigarette.	その男性はついに誘惑に負けてタバコを吸った。
Their names did not **tally** with those on the guest list.	彼らの名前は来賓名簿にある名前と符合しなかった。
The country was **teetering** on the edge of a war with its neighbor.	その国は，隣国との戦争の間際でぐらついていた。
Some men at the station were **touting** tickets for the concert.	駅で何人かの男がコンサートのチケットをしつこく売り込んでいた。
It took the explorers longer than expected to **traverse** the terrain.	探検家たちがその地域を横断するのに，予想よりも長く時間がかかった。
The driver **veered** to avoid a cat and crashed into the fence.	運転手はネコをよけようとして進路を変え，フェンスに激突した。
The President **vetoed** the Congressional bill cutting welfare to the poor.	大統領は貧困層への福祉を削減する議会法案に拒否権を行使した。
The automobile company **weathered** a period of record high oil prices.	その自動車会社は，記録的な石油高価格の時期を切り抜けた。

weather「天候」は変化するので「(難局)を切り抜ける」というイメージで覚えましょう。

0210

wince
[wíns]

顔をしかめる, たじろぐ [= shrink]

0211

scuttle
[skʌ́tl]

急ぎ足で歩く
▶ scuttle in all directions
(四方八方に急いで逃げ散る)

0212

agonize
[ǽgənàɪz]

(〜で) 苦悶する〈over〉 ひどく苦しむ
图 agony 形 agonizing

0213

bask
[bǽsk]

日光浴をする [= sunbathe],
享受する [= delight]

0214

concoct
[kənkɑ́(ː)kt]

(話・言い訳など)
をでっち上げる [= fabricate, cook up],
を混ぜ合わせて作る (スープ・飲食物 etc)
图 concoction

0215

delve
[délv]

(〜を) (徹底的に) 調査する [= search]〈into〉

0216

evade
[ɪvéɪd]

を避ける
图 evasion

0217

interject
[ìntərdʒékt]

(言葉)を差し挟む [= interpose]
图 interjection (間投詞)
語源 inter (間に) + ject (投げる)

0218

linger
[líŋgər]

ぶらぶらする [= loiter],
ぐずぐずする [= delay]

0219

pawn
[pɔ́ːn]

を質[担保]に入れる
图 pawn (人質, 抵当)

As the dentist inserted the needle, the patient **winced**.	歯科医が注射針を刺した時，患者は顔をしかめた。
The man **scuttled** after his boss, taking notes of what he said.	その男性は上司の言ったことのメモを取りながら，彼の後を急ぎ足で歩いた。
She told him to stop **agonizing** over the decision and to make up his mind.	決断にあたって苦悶することをやめて腹を決めなさいと，彼女は彼に言った。
In the summer, seals could be seen **basking** on the rocks.	夏には，岩の上で日光浴をするアザラシの姿を見ることができる。
He tried to **concoct** a good excuse for not having done his homework.	彼は宿題をやっていなかったことに対するうまい言い訳をでっち上げようとした。
I **delved** into that question for over a week but never found an answer.	その疑問点を1週間以上調べたが，答えは見つからなかった。
In order to **evade** the police, the fugitive wore a disguise.	警官を避けるために，逃亡者は変装をした。
Please wait until I have finished talking and do not **interject** any comments.	批評を差し挟むのは，私が話を終えてからにしてください。
Even after school is over, that group of students likes to **linger** around.	放課後になっても，その学生たちのグループはぶらぶら残っていたがる。
He had to **pawn** his wife's jewelry in order to cover his debts.	彼は借金を補填するため，妻の宝石類を質に入れなければならなかった。

0220 procure
[prəkjúər]

を入手する，を調達する
[= obtain, secure]
(御・苦労して)〈物〉を手に入れる

0221 reclaim
[rìːkléɪm]

を取り戻す，を更生させる，を埋め立てる
图 reclamation
語源 re(再び) + claim(主張する)

0222 recur
[rɪkə́ːr]

再び起こる [= occur again]
图 recurrence 形 recurrent
語源 re(再び) + cur(走る)

0223 reminisce
[rèmɪnís]

(〜の)思い出を語る〈about〉，思い出にふける
形 reminiscent

0224 replenish
[rɪplénɪʃ]

を補充する
[= fill up]

0225 scrawl
[skrɔːl]

をぞんざいに書く
[= scribble, write carelessly]

0226 hurtle
[hə́ːrtl]

(猛スピードで)突進する [= career]，
びゅーんと飛ぶ

0227 disparage
[dɪspǽrɪdʒ]

を見くびる [= undervalue]
图 disparagement 形 disparaging

0228 incur
[ɪnkə́ːr]

(負債・損害など)を負う，
(怒りなど)を買う [= invite]

0229 tarnish
[táːrnɪʃ]

を損なわせる [= stain]
▶ tarnish one's corporate image
(会社のイメージを傷つける)

I was able to **procure** my visa in three weeks so I could visit the country.	3週間ほどでビザを入手できたので、私はその国を訪問できた。
He went to **reclaim** his suitcase from the lost property office.	彼は遺失物取扱所にスーツケースを取り戻しに行った。
Doctors hoped her illness would not **recur** after a long series of treatments.	一連の長期にわたる治療の後、彼女の病気が再発しないことを医師たちは願った。
We still meet every two years and **reminisce** about old times.	私たちは今でも2年ごとに会い、昔の思い出を語り合う。
Once a week the farmers drive to town to **replenish** their supplies.	週に1度、農場主たちは生活必需品を補充するために、車で町へ出る。
His signature is unintelligible because he always **scrawls** his name.	彼はいつも自分の名前を走り書きするので、署名が判読しにくい。
He **hurtled** down the hill on his bicycle and crashed into a wall.	彼は自転車で丘を猛スピードで走り下り、壁に激突した。
Even members of the scientific community **disparaged** the cloning of a sheep.	科学団体の人々でさえ、羊のクローン化を見くびっていた。
The student **incurred** substantial debts as a result of going to college.	その学生は大学進学の結果として多額の借金を負った。
The bribery accusation **tarnished** his reputation forever.	賄賂容疑の告発が長いこと彼の評判を台無しにした。

bribery = 贈賄行為 (≒ payoff)

0230 ～ 0233

0230 **deplete** [dɪplíːt]	を使い果たす [= exhaust]
0231 **project** [prədʒékt]	を見積もる [= guess, estimate]，を提示する [= propose] 語源 pro (前に) + ject (投げる)
0232 **founder** [fáundər]	失敗する [= fail, blunder]，(船が) 浸水して沈没する
0233 ✓ **justify** [dʒʌ́stɪfàɪ]	を正当化する，の正当性を示す 名 justification 形 justifiable 語源 just (正しい) + fy

The explorer doubted if he could survive on his **depleted** supplies.	その探検家はわずかになってしまった食糧で生存していけるかどうか自信がなかった。
The company has **projected** record sales for the next quarter.	その会社は次の四半期に記録的な売上高を見積もっている。
The students all **foundered** badly on their latest exams.	学生たちはみな最近の試験でひどく失敗した。
The university president tried to **justify** the rise in fees to the students.	大学学長は学生たちに対して、授業料値上げを正当化しようとした。

plete (満たす) の前に com (完全に) がつくと complete「完成する」, de (分離) がつくと deplete (0230)「使い果たす」です。

でる度 A よくでる重要単語

名詞 239語

0234〜0242

0234
diversity
[dəvə́ːrsəti]

多様性 [= variety]
動 diversify
語源 di(離れて) + verse(向ける) + ity

0235
extinction
[ɪkstíŋkʃn]

絶滅
[= disappearance]
形 extinct

0236
specimen
[spésəmɪn]

標本
[= sample]
語源 spec(見る) + men(物)

0237
perspective
[pərspéktɪv]

観点 [= viewpoint, standpoint], 遠近法, 展望 [= vista]
語源 per(完全に・〜を通して) + spect(見る) + ive

0238
enforcement
[ɪnfɔ́ːrsmənt]

(法律などの)施行
動 enforce

0239
breakthrough
[bréɪkθrùː]

大進歩 [= significant advance or achievement], 突破

0240
myriad
[míriəd]

無数
▶a myriad of 〜（無数の〜）

0241
perception
[pərsépʃn]

認識 [= discernment], 知覚
動 perceive

0242
endowment
[ɪndáʊmənt]

寄付(金)
[= contribution, donation of money]

The **diversity** of the students added much interest to classroom discussions.	生徒の多様性はクラス討議をさらに興味深いものにした。
The rapid **extinction** of the dinosaurs remains a scientific mystery.	恐竜の急激な絶滅はいまだ科学的な謎である。
The museum contained many **specimens** of rare plants.	その博物館には多くの希少植物の標本があった。
The specialist provided a sociological **perspective** on the problems of the inner city.	その専門家はスラム街の抱える問題について社会学的観点を提示した。
The government ordered a stricter **enforcement** of the law to prevent any further incidents.	政府はこれ以上の紛争を回避するため、その法律をより厳格に施行するように指示した。
It took several years to achieve any **breakthroughs** in AIDS research.	エイズ研究に大進歩が実現するまでに数年かかった。
There were a **myriad** of famous names at the high society wedding.	その上流社会の結婚式には、無数の著名人が勢ぞろいした。
Perception involves more than merely the physiological aspects of the senses.	認識とは、単なる生理学上の知覚以上のものを含む。
A wealthy graduate had left the college a huge **endowment**.	裕福な卒業生は、大学に高額の寄付をした。

0243 **gist** [dʒɪst]	要点, 骨子 [= essence] ▶get [understand] the gist of ~ (〜の要点を理解する)
0244 **influx** [ínflʌks]	流入 [= inflow] (⇔efflux 流出)
0245 **backlash** [bǽklæʃ]	(思想などへの)反発, 反動 [= reaction] ⟨against⟩, (機械の)緩み
0246 **onset** [á(:)nsèt]	始まり [= start, beginning], 兆候 ▶the onset of a disease (発病)
0247 **paternity** [pətə́ːrnəti]	父親であること [= fatherhood] (⇔maternity 母親であること) ▶paternity leave (父親が取る出産休暇)
0248 **preservation** [prèzərvéɪʃən]	保存, 保護 [= conservation] 動 preserve 名 preservative (防腐剤, 保存料)
0249 **verdict** [və́ːrdɪkt]	(陪審員の)評決, 決定 [= decision], 判断 [= judgment] 語源 ver (真実) + dict (言う)
0250 **credibility** [krèdəbíləti]	信頼, 信憑性 [= reliability], 確実性 名 credential (証明書) 形 credible
0251 **momentum** [mouméntəm]	勢い [= impetus], 運動量
0252 **brevity** [brévəti]	(時の)短さ, 簡潔さ [= shortness, briefness, conciseness, terseness] 形 brief

The **gist** of his speech was that he was against the plan.	彼の演説の要点は，その計画には反対だということだった。
Recently, there has been a large **influx** of foreign investment into the U.S.	最近，合衆国への海外からの投資の大量流入が見られる。
Many feminists complained that there had been a **backlash** against policies designed to help women.	女性を支援しようとする諸政策に対する反発があったと，フェミニストたちの多くは不満を表した。
With the **onset** of winter, fuel prices rose dramatically.	冬の到来とともに，燃料価格が急騰(きゅうとう)した。
A test was carried out to determine the **paternity** of the child.	子どもの父親であることを決定するために検査が行われた。
The famous artist dedicated much of his life to the **preservation** of ancient buildings.	その有名な芸術家は，古い建造物の保存に人生の大半をささげた。
The public was shocked by the jury's **verdict** of 'guilty'.	公衆は陪審員の「有罪」判決にショックを受けた。
It seems his **credibility** has not been damaged despite the scandal.	スキャンダルにもかかわらず，彼に対する信頼は傷ついていないようだ。
Coaches often say that **momentum** is an important part of winning a game.	勢いは試合に勝つ重要な要素だと，コーチはよく言っている。
Haiku poets often suggest, at least indirectly, the **brevity** of life.	俳人は，少なくとも間接的に，人生のはかなさを詠むことが多い。

gist (0243) は「要点」です。summary「要約」との違いはしっかりと覚えましょう。

#	単語	意味
0253	**buffer** [bʌ́fər]	衝突を和らげる人[物]，緩衝器 [= shield, cushion, shock absorber]
0254	**knack** [næk]	(〜の)こつ〈of, for〉，要領
0255	**viability** [vàiəbíləti]	実現可能性 [= feasibility] 形 viable
0256	**auspice** [ɔ́:spɪs]	保護，後援 [= patronage, aegis, support]
0257	**requisite** [rékwɪzɪt]	(〜の)必要条件 [= requirement] 〈for〉 動 require
0258	**prerequisite** [pri:rékwəzɪt]	(〜に)(前もって)必要なもの〈for〉，前提条件
0259	**feat** [fi:t]	偉業 [= achievement]
0260 ✓	**gravity** [grǽvəti]	重力，引力 [= gravitation]，重さ [= weight]，重大さ [= seriousness]
0261	**jinx** [dʒɪŋks]	悪運 [= bad luck]
0262	**omen** [óumən]	前兆 [= prognostic, augury, foreboding]

The manager used his assistant as a **buffer** between himself and the public.	監督は自分と一般人の間の<u>クッション役</u>に助手を利用した。
It took the little girl a few days to get the **knack** of how to ride her bike.	自転車に乗る<u>こつ</u>を会得するのに,その幼い少女は数日を要した。
Many questions were raised about the **viability** of the policy.	その方針の<u>実現可能性</u>に関して多くの疑問点が挙げられた。
Noh flourished in the Muromachi Period under the **auspices** of the shogunate.	能は,幕府の<u>保護</u>のもとで,室町時代に栄えた。
One **requisite** for entering Harvard University is an acceptable score on the entrance exam.	ハーバード大学入学の<u>必要条件</u>の1つは,入試で満足な点数を取ることである。
Strong walking boots are considered a **prerequisite** for anyone planning to climb the mountain.	丈夫なウォーキングブーツは,山登りをしようとするすべての人にとって<u>必需品</u>である。
Very few climbers have managed the **feat** of climbing Everest.	エベレスト山を登りきる<u>偉業</u>を成し遂げた者は,ごくわずかしかいなかった。
The force of **gravity** is much weaker on the moon because of its smaller mass.	月面では質量が小さいために,<u>重力</u>がずっと小さい。
The ship was rumored among sailors to have a **jinx** on it.	その船は船員たちの間で<u>悪運</u>を持っているとうわさされていた。
The signs of recent economic instability may be serious **omens** for the future.	最近の経済不安の表れは,未来への重大な<u>前兆</u>かもしれない。

#		
0263 **precedent** [présɪdənt]	前例 [= previous case] 語源 pre (前に) + cede (進む) + enct	
0264 **prelude** [prélju:d]	前兆 [= forerunner]	
0265 **harbinger** [háːrbɪndʒər]	前触れ [= signal] ▶harbinger of the arrival of spring (春の到来の前触れ)	
0266 **philanthropy** [fɪlǽnθrəpi]	慈善（事業） [= benevolence] 形 philanthropic	
0267 **camaraderie** [kàːmərάːdəri]	友愛 [= friendship] (⇔ hostility 敵意)	
0268 **phase** [feɪz]	段階，局面 [= stage]，面 [= aspect, side, part]	
0269 **facet** [fǽsɪt]	（物事の）一面 [= face, aspect]	
0270 **facade** [fəsάːd]	（いつわりの）外見 [= pretense]，（建物の）正面	
0271 **incentive** [ɪnséntɪv]	刺激 [= stimulus, spur, encouragement]，動機 [= motive]，報奨金	
0272 **morale** [mərǽl]	勤労意欲，士気 *cf.* demoralize（の士気をくじく）	

His request was refused because there was no **precedent**.	<u>前例</u>がなかったので彼の要求は拒否された。
The busy week turned out to be a **prelude** to a frantic year.	その忙しい週は慌ただしい1年の<u>前触れ</u>だった。
The border clash proved to be a **harbinger** of full-scale war.	国境の衝突は,全面戦争の<u>前触れ</u>だということが判明した。
The orphanage depended on the **philanthropy** of a wealthy businessman.	その児童養護施設は裕福な実業家の<u>慈善事業</u>に頼っている。
After he left the army, he missed the **camaraderie** that he had shared with the soldiers.	軍を除隊した後,彼は兵士たちと共有していた<u>友愛</u>を懐かしく思った。
He was very lucky that his illness was detected in its early **phase**.	彼は病気が早い<u>段階</u>で見つかって,本当に幸運だった。
The committee was asked to look at every **facet** of the problem.	委員会はその問題のすべての<u>側面</u>を検討するように求められた。
Beneath a **facade** of respectability, the businessman was engaged in criminal activities.	立派な<u>表向きの顔</u>の裏で,その実業家は犯罪活動に手を染めていた。
The birth of his first child was an **incentive** for him to settle down and work harder.	最初の子どもが誕生したことは,彼にとって腰を据えてもっと熱心に働く<u>刺激</u>となった。
In an effort to improve **morale**, the boss announced a picnic for all his employees.	<u>勤労意欲</u>を高める努力の一環として,上司は全社員参加のピクニックを発表した。

0273
gratuity
[grətjúːəti]

チップ，心付け [= tip]

0274
proponent
[prəpóunənt]

支持者 [= adherent] (⇔ opponent)，提唱者

0275
advocate
[ædvəkət]

支持者 [= proponent]，擁護者
動 advocate
名 advocacy

0276
recipient
[rɪsípiənt]

受賞者，受取人 [= receiver]
▶ recipient of an award (受賞者)

0277
pundit
[pʌ́ndɪt]

専門家
[= expert]

0278 ✓
descendant
[dɪséndənt]

子孫 [= offspring] (⇔ ancestor)
動 descend (遺伝する, 下降する)
名 descent (家系)

0279
prosecutor
[prɑ́(ː)sɪkjùːtər]

検察官

0280
consort
[kɑ́(ː)nsɔːrt]

(特に国王・女王の) 配偶者
[= spouse]

0281
culprit
[kʌ́lprɪt]

容疑者，罪人
[= criminal]
▶ principal culprit (主犯)

0282
fugitive
[fjúːdʒətɪv]

逃亡者，脱走者
[= runaway, deserter]

At many restaurants, the expected amount of **gratuity** is 15 percent of the meal's cost.	多くのレストランでは，**チップ**の金額は食事代の15パーセントが見込まれている。
The pop star is known as an ardent **proponent** of vegetarianism.	その人気歌手は菜食主義の熱心な**支持者**として知られている。
The missionary is a well-known **advocate** of prison reform.	その宣教師は，刑務所改革の有名な**支持者**である。
The **recipient** of the Nobel Prize for literature has been announced.	ノーベル文学賞の**受賞者**が発表された。
Well-known **pundits** were invited to give their views on the election.	有名な**専門家たち**が選挙についての見解を述べるために招待された。
DNA analysis showed that some inhabitants were **descendants** of Vikings.	DNA分析によって住民の中にはバイキングの**子孫**も存在することが判明した。
The **prosecutor** did his best to show the witness was lying.	**検察官**は，目撃者が嘘をついていることを証明するために全力を尽くした。
The millionaire's **consort** was a beautiful young woman.	大富豪の**配偶者**は若くて美しい女性だった。
After a long police search, the **culprit** was apprehended.	長い期間警察が捜索を行った後，その**容疑者**が逮捕された。
How could anyone know that such a nice young man was a **fugitive** from justice?	そのようなすてきな若者が**逃亡犯**だったなんて，いったい誰が気付くだろうか。

proponent (0274) は pro (前に) + pone (置く) + ent (人) →自分の前に置く人だから「支持者」と覚えましょう！

0283
adherent
[ədhíərənt]

信奉者
[= follower]
語源 ad（〜の方へ）+ here（付く）+ nt

0284
mentor
[méntɔːr]

良き助言者
[= counselor, wise adviser]
▶ mentor for life（人生の指導者）

0285
novice
[ná(:)vəs]

初心者 [= beginner]，
見習い生
▶ novice teacher（新米教師）

0286
recluse
[réklu:s]

隠遁者
[= hermit]

0287
surrogate
[sə́:rəgət]

代理人
[= replacement]

0288
throng
[θrɔ(:)ŋ]

群集 [= crowd]
動 throng（に群がる）

0289
peer
[pɪər]

仲間，同輩 [= equal]，
貴族 [= nobleman]
形 peerless（比類ない）

0290
prodigy
[prá(:)dədʒi]

神童
[= child genius]

0291
counterpart
[káʊntərpàːrt]

（〜に）対応する物［人］[= equivalent]〈of〉，
写し [= copy, duplicate]，
対の一方

0292
aptitude
[ǽptɪtjùːd]

適性 [= fitness]，素質 [= talent]
形 apt
▶ aptitude test（適性検査）

He became a strong **adherent** of the new religion.	彼は新興宗教の熱心な<u>信奉者</u>になった。
Most people have found at least one **mentor** who has helped guide them through life.	たいていの人は，人生の手助けとなってくれた<u>良き助言者</u>を，少なくとも1人は見つけている。
From the first moves, the chess expert could see that his opponent was a **novice** at the game.	最初の数手の駒の動きを見て，チェスの名人は相手がゲームの<u>初心者</u>だとわかった。
The famous novelist now lived as a **recluse** on his own island.	その有名な小説家は今や自分の島で<u>隠遁者</u>として暮らしていた。
He appointed a **surrogate** to run the office while he was away.	彼は，自分の留守中に事務所を管理してくれる<u>代理人</u>を指定した。
He pushed through the **throng** of waiting reporters and walked quickly away.	待機しているリポーターたちの<u>群れ</u>をかき分けて，彼は素早く歩き去った。
Children at a certain age are more influenced by their **peers** than by their parents.	一定の年齢に達した子どもたちは，親よりも<u>仲間</u>により影響される。
Like many **prodigies**, his abilities declined as he became an adult.	多くの<u>神童</u>と同様に彼の才能は大人になるにつれて低下した。
The sales manager contacted his **counterpart** in the other company.	営業部長は，他社の<u>同じ地位の人物</u>と連絡を取った。
The SAT is designed to test **aptitude** rather than the memorization of facts.	SAT（大学進学適性試験）は，事実の記憶よりも<u>適性</u>をテストするように作られている。

0293 **caliber** [kǽləbər]	能力(の程度) [= faculty]，銃の口径 图 calibration（目盛り） ▶ high-caliber researcher（能力のある研究者）
0294 **demeanor** [dɪmíːnər]	振る舞い，品行 [= deportment, conduct] *cf.* misdemeanor 非行，軽犯罪
0295 **posture** [pá(ː)stʃər]	姿勢 [= pose]，態度 [= bearing]，状態
0296 **prudence** [prúːdəns]	慎重 [= judiciousness]
0297 **zeal** [ziːl]	熱心さ，熱意 [= fervor, ardor, zest] 形 zealous
0298 **prestige** [prestíːʒ]	名声 [= reputation, distinction, renown] 形 prestigious
0299 **eminence** [émɪnəns]	高名 [= renown] 形 eminent
0300 **conviviality** [kənvìviǽləti]	陽気な行動 形 convivial（陽気な）
0301 **elocution** [èləkjúːʃən]	雄弁術 語源 ex（外へ）+ locution（話し方）
0302 **agility** [ədʒíləti]	敏捷性，機敏さ [= nimbleness] 形 agile（鋭敏な）

There are not many lawyers of his **caliber** in the company.	その会社には彼ほどの高い能力のある弁護士はそれほど多くはいない。
His **demeanor** always appears serious, but actually he is quite a wit.	彼の振る舞いはいつも堅苦しく見えるが,実際には,彼は機知に富んだ男だ。
His father made him sit with a straight back to improve his **posture**.	彼の父親は,彼の姿勢を良くするために,背筋を真っすぐにして座らせた。
The bank was known for the **prudence** of its investment decisions.	その銀行は投資決定が慎重であることで有名だった。
While appreciating his **zeal**, his boss would prefer more care and accuracy.	彼の熱心さは評価していても,上司は,もっと注意力と正確さがあればと思うだろう。
At the peak of his career, his **prestige** was unrivaled.	彼がキャリアの頂点にあった時,彼と名声を競う者はいなかった。
Following his retirement, the professor's **eminence** grew even greater.	退職後,教授の高名はさらに上がった。
The **conviviality** of the party was spoiled by an argument.	パーティーのお祭り気分は,口論によって台無しにされた。
The young actress studied **elocution** in order to improve her accent.	その若い女優は,アクセントを直すために雄弁術を学んだ。
The old man showed surprising **agility** as he climbed the mountain.	その老人は登山をした時に,驚くべき敏捷性を見せた。

0303
allure
[əlúər]

魅力
[= attractiveness]
名 allurement（誘惑）

0304
candor
[kǽndər]

率直
[= frankness, candidness, openness]

0305
decorum
[dɪkɔ́:rəm]

礼儀正しさ
[= decency]
▶ perfect decorum（完璧な礼儀作法）

0306
fidelity
[fɪdéləti]

忠誠心
[= loyalty]

0307
dexterity
[dekstérəti]

器用さ [= skill, adroitness],
利口さ [= cleverness]
形 dexterous

0308
ebullience
[ɪbúliəns]

あふれる元気
[= cheerfulness]

0309
exhilaration
[ɪgzɪləréɪʃən]

大喜び
[= exultation]
動 exhilarate

0310
duplicity
[djuplísəti]

二枚舌 (謝罪に) 裏表があること
[= deceit, double-dealing]

0311
indiscretion
[ɪndɪskréʃən]

軽率な行為
[= imprudence]（⇔discretion 慎重さ）

0312
indolence
[índələns]

怠惰
[= idleness]

The young actress could not resist the **allure** of Hollywood.	その若い女優はハリウッドの魅力にあらがえなかった。
As usual, we spoke with absolute **candor** about our different perspectives.	いつものように,我々は異なった見方について極めて率直に話し合った。
Students at the girls' school were told to maintain **decorum** at all times.	その女子校の生徒たちは,常に礼儀正しさを保つように教えられていた。
The assistant was known for his intense **fidelity** to his boss.	そのアシスタントは,自分の上司に対する高い忠誠心で知られていた。
The **dexterity** required for certain traditional arts takes years to acquire.	ある種の伝統芸術に必要な器用さは,習得に何年もを要する。
Despite failing the audition, the girl's natural **ebullience** soon returned.	オーディションに落ちたにもかかわらず,その少女はすぐに生まれながらの情熱を取り戻した。
The boy's **exhilaration** at his exam results was clear.	少年がテスト結果に大喜びしている様子は,一目瞭然だった。
When we could no longer tolerate her **duplicity**, we confronted her directly.	彼女の二枚舌にもはや我慢できず,我々は彼女と直接対決した。
The politician's meeting with a gangster was a serious **indiscretion**.	その政治家の暴力団員との会合は,ただでは済まない軽率な行為だった。
The teacher felt irritated by the **indolence** of his students.	その教師は生徒たちの怠惰にいらだちを感じた。

0313
audacity [ɔ́ːdæsəti]
厚かましさ [= impudence, insolence], 大胆さ [= boldness]
形 audacious

0314
grudge [grʌdʒ]
恨み
副 grudgingly (しぶしぶ)
▶ bear [have] a grudge against ~ (~を恨む)

0315
tenure [ténjər]
(大学教授の)終身在職権, 保有(期間)

0316
duration [djuəréɪʃən]
継続[持続]期間
[= period]

0317
affinity [əfínəti]
相性 [= chemistry, compatibility], 類似性 [= similarity]

0318
proximity [prɑ(ː)ksíməti]
近接 [= nearness, neighborhood] ⟨to, of⟩
語源 proxim (最も近い) + ity

0319
hoax [hoʊks]
作り話, 悪ふざけ
[= trick]
▶ hoax call (いたずら電話)

0320
allegory [æləgɔ̀ːri]
寓話, たとえ話
[= story with a symbolic meaning]

0321
apex [éɪpeks]
絶頂 [= peak]

0322
zenith [zíːnəθ]
絶頂 [= culmination, peak, summit], 天頂 (⇔ nadir どん底)

Although I knew she was bold, one time her **audacity** really took me by surprise.	彼女が出しゃばりなことは知っていたが，ある時，彼女の厚かましさには本当にびっくりした。
Despite his ill treatment, he did not bear a **grudge** against his former employers.	ひどい扱いを受けたにもかかわらず，彼は以前の雇い主たちに対して恨みを抱かなかった。
American university professors must earn **tenure** to ensure their jobs.	アメリカの大学教授は，仕事を確保するためには終身在職権を得なければならない。
The politician was imprisoned for the **duration** of the war.	その政治家は，戦時中，投獄されていた。
Although we had only met each other twice, we felt a great **affinity** for each other.	それまでに2度しか会ったことがなかったが，私たちは互いに強い親近感を持った。
Those favoring America's free trade with Mexico always stress its close **proximity**.	メキシコとアメリカの自由貿易に賛成する人たちは，両国が非常に近いことをいつも強調する。
The UFO sighting turned out to be a student **hoax**.	UFOの目撃情報は生徒の作り話だと判明した。
I explained to the students Plato's **allegory** of the cave.	私は，学生たちにプラトンの洞穴の寓話を説明した。
At the **apex** of his career, the champion suffered a run of defeats.	そのチャンピオンはキャリアの絶頂期に連敗してしまった。
At the very **zenith** of his career, he got involved in scandal.	キャリアの絶頂期に，彼はスキャンダルに巻き込まれた。

0323	**ascension** [əsénʃən]	上昇, 即位 [= enthronement] ▶ The Ascension (キリストの昇天)
0324	**conglomerate** [kənglá(:)mərət]	巨大複合企業
0325	**offshoot** [ɔ́(:)fʃùːt]	派生物, 子会社 [= subsidiary]
0326	**consignment** [kənsáɪnmənt]	託送, 委託商品 動 consign (を託送する)
0327	**conveyance** [kənvéɪəns]	輸送(機関), (権利の)譲渡 [= transfer] 動 convey 名 conveyor (コンベヤー)
0328	**durability** [djùərəbíləti]	耐久性 [= ability to last] 形 durable
0329	**footage** [fútɪdʒ]	映画・テレビの特定の場面
0330	**gadget** [gǽdʒɪt]	機器 [= appliance]
0331	**glitch** [glɪtʃ]	(機器などの)故障 [= breakdown], 小さな技術上の問題
0332	**echelon** [éʃəlà(:)n]	地位, (組織などの)階層 [= rank]

The singer's **ascension** to the rank of superstar was unusually quick.	その歌手はスーパースターの座へ昇りつめるのが並外れて早かった。
His small business was taken over by a huge **conglomerate**.	彼の小さな会社は巨大複合企業に買収された。
The new series was an **offshoot** of the original drama series set in the same hospital.	新しいシリーズは、同じ病院の設定の原作ドラマシリーズから派生したものである。
The storekeeper said he was expecting a fresh **consignment** of eggs that day.	店主はその日、新鮮な卵の入荷があるだろうと言った。
The millionaire paid for the **conveyance** of the tents to the area affected by the earthquake.	その大富豪は、地震の被災地に送るテントの輸送の費用を負担した。
Doubts were raised as to the **durability** of the new storehouse.	新倉庫の耐久性について懸念が持ち上がった。
The police released **footage** of the riot to the television companies.	警察は暴動の映像をテレビ局に公開した。
The young man's room was full of IT **gadgets**.	その若者の部屋は、IT機器でいっぱいだった。
Suddenly a **glitch** in the lighting system threw the theater into darkness.	突然の照明装置の故障で、映画館が真っ暗になった。
People from the company's higher **echelons** rarely visited the branch.	会社で高い地位にいる人はめったに支社を訪れなかった。

consignment (0326) のsignは「印をつける」を意味します。ほかの例としてはdesignation「指名」やassignment「割り当て」があります。

0333 speculation [spèkjuléɪʃən]	投機, 考察 [= thought], 推測 [= conjecture] 動 speculate ▶speculation in stocks（株式投資）
0334 hype [haɪp]	誇大宣伝 *cf.* hyperbole（誇張表現）
0335 benchmark [béntʃmàːrk]	基準 [= standard]
0336 integration [ìnṭəgréɪʃən]	統合, 差別撤廃による人種統合 (⇔ segregation) 動 integrate
0337 contraband [káː)ntrəbænd]	密輸品 [= smuggled goods] 語源 contra（反）+ ban（禁止する）
0338 liability [làɪəbíləṭi]	（～に対する）責任 [= responsibility]〈for〉, 負債 [= debt] 形 liable
0339 libel [láɪbəl]	名誉毀損, 中傷 形 libelous
0340 quota [kwóʊṭə]	割り当て, ノルマ [= norm]
0341 perk [pəːrk]	諸手当 [= perquisite, fringe benefit] ▶receive a perk（手当を受ける）
0342 annotation [ænətéɪʃən]	注釈 [= footnote] 動 annotate

Speculation in currency is a risky but potentially lucrative business.	通貨への投機はリスクがあるが潜在的には金になるビジネスだ。
He refused to believe all the **hype** about the new invention.	彼はその新しい発明品についてのすべての誇大宣伝を信じようとしなかった。
The program was said to have set a new **benchmark** for documentaries.	その番組がドキュメンタリー番組の新しい基準を定めたと言われた。
Racial **integration** of schools was eventually mandated by the American government.	学校の人種統合は，最終的にアメリカ政府の権限で実施された。
It was suspected that the boat carried **contraband**, though none was found.	その船は密輸品を運んだのではないかと疑いをかけられたが，何も見つからなかった。
The judge ordered the man to assume **liability** for the accident.	判事は，その男に事故の責任を取るように命じた。
The tabloid went bankrupt because so many people won **libel** suits against it.	そのタブロイド紙は，あまりにも多くの人が同紙に名誉毀損訴訟で勝訴したので破産した。
Each student was given a **quota** for how many boxes of cookies they should sell.	各学生は，売るべきクッキーの箱の数を割り当てられた。
One of the **perks** of the job was regular meals at restaurants.	仕事の諸手当の1つは食堂での三度三度の食事である。
The scholar's **annotations** to the play were full of errors.	その劇に関する学者の注釈は，間違いだらけだった。

0343
backlog
[bǽklɔ̀(:)g]

未処理の山
[= accumulation]
▶ backlog of work (たまった仕事)

0344
collation
[kəléɪʃən]

照合作業, (書物の)ページ合わせ
動 collate

0345
counterfeit
[káʊntərfìt]

偽造通貨, 模造品
[= imitation]

0346
forgery
[fɔ́:rdʒəri]

偽造(罪), 偽造品
[= counterfeit]
動 forge

0347
asylum
[əsáɪləm]

(政治犯の)亡命に対する庇護,
避難所 [= shelter]

0348
haven
[héɪvən]

避難所, 停泊所
[= refuge, shelter]
▶ tax haven (租税回避地)

0349
hub
[hʌb]

中心 [= center],
商業や輸送の中心 [= focus of commerce or transportation]

0350
venue
[vénju:]

開催地, (犯行などの)現場

0351
vicinity
[vəsínəti]

近所
[= neighborhood]

0352
validity
[vəlídəti]

効力 [= effectiveness],
正当性 [= lawfulness]

Returning from his holiday, he found a **backlog** of work waiting for him.	彼が休暇から戻ってくると，仕事の<u>未処理の山</u>が待ち受けていることがわかった。
The **collation** of the different texts took a long time.	異なったテキストの<u>照合作業</u>にはかなりの時間を要した。
Although a **counterfeit**, the hundred-dollar bill fooled almost everyone.	<u>偽札</u>であるにもかかわらず，その100ドル紙幣にはほとんど誰もがだまされた。
I did not know he had been convicted of **forgery** when I accepted his personal check.	私は彼から個人用小切手を受け取った時，彼が<u>偽造</u>で有罪になっていたのを知らなかった。
The refugees applied for political **asylum** as soon as they landed.	難民たちは，上陸すると同時に，政治的な<u>亡命に対する庇護</u>を申請した。
In the last days of the Bosnian conflict the U.N. established 'safe **havens**.'	ボスニア紛争の終わり頃に，国連は「安全<u>避難所</u>」を設けた。
New York is not the American capital but it is the **hub** of modern American life.	ニューヨークはアメリカの首都ではないが，現代のアメリカの生活の<u>中心</u>となっている。
The sports stadium is also a popular **venue** for concerts.	その競技場は，よく知られたコンサートの<u>開催地</u>でもある。
The only drawback to the new house was there were no shops in the immediate **vicinity**.	新しい家の唯一の欠点は，すぐ<u>近所</u>に店が1軒もないことだった。
The court said the company's regulations had no legal **validity**.	裁判所はその会社の規則は法的<u>効力</u>がないと言った。

backにおいてあるlog「材木」は使っていないのでbacklog「未処理の山」(0343)，というイメージで覚えよう。

#	語	意味
0353	**efficacy** [éfɪkəsi]	効力, 有効性 [= effectiveness]
0354	**longevity** [lɑ(:)ndʒévəti]	長寿, 長命 [= long life]
0355	**mortality** [mɔːrtǽləti]	死亡率, 死ぬ運命 (⇔ immortality 不死, 不朽) 形 mortal
0356	**demise** [dɪmáɪz]	死去 [= decease, death], 終焉 [= end, termination]
0357	**immunity** [ɪmjúːnəti]	(〜の)免疫 [= resistance] 〈to〉 形 immune
0358	**remedy** [rémədi]	(〜の)治療(薬), 治療法 [= cure] 〈for〉 形 remedial
0359	**transfusion** [trænsfjúːʒən]	輸血 [= blood transfusion] 動 transfuse 語源 trans(超えて) + fuse(注ぐ) + ion
0360	**bout** [baʊt]	発作 [= attack], 短い期間 [= spell]
0361	**quarantine** [kwɔ́(ː)rəntiːn]	隔離(期間), 検疫
0362	**contingency** [kəntíndʒənsi]	不慮の出来事 [= accident, contingent], 偶然 [= chance], 不確実 [= uncertainty]

One must often doubt the **efficacy** of the United Nations in world governance.	国連の世界統治における<u>効力</u>はしばしば疑う必要がある。
In Japan, the pine tree is a symbol of **longevity**.	日本では，松の木は<u>長寿</u>のシンボルだ。
The charity made great efforts to decrease infant **mortality** among the poor.	その慈善団体は，貧困層の幼児<u>死亡率</u>を減らすことに多大なる努力をしていた。
Smoking and drinking to excess can bring about an early **demise**.	タバコの吸い過ぎ，酒の飲み過ぎは早期<u>死亡</u>の原因になることがある。
Some people have a natural **immunity** to the disease.	その病気に対する自然<u>免疫</u>が備わっている人たちもいる。
Honey and lemon is a traditional **remedy** for a sore throat.	ハチミツとレモンは，のどの痛みに対する伝統的<u>治療薬</u>である。
The accident victim needed an immediate **transfusion** of a rare blood type.	その事故の被害者は，稀少な血液型の<u>輸血</u>を即時に必要とした。
A **bout** of malaria generally leaves the victim much weakened.	マラリアの<u>発作</u>は概して被害者をさらに衰弱させる。
All dogs have to spend two weeks in **quarantine** before they enter the country.	すべての犬は入国前に2週間の<u>隔離期間</u>を経なくてはならない。
The mayor insisted on preparing the city for any **contingency**.	市長は，市が<u>不慮の出来事</u>に備えることを主張した。

0363
concussion
[kənkʌ́ʃən]

脳震盪(のうしんとう)

0364
blister
[blístər]

水膨れ,火膨れ
[= vesicle on the skin]

0365
prognosis
[prɑ(:)gnóusəs]

(病気の)予後 (⇔ diagnosis 診断)

0366
penchant
[péntʃənt]

(〜の)傾向,(〜の)好み
[= preference] ⟨for⟩

0367
propensity
[prəpénsəti]

(〜の)(しばしば好ましくない)傾向,
(〜の)性癖 [= tendency, inclination] ⟨for⟩

0368
savor
[séivər]

(〜を)思わせるもの⟨of⟩,
風味,嗜好(しこう) [= taste, relish]

0369
banter
[bǽntər]

冗談,ひやかし
[= joke, badinage]

0370
jest
[dʒest]

冗談
[= funny remarks]

0371
animosity
[ænimɑ́(:)səti]

憎悪 [= hatred],
敵意 [= enmity, hostility, antagonism]

0372
aversion
[əvə́:rʒən]

(〜への)嫌悪感
[= repulsion] ⟨to⟩

After falling from her horse, she suffered a severe **concussion**.	彼女は落馬してから，激しい脳震盪にかかった。
We developed **blisters** because it was cold and dry.	寒くて乾燥していたので，私たちは水膨れができた。
After he had taken some medical tests, the doctor told him that the **prognosis** was good.	いくつかの医学的検査を受けた後に，医師は予後は順調だと彼に告げた。
The professor had a **penchant** for expensive French restaurants.	その教授は高価なフランス料理店を好む傾向があった。
Despite his **propensity** for anger, he was a generous and basically kind person.	彼は怒りっぽい傾向があるが，寛大で基本的には親切な人だった。
There was a **savor** of sarcasm in Dr. Record's speech.	レコード博士の講演には皮肉の香りが漂っていた。
One eventually tires of mere **banter** and wants to talk seriously.	人は単なる冗談にはいつか飽きて，まじめな話がしたくなるものだ。
The announcer's casual **jest** offended many viewers.	そのアナウンサーの不用意な冗談は，多くの視聴者の怒りを買った。
It has been hard to overcome the **animosity** between Israel and its Arab neighbors.	イスラエルとアラブ近隣諸国との間の憎悪を抑えることは難しかった。
The woman said she had an **aversion** to people smoking near her.	その女性は彼女のそばで喫煙する人に嫌悪感を抱くと言った。

#	単語	意味
0373	**acrimony** [ækrəmòuni]	とげとげしさ, 辛辣さ [= asperity] 形 acrimonious
0374	**affront** [əfrʌ́nt]	(公然の)侮辱 [= insult, scorn, slight]
0375	**misgiving** [mìsgívɪŋ]	(将来の結果に関しての)不安 [= uneasiness] ⟨about⟩, 疑念 [= doubt]
0376	**scruple** [skrúːpl]	罪の意識, 良心の呵責 [= twinge of conscience]
0377	**grievance** [gríːvəns]	不満, 苦情 [= complaint] 動 grieve (を嘆く) 名 grief (悲嘆) 形 grievous (悲痛な)
0378	**eulogy** [júːlədʒi]	追悼 [= memorial address], 賛辞 [= speech of praise]
0379	**flattery** [flǽtəri]	お世辞, おべっか 動 flatter 形 flattering
0380	**homage** [há(ː)mɪdʒ]	敬意 [= respect, reverence]
0381	**defiance** [dɪfáɪəns]	反抗, 挑戦 [= challenge] ▶in defiance of ~ (~を無視して)
0382	**deportation** [dìːpɔːrtéɪʃən]	国外追放 [= banishment, expulsion] 動 deport 語源 de (離れて) + port (運ぶ) + ate + ion

The problems were finally resolved but not without some **acrimony**.	問題はやっと解決したが、いくらかの<u>とげとげしさ</u>が残った。
The way he was treated at the hotel was an **affront** to his dignity.	そのホテルの彼に対する扱いは、彼の尊厳を<u>侮辱</u>するものだった。
Many had serious **misgivings** about the new plan to restructure the company.	会社再建の新計画には、多くの人が非常に<u>不安</u>を覚えた。
The man felt no **scruples** about betraying his country.	男性は母国を裏切ったことに対して<u>罪の意識</u>を感じなかった。
He has a **grievance** against his company, which had never rewarded him for all his hard work.	彼は、自分の激務に一度も報いてくれたことがない会社に<u>不満</u>を感じている。
At the funeral, a friend delivered a **eulogy** to the deceased worker.	葬儀でひとりの友人が亡くなった労働者への<u>弔辞</u>を述べた。
The professor usually dismissed the students' compliments as **flattery** designed to get a better grade.	教授は学生たちの褒め言葉を、成績を上げてもらうための<u>お世辞</u>としていつも退けた。
Although we didn't always agree with his views, we never ceased to pay him **homage**.	我々は彼の見解に必ずしも賛成したわけではなかったが、彼には常に<u>敬意</u>を払っていた。
In a gesture of **defiance**, the terrorists pledged to strike again.	<u>反抗</u>的な身ぶりで、テロリストたちは再び攻撃することを誓った。
The government announced the immediate **deportation** of five diplomats.	政府は、5人の外交官を直ちに<u>国外追放</u>すると発表した。

0383 **decadence** [dékədəns]	堕落 [= corruption]
0384 **derision** [dɪríʒən]	嘲笑 [= mockery] 動 deride
0385 ✓ **disguise** [dɪsgáɪz]	変装 [= camouflage] 動 disguise (を変装させる)
0386 **conjecture** [kəndʒéktʃər]	憶測, 推測 [= guess, surmise, inference]
0387 **fallacy** [fæləsi]	誤った推論 [= misconception]
0388 **decree** [dɪkríː]	法令, 布告 [= edict]
0389 **ordinance** [ɔ́ːrdənəns]	条例 [= regulation], 法令 [= statute] 動 ordain (を命じる, を規定する)
0390 **precept** [príːsept]	命令書, 行動上の指針, 格言 [= maxim]
0391 **elimination** [ɪlìmɪnéɪʃən]	除去 [= removal, abolition, deletion], 予選 動 eliminate
0392 **exorcism** [éksɔːrsɪzm]	悪魔払い 動 exorcize 名 exorcist (悪魔払い祈祷師)

The preacher denounced the **decadence** of the media.	牧師はマスコミの堕落を公然と非難した。
Despite the **derision** of the critics, the movie was a big success.	批評家たちの嘲笑にもかかわらず,映画は大ヒットとなった。
Nobody recognized the famous pop star through his **disguise**.	変装していたので,有名なポップスターに誰も気づかなかった。
The defense attorney insisted that his client be convicted on facts, not on **conjecture**.	依頼人は憶測ではなく事実に基づいて判決を出されるべきであると,被告側の弁護士は主張した。
He said that the idea that price always indicated quality was a **fallacy**.	価格が常に品質を示しているという考えは,誤った推論だと彼は言った。
The dictator issued a **decree** banning all political parties.	独裁者はすべての政党を禁止する法令を発動した。
A recent **ordinance** against smoking in public places has pleased many citizens.	公的な場所での喫煙を禁じる最近の条例が,多くの市民を喜ばせた。
The mayor issued a formal **precept** regulating the use of firearms within the city limits.	市長は市内における銃器使用を規制する正式の令状を発行した。
Green Peace seeks the complete **elimination** of all nuclear testing.	グリーン・ピースはあらゆる核実験の完全撤廃を求めている。
Even today, **exorcisms** are sometimes held in haunted houses.	今日ですら幽霊屋敷ではときどき悪魔払いが行われている。

0393
transgression
[trænsgréʃən]

違反
[= offense]
動 transgress

0394
infringement
[ɪnfríndʒmənt]

侵害 [= violation]
▶ infringement of the freedom of the press
（報道の自由の侵害）

0395
disparity
[dɪspǽrəṭi]

差異 [= difference],
不均衡 [= incongruity]
形 disparate（本質的に異なる）

0396
dissension
[dɪsénʃən]

意見の衝突
[= disagreement]

0397
discrepancy
[dɪskrépənsi]

不一致
[= disagreement, difference, inconsistency]

0398
dearth
[də:rθ]

不足，欠乏 [= scarcity],
飢饉(ききん) [= famine]

0399
deluge
[délju:dʒ]

大洪水 [= great flood],
豪雨

0400
conflagration
[kɑ̀(:)nfləgréɪʃən]

大火
[= fire]

0401
spillage
[spílɪdʒ]

流出
[= leakage]

0402
outage
[áʊṭɪdʒ]

停止，停電

In the prison, even minor **transgressions** were severely punished.	刑務所では小さな違反でさえ厳しく処罰された。
The article was considered an **infringement** of the celebrity's privacy.	その記事は有名人のプライバシーの侵害だと見なされた。
Despite the **disparity** in their ages, the little boy got on very well with his grandfather.	年齢の差があるにもかかわらず,その小さな男の子は祖父と仲良しだった。
There was much **dissension** when women were admitted to the club.	女性たちがそのクラブに入会を許可された時,多くの意見の衝突が起こった。
An auditor found a large **discrepancy** in the accounts of the bank's transactions.	会計検査官は,その銀行の取引の貸借勘定に大きな不一致を見つけた。
A **dearth** of fresh water required that barren farmland undergo irrigation.	淡水不足のため,不毛な農地は灌漑しなくてはならなかった。
The Biblical story of Noah's Ark describes a great **deluge** that floods the earth.	ノアの箱舟についての聖書の物語は,地上に氾濫する大洪水を描いている。
Massive **conflagrations** have nearly destroyed the city on several occasions.	過去何回も,大火災がその都市を壊滅に近い状態にしてきた。
The accident led to a **spillage** of dangerous chemicals.	事故は危険な化学薬品の流出を引き起こした。
The typhoon caused power **outages** across the whole region.	台風は地域全体の停電を引き起こした。

transgression (0393) のgressは (行く) を意味します。同じようにgressの入った単語にはregression「後退」やdigression「脱線」があります。

0403 hazard
[hǽzərd]

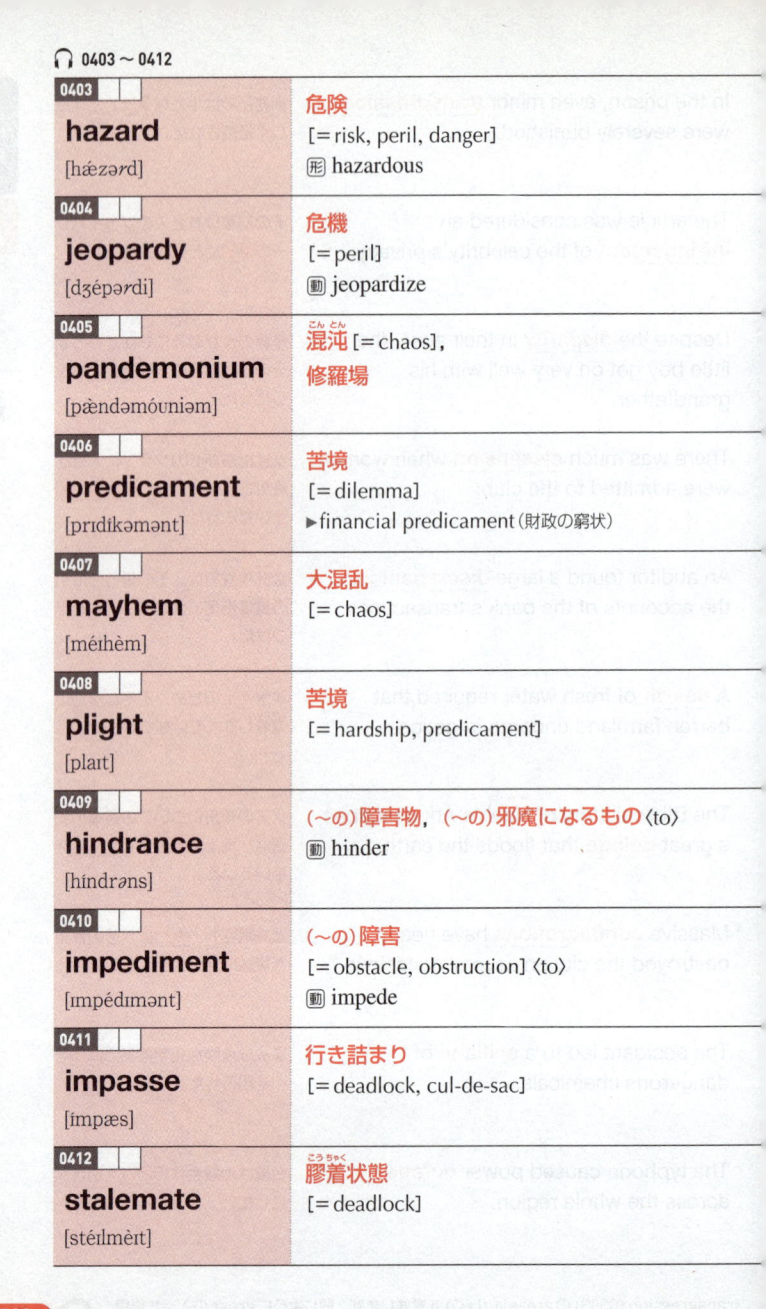

危険
[= risk, peril, danger]
形 hazardous

0404 jeopardy
[dʒépərdi]

危機
[= peril]
動 jeopardize

0405 pandemonium
[pæ̀ndəmóuniəm]

混沌 [= chaos], 修羅場

0406 predicament
[prɪdíkəmənt]

苦境
[= dilemma]
▶financial predicament (財政の窮状)

0407 mayhem
[méɪhèm]

大混乱
[= chaos]

0408 plight
[plaɪt]

苦境
[= hardship, predicament]

0409 hindrance
[híndrəns]

(〜の)障害物, (〜の)邪魔になるもの〈to〉
動 hinder

0410 impediment
[ɪmpédɪmənt]

(〜の)障害
[= obstacle, obstruction] 〈to〉
動 impede

0411 impasse
[ímpæs]

行き詰まり
[= deadlock, cul-de-sac]

0412 stalemate
[stéɪlmèɪt]

膠着状態
[= deadlock]

The dump site was deemed a health **hazard** to people in the community.	ごみ投棄場は、地域住民にとって健康上**危険**であるとされた。
The scandal put the businessman's career in **jeopardy**.	そのスキャンダルは実業家の経歴を**危機**に陥れた。
Pandemonium broke out when officials announced that the game would be postponed.	審判が試合は延期されると発表すると、**混沌状態**となった。
He was saved from his **predicament** by a loan from his father-in-law.	義父からの融資によって彼は**苦境**から救われた。
People began to fight and the meeting became **mayhem**.	人々はけんかを始めたので、会議は**大混乱**となった。
Moved by the **plight** of the refugees, the millionaire donated a large sum to help them.	難民たちの**苦境**に心を動かされて、その大富豪は彼らの援助のために多額の寄付をした。
The greatest **hindrance** to their studies was a lack of up-to-date textbooks.	彼らの勉学に対する最大の**障害**は、最新の教科書が不足していることだった。
A series of environmental disasters created additional **impediments** to economic recovery.	一連の環境災害が経済復興のさらなる**障害**となった。
We were locked in an ideological **impasse** that made it difficult to come to an agreement.	我々はイデオロギー上の**行き詰まり**に陥り、合意に達するのが難しかった。
After days of fighting, the armies reached a **stalemate**.	何日間にもわたる戦いの後、両軍は**膠着状態**に陥った。

pass (通路) を通ることができない (impossible) のでimpasse (0411) は「行き詰まり」というイメージで覚えましょう。

0413
blunder
[blʌ́ndər]

重大なミス
[= mistake]

0414
fiasco
[fiǽskou]

大失敗
[= blunder, total or ridiculous failure]

0415
culpability
[kʌ̀lpəbíləṭi]

過失の原因 [= responsibility]
形 culpable

0416
catalyst
[kǽṭəlɪst]

きっかけ, 触発するもの
[= trigger]

0417
dispute
[dɪspjúːt]

論争
[= controversy, argument]
形 disputable

0418
feud
[fjuːd]

確執
[= conflict]
▶ wage a feud with ~ (~と反目している)

0419
hassle
[hǽsl]

口論 [= squabble, dispute, quarrel],
わずらわしいこと [= bother, nuisance]

0420
antipathy
[æntípəθi]

(~への)反感 (⇔sympathy 共感) ⟨to⟩
形 antipathetic
語源 anti (反) + pathy (感情)

0421
atrocity
[ətrɑ́(ː)səṭi]

残虐
[= brutality, cruelty]
形 atrocious

0422
vandalism
[vǽndəlìzm]

芸術品・公共物などの破壊

The investigation blamed a series of **blunders** for the accident.	調査はその事故の原因に一連の重大ミスを挙げた。
Our expedition to the Himalayas was a complete **fiasco**.	我々のヒマラヤ遠征は大失敗だった。
The report failed to determine **culpability** for the accident.	報告ではその事故の過失の原因を特定することができなかった。
The minister's resignation proved to be the **catalyst** for a general election.	大臣の辞任が総選挙のきっかけとなったことがわかった。
The government said it could not interfere in an industrial **dispute**.	労働争議に介入することはできないと，政府は発言した。
The two families had been waging a **feud** for years.	両家には多年にわたる確執があった。
I got into a **hassle** with the tax office over my tax liability.	私は，私の納税義務をめぐって税務署と口論をした。
She felt an **antipathy** to her new boss from the moment she met him.	会ってすぐに，彼女は新しい上司に反感を覚えた。
The **atrocity** of the mass killings still causes the survivors to have nightmares.	大量殺戮の残虐性が原因で，生存者たちは今でも悪夢を見る。
The art critic said that the plans for the new city center were simply bureaucratic **vandalism**.	その美術批評家は，新しい都市センターの計画は官僚的な文化芸術への破壊行為にすぎないと発言した。

0423 **devastation** [dèvəstéɪʃən]	破壊 [= destruction], 荒廃 [= desolation] 動 devastate 語源 de(完全に) + vast(空の) + ate + ion
0424 **havoc** [hǽvək]	大混乱, 破壊 ▶play havoc with ~ (~をめちゃくちゃに破壊する)
0425 **wreckage** [rékɪdʒ]	残骸 [= debris] 動 wreck (を破壊する)
0426 **rubble** [rʌ́bl]	瓦礫, 石片 [= debris, fragments of rock] ▶rubble of war (戦争の瓦礫)
0427 **regime** [rəʒíːm]	政権 [= reins of government], 政体 [= system of government]
0428 **exodus** [éksədəs]	大量出国, 移住, (the E-) (イスラエル人の) エジプト脱出
0429 **onslaught** [ɑ́(ː)nslɔ̀ːt]	猛攻撃 [= assault]
0430 **amnesty** [ǽmnəsti]	恩赦 [= pardon]
0431 **barrage** [bərɑ́ːʒ]	(質問などの) 集中砲火, 弾幕
0432 **brunt** [brʌnt]	矢面, 攻撃の矛先 ▶bear [take] the brunt of ~ (~の矢面に立つ)

Devastation from natural forces can exceed our wildest projections.	自然の力が持つ破壊力は，我々の大胆な予測をも超えることすらある。
The riot at the stadium created general **havoc** for the fans and officials.	スタジアムの騒動がファンと係員を巻き込む大混乱を引き起こした。
Experts searched the **wreckage** of the crashed airplane for clues.	専門家たちは(事故の原因の)手がかりを得るために，墜落した飛行機の残骸を探した。
Clearing away **rubble** after the accident was itself a huge task.	事故の後，瓦礫を片付けること自体が大変な仕事だった。
The country was ruled by a military **regime** led by a general.	その国は将軍によって率いられた軍事政権に統治されていた。
During the civil war there was a mass **exodus** by the villagers into neighboring countries.	内戦の間，村人による隣国への大量出国があった。
The little town withstood the enemy's **onslaught** for three days.	その小さな町は，敵軍の3日間にわたる猛攻撃に耐え抜いた。
An **amnesty** for all political prisoners was announced by the new government.	すべての政治犯の恩赦が，新政府によって発表された。
The film star was faced with a **barrage** of questions about his upcoming divorce.	その映画俳優は今度の離婚に関する質問の集中砲火に直面した。
The capital city bore the **brunt** of the enemy's bombing campaign.	首都が敵国の爆撃作戦の矢面に立った。

0433
cessation
[seséɪʃən]

停止 [= halt, suspension, discontinuance]

0434
cipher
[sáɪfər]

暗号 [= code]
(⇔ decipher 判読, 解読)

0435
retribution
[rètrɪbjúːʃən]

報い [= requital],
仕返し [= reprisal]

0436
repeal
[rɪpíːl]

撤廃, 破棄

0437
provision
[prəvíʒən]

配給
[= distribution]
語源 pro (前を) + vide (見る) + ion

0438
repercussion
[rìːpərkʌ́ʃən]

影響, (音の) 反響
[= reverberation, aftereffect, rebound]

0439
reprisal
[rɪpráɪzəl]

報復

0440
faction
[fǽkʃən]

派閥
[= clique]
▶ faction leader (派閥のリーダー)

0441
rampage
[rǽmpeɪdʒ]

狂暴な行動
▶ go on a rampage (荒れ狂う)

0442
menace
[ménəs]

(〜に対する) 脅威
[= threat] 〈to〉
動 menace 形 menacing

The first step in any peace process is an initial **cessation** of hostilities.	いかなる和平交渉においても第一歩は，まず敵対行為を停止することである。
During the war, the mathematician had created **ciphers** for the army.	戦時中，数学者は軍隊のために暗号を作り出した。
Christians are supposed to believe that **retribution** is the right of God alone.	キリスト教徒は，（悪事の）報いは神のみに許された権利と信じるべきとされる。
Many people were calling for the **repeal** of the harsh new anti-terrorism laws.	新たに制定された厳し過ぎる反テロリズム法の撤廃を，多くの人々が要求していた。
The army was made responsible for the **provision** of food to the refugees.	軍隊は避難民への食料品の配給の責任を担った。
The **repercussions** of the debt crisis included a fall in stock prices.	債務危機の影響は，株価下落を招いた。
Following the rebellion, the government carried out savage **reprisals**.	反乱の後をたどるように，政府は激しい報復をした。
Each **faction** in the party wanted its candidate to have the job.	その党内の派閥それぞれが，その立候補者にその職に就くことを望んだ。
The soccer fans went on a **rampage**, breaking shop windows.	サッカーファンは，狂暴な行動に出て，店の窓を割った。
The politician said that young hooligans were becoming an increasing **menace** to society.	不良少年たちがますます社会に対する脅威になりつつあると，その政治家は発言した。

0443	**upheaval** [ʌphíːvəl]	(社会・政治などの) 激変 [= disruption], (地殻の) 隆起
0444	**commotion** [kəmóuʃən]	騒動, 動揺 [= tumult, uproar, disturbance]
0445	**concession** [kənséʃən]	譲歩 [= compromise]
0446 ✓	**curfew** [kə́ːrfjuː]	夜間外出禁止令, 門限
0447	**ultimatum** [ʌ̀ltɪméɪṭəm]	最終通告 [= last offer] 形 ultimate
0448	**truancy** [trúːənsi]	無断欠席, ずる休み [= absenteeism] ▶truancy rate (生徒の無断欠席率)
0449	**hindsight** [háɪndsàɪt]	後知恵 (⇔foresight 先見の明) 語源 hind (後ろ) + sight (視覚) ▶with [in] hindsight (後から考えると)
0450	**maxim** [mǽksɪm]	行動原理 [= principle], 格言 [= axiom, dictum]
0451	**memento** [məméntou]	記念品, 形見 [= keepsake]
0452	**cinch** [sɪntʃ]	簡単なこと

Scientists theorize that an environmental **upheaval** caused by a huge meteorite destroyed the dinosaurs.	科学者は，巨大な隕石による環境の**激変**で恐竜が死に絶えたという理論を立てている。
The teacher heard a **commotion** going on in a neighboring classroom.	その教師は隣の教室で**騒動**が起こっているのを聞いた。
However long we negotiated, the enemy refused to make any **concessions**.	長時間の交渉にもかかわらず，敵軍は**譲歩**することを拒否した。
The government imposed a **curfew** in an attempt to prevent further protests.	政府は，それ以上の抗議行動を防ぐべく，**夜間外出禁止令**を敷いた。
The company finally issued him an **ultimatum** to work harder or be fired.	会社はついに，もっと一生懸命働くかクビになるかの**最後通告**を彼に出した。
Parents are held responsible for the **truancy** of their children.	子どもの**無断欠席**の責任は両親にある。
With **hindsight**, the company realized that it could have prevented a grave mistake.	**後から考えると**，その会社は重大な過ちを防げたはずだったということに気がついた。
His **maxim** in business had always been that honesty was the best policy.	仕事における彼の**行動原理**はずっと，正直こそ最善の策というものだった。
The students gave their teacher a **memento** in appreciation of his great teaching.	学生たちは素晴らしい授業に感謝して，先生に**記念品**を贈った。
After the exam, he said it had been a **cinch** and he was sure that he had passed.	試験が終わると，彼は，試験は**朝飯前**だったし合格を確信していると言った。

0453 **vent** [vent]	通気孔 [= air hole], 穴 [= aperture], はけ口 [= outlet, escape]	
0454 **solace** [sá(:)ləs]	慰め, 癒やし	
0455 **trance** [træns]	昏睡状態 [= coma]	
0456 **felicity** [fəlísəti]	慶事 [= glad occasion] 形 felicitous	
0457 **entity** [éntəti]	独立体, 存在 [= being, existence], 本質 [= essence]	
0458 **premises** [prémɪsɪz]	(建物を含めた)土地 [= building and its adjuncts]	
0459 **pretext** [príːtekst]	口実 [= excuse]	
0460 **creed** [kriːd]	信条 [= belief]	
0461 **quandary** [kwá(:)ndəri]	板挟み [= dilemma], 苦境 [= predicament, crunch]	
0462 **depiction** [dɪpíkʃən]	描写 [= delineation] 語源 de(下に) + pict(描く) + ion	

A blockage in the **vents** rendered the air-conditioning system ineffective.	通気孔部分がふさがって、エアコンが効かなくなった。
After his wife died, the man sought **solace** in his work.	妻を亡くしてから、男は仕事に慰めを求めた。
The hypnotist put the volunteer into a deep **trance**.	催眠術師はその志願者を深い昏睡状態に陥らせた。
Beneath a facade of domestic **felicity**, the marriage was in trouble.	家庭の慶事の見せかけの裏で、その結婚は危機に陥っていた。
The university's publishers are a separate **entity** from the university and manage their own finances.	大学出版局は大学とは別個の事業体であり、独自に会計を行っている。
No one can enter his **premises** without formal approval.	正式な許可なしには、誰も彼の土地に立ち入ることはできない。
He called me under the **pretext** of inviting me to a party.	彼は、私をパーティーに招くことを口実に、私に電話をかけてきた。
Although they follow different **creeds**, they still decided to marry.	2人は信条は異なるが、それでも結婚することに決めた。
When he was offered both jobs, he found himself in a **quandary**.	両方の仕事の申し出を受けて、彼は板挟みの状態に自分がいることに気付いた。
Some felt that the film's **depiction** of the queen was disrespectful.	映画での女王の描写が失礼だと感じる人たちもいた。

#	単語	意味
0463	**farce** [fɑːrs]	道化芝居 [= slapstick comedy]
0464	**juncture** [dʒʌ́ŋktʃər]	(決定的な)時点，岐路 ▶at this (critical) juncture (この重大時に)
0465	**misnomer** [mìsnóumər]	誤った名称 [= unsuitable name] 語源 mis(誤る) + nomer(名付ける)
0466	**clique** [kliːk]	小集団，派閥 [= inner circle]
0467	**clout** [klaut]	殴ること，権力，影響力
0468	**gimmick** [gímɪk]	巧妙な仕掛け
0469	**ordeal** [ɔːrdíːl]	厳しい試練，苦難 [= affliction, anguish, torment, tribulation]
0470	**polarization** [pòulərəzéɪʃən]	二極化 動 polarize 形 polar (極地の)
0471	**prerogative** [prɪrɑ́(ː)gətɪv]	特権 [= privilege]，大権
0472	**ramification** [ræ̀mɪfɪkéɪʃən]	厄介事，派生問題，分枝

The comedian first made his name in a theatrical **farce**.	その喜劇役者が初めて有名になったは，劇場で演じた<u>道化芝居</u>だった。
At this **juncture**, the chairman of the conference announced a short break.	この<u>重大時</u>に，会議の議長は短い休憩を取ると発表した。
It would be a **misnomer** to describe him as a specialist in the subject.	彼をその分野の専門家と評することは<u>間違った呼び方</u>となるだろう。
The group of boys formed an exclusive **clique** in the school.	少年のグループは学校で排他的な<u>小集団</u>を作った。
The heavyweight boxer could deliver an incredible **clout** with either fist.	そのヘビー級ボクサーは，どちらのこぶしでも，とてつもない<u>パンチ</u>を繰り出すことができた。
He dismissed the new policy as just a **gimmick** to attract voters.	新たな政策は有権者を引きつける<u>巧妙な仕掛け</u>にすぎないと，彼は退けた。
She found giving evidence in the trial a terrible **ordeal**.	裁判で証言するのは恐ろしい<u>試練</u>だと彼女は感じた。
The growing **polarization** between rich and poor is threatening the country's social stability.	貧富の<u>二極化</u>の拡大が，その国の社会的安定を脅かしている。
It was the professor's **prerogative** to decide the textbook for the course.	講座の教材を決めるのは，教授の<u>特権</u>だった。
The full **ramifications** of cloning are yet to be understood.	クローンの<u>厄介な問題</u>がどうなるか，すべてわかるのはこれからだ。

でる度 A よくでる重要単語
形容詞・副詞　228語

0473〜0481

0473 **altruistic** [æltruístɪk]	利他的な [= unselfish] (⇔egoistic) 語源 alter (ほかの) + tic	
0474 **profound** [prəfáund]	深い，深遠な [= deep, esoteric, inscrutable] (⇔shallow 浅い) 副 profoundly	
0475 ✓ **skeptical** [sképtɪkəl]	懐疑的な [= doubtful] 名 skepticism 副 skeptically	
0476 ✓ **widespread** [wáɪdsprèd]	広範な [= extensive], 広く知られた [= well-known]	
0477 **anonymous** [ənɑ́(ː)nɪməs]	作者不詳の，匿名の [= with no name given] 名 anonymity	
0478 **contentious** [kənténʃəs]	論争好きな [= controversial, quarrelsome] 動 contend 名 contention	
0479 **authentic** [ɔːθéntɪk]	本物の [= genuine], 確実な，信頼できる [= reliable, trustworthy]	
0480 **paramount** [pǽrəmàunt]	最高(位)の [= supreme, preeminent, highest in rank]	
0481 **replicate** [réplɪkət]	複製された 名 replica (複製) 語源 re (再び) + pli (重なる) + ate	

The businessman said his donations had been **altruistic** in nature.	その実業家は，自分の寄付は本質的に利他的な性質のものだと述べた。
His last novels are considered **profound** meditations on the nature of human evil.	彼の最近の小説は，人間の邪悪さの本質を深く熟考したものと見なされている。
Although he assured me he would help, I remained **skeptical**.	彼は助けてくれることを請け合ったが，私は懐疑的なままだった。
The move provoked **widespread** opposition throughout the country.	その運動は，国中で広範な反対を引き起こした。
Scholars are studying an **anonymous**, fifth-century B.C. manuscript.	学者たちは作者不詳の紀元前5世紀の写本を調べている。
It's often hard to deal with his **contentious** attitude.	彼の論争好きな態度は，往々にして御しがたい。
Van Gogh's "Sunflowers", now in a Tokyo museum, was proven to be **authentic**.	ヴァン・ゴッホの『ひまわり』は今東京のさる美術館にあるが，本物であることが証明された。
Mao Zedong was the **paramount** leader of the Chinese communist revolution.	毛沢東は中国共産革命の最高指導者だった。
He created a **replicate** volume that looked exactly like the original book.	彼は原本とうり二つの複製版を作った。

#		
0482 **lucrative** [lú:krətɪv]	**儲かる** [= profitable]	
0483 **clumsy** [klʌ́mzi]	**不器用な** [= awkward] (⇔ adroit 器用な)	
0484 **defunct** [dɪfʌ́ŋkt]	**使用されていない** [= disused]	
0485 **discernible** [dɪsə́:rnəbl]	**認識できる** [= recognizable] 動 discern	
0486 **futile** [fjú:təl]	**無駄な** [= worthless, useless] 名 futility	
0487 **prolific** [prəlífɪk]	**多作の** [= fruitful, fecund, highly productive] ▶ prolific writer (多作の作家)	
0488 **inscrutable** [ɪnskrú:təbl]	**謎めいた, 不可解な** [= enigmatic, unfathomable, inexplicable]	
0489 **manifest** [mǽnɪfèst]	**明らかな** [= evident, clear, plain, obvious] 名 manifestation (明示, 表明)	
0490 **ubiquitous** [jubíkwətəs]	**遍在する** [= omnipresent, universal] 名 ubiquity	
0491 **occidental** [à(:)ksədéntəl]	**西洋の** [= western] (⇔ oriental) 名 Occident	

I knew a man who built a very **lucrative** business from the repair and resale of junk appliances.	私は，ガラクタの電化製品を修理・販売して，非常に儲かる商売を築き上げた男を知っていた。
She was a **clumsy** girl who often dropped or spilled things.	彼女は，たびたび物を落としたりこぼしたりするような，不器用な女の子だった。
The factory had long been **defunct** and was now a ruin.	工場は長い間，使用されていなかったので，今では荒廃した状態になっていた。
His teacher said there had been no **discernible** improvement in his work.	彼の学業成績に認識できる成果は上がっていないと先生は言った。
Having failed to get into university, the students' years of study appear to have been **futile**.	その学生たちは大学に入れなかったので，長年の勉強が無駄だったように思われる。
The author Isaac Asimov astonished everyone with his **prolific** output.	作家アイザック・アシモフはその多作で皆を驚かせた。
The smile of the "Mona Lisa" is said to be **inscrutable**.	『モナリザ』の微笑みは謎とされている。
The problem was **manifest** to all those at the conference.	会議に出席しているすべての人々にとって，その問題は明らかだった。
At certain times of the year in Bali, tourists seem to be **ubiquitous**.	バリ島では毎年ある時期になると観光客が至る所にいるようだ。
That professor is well versed in both Oriental and **Occidental** philosophy.	その教授は東洋，西洋両方の哲学に詳しい。

---

ubiquitous (0490) は日本語化しています。「ユビキタス社会」とは情報ネットワークにどこでもアクセスできる社会という意味です。

0492		
exemplary [ɪgzémpləri]	模範的な [= model]	

0493		
commensurate [kəménsərət]	(〜に)釣り合った [= proportional], (〜と)同程度の 〈with〉 名 commensuration	

0494		
transient [trǽnziənt]	はかない [= passing, transitory, temporary, evanescent, fleeting]	

0495		
ostensible [ɑ(:)sténsəbl]	表向きの, 見せかけの, 明らかな [= apparent] 副 ostensibly	

0496		
aesthetically [esθétɪkəli]	美的に [= ornamentally]	

0497		
marginally [mάːrdʒənəli]	かろうじて, わずかに [= slightly]	

0498		
indigenous [ɪndídʒənəs]	土着の, (その土地に)固有の [= native], 生まれながらの [= innate]	

0499		
inherent [ɪnhíərənt]	生来の, 固有の [= intrinsic, innate] ▶ one's inherent character (生まれながらの性格)	

0500		
intrinsic [ɪntrínsɪk]	固有の [= inherent], 本質的な [= essential] (⇔ extrinsic 非本質的な)	

0501		
latent [léɪtənt]	潜在的な [= lying, hidden, potential] 名 latency ▶ one's latent abilities (潜在能力)	

She was an **exemplary** student who gained straight 'A's.	彼女は成績がオールAの模範的な学生だった。
We want to keep our expenditures **commensurate** with our income.	支出を収入に釣り合ったものにし続けたい。
The **transient** nature of all living things is the essence of Buddhism.	すべての生きとし生けるものははかないという自然の理法は、仏教の本質である。
His **ostensible** purpose was to deliver a present, but actually he had another aim.	彼の表向きの目的は贈り物を届けることだったが、彼には実は別の目的があった。
The car was cheap and yet had an **aesthetically** satisfying design.	その車は安かったが、それにもかかわらず美的な満足感を与えてくれるデザインだった。
The student's grades improved **marginally** in his second year.	その生徒の成績は2年生の時にかろうじて上がった。
The **indigenous** peoples of many countries have been persecuted or killed.	多くの国の先住民が迫害されたり殺害されたりしてきた。
Human beings possess an **inherent** ability to acquire language.	人類は言語を習得する生来の能力を持っている。
Humans and some apes have an **intrinsic** ability to walk on two legs.	人類とある種の類人猿は2足歩行という固有の能力を持っている。
All his **latent** hostility to his father was brought out by the incident.	父親に対して抱いていた彼の潜在的な憎悪が全部、その出来事によって噴出した。

intrinsic(0500)と、次ページのextrinsicはペアで覚えましょう。trinsic（並んでいる）にin（中に）がつくと「本質的な」、ex（外に）がつくと「非本質的な」の意味になります。

0502	**extrinsic** [ekstrínsɪk]	外的な，非本質的な [= unessential] (⇔ intrinsic)
0503	**covert** [kóuvəːrt]	秘密の [= hidden, concealed, disguised] (⇔ overt)
0504	**clandestine** [klændéstɪn]	秘密の [= secret, hidden]，人目をはばかる [= underhand]
0505	**classified** [klǽsɪfàɪd]	機密扱いの [= secret, clandestine]，分類された
0506	**ulterior** [ʌltíəriər]	隠された [= hidden, covert]，ずっと遠い [= further, remote]
0507	**surreptitiously** [sə̀ːrəptíʃəsli]	こっそりと [= furtively]
0508	**equivalent** [ɪkwívələnt]	(〜と) 等価の [= equal] ⟨to⟩　图 equivalence, equivalency
0509	**tantamount** [tǽnṭəmàunt]	(〜と) 等しい [= equivalent, equal] ⟨to⟩
0510	**rigorous** [rígərəs]	厳しい [= austere, merciless, unyielding]　图 rigor
0511	**stringent** [stríndʒənt]	厳しい [= strict, rigorous, exacting]

He studied hard not because he enjoyed it but for the **extrinsic** rewards good grades would bring.	彼が一生懸命勉強したのは，勉強が楽しいからではなく，良い成績がもたらす外的な褒美のためであった。
The **covert** activities of the CIA have been roundly condemned.	CIAの秘密工作が厳しく非難された。
Their meeting always had to be **clandestine** and brief.	彼らの会議は，いつも秘密裡に行われ，かつ手短でなくてはならなかった。
The clerk said that the information was **classified** and so could not be released.	情報は機密扱いなので公表できないと，その事務員は言った。
Their job offer to me was so generous that I suspected an **ulterior** motive.	彼らの仕事の条件はあまりに気前よかったので，私は隠された目的があるのではないかと疑った。
He tried to read the letter **surreptitiously** but his wife noticed it.	彼はその手紙をこっそり読もうとしたが，彼の妻は気付いた。
The scientist said that the cut in funding was **equivalent** to canceling the research altogether.	この財政的支援の削減は研究の完全中止に等しいと，その科学者は発言した。
His silence was **tantamount** to an admission of guilt.	彼の沈黙は罪を認めたことに等しかった。
Medical science is usually thought to be a **rigorous** intellectual challenge.	医学は厳しい知的な試練の場だと普通は考えられている。
The standards set for passing the exam were quite **stringent**.	その試験の合格基準は極めて厳しかった。

classified (0505) はclassに分けるから「分類された」，大切な「機密扱いの」という2つの意味があります。

0512 austere [ɔ:stíər]	厳しい [= stern, severe, rigid, harsh]
0513 caustic [kɔ́:stɪk]	辛辣な [= biting, stinging, cutting, sarcastic]
0514 scarce [skeərs]	希少な [= rare, scanty, sparse], 珍しい 图 scarcity 副 scarcely
0515 subtle [sʌ́tl]	微妙な [= delicate], 鋭い [= sharp, acute] 图 subtlety
0516 meager [mí:gər]	(収入・食事などが)乏しい [= lean, scanty, paltry], やせた ▶ a meager meal (乏しい食事)
0517 sophisticated [səfístɪkèɪtɪd]	洗練された [= refined], 複雑な [= complex, intricate]
0518 sublime [səbláɪm]	荘厳な, 崇高な [= magnificent] 图 sublimity
0519 exquisite [ɪkskwízɪt]	絶妙な, 洗練された [= refined]
0520 susceptible [səséptəbl]	(〜に)影響されやすい [= vulnerable] 〈to〉 图 susceptibility 形 susceptive
0521 vulnerable [vʌ́lnərəbl]	(〜に)傷つきやすい 〈to〉, もろい [= sensitive, susceptible]

His **austere** expression and manner belied the kindness underneath.	彼の厳しい表情と態度のために，根底にある親切心が伝わらなかった。
Susie was offended by his **caustic** remarks.	スージーは彼の辛辣な批評に気分を害していた。
Crows used to be common here, but now they have grown quite **scarce**.	カラスはこの辺りによくいたものだが，現在ではかなり希少になっている。
He learned to recognize the **subtle** differences between one butterfly and another.	彼はチョウとチョウとの微妙な違いを見分けられるようになった。
The young couple can barely live on their **meager** income.	その若い夫婦は乏しい収入でやっと暮らしていくことができる。
Her manner is charming but not what one would call **sophisticated**.	彼女の振る舞いは愛嬌があるが，洗練されていると言えるものではない。
The poetry of Dante's "Divine Comedy" is **sublime**.	ダンテの『神曲』の詩は荘厳だ。
This lady's spring kimono is of **exquisite** design and quality.	この女性用の春物の着物は絶妙なデザインと品質だ。
People with a poor diet are especially **susceptible** to colds and the flu.	貧弱な食生活をしている人たちは，特に風邪やインフルエンザにかかりやすい。
The AIDS virus makes its victims **vulnerable** to normally minor illnesses.	エイズ・ウイルスに感染すると，患者は普通は大したことのない病気にも弱くなる。

0522
impervious
[ɪmpə́ːrviəs]

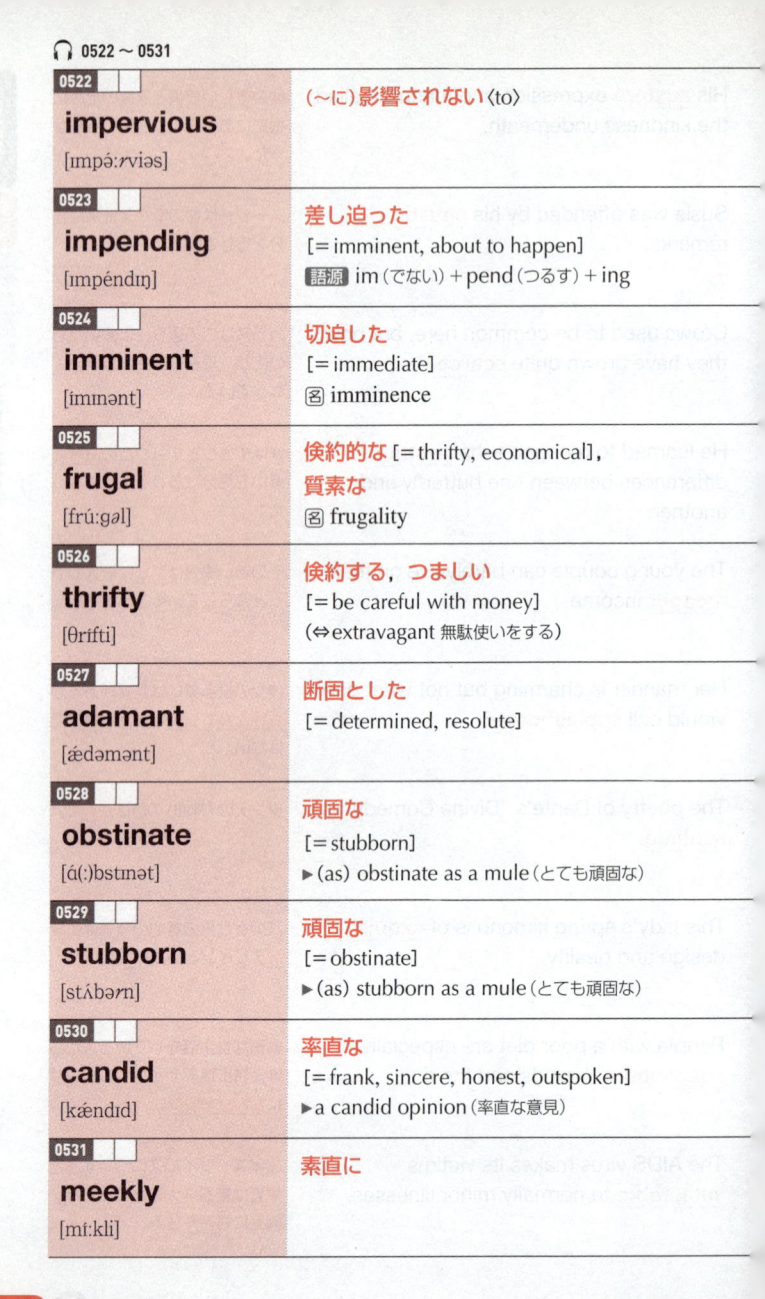

(〜に)影響されない 〈to〉

0523
impending
[ɪmpéndɪŋ]

差し迫った
[= imminent, about to happen]
語源 im (でない) + pend (つるす) + ing

0524
imminent
[ímɪnənt]

切迫した
[= immediate]
名 imminence

0525
frugal
[frúːgəl]

倹約的な [= thrifty, economical],
質素な
名 frugality

0526
thrifty
[θrífti]

倹約する, つましい
[= be careful with money]
(⇔ extravagant 無駄使いをする)

0527
adamant
[ǽdəmənt]

断固とした
[= determined, resolute]

0528
obstinate
[á(ː)bstɪnət]

頑固な
[= stubborn]
▶ (as) obstinate as a mule (とても頑固な)

0529
stubborn
[stʌ́bərn]

頑固な
[= obstinate]
▶ (as) stubborn as a mule (とても頑固な)

0530
candid
[kǽndɪd]

率直な
[= frank, sincere, honest, outspoken]
▶ a candid opinion (率直な意見)

0531
meekly
[míːkli]

素直に

His mother begged him to study but he was **impervious** to her appeals.	母親は彼に勉強するように願ったが、彼は母親の訴えに耳を貸さなかった。
Weather forecasters warned of an **impending** storm from the hurricane.	気象予報士たちはハリケーンによる差し迫った暴風雨を警告した。
Most seismologists predict that a big earthquake is **imminent** in the country.	ほとんどの地震学者は、大地震がその国に迫っていると予測している。
Despite years of **frugal** management, the company is still struggling.	倹約的な経営を何年も続けたにもかかわらず、会社は依然として苦闘している。
Even after he made his fortune, he remained very **thrifty** about money.	彼は一財産築いた後でさえ、お金に対してとても倹約家のままだった。
The accused man was **adamant** that he was innocent despite the evidence against him.	被告人は証拠が不利であるにもかかわらず、自分は無罪であるとして譲らなかった。
She knew that her husband, with his **obstinate** character, would be difficult to persuade.	頑固な性格の夫の説得が難しいであろうことを、彼女はわかっていた。
Her husband's **stubborn** refusal even to listen to her suggestion infuriated her.	彼女の忠告に耳を貸すことさえも頑固に拒絶する夫に、彼女は激怒した。
Political meetings hardly ever seem to be constructive and **candid**.	政治集会が建設的で率直であることはほとんどないようだ。
Despite his fame, the scientist **meekly** accepted the student's criticisms.	名声があるにもかかわらず、その科学者は素直に学生の批判を受け入れた。

0532 ~ 0541

0532	**affluent** [ǽfluənt]	裕福な [= rich, opulent], 豊富な [= ample, abundant] 图 affluence
0533	**superfluous** [supə́ːrfluəs]	過剰の, 余分な [= excessive, unnecessary, redundant] 图 superfluity
0534	**engrossed** [ɪngróʊst]	(~に)夢中になって ⟨in⟩
0535	**exuberant** [ɪgzjúːbərənt]	熱狂的な [= fervent, enthusiastic], あふれるばかりの 图 exuberance
0536	**frenetic** [frənétɪk]	熱狂した [= frantic, frenzied, rapturous]
0537	**infatuated** [ɪnfǽtʃuèɪtɪd]	(~に)夢中な [= obsessed] ⟨with⟩ 图 infatuation
0538	**ecstatic** [ɪkstǽtɪk]	有頂天の, 恍惚とした 图 ecstasy
0539	**dubious** [djúːbiəs]	半信半疑の [= skeptical, doubtful]
0540	**ambivalent** [æmbívələnt]	相反する感情を持った, 曖昧な [= uncertain] 图 ambivalence (両面性)
0541	**precarious** [prɪkéəriəs]	不安定な [= unsure, uncertain, unstable] ▶ precarious position (不安定な立場)

As a population grows more **affluent**, it naturally begins to buy more luxury goods.	人々が裕福になればなるほど，必然的によりぜいたくなものを買い始める。
Sometimes we tire of **superfluous** rules and regulations.	私たちは時に過度の決まりや規則が嫌になる。
He was so **engrossed** in the movie that he failed to hear the doorbell.	彼はその映画にとても夢中になっていたので，ドアのベルが聞こえなかった。
Her **exuberant** and passionate acting debut won her wide acclaim.	彼女の熱狂的で情熱的な演技のデビューは広く喝采を浴びた。
With his rural background, he found it hard to adjust to the **frenetic** pace of the city.	彼は地方出身で，都会の熱狂したようなペースに適応するのに困難を覚えた。
The student became **infatuated** with her glamorous literature professor.	学生は（彼女の）魅力的な文学の教授に夢中になった。
When the president saw the excellent sales figures, he felt **ecstatic**.	ずば抜けた売上高の数字を見て，社長は有頂天になった。
He assured me that things were fine, but I remained somewhat **dubious**.	事態はうまくいっていると彼は私に断言したが，私はいくぶん半信半疑のままだった。
He felt **ambivalent** about his promotion because it would involve more work.	昇進すると仕事が増えるので，彼は曖昧な感情を抱いていた。
Peace in this country depends on a **precarious** balance of force and diplomacy.	この国の平和は武力と外交の危ういバランスに依存している。

precarious (0541) は前が (pre) 危ないので，注意 (care) しようと覚えましょう。

0542 **inclusive** [ɪnklúːsɪv]	包括的な (⇔exclusive) 動 include 名 inclusion 語源 in (中に) + clude (閉じる) + sive
0543 **exclusive** [ɪksklúːsɪv]	独占的な, (〜に) 専用の (⇔inclusive) ⟨to⟩ 動 exclude 名 exclusion 語源 ex (外へ) + clude (閉じる) + sive
0544 **abject** [ǽbdʒekt]	絶望的な, 悲惨な [= wretched]
0545 **deplorable** [dɪplɔ́ːrəbl]	嘆かわしい [= shameful] 動 deplore
0546 **abridged** [əbrídʒd]	要約された [= condensed]
0547 **succinct** [sʌksíŋkt]	簡潔な [= concise, compact] 副 succinctly
0548 **adroit** [ədrɔ́ɪt]	巧みな [= adept, skillful], 器用な
0549 **adept** [ədépt]	(〜に) 熟練した ⟨at, in⟩
0550 **inept** [ɪnépt]	不適切な [= unsuitable, inappropriate] 名 ineptitude
0551 **vigorous** [vígərəs]	積極的な [= aggressive]

He said he wanted to create an **inclusive** society in which everybody felt valued.	誰もが自分が尊重されていると実感できるような包括的な社会を作りたいと，彼は言った。
The prime minister granted an **exclusive** interview to one newspaper.	首相は新聞社1社に対して独占インタビューを許可した。
In his later years, the artist fell into **abject** poverty and died penniless.	その芸術家は晩年には絶望的な貧困に陥り，無一文で亡くなった。
The decision to expel the refugees was a **deplorable** one.	難民を国外に追放するという決定は嘆かわしいものだった。
An **abridged** edition for non-specialists was also published.	専門家でない人たちのための要約版も出版された。
The White House issued a **succinct** statement denying all allegations.	ホワイトハウスはすべての申し立てを否定する簡潔な声明を発表した。
In the final moments of the game he made an **adroit** pass that led to a winning goal.	試合のラスト数分で，彼は巧みなパスを出して，決勝点を導いた。
The spokesperson was **adept** at handling difficult questions and answered smoothly.	その広報担当官は，難しい質問を処理することにたけており，よどみなく答えた。
The coach admitted to the press that his team's play had been **inept**.	コーチは自分のチームのプレーが不適切だったことを報道陣に対して認めた。
The new government took a **vigorous** approach and cut taxes sharply.	新政府は積極的な取り組みを行い，大幅減税を行った。

0552 **avid** [ǽvɪd]	熱心な，渇望している
0553 **antagonistic** [æntæ̀gənístɪk]	敵対的な [= opposing] 動 antagonize 名 antagonism, antagonist（敵対者）
0554 **arbitrary** [ɑ́ːrbətrèri]	独断的な，専制的な [= despotic, tyrannical]，気まぐれな [= capricious]
0555 **belligerent** [bəlídʒərənt]	けんか腰の，好戦的な [= quarrelsome]，交戦中の 名 belligerence
0556 **sinister** [sínɪstər]	陰険な，邪悪な [= wicked]，不吉な [= ominous, portentous]
0557 **blatantly** [bléɪtəntli]	露骨に [= broadly] 形 blatant（ずうずうしい）
0558 **bluntly** [blʌ́ntli]	ぶっきらぼうに，そっけなく [= abruptly]
0559 **curtly** [kə́ːrtli]	ぶっきらぼうに，そっけなく [= abruptly]
0560 **aloof** [əlúːf]	よそよそしい，冷淡な
0561 **apathetic** [æ̀pəθétɪk]	無関心な [= indifferent] 名 apathy

The professor was an **avid** reader of detective fiction in his spare time.	その教授は余暇には，探偵小説を熱心に読んでいた。
He made some **antagonistic** remarks, designed to show his opposition to the new policy.	彼は敵意に満ちた発言をいくつか行ったが，それは新政策に対する自分の異議を示すためのものであった。
The President was criticized for the **arbitrary** nature of his decisions.	大統領は，決定の際の独断的な性向を非難された。
The tone of his voice sounded unnecessarily **belligerent** given the circumstances.	状況から考えて，彼の声のトーンは不必要にけんか腰のように聞こえた。
I was taken aback by the **sinister** look in his eyes.	彼の陰険な目つきに，私はびっくりした。
Even some of the president's supporters were **blatantly** critical of him.	支持者でさえ露骨に大統領を非難する者がいる。
The woman told the man **bluntly** that she did not like him.	その女性は男性に，彼のことを好きではないとぶっきらぼうに言った。
He answered **curtly**, signaling his irritation with the journalist.	彼はぶっきらぼうに答え，そのジャーナリストにいらだちを見せた。
Some of his colleagues resented his **aloof** attitude towards them.	彼の同僚の中には，自分たちに対する彼のよそよそしい態度に腹を立てた者もいた。
He did his best to stimulate the students but they remained **apathetic**.	彼は生徒たちにやる気を起こさせるために最善を尽くしたが，生徒たちは無関心なままだった。

0562	**contagious** [kəntéɪdʒəs]	伝染性の [= transmittable]
0563	**epidemic** [èpɪdémɪk]	蔓延している，伝染性の 名 epidemic（病気の流行） 語源 epi（〜の間に）+ dem（人々）+ ic
0564	**endemic** [endémɪk]	特有の 語源 en（中に）+ dem（人々）+ ic
0565	**infectious** [ɪnfékʃəs]	伝染性の [= catching, easily transmitted] 名 infection
0566	**infested** [ɪnféstɪd]	はびこっている [= overrun]
0567	**pandemic** [pændémɪk]	（世界的に）流行性の [= rampant, worldwide or nationwide]
0568	**pervasive** [pərvéɪsɪv]	蔓延する
0569	**rife** [raɪf]	（好ましくないことに）満ちて〈with〉, 広まって [= prevalent, widespread]
0570	**contemplative** [kəntémplətɪv]	沈思黙考する [= reflective], めい想する [= meditative] 動 contemplate
0571	**scrupulous** [skrúːpjʊləs]	慎重な [= cautious, circumspect, minutely careful]

As the disease was **contagious**, the patients were isolated from others.	その病気は伝染性のものなので，患者たちはほかの人から隔離された。
The report said that drug use was **epidemic** among the prison population.	その報告書には，ドラッグの使用が囚人たちに蔓延していることが記されていた。
One problem was the **endemic** corruption in the bureaucracy.	一つの問題は官僚制に特有の腐敗だった。
The most essential aspect of controlling **infectious** diseases is sanitation.	伝染性の病気を抑制するのに最も不可欠な点は，公衆衛生である。
The deserted house turned out to be **infested** with mice.	人の住んでいないその家は，ネズミがはびこっていることがわかった。
The disease was once **pandemic** but is now quite rare.	その病気はかつては流行性のものだったが，今ではめったに発生しない。
Amid the **pervasive** gloom, the good news was very welcome.	蔓延する沈滞ムードの中で，良いニュースが歓迎された。
The news agency claimed that Iran was **rife** with spies.	その通信社は，イランにはスパイがはびこっていると主張した。
He was a **contemplative** boy, mainly interested in philosophy.	彼は沈思黙考するタイプの男の子で，主に哲学に興味があった。
Her **scrupulous** attention to detail makes her an excellent editor.	彼女は細かな点に慎重な配慮ができるので，優秀な編集者である。

pandemic (0567) のpanは「すべての」の意味を持ちます。
例. Pan American Union (米州連合)

#	単語	意味
0572	**meticulous** [mətíkjuləs]	細かいことに気を遣う [= scrupulous, excessively careful about details]
0573	**cursory** [kə́ːrsəri]	大ざっぱな，ぞんざいな [= hastily done], 上っ面の [= superficial]
0574	**erratic** [ɪrǽṭɪk]	不規則な [= irregular], 風変わりな [= eccentric, odd]
0575	**erroneous** [ɪróuniəs]	誤った，間違った [= incorrect] 動 err 名 error ▶erroneous assumption (間違っている前提)
0576	**derogatory** [dɪrá(ː)gətɔ̀ːri]	軽蔑的な [= dismissive, disdainful]
0577	**detrimental** [dètrɪméntl]	(〜に)有害な ⟨to⟩ [= damaging] 名 detriment (損失)
0578	**diffident** [dífɪdənt]	自信のない [= bashful, hesitant, timid] (⇔confident)
0579	**dissident** [dísɪdənt]	異論を持つ，反体制の 名 dissident (反体制派), dissidence (反対)
0580	**disgruntled** [dɪsgrʌ́ntld]	不満な [= discontented, displeased], 不機嫌な [= sulky]
0581	**demoralized** [dɪmɔ́(ː)rəlàɪzd]	意気消沈して [= dispirited, disappointed]

Gene mapping involves a **meticulous** procedure to isolate human genes.	遺伝子地図作製には，人の遺伝子を分離する<u>綿密な</u>作業が含まれる。
I could see that the job was poorly done after only a **cursory** glance.	<u>大ざっぱに</u>見ただけでも，その仕事はきちんとできていないことがわかった。
Since his wife passed away, his habits have become quite **erratic**.	妻が亡くなって以来，彼の生活習慣は極めて<u>不規則</u>になってきた。
They came to the **erroneous** conclusion that he was responsible for the accident.	彼らは，その事故の責任が彼にあるという<u>誤った</u>結論に達した。
I read an extremely **derogatory** column about the President in a local paper.	私は地元の新聞で，大統領についての極めて<u>軽蔑的な</u>コラムを読んだ。
The boy's bad behavior was **detrimental** to the school's atmosphere.	少年の悪い行動は学校の雰囲気に<u>有害な</u>ものだった。
He always seemed so **diffident**, so his speech was all the more impressive.	彼はいつもは<u>自信なさげに</u>見えたので，彼のスピーチはなおさら印象的だった。
Despite a few **dissident** voices, most people supported the prime minister's reforms.	2，3の<u>反対</u>意見はあったものの，大多数の人々は首相の改革を支持した。
I knew he had become **disgruntled**, but not that he was going to resign.	彼が<u>不満を持つ</u>ようになったことは知っていたが，辞めるつもりだとは知らなかった。
The fans felt **demoralized** by their team's weak performance.	ファンたちはそのチームの低迷している成績に<u>意気消沈した</u>。

0582	**destitute** [déstɪtjùːt]	極貧の [= extremely poor], (〜を)全く持たない [= devoid] ⟨of⟩ 图 destitution
0583	**dilapidated** [dɪlǽpɪdèɪtɪd]	荒廃した [= tumbledown]
0584	**emaciated** [ɪméɪʃièɪtɪd]	やつれた [= lean, thin, lank] 图 emaciation
0585	**unscathed** [ʌnskéɪðd]	痛手を受けていない [= unharmed]
0586	**unprecedented** [ʌnprésɪdènṭɪd]	前例のない [= unparalleled] (⇔common)
0587	**ferocious** [fəróʊʃəs]	凶暴な [= fierce, savage] 图 ferocity
0588	**filthy** [fílθi]	不潔な [= unclean, dirty], わいせつな [= obscene]
0589	**flagrant** [fléɪɡrənt]	目に余る [= outrageous], 極悪の [= notorious]
0590	**grueling** [ɡrúːəlɪŋ]	極度にきつい [= exhausting] ▶grueling schedule (厳しいスケジュール)
0591	**immaculate** [ɪmǽkjulət]	汚れのない [= pure, spotless, undefiled], 欠点のない [= impeccable, perfect]

After the war, many soldiers found themselves **destitute** and homeless.	終戦後，兵士たちの多くは自分たちが極貧で家すらないと気付いた。
The valuable papers were found in a **dilapidated** hut in the garden.	貴重な書類が庭にある荒れ果てた小屋で見つかった。
The hostages finally were rescued alive but dangerously **emaciated**.	人質たちはついに生きて救助されたが，危険なほどにやつれていた。
He seemed **unscathed** by his long years serving a prison sentence.	彼は長い刑務所での服役後も，痛手を受けていないように見えた。
The political party won an **unprecedented** share of the vote.	その政党は前例のない得票率を得た。
It can be argued that the most **ferocious** animals on earth are people.	地上で最も凶暴な動物は人間であると言えよう。
My apartment was so **filthy** when I first moved in I had to clean it twice.	私のアパートは，初めて引っ越してきた時，あまりに汚れていて，2度も掃除を必要とした。
Such **flagrant** disregard for international law will not be tolerated.	国際法に対するそのような甚だしい無視は許されない。
After their **grueling** journey across the mountains, they were exhausted.	彼らは極度にきつい山岳旅行の後で疲れ果てていた。
That politician was elected because of his **immaculate** reputation.	その政治家は汚れのない名声のおかげで当選した。

#		
0592 **impeccable** [ɪmpékəbl]	申し分のない [= faultless, flawless, perfect] 副 impeccably	
0593 **pristine** [prísti:n]	汚されていない, 初期の	
0594 **intangible** [ɪntǽndʒəbl]	不可解な, 無形の [= non-physical] (⇔ tangible)	
0595 **invincible** [ɪnvínsəbl]	不屈の, 克服しがたい [= unconquerable, insuperable, insurmountable]	
0596 **incoherent** [ɪnkouhíərənt]	取り乱した [= confused], 支離滅裂な [= illogical]	
0597 **incessant** [ɪnsésənt]	絶え間ない [= ceaseless, continual, constant]	
0598 **intermittently** [ìntərmítəntli]	断続的に [= fitfully]	
0599 **sporadic** [spərǽdɪk]	散発的な [= occasional, scattered], 突発的な [= not constant]	
0600 **omniscient** [ɑ(:)mníʃənt]	博学な, 全知の [= all-knowing]	
0601 **pedantic** [pɪdǽntɪk]	知識をひけらかすような, 衒学的な 名 pedant (学者ぶる人)	

Although his financial judgment is poor, his personal taste is **impeccable**.	彼のお金に対する判断は駄目だが，個人的嗜好は申し分ない。
Just walking on the **pristine** white carpet made him feel uncomfortable.	汚れのない白いじゅうたんの上を歩くだけで，彼は窮屈な思いをした。
He sensed an **intangible** atmosphere of tension in the room.	彼はその部屋の中で緊張した不可解な雰囲気を感じ取った。
The man we thought to be **invincible** suddenly died from heart failure.	我々が不屈だと思っていた人が心不全で急死した。
He was so excited that he became quite **incoherent**.	彼はとても興奮していたので全く取り乱してしまった。
The teachers' **incessant** complaining made life difficult for the principal.	先生たちが絶えず文句を言ったので，校長の生活は厳しいものとなった。
During his final illness, he was only **intermittently** conscious.	死に至る病の床で，彼は途切れ途切れにしか意識がなかった。
He made only **sporadic** efforts to prepare for the entrance examinations.	彼は入試の準備には時たま努力をしただけだった。
The expert had an apparently **omniscient** knowledge of his field.	その専門家は自分の分野において明らかに博学な知識を持っていた。
The professor dismissed the criticisms of his book as trivial and **pedantic**.	教授は自著に対する批判を，末梢的でありかつ知識をひけらかしているとして退けた。

science（科学）のsciは（知る）という意味です。omni（すべての）とあわせて，omniscient (0600)「全知の」です。

0602 **inquisitive** [ɪnkwízətɪv]	好奇心が強い [= curious, prying]
0603 **insatiable** [ɪnséɪʃəbl]	貪欲な [= greedy] (⇔ satiable 満足させられる) *cf.* satiate (を満たす)
0604 **perceptible** [pərséptəbl]	目に見えた [= discernible] 图 perception
0605 **notable** [nóʊṭəbl]	目立った [= conspicuous] 副 notably
0606 **benign** [bənáɪn]	優しい, 温和な [= mild], (気候などが) 穏やかな, (病理学的に) 良性の (⇔ malignant)
0607 **affable** [ǽfəbl]	愛想のよい, 気軽に話せる [= sociable, amiable]
0608 **robust** [roʊbʌ́st]	強健な [= hardy, sturdy, vigorous, sinewy]
0609 **buoyant** [bɔ́ɪənt]	活気がある [= perky, cheerful], 浮かんでいる [= floating] 图 buoyancy
0610 **resplendent** [rɪspléndənt]	光輝くばかりの [= brilliant], まばゆい [= dazzling]
0611 **tenacious** [tɪnéɪʃəs]	粘り強い [= persevering, retentive, clinging] 图 tenacity

Young mammals are characteristically and relentlessly **inquisitive**.	哺乳動物の子どもは，特性として，どこまでも好奇心が強い。
King Henry the Eighth of England was an **insatiable** glutton.	イングランドのヘンリー8世は，貪欲な大食漢だった。
After the speech, there was a **perceptible** change in the audience's attitude.	スピーチの後で聴衆の態度には目に見えた変化があった。
There was a **notable** absence of young people at the party.	そのパーティーでは若者の欠席が目立っていた。
His intentions are always **benign**, though sometimes poorly communicated.	彼の意志は，時にはよく伝わっていないが，いつも優しい。
Although the stranger seemed **affable**, Bill sensed an underlying hostility.	そのよそ者は愛想のよい感じがしたが，ビルは隠れた敵意を感じ取った。
Even at the age of eighty, Picasso was intellectually and physically **robust**.	80歳になってもピカソは知的にも肉体的にも強健だった。
When she won first prize in the speech contest, she felt **buoyant**.	彼女はスピーチ・コンテストで優勝した時，浮き浮きした気持ちだった。
The bride wore a **resplendent** dress made of lace.	花嫁はレースでできた光輝くばかりのドレスを着ていた。
The **tenacious** effort of our team finally won us the match in overtime.	チームの粘り強い努力の結果，我々は延長戦でようやく試合に勝った。

0612 lenient [líːniənt]	寛大な [= generous, tolerant]
0613 negligent [néglɪdʒənt]	不注意な, 怠慢な [= neglectful] 名 negligence
0614 perfunctory [pərfʌ́ŋktəri]	おざなりの, いい加減な [= cursory, negligent] (⇔ careful)
0615 spurious [spjúəriəs]	うさん臭い, にせの [= sham, bogus, counterfeit, mock, phony]
0616 treacherous [trétʃərəs]	不誠実な, 裏切りの, 当てにならない 名 treachery (裏切り, 不信, 背信)
0617 devious [díːviəs]	不誠実な [= deceitful]
0618 drab [dræb]	くすんだ [= dull, not bright], 単調な [= monotonous]
0619 eerie [íəri]	不気味な [= weird, uncanny]
0620 menial [míːniəl]	(仕事が) 単純で退屈な, 卑しい [= servile, low]
0621 morbid [mɔ́ːrbɪd]	病的な [= sickly, unhealthy]

The students admitted to breaking the rules but asked that we be **lenient**.	学生たちはルールを破ったことを認めたが、私たちに寛大な処置を願った。
Although he was not guilty of murder, his behavior was certainly **negligent**.	彼は殺人罪では無実となったが、彼の行為は確かに不注意だった。
Her attitude in the classroom seems **perfunctory** and mechanical.	教室での彼女の態度はおざなりで自発性に欠けているように思える。
The defendant told the court a story too **spurious** to be believed.	被告は法廷でいかにもうさん臭い信じられないような話をした。
He made a **treacherous** speech in which he attacked his former boss.	彼は以前の上司を攻撃するような不誠実な話をした。
Few people believed the man's **devious** explanations for his behavior.	男性の行動についての不誠実な弁明を信じる者はほとんどいなかった。
The gray walls with green trim gave the room such a **drab** appearance.	緑の縁取りがついた灰色の壁のために、その部屋はとてもくすんで見えた。
The sound of the wind over the dark moor has an **eerie** effect.	暗い荒地の上を吹く風の音が不気味さを加える。
Despite his qualifications, the immigrant doctor was forced to take **menial** jobs to survive.	移住してきた医者は、資格があるにもかかわらず、生存するために単純労働をすることを強いられた。
The American poet Emily Dickinson had a **morbid** fascination with death.	アメリカの詩人、エミリー・ディキンソンは、死について病的なまでに魅せられていた。

---

perfunctoryのperは(完全に)、functは(実行する)、oryは(ような)を表します。「完全に実行したような」、つまり、「うわべだけの、おざなりの」となります。

0622	**lethargic** [ləθɑ́ːrdʒɪk]	気だるい, 昏睡状態の [= comatose]
0623	**subdued** [səbdjúːd]	沈んだ, 控え目な [= dejected, low-spirited] 動 subdue (を制圧する)
0624	**tepid** [tépɪd]	生ぬるい [= lukewarm, half-hearted]
0625	**gullible** [ɡʌ́ləbl]	だまされやすい [= credulous, easily gulled or cheated]
0626	**imprudent** [ɪmprúːdənt]	軽率な [= incautious] (⇔ prudent) 名 imprudence
0627	**heedless** [híːdləs]	(〜に) 無頓着な〈of〉, 不注意な 動 heed (に気を付ける)
0628	**inadvertently** [ɪnədvə́ːrtəntli]	不注意に [= accidentally]
0629	**haphazardly** [hæphǽzərdli]	無計画に 形 haphazard (偶然の, でたらめの)
0630	**gaudy** [ɡɔ́ːdi]	けばけばしい [= over-bright]
0631	**flamboyantly** [flæmbɔ́ɪəntli]	華麗に

The humid weather made him feel **lethargic** and irritable.	湿気を含んだ天気が、彼を気だるくいらいらとさせた。
After the election defeat, the atmosphere in the party was **subdued**.	選挙での敗北後、党の雰囲気は沈んでいた。
The water was too **tepid** to make a nice cup of tea with.	おいしいお茶を入れるには、湯が生ぬる過ぎた。
Those children are too **gullible** for their own good.	その子どもたちは、だまされやすくて損している。
His **imprudent** criticisms of his boss got him into trouble.	上司に対する軽率な批判が彼をトラブルに巻き込んだ。
The man walked casually up to the lion, apparently **heedless** of the danger he was in.	男は自分が置かれている危険には無頓着らしく、気安くライオンの方に歩いて行った。
On the train, he **inadvertently** stepped on another passenger's foot.	電車の中で彼はうっかりほかの乗客の足を踏んでしまった。
The cheap furniture was arranged **haphazardly** around the room.	安い家具が無計画に部屋中に配置されていた。
The disco was full of teenagers wearing **gaudy** clothes.	そのディスコはけばけばしい服を着た10代の若者でいっぱいだった。
The film star dressed **flamboyantly** for every occasion.	その映画スターはどんな場合も華麗に着飾っていた。

happenやperhapsのhapは（偶然）という意味です。haphazardly (0629) はさらにhazard「偶然」がつきます。つまり、「偶然に任せて、無計画に」となります。

0632 **hereditary** [hərédətèri]	遺伝する [= genetically transmitted], 世襲の [= passed down by inheritance]
0633 **homogeneous** [hòumədʒí:niəs]	同質の [= unmixed] (⇔ heterogeneous 異質の)
0634 **hygienic** [hàɪdʒiénɪk]	衛生的な [= sanitary, clean] 图 hygiene (衛生状態)
0635 **deceased** [dɪsí:st]	亡くなった [= dead] ▶ the dead (故人)
0636 **terrestrial** [təréstriəl]	地球上の [= earthly]
0637 **torrid** [tɔ́(:)rəd]	灼熱の [= scorching]
0638 ✓ **traumatic** [trəmǽtɪk]	精神的外傷を引き起こす 图 trauma
0639 **gregarious** [grɪgéəriəs]	群れを成す,社交的な [= social, outgoing, extroverted]
0640 **palatable** [pǽlətəbl]	美味な,口に合う [= delicious, savory, tasty],好ましい *cf.* palate (口蓋, 味覚)
0641 **fiscal** [fískəl]	財政の [= financial],国庫の ▶ fiscal year (会計年度)

Scientists have learned that Alzheimer's disease is often **hereditary**.	アルツハイマー病は遺伝性であることが多いと,科学者たちは知った。
Despite having distinct ethnic groups, Japan is considered a **homogeneous** society.	明らかに異なる民族集団がいるにもかかわらず,日本は同質の社会と見なされている。
The old hospital was not as **hygienic** as it should have been.	その古い病院は,本来そうであるべきほどには衛生的ではなかった。
Now that his siblings are all **deceased**, he feels completely alone.	兄弟姉妹が全員亡くなって,彼は完全な孤独感を味わっている。
Any alien life form would likely differ dramatically from **terrestrial** ones.	地球外の生物はどれでも,地球上の生物と著しく異なるだろう。
Years of life in the **torrid** climate damaged his health.	長年の灼熱の気候下での生活ために彼は健康を害した。
War sometimes leads to a lifetime of **traumatic** memories.	戦争は時として,一生精神的外傷を引き起こす記憶として残る。
Dogs are **gregarious** creatures that travel in packs.	犬は群れになって移動する群居性の動物だ。
I seldom find British cuisine very **palatable**.	私はイギリスの料理が本当においしいとはめったに思わない。
Leaders of many nations in the world ignore their **fiscal** responsibilities.	世界の多くの国々の指導者は,財政上の責任を無視している。

0642	**indicative** [ɪndíkətɪv]	(〜を)示す〈of〉 動 indicate 名 indication (徴候), indicator (尺度)
0643	**auspicious** [ɔːspíʃəs]	縁起のよい [= fortunate, propitious] 名 auspice
0644	**illustrious** [ɪlʌ́striəs]	著名な [= eminent, distinguished] (⇔ unknown, obscure)
0645	**pinpoint** [pínpɔ̀ɪnt]	非常に正確な [= exact, precise]
0646	**eloquent** [éləkwənt]	雄弁な [= silver-tongued]
0647	**arduous** [áːrdʒuəs]	(仕事などが)骨の折れる, 大変な [= demanding]
0648	**laudable** [lɔ́ːdəbl]	称賛に値する [= commendable, admirable] 動 laud
0649	**dainty** [déɪnṭi]	優美な, きゃしゃな [= delicate]
0650	**conducive** [kəndjúːsɪv]	(〜に)貢献する〈to〉 動 conduce (至る, 貢献する) 語源 con (共に) + duc (導く) + ive
0651	**innocuous** [ɪnɑ́(ː)kjuəs]	無害な [= harmless]

That new policy was **indicative** of the government's indifference to environmental issues.	その新しい政策は政府の環境問題に対する無関心を示すものであった。
His first match was an **auspicious** start for the spring sumo tournament.	彼の初日の取組は，大相撲春場所の幸先のよい始まりとなった。
The college boasts many **illustrious** graduates.	その大学は多くの著名な卒業生を誇りとしている。
Technology now allows **pinpoint** military strikes from the air.	技術が発達したため，今や，空からの極めて正確な軍事攻撃が可能である。
The young lecturer was known as a witty and **eloquent** debater.	その若い講師は機知に富んだ雄弁な討論者として知られていた。
Although the task of digging the pond was **arduous**, he enjoyed it.	池を掘る作業は骨の折れるものだったが，彼は楽しんでやっていた。
The team made a **laudable** effort but they could not win the match.	そのチームは称賛に値する努力をしたが，試合に勝つことはできなかった。
The cat walked among the flowers with **dainty** steps.	そのネコは優美な足取りで花の間を歩いた。
The beautiful new university library is very **conducive** to study.	その美しい新大学図書館は研究に大いに貢献する。
He seemed so **innocuous**, no one believed he could actually harm anyone.	彼はあまりに無害に見えたので実際に人を傷つけるとは誰も思わなかった。

0652	**integral** [íntɪɡrəl]	不可欠の [= essential]，完全な [= perfect]，整数の 图 integral（積分）
0653	**valiant** [vǽljənt]	勇敢な [= chivalrous, dauntless, gallant]
0654	**serene** [sərí:n]	平穏な [= tranquil] 图 serenity（落ち着き）
0655	**fraught** [frɔ:t]	(〜を)伴う，(〜に)満ちた [= filled, loaded, charged]〈with〉
0656	**reclusive** [rɪklú:sɪv]	隠遁している 图 recluse（隠遁者）
0657	**flimsy** [flímzi]	見え透いた [= makeshift]，壊れやすい [= fragile]
0658	**catastrophically** [kæ̀təstrɑ́(:)fɪkəli]	恐ろしいまでに [= disastrously]
0659	**dogmatic** [dɔ(:)ɡmǽtɪk]	独断的な [= assertive]
0660 ✓	**insular** [ínsələr]	偏狭な [= close-minded]，(島のように)孤立した 動 insulate（を隔離する）
0661	**intimidated** [ɪntímɪdèɪtɪd]	恐れて [= threatened] 動 intimidate（を脅す）

An **integral** part of athletic excellence is a knowledge of the fundamentals.	運動能力に優れるための<u>不可欠な</u>要素は基礎知識である。
The firefighter made a **valiant** attempt to enter the house but he was driven back by the heat.	消防士は<u>勇敢</u>にも家の中に入ろうとしたが，熱で追い返された。
He enjoyed the **serene** atmosphere of the little country village.	彼は小さな田舎の村の<u>平穏な</u>雰囲気を楽しんだ。
The direction of this policy is **fraught** with dangers.	この政策のやり方には危険が<u>伴う</u>。
After the film star retired, she lived a **reclusive** life on her own in the country.	映画スターは引退した後，田舎に1人で<u>隠遁して</u>暮らした。
The teacher refused to believe the boy's **flimsy** excuse.	その教師は少年の<u>見え透いた</u>言い訳を信じようとしなかった。
The nuclear scientist had made a **catastrophically** foolish error.	原子物理学者は<u>恐ろしいまでに</u>愚かな間違いを犯した。
He criticized the economist's **dogmatic** belief in free trade.	彼はそのエコノミストの自由貿易についての<u>独断的な</u>考えを批判した。
The young woman felt irritated by the villagers' **insular** attitudes.	その若い女性は村人たちの<u>偏狭な</u>態度にいらだった。
The boy was so **intimidated** by the man he could hardly speak.	その少年は男性をとても<u>恐れて</u>いたので，ほとんど話すことができなかった。

#	単語	意味
0662	**languishing** [lǽŋgwiʃiŋ]	沈滞する [= weakening]
0663	**obsequious** [əbsíːkwiəs]	こびへつらうような [= fawning]
0664	**squeamish** [skwíːmiʃ]	神経質な [= fastidious]、（血などを見て）すぐ吐き気を催す [= nauseous]
0665	**uncouth** [ʌnkúːθ]	粗野な [= ungraceful, crude, coarse]、ぎこちない [= awkward, clumsy]（⇔ refined）
0666	**petrified** [pétrɪfàɪd]	石のように固い、怖がる [= terrified]
0667	**ponderous** [pá(ː)ndərəs]	冗長な [= redundant]、重苦しい
0668	**rowdy** [ráʊdi]	騒々しい
0669	**somber** [sá(ː)mbər]	重苦しい [= gloomy, depressing]、薄暗い [= dusky]
0670	**banal** [bənάːl]	通俗な [= commonplace, vulgar]、陳腐な [= hackneyed, trite]
0671	**relentless** [rɪléntləs]	容赦ない [= severe, harsh, unrelenting] 動 relent（和らぐ、弱まる）

The finance ministry attempted to revive the <u>languishing</u> economy.	財務省は<u>沈滞する</u>経済を復興させようとした。
Wearing an <u>obsequious</u> expression, the man apologized.	<u>こびへつらうような</u>表情で、その男性は謝罪した。
This movie is not for the <u>squeamish</u>.	この映画は<u>神経質な</u>人には向かない。
Though uneducated and <u>uncouth</u>, this young man is quite intelligent.	教育もなく<u>粗野だ</u>が、この若い男は極めて頭がよい。
The girl was <u>petrified</u> to find a snake on her pillow.	その少女は枕の上にヘビを見つけて<u>石のように固くなって</u>いた。
Despite its <u>ponderous</u> style, the book was actually very interesting.	その本は<u>冗長な</u>スタイルにもかかわらず、実際はとても面白かった。
On the last day of the term, the students became quite <u>rowdy</u>.	学期の最終日には生徒たちはかなり<u>騒々しく</u>なった。
The growing international tension gave a <u>somber</u> atmosphere to the negotiations.	国際的な緊迫の高まりのために、交渉には<u>重苦しい</u>雰囲気が漂っていた。
His speech was well-enough organized, but its content was rather <u>banal</u>.	彼の演説はしっかり構成されていたが、内容はかなり<u>通俗的</u>だった。
It is hard to endure the <u>relentless</u> winter cold of the American Midwest.	アメリカ中西部の<u>容赦ない</u>冬の寒さに耐えるのは厳しい。

#		
0672 **elusive** [ɪlúːsɪv]	理解しにくい，捕まえにくい	[= difficult to catch] 動 elude
0673 **excruciatingly** [ɪkskrúːʃiètɪŋli]	極度に	動 excruciate（を苦しめる）
0674 **fraudulent** [frɔ́ːdʒələnt]	詐欺的な	[= dishonest, deceitful] 名 fraud, fraudulence
0675 **irreparably** [ɪrépərəbli]	修復できないほど	
0676 **lackluster** [lǽklÀstər]	精彩を欠いた，ぱっとしない	*cf.* luster（光沢，つや）
0677 **lurid** [lúrəd]	ぞっとするような [= horrible, gruesome]，燃えるように真っ赤な [= glowing]	
0678 **roundabout** [ráʊndəbàʊt]	回りくどい，遠回しの	[= euphemistic]
0679 **shrewd** [ʃruːd]	鋭い [= astute]，抜け目のない [= clever]	▶a shrewd politician（抜け目のない政治家）
0680 **voraciously** [vəréɪʃəsli]	むさぼるように	[= insatiably] 名 voracity（大食）
0681 **sedentary** [sédəntèri]	座りがちの [= sitting]，ほとんど体を動かさない	

Many readers found his argument in the book somewhat **elusive**.	多くの読者は，その本の中における彼の論点を理解しにくいと思った。
The paintings in the exhibition were **excruciatingly** bad.	展示されている絵画は極端にひどかった。
When I suspected his dealings were **fraudulent**, I cut off all negotiations.	彼の取引は詐欺的だと思って，私はすべての交渉を打ち切った。
The technician said the computer was **irreparably** damaged.	技術者はコンピューターが修復できないほど損傷してしまっていると言った。
Following a **lackluster** season, the footballer announced that he was retiring.	精彩を欠いたシーズンの後，そのフットボール選手は引退を宣言した。
The face of Count Dracula appeared **lurid** and evil in the candlelight.	ドラキュラ伯の顔がろうそくの灯火の中でぞっとするような邪悪な相を呈した。
The man spoke in such a **roundabout** way that it was hard to understand just what his complaint was.	男はあまりにも回りくどい話し方をしたので，彼の不満が正確には何なのか，理解するのは難しかった。
Though now criticized, Freud was a **shrewd** observer of human behavior.	今では批判はあるが，フロイトは人間行動の鋭い観察者であった。
As a young man, he read **voraciously** about his subject.	若かりし頃，彼は専攻科目についての本をむさぼるように読んだ。
A **sedentary** life can lead to heart problems and other health disorders.	座りがちの生活をしていると，心臓病やほかの健康障害につながることがあり得る。

光沢 (luster) を欠く (lack) と「精彩を欠く」のは lackluster というイメージです。

0682	**archaic** [ɑːrkéɪɪk]	古風な [= antiquated, old-fashioned], 古代の [= ancient]
0683	**embedded** [ɪmbédɪd]	埋め込まれた [= implanted]
0684	**inclement** [ɪnklémənt]	(天候が)荒れ模様の,厳しい [= rough, severe, stormy, tempestuous] (⇔ clement)
0685	**facetious** [fəsíːʃəs]	滑稽な,ひょうきんな [= jocular]
0686	**docile** [dá(ː)səl]	従順な [= tame, submissive, obedient]
0687	**momentous** [moʊméntəs]	重大な [= important]
0688	**nonchalant** [nà(ː)nʃəláːnt]	平然としている [= calm] 副 nonchalantly
0689	**pragmatic** [prægmǽtɪk]	実利的な,実用的な,実用主義の 名 pragmatism (実利主義), pragmatics (語用論)
0690	**retroactively** [rètroʊǽktɪvli]	遡及して 形 retroactive (遡及力のある)
0691	**salient** [séɪliənt]	目立った,顕著な [= striking, prominent, conspicuous]

Using <u>archaic</u> language in writing is usually considered poor style.	書き言葉に<u>古風な</u>言語を使うことは、普通は悪文と考えられている。
A number of fossils were **<u>embedded</u>** deep within the rock.	多くの化石が岩の中にしっかりと<u>埋まっていた</u>。
The tournament was cancelled due to the <u>inclement</u> weather.	<u>荒れ模様の</u>天候のため、試合は中止された。
I didn't realize at first that his comments were intended to be <u>facetious</u>.	私は最初のうちは、彼の発言が<u>滑稽である</u>ことを狙ったものとは気付かなかった。
The farmer said that the dog was usually <u>docile</u> but could attack if threatened.	その犬は普段は<u>従順だ</u>が脅されると攻撃する可能性があると、農場主は言った。
The **<u>momentous</u>** decision to go to war was made.	戦争を始めるという<u>重大な</u>決定が下された。
The woman seemed quite <u>nonchalant</u> before her job interview.	その女性は就職の面接の前にずいぶん<u>平然としている</u>ように見えた。
Despite his strong religious convictions, he took a **<u>pragmatic</u>** attitude toward the issue.	強い宗教的な信念を持っているにもかかわらず、彼はその問題に対しては<u>実利的な</u>態度をとった。
To the annoyance of the business world, the tax was applied <u>retroactively</u>.	財界にとって非常に困ったことに、税金が<u>遡及して</u>適用された。
The most <u>salient</u> aspect of our trip was the incessant rainfall.	我々の旅行で最も<u>目立った</u>ことと言えば、絶え間なく降る雨だった。

0692
prostrate [prá(:)streɪt]
伏せた
[= lying flat, lying face down]
名 prostration (屈服)

0693
obligatory [əblígətɔ̀ːri]
義務的な, 強制的な
[= mandatory]
動 oblige 名 obligation

0694
oblivious [əblíviəs]
(~に)気付いていない⟨of⟩,
(~を)忘れている [= unmindful]⟨of⟩
名 oblivion

0695
teeming [tíːmɪŋ]
あふれている
[= filled]

0696
appalled [əpɔ́ːld]
唖然としている
[= shocked]

0697
implicit [ɪmplísɪt]
暗に示された [= implied],
暗黙の (⇔ explicit 明確な),
絶対の [= absolute]

0698
bellicose [bélɪkòus]
好戦的な [= warlike, belligerent],
けんか好きな [= pugnacious, quarrelsome]
名 bellicosity

0699
vibrant [váɪbrənt]
活気のある [= spirited, vivacious],
反響する

0700
subsequent [sʌ́bsɪkwənt]
その後の [= succeeding]
副 subsequently
語源 sub (後に) + seq (続く) + ent

He tripped while descending the stairs and fell **prostrate** on the floor.	彼は階段を降りる時につまずき,床にうつ伏せに倒れた。
Attendance at faculty meetings is **obligatory** for all staff members.	教授会への出席は,全教員に義務付けられている。
She was so intoxicated that she seemed **oblivious** of her actions.	彼女はあまりにも酒が回り過ぎて,自分のしていることに気付いていないようだった。
The square was **teeming** with pop fans going to a concert.	その広場はコンサートに行くポピュラーミュージックファンであふれていた。
She looked **appalled** by the news of her husband's accident.	彼女は夫の事故の知らせに唖然としているように見えた。
The country's actions were an **implicit** rejection of the request for compromise.	その国の行為は歩み寄りの要請に対する拒絶を暗に示すものであった。
Even if one disagrees, one need not be **bellicose** about expressing it.	たとえ不賛成であっても,それを表現するのに好戦的になる必要はない。
The city has a **vibrant** night life, with plenty of clubs and bars.	その都市にはたくさんのクラブやバーがあって,夜遊びに活気がある。
We hope that all his **subsequent** novels will be turned into films.	彼のその後の小説がすべて映画化されるといいが。

1分間 mini test

1 1分間

(1) Even though he (　　) broccoli, his wife often served it.

(2) Although a (　　), the hundred-dollar bill fooled almost everyone.

(3) After he had taken some medical tests, the doctor told him that the (　　) was good.

(4) There was much (　　) when women were admitted to the club.

(5) Just when we thought we had reached an agreement, the other party began to (　　).

(6) His signature is unintelligible because he always (　　) his name.

(7) Using (　　) language in writing is usually considered poor style.

(8) The little town withstood the enemy's (　　) for three days.

(9) The comedian first made his name in a theatrical (　　).

(10) All new employees are required to (　　) a medical examination.

ここから選んでね。※選択肢はすべて原形で表示しています。

① farce　　② prognosis　　③ haggle
④ detest　　⑤ scrawl　　⑥ undergo
⑦ dissension　⑧ archaic　　⑨ counterfeit
⑩ onslaught

2 1分間

(11) To the annoyance of the business world, the tax was applied (　　　).

(12) The comedian made his name by (　　　) politicians and other powerful figures.

(13) The square was (　　　) with pop fans going to a concert.

(14) She took a holiday after the tournament to (　　　) her energy.

(15) The paintings in the exhibition were (　　　) bad.

(16) The face of Count Dracula appeared (　　　) and evil in the candlelight.

(17) The sports stadium is also a popular (　　　) for concerts.

(18) The defense attorney insisted that his client be convicted on facts, not on (　　　).

(19) Even if one disagrees, one need not be (　　　) about expressing it.

(20) The city has a (　　　) night life, with plenty of clubs and bars.

ここから選んでね。

① vibrant　　② conjecture　　③ mock
④ recoup　　⑤ lurid　　⑥ teeming
⑦ venue　　⑧ retroactively　　⑲ excruciatingly
⑳ bellicose

1分間 mini test 答え

1 P. 168

(1)	④	0005 detest(detested)	(⇒p. 26)
(2)	⑨	0345 counterfeit	(⇒p. 96)
(3)	②	0365 prognosis	(⇒p. 100)
(4)	⑦	0396 dissension	(⇒p. 106)
(5)	③	0194 haggle	(⇒p. 64)
(6)	⑤	0225 scrawl(scrawls)	(⇒p. 70)
(7)	⑧	0682 archaic	(⇒p. 164)
(8)	⑩	0429 onslaught	(⇒p. 112)
(9)	①	0463 farce	(⇒p. 120)
(10)	⑥	0031 undergo	(⇒p. 32)

2 P. 169

(11)	⑱	0690 retroactively	(⇒p. 164)
(12)	⑬	0006 mock(mocking)	(⇒p. 26)
(13)	⑯	0695 teeming	(⇒p. 166)
(14)	⑭	0071 recoup	(⇒p. 40)
(15)	⑲	0673 excruciatingly	(⇒p. 162)
(16)	⑮	0677 lurid	(⇒p. 162)
(17)	⑰	0350 venue	(⇒p. 96)
(18)	⑫	0386 conjecture	(⇒p. 104)
(19)	⑳	0698 bellicose	(⇒p. 166)
(20)	⑪	0699 vibrant	(⇒p. 166)

でる度

A

B

C

単語編

覚えておきたい単語 **700**

動詞 (219語) ……………… 172
名詞 (258語) ……………… 216
形容詞・副詞 (223語) ……… 268
1分間 mini test ……………… 314

でる度Bは，1級受験者であれば，ぜひとも覚えておきたい単語です。合格レベルの力をつけるのに必要となる単語ですので，掲載されている700語を身につけましょう。

	1周目	2周目
動	/	/
名	/	/
形・副	/	/

でる度 B 覚えておきたい単語
動詞　219語

0701〜0709

0701 stimulate [stímjulèɪt]
を刺激する [= activate]
名 stimulation

0702 retrieve [rɪtríːv]
を取り戻す [= recover, get back], を検索する
名 retrieval (回復)

0703 fuel [fjúːəl]
を煽る [= agitate], に燃料を補給する
名 fuel (燃料)

0704 halt [hɔːlt]
止まる, を止める
[= stop]
▶ halt traffic (交通を一時止める)

0705 heed [hiːd]
に気を付ける
[= pay attention to]
▶ heed one's warning (〜の警告に耳を傾ける)

0706 expand [ɪkspǽnd]
を拡大する
名 expansion, expanse　形 expansive

0707 forebode [fɔːrbóud]
(悪いこと)を予言する, 虫が知らせる
[= portend]
名形 foreboding

0708 clarify [klǽrəfàɪ]
を明らかにする [= make clear]
名 clarification

0709 elongate [ɪlɔ́ːŋgeɪt]
を長くする
[= lengthen]

The economist said the tax cuts should **stimulate** the economy.	減税は当然経済を刺激するだろうと,そのエコノミストは語った。
It took years of hard work to **retrieve** his family's former wealth.	彼の家族の昔の資産を取り戻すには,何年にも及ぶ大変な努力を要した。
The dismal economic news only **fueled** the widespread dissatisfaction with the government.	その悪い状況の経済ニュースは,政府に対する広範な不満を煽るだけだった。
The weary climbers decided to **halt** for a brief rest.	疲れきった登山者たちは少し休むために立ち止まることにした。
If he had **heeded** his parents' warning, the accident would never have happened.	彼が両親の注意に気を付けていたら,事故は起こらなかっただろうに。
The university has decided to **expand** its popular MBA program by 50 places.	その大学は,人気の MBA(経営学修士)課程を50か所に拡大することを決定している。
The oracles at Delphi often **foreboded** ill fortune for ancient Greeks.	デルフォイの神託は,しばしば,古代ギリシャ人に凶事を予言した。
The professor asked the student to **clarify** one or two points in his explanation.	教授は学生に彼の説明のうち1,2点を明確にするように言った。
He used tongs to **elongate** and shape the soft glass.	彼はやわらかいガラスを長くし成形するためにトングを使用した。

0710
liken
[láɪkən]

を (〜に) 例える
[= compare] 〈to〉
图 likeness (類似点)

0711
spurn
[spəːrn]

をきっぱりと拒絶する
[= refuse, reject]

0712
stray
[streɪ]

(〜から) はぐれる
[= wander off, move away] 〈from〉
形 stray (迷った)

0713
predominate
[prɪdɑ́(ː)mɪnèɪt]

優位を占める [= be in the majority]
图 predominance
語源 pre (先に) + dominate (支配する)

0714
elaborate
[ɪlǽbərèɪt]

(〜について) 詳述する
[= expand] 〈on〉
形 elaborate (入念な)

0715
retain
[rɪtéɪn]

を保つ [= keep, maintain]
图 retention

0716
bestow
[bɪstóʊ]

(称号・栄誉など) を (〜に) 授ける
[= confer, grant] 〈on〉

0717
improvise
[ímprəvàɪz]

即興で演奏する,
を即席で作る [= extemporize]
图 improvisation

0718
uphold
[ʌphóʊld]

を守る,支持する [= support]
图 upholder (支持者)

0719
mesmerize
[mézməràɪz]

を魅了する [= fascinate, spellbind],
に催眠術をかける [= hypnotize]

The minister **likened** the economy to a ship in a violent storm.	大臣は経済を激しい嵐の中の船に例えた。
She **spurned** the offer of a job at her company's chief rival.	彼女は最大のライバル会社の仕事の誘いをきっぱりと拒絶した。
Visitors who **stray** from the path sometimes get lost in the woods.	観光客は道から外れると，森の中で迷子になってしまうことが時々ある。
By and large, male students still **predominate** in engineering courses.	概して，工学課程ではいまだ男子学生が数の上で優位を占めている。
The committee asked her to **elaborate** on her proposals for reform.	委員会は彼女にその改革の提案について詳述するように依頼した。
Although she lost her fortune, she **retained** the mansion and surrounding fields.	彼女は財産を失ったが，大邸宅と周囲の畑を手放さなかった。
His family still owns the land that the king **bestowed** on them in the 17th century.	彼の家族は，17世紀に王が与えた土地をいまだに所有している。
Jazz musicians must **improvise** as they play their music.	ジャズ音楽家は演奏中に即興で演奏しなければならない。
The principal promised to **uphold** the school's tradition of excellence.	校長先生は質の高い学校の伝統を守ることを約束した。
Students were **mesmerized** by his astonishing lectures.	学生たちは彼の驚くべき講義に魅了された。

retain (0715) のtainは (保管する) の意味を持ちます。tainを含むそのほかの動詞は，contain「を含む」，maintain「を維持する」などがあります。

0720
stipulate
[stípjulèit]

を明記する [= state, specify]
图 stipulation
▶ stipulate a price(値段を明記する)

0721
guarantee
[gæ̀rəntí:]

を確約する, を保証する

0722
reconcile
[rékənsàil]

を(〜と)和解させる ⟨with⟩
图 reconciliation

0723
revert
[rɪvə́ːrt]

(財産などが)(〜に)復帰する, (元の状態に)戻る [= go back] ⟨to⟩

0724
rebate
[rɪbéɪt]

を払い戻す

0725
reimburse
[rìːɪmbə́ːrs]

に払い戻す
[= refund, pay back]
图 reimbursement

0726
remit
[rɪmɪ́t]

を送金する [= send], を免じる [= pardon, forgive]
图 remittance(送金), remission(免除, 容赦)

0727
reciprocate
[rɪsɪ́prəkèit]

に返礼する, を交換する
图 reciprocation
形 reciprocal(相互の)

0728
redeem
[rɪdíːm]

(紙幣)を兌換する, を買い戻す, (名誉など)を回復する
图 redemption

0729
accentuate
[əkséntʃuèit]

を強調する
[= highlight]

The rule **stipulates** that students can not use calculators.	規則では生徒は計算機を使うことはできないと明記している。
The government **guaranteed** to compensate bank account holders.	政府は銀行の口座保有者に対して預金保障を行うことを確約した。
After a bloody and bitter war, the two enemies were finally **reconciled**.	血なまぐさい激戦の末、その敵軍両者はついに和解した。
On his death, the house would **revert** to its original owners.	彼の死によって、家は元の所有者に復帰することになるだろう。
The city council decided to **rebate** local taxes by ten percent.	市議会は、地方税を10パーセント払い戻すことを決定した。
The company agreed to **reimburse** him for his travel expenses.	会社は旅費を彼に払い戻すことを承諾した。
I agreed to **remit** the balance of my account within thirty days.	私は30日以内に勘定の残高を送金することに同意した。
He felt obligated to **reciprocate** the giving of any gifts he received.	彼は、受け取ったすべての贈り物に返礼しなければならない義務があると感じていた。
Theoretically, American dollars can be **redeemed** in gold at certain banks.	理論的には、アメリカのドルは特定の銀行で金と兌換することができる。
The politician tried to **accentuate** the positive achievements of the government.	その政治家は政府の上向きの業績を強調しようとした。

#	語	意味
0730	**accelerate** [əksélərèɪt]	加速する [= speed up] (⇔ decelerate)
0731	**rejuvenate** [rɪdʒúːvənèɪt]	を再活性化させる [= revitalize]
0732	**revitalize** [riːváɪṭəlàɪz]	に新しい活力を与える *cf.* vitality (活力, 生命力) vital (命の)
0733	**emigrate** [émɪgrèɪt]	(〜へ) 移住する [= migrate] ⟨to⟩
0734	**migrate** [máɪgreɪt]	(鳥などが) 渡る, 移住する [= immigrate, emigrate] 图 migration, migrant (移住者)
0735	**reinforce** [rìːɪnfɔ́ːrs]	を補強する [= strengthen] 图 reinforcement
0736	**recapitulate** [rìːkəpítʃulèɪt]	を要約する [= summarize] 图 recapitulation
0737	**revise** [rɪváɪz]	を改訂する [= reedit], を改正する 图 revision
0738	**redress** [rɪdrés]	(損害など) を償う, (問題など) を是正する [= rectify, remedy] ▶ redress the balance (均衡を取り戻す)
0739	**refurbish** [riːfə́ːrbɪʃ]	を改装する, を一新する [= renovate] *cf.* furbish (を研ぐ)

As the police tried to overtake the car, it suddenly **accelerated**.	警察が車に追いつこうとすると、その車は突然、加速した。
The new young chairman set about **rejuvenating** the old company.	その若い新取締役社長はその古い会社を再活性化することに取り掛かった。
The government moved some ministries there in order to **revitalize** the local economy.	政府は地域経済を再活性化するために、いくつかの省庁をそこへ動かした。
As the economy worsened, many people **emigrated** to other countries.	経済状態が悪化したので、多くの人たちがほかの国々へ移住した。
The geese were beginning to **migrate** south for the winter.	ガンは冬に備えて、南へ渡り始めていた。
The architect had to **reinforce** the foundations of his latest building.	その建築家は自分が最近建てた建物の基礎を補強しなければならなかった。
At the end of his lecture, the professor always **recapitulates** his main points.	教授はいつも講義の終わりに主要な点を要約する。
The science textbook had to be **revised** every few years.	科学の教科書は数年ごとに改訂されなければばらない。
The victims demanded that their pain and suffering be **redressed**.	被災者たちは、痛みと苦しみが償われることを要求した。
He bought the house, intending to **refurbish** it completely.	彼は、そっくり改装するつもりでその家を購入した。

0740 ~ 0749

0740
suffocate
[sʌ́fəkèɪt]

窒息(死)する
[= smother]

0741
smother
[smʌ́ðər]

(火)を(~で)覆って消す〈with〉,
を窒息(死)させる [= choke, stifle, suffocate]

0742
drain
[dreɪn]

の水を排出する [= draw off]
名 drainage
▶ drain the bath water (浴槽の湯を流す)

0743
drench
[drentʃ]

びしょぬれになる, 水浸しになる
▶ get drenched in the rain (雨でずぶぬれになる)

0744
decant
[dɪkǽnt]

を(~へ)注ぐ
[= pour out] 〈into〉
名 decantation

0745
deregulate
[diːrégjulèɪt]

の規制を緩和する
[= remove government controls from]

0746
extract
[ɪkstrǽkt]

を(~から)抽出する,
を(~から)抜粋する
[= quote, excerpt] 〈from〉

0747
exterminate
[ɪkstə́ːrmɪnèɪt]

を絶滅させる
[= extinguish]
▶ exterminate poverty (貧困を一掃する)

0748
extort
[ɪkstɔ́ːrt]

(金)をゆすり取る
名 extortion (強要)
語源 ex (外へ) + tort (ねじる)

0749
repel
[rɪpél]

を追い払う [= expel, reject, spurn]
名形 repellent
▶ repel an enemy (敵を撃退する)

Most of the fire's victims had **suffocated** in the smoke.	火事の犠牲者のほとんどは煙で<u>窒息死した</u>。
When the oil in the pan caught fire, she tried to **smother** the flames with a blanket.	フライパンの中の油が引火した時、彼女は炎を毛布で<u>覆って消そ</u>うとした。
The swimming pool was **drained** and cleaned once a month.	その水泳プールは、1か月に1度<u>水を抜き取ら</u>れ清掃された。
He caught a cold after becoming **drenched** in a sudden rainstorm.	突然の暴風雨で<u>ずぶぬれ</u>になった後に、彼は風邪をひいた。
He **decanted** some of the wine from the barrel into a jug.	彼は樽から水差しにいくらかワイン<u>を注いだ</u>。
America frequently asks Japan to **deregulate** its economy.	アメリカは日本に経済<u>を自由化する</u>よう、頻繁に求めている。
Researchers are continuously **extracting** new medicines from tropical plants.	研究者たちは絶えず熱帯植物から新しい薬<u>を抽出</u>している。
The wolves were eventually **exterminated** by settlers in the area.	オオカミはその地域の入植者によって、ついに<u>絶滅させら</u>れた。
The criminal gang was **extorting** money from local shopkeepers.	その犯罪者集団は、地元の商店主たちから金<u>をゆすり取って</u>いた。
In the tropics, we must use special ointments to **repel** disease-bearing insects.	熱帯地方では、病気を運ぶ昆虫<u>を追い払う</u>ために、特別な塗り薬を使わなければならない。

0750	**retort** [rɪtɔ́ːrt]	言い返す，に反論する [= counter] 語源 re (後ろへ) + tort (ねじる)
0751	**encapsulate** [ɪnkǽpsəlèɪt]	を要約する [= summarize]
0752	**entrust** [ɪntrʌ́st]	を (〜に) 預ける，を (〜に) ゆだねる 〈to〉
0753	**entail** [ɪntéɪl]	を (必然的に) 伴う [= include, involve]，を余儀なくさせる [= require]
0754	**induce** [ɪndjúːs]	に (〜をするように) 説得する [= persuade, motivate] 〈to do〉 語源 in (中へ) + duce (導く)
0755	**integrate** [ɪ́nṭəgrèɪt]	(〜に) 溶け込む [= harmonize]，を (〜に) 統合する 〈into〉 (⇔ segregate)
0756	**ingratiate** [ɪngréɪʃièɪt]	(〜に) 気に入られるようにする 〈with〉 副 ingratiatingly ▶ ingratiate *oneself* with 〜 (〜に取り入る)
0757	**jeer** [dʒɪər]	(〜を) あざける [= mock, gibe] 〈at〉
0758	**sneer** [snɪər]	(〜を) あざ笑う [= scoff, jeer, gibe] 〈at〉
0759	**deride** [dɪráɪd]	を嘲笑する，をあざける 名 derision 形 derisive (嘲笑的な)

The comedian could always **retort** in a witty way to any comment.	その喜劇役者はいつも，どんなコメントにも機知に富んだ答えを返すことができた。
The professor began by **encapsulating** his previous lectures on the subject.	教授はその主題について，彼の以前の講義を要約することから始めた。
Before he left, the man **entrusted** the key to his safe to his deputy.	出発する前に，男は代理人に金庫の鍵を預けた。
At the interview, the girl took the chance to ask just what the job **entailed**.	面接で，彼女は仕事に伴う内容を尋ねる機会を得た。
The teacher **induced** his students to study abroad to broaden their views.	先生は生徒たちに視野を広げるために留学するよう説得した。
The students quickly **integrated** into the life of their new school.	生徒たちは，新しい学校生活に素早く溶け込んだ。
The employee did her best to **ingratiate** herself with her older colleagues.	その従業員は，先輩に気に入れるようにベストを尽くした。
The unruly soccer fans **jeered** at the referee and threw bottles.	乱暴なサッカーファンが審判にやじを飛ばし，びんを投げた。
Some scientists simply **sneered** at Einstein's early theories of relativity.	一部の科学者はアインシュタインの初期の相対性理論をただあざ笑った。
The government's policy on global warming was **derided** as farcical by environmentalists.	地球温暖化に対する政府の政策は，環境問題専門家たちから茶番だとして嘲笑された。

0760
discharge
[dɪstʃɑ́ːrdʒ]
を退院させる，を解雇する [=dismiss]，を放出する [=emit]

0761
dispel
[dɪspél]
を追い散らす
[=disperse, scatter, drive away]

0762
displace
[dɪspléɪs]
を強制退去させる，を移動させる
名 displacement

0763
distend
[dɪsténd]
膨らむ，を膨らませる [=swell]
名 distention

0764
oust
[aʊst]
を追い出す，(財産など)を取り上げる

0765
evict
[ɪvíkt]
を立ち退かせる [=expel by legal procedure]
名 eviction

0766
expel
[ɪkspél]
を追放する
[=drive out, force out]
▶expel air from lungs (肺から息を吐き出す)

0767
evacuate
[ɪvǽkjuèɪt]
を(～から)避難させる，
を(～から)立ち退かせる 〈from〉
名 evacuation

0768
relegate
[réləɡèɪt]
を(～に)追いやる [=demote]，
を(～に)委託する [=delegate] 〈to〉
名 relegation (追放)

0769
dismantle
[dɪsmǽntl]
を分解する
[=take apart]
語源 dis(ない) + mantle(覆い隠す)

After a few days' rest, the patient was **discharged** from the hospital.	数日の静養を経て，患者は病院から退院した。
The arrival of soldiers **dispelled** the angry crowd.	兵士たちが到着すると，怒れる群衆は追い払われた。
Thousands of people were **displaced** from their homes by the flood.	洪水のため，何千人もの人々が自宅から強制退去させられた。
The sight of the children, their stomachs **distended** with hunger, moved the journalist to tears.	飢餓のために腹を膨らませている子どもたちの光景は，ジャーナリストを涙ぐませた。
The army **ousted** the government and began to rule the country itself.	軍隊は政府を追い出して，自ら国を統治し始めた。
It took over six months to **evict** them legally from the property.	その土地から合法的に彼らを立ち退かせるのに半年以上かかった。
After the boy was caught cheating, he was **expelled** from the school.	カンニングが見つかった後にその少年は退学になった。
People were **evacuated** from their homes because of the danger of an eruption.	噴火の危険があるので，人々は自宅から避難させられた。
The once-great star was **relegated** to a reserve position on the national soccer team.	かつての偉大なスターは，サッカーの代表チームの控えの地位に追いやられた。
The new recruits were taught how to **dismantle** and clean their guns.	新兵たちは，銃を分解し掃除する方法を教えられた。

0770
disrupt [dɪsrʌ́pt]

を中断[混乱]させる [= interrupt]
▶disrupt a relation between A and B
（AとBの関係を引き裂く）

0771
discard [dɪskɑ́ːrd]

を捨てる [= dump, throw away],
を解雇する [= fire, dismiss]

0772
ditch [dɪtʃ]

を捨てる
[= discard, desert, abandon]
名 ditch（溝）

0773
soar [sɔːr]

舞い上がる [= rise high],
（価格が）急騰する [= skyrocket]
▶soaring unemployment（上昇し続ける失業率）

0774
surge [səːrdʒ]

（波が）押し寄せる [= billow],
急上昇する

0775
skyrocket [skáɪrɑ̀(ː)kət]

急騰する
[= shoot through the roof]

0776
contend [kənténd]

(〜を)競う
[= compete]
語源 con（共に）+ tend（伸ばす）

0777
contradict [kɑ̀(ː)ntrədíkt]

に反論する [= dispute], と矛盾する
語源 contra（反対に）+ dict（言う）

0778
belittle [bɪlɪ́t̬l]

を見くびる，を卑下する
[= debase]
▶belittle *oneself*（卑下する）

0779
deprecate [déprəkèɪt]

を軽んじる
[= depreciate, belittle, make light of]
名 deprecation

A group of demonstrators attempted to **disrupt** the meeting.	デモ参加者の一団が会議を中断させようとした。
We were surprised to see that someone had **discarded** such nice furniture.	我々は，誰かがそのような立派な家具を捨てたのを見て驚いた。
The bicycle was broken so he **ditched** it and carried on on foot.	自転車が壊れたので，彼はそれを捨て，歩き続けた。
The eagle looks proud and majestic as it **soars** above the mountains.	ワシが山の上空に舞い上がる時，それは誇らしく堂々として見える。
The waves began to **surge** and toss as the storm grew more intense.	嵐が強くなるにつれて，波が押し寄せてうねり始めた。
During the crisis, oil prices **skyrocketed** throughout the globe.	石油危機の時，石油価格が世界中で急騰した。
A number of professors were **contending** for the post of dean.	複数の教授が学部長の座を目指して競っていた。
He hesitated to **contradict** openly what his superior had said.	彼は上司の発言に対して，あからさまに反論することをためらった。
In his speech, the politician tried to **belittle** his rival's achievements.	スピーチの中で，その政治家はライバルの業績をけなそうとした。
He **deprecated** his own work as something of little value.	彼は価値がほとんどないと自分の仕事を軽んじた。

sky（空）に向けてrocketのように上がっていくからskyrocket「急上昇する，急騰する」(0775) と覚えましょう。

0780	**deface** [dɪféɪs]	の表面を(〜で)汚す [= tarnish] 〈with〉 語源 de (悪化) + face (顔)
0781	**defame** [dɪféɪm]	の名誉を傷つける [= slander] ▶defame the politician (その政治家を中傷する)
0782	**mediate** [míːdièɪt]	(〜を)調停する〈in〉, とりなす [= intercede] 名 mediation
0783	**meditate** [médɪtèɪt]	(〜について)熟考する, めい想する [= ponder, muse] 〈on〉 名 meditation
0784	**contemplate** [ká(ː)ntəmplèɪt]	を熟考する, 沈思黙考する 名 contemplation 形 contemplative
0785	**deteriorate** [dɪtíəriərèɪt]	悪化する [= worsen]
0786	**decay** [dɪkéɪ]	崩壊する [= become weak, disintegrate], 腐食する
0787	**adorn** [ədɔ́ːrn]	を(〜で)飾る [= decorate] 〈with〉 名 adornment
0788	**emblazon** [ɪmbléɪzən]	を(〜で)飾る [= ornament] 〈with〉 名 emblazonment
0789	**divert** [dəvə́ːrt]	を(〜から)そらす [= deviate] 〈from〉 名 diversion (迂回路, 転換)

A gang of youths **defaced** the statue with spray paint.	若者の一団はスプレー式塗料でその像を汚した。
The journalist was accused of **defaming** an honest businessman.	そのジャーナリストは、誠実な実業家の名誉を傷つけたとして告訴された。
The superpower attempted to **mediate** in the dispute between its allies.	その超大国は同盟国間の紛争を調停しようとした。
The great actor would **meditate** on a new part for weeks before he started rehearsals.	その大物俳優は、リハーサルに入る数週間も前から、新しい役について熟考したものだった。
His heart sank as he **contemplated** the pile of work that lay on his desk.	机の上に積まれた仕事の山のことを考えるにつけ、彼の気持ちは沈んだ。
As the war continued, the food situation began to **deteriorate**.	戦争が続くにしたがって、食糧事情は悪化し始めた。
The valuable wooden furniture had been left to **decay**.	高価な木製の家具は放置されていたためにぼろぼろになった。
To welcome the soldiers home, the station was **adorned** with flags.	兵士の帰国を歓迎するために、駅は国旗で飾られた。
The walls of the castle were **emblazoned** with bright banners.	城壁は明るい色の旗で飾られていた。
Police were posted near the accident site to **divert** curiosity seekers.	やじ馬を退けるため、事故現場近くに警察官が配置された。

#	単語	意味
0790	**deflect** [dɪflékt]	をそらす [= divert], 外れる [= swerve] 語源 de(分離) + flect(曲げる)
0791	**diverge** [dəvə́ːrdʒ]	分岐する, をそらす [= deviate] 形 divergent
0792	**empathize** [émpəθàɪz]	(に)共感する [= sympathize, identify] ⟨with⟩ 名 empathy
0793	**empower** [ɪmpáuər]	に権力を持たせる [= authorize], を力づける
0794	**embolden** [ɪmbóuldən]	を励ます, を大胆にする *cf.* boldness(大胆さ)　bold(ずうずうしい)
0795	**embody** [ɪmbá(ː)di]	を体現する, を具体的に表現する 名 embodiment
0796	**materialize** [mətíəriəlàɪz]	具体化する [= concretize] ▶ materialize an ambition(野望を実現する)
0797	**embezzle** [ɪmbézl]	を横領する [= steal, appropriate fraudulently] 名 embezzlement
0798	**embark** [ɪmbáːrk]	(事業などに)乗り出す [= launch out] ⟨on⟩, 乗船する [= go on board], を乗せる
0799	**embrace** [ɪmbréɪs]	を受諾する [= accept], を抱きしめる [= hug]

Sunglasses are designed to **deflect** UV rays of direct sunlight.	サングラスは直射日光の紫外線をそらすことを目的として作られている。
As they grew older, their interests **diverged** and the two friends lost contact.	その2人の友人は，年を取るにつれて関心が分かれ，連絡を取らなくなった。
Although he **empathized** with the protestor's feelings, he did not support them.	彼はその抗議者の感情に共感したが，支持しなかった。
The project was designed to **empower** local women farmers.	そのプロジェクトは地元の女性農業者たちに権限を持たせるために計画された。
Emboldened by the success of the product, the company decided to produce two more models.	製品の成功に励まされ，その企業はさらに2つのモデルを生産することを決定した。
His professor **embodied** everything he admired in a scholar.	その教授は彼が称賛する学者としてのあらゆるものを体現していた。
If funding **materializes**, they will start the research the following year.	資金(調達)が具体化したら彼らは次の年に研究を始めるだろう。
The banker was eventually sent to prison because he **embezzled** funds.	その銀行家は預金を横領したため，結局は刑務所に入れられた。
They **embarked** on a journey to the moon.	彼らは月旅行の事業に乗り出した。
To the ecologist's surprise, the government **embraced** his proposals for cutting carbon emissions.	環境保護論者が驚いたことには，政府は二酸化炭素排出削減に関する彼の提案を受け入れた。

0800 obstruct
[əbstrʌ́kt]

を妨害する
[= hinder, impede, hamper, retard]
图 obstruction

0801 hamper
[hǽmpər]

を妨げる [= hinder, impede, encumber, prevent, obstruct]

0802 hinder
[híndər]

を妨げる
[= hamper]
图 hindrance

0803 transcend
[trænsénd]

を越える
[= outgo, exceed, rise above]

0804 transpose
[trænspóuz]

を(〜に)置き換える〈to〉
图 transposition

0805 uncover
[ʌnkʌ́vər]

を暴露する [= reveal],
を見いだす [= discover] (⇔conceal 隠す)

0806 undertake
[ʌ̀ndərtéik]

を引き受ける
(⇔refuse 断る)

0807 unearth
[ʌnə́ːrθ]

を発掘する
[= excavate] (⇔bury 埋める)
▶ unearth fossils (化石を発掘する)

0808 unfold
[ʌnfóuld]

を広げる
[= open]
▶ unfold the newspaper (新聞を広げる)

0809 unsettle
[ʌnsétl]

を動揺させる
[= discompose]
图 unsettlement

The government was accused of trying to **obstruct** the inquiry.	政府はその調査を妨害しようとしたことを非難された。
The police investigation was **hampered** by the uncooperative attitude of local people.	警察の捜査は地元の人々の非協力的な態度により妨げられた。
Work on repairing the bridge was **hindered** by strong winds.	橋の修理工事は強風によって妨げられた。
In order to succeed, we must **transcend** our greatest weaknesses.	成功するには、我々は自己の最大の弱みを超越しなければならない。
The setting of the classic novel was **transposed** to a modern one.	その古典小説の舞台は現代に置き換えられた。
A persistent journalist had first **uncovered** the crime.	粘り強いジャーナリストが最初にその犯罪を暴いた。
The soldiers **undertook** the responsibility to defend their country.	兵士たちは、母国を守る責任を引き受けた。
The construction workers accidentally **unearthed** the remains of a Roman villa.	建設現場の労働者たちは、たまたま古代ローマの大邸宅の遺跡を掘り当てた。
The guide **unfolded** a large map and showed them the route.	ガイドは大きな地図を広げて、彼らにルートを教えた。
Reports of a series of burglaries **unsettled** the local inhabitants.	一連の強盗事件の報道は地元の住民たちを動揺させた。

transcend (0803) のscendは〔上る〕の意味を持ちます。ascendは「上る」、descendは「下る」とペアで覚えましょう。

0810 ~ 0819

0810 incriminate
[ɪnkrímɪnèɪt]

に罪を負わせる, を告発する
[= accuse, charge with a crime]
图 incrimination

0811 instill
[ɪnstíl]

を教え込む
[= inculcate]
語源 in (中に) + still (したたる)

0812 enroll
[ɪnróul]

(~に) 入学 [入会] する ⟨in⟩,
を登録する [= register]
图 enrollment

0813 engulf
[ɪngʌ́lf]

を飲み込む
[= swallow up]

0814 engender
[ɪndʒéndər]

を生み出す
[= cause, generate, give rise to, produce]

0815 ensue
[ɪnsjúː]

結果として起こる
[= follow (immediately), come after]

0816 enforce
[ɪnfɔ́ːrs]

(法律など)を執行する
[= dispense]

0817 stagger
[stǽgər]

よろめく [= totter, waver],
(勤務時間など)をずらす
▶ stagger business hours (時差出勤にする)

0818 waver
[wéɪvər]

(信念などの点で) 心が揺らぐ [= vacillate] ⟨in⟩,
動揺する

0819 exasperate
[ɪgzǽspərèɪt]

を憤慨させる [= infuriate, irritate]
形 exasperation

In American courts, suspects cannot be forced to **incriminate** themselves.	アメリカの法廷では，容疑者は自分の罪を認めるように強いられることはない。
We always try to **instill** strong moral values in our children.	我々は常に子どもたちに強い倫理観を教え込もうとする。
My brother will **enroll** in Stanford University next fall.	私の弟は，来秋スタンフォード大学に入学する。
The typhoon totally **engulfed** that small fishing community.	台風は完全にその小さな漁村を飲み込んだ。
They hoped that our research would **engender** further efforts to cure cancer.	我々の研究が，がん治療のさらなる努力を喚起することを，彼らは期待した。
She spoke her mind clearly, not caring what might **ensue**.	彼女は何が結果として起きるかを気にせず，気持ちをはっきりと打ち明けた。
The police rarely **enforced** the local laws against fishing.	警察は釣りに関しては地域法を執行することはほとんどなかった。
The intoxicated man was **staggering** dangerously near the train tracks.	その酔った男は鉄道線路の近くで危なっかしくよろよろ歩いていた。
No matter how much pressure he felt, he never **wavered** in his decision.	いかに多くの圧力を感じても，彼の決心は揺るがなかった。
She was so **exasperated** by her husband's complaints that she threw the meal at him.	彼女は夫の言う不満にとても憤慨したので，食べ物を夫に投げつけた。

engulf (0813) は，en (中に) + gulf (湾)「湾の中へ包み込む」からイメージを膨らませて「飲み込む」と覚えましょう。

0820
resent
[rɪzént]

に憤る [= show indignation at], を恨みに思う [= have a grudge against]
名 resentment

0821
surmount
[sərmáunt]

に打ち勝つ
[= overcome, get the better of]

0822
surpass
[sərpǽs]

を上回る
[= exceed, excel, transcend]

0823
impair
[ɪmpéər]

を損なう [= deteriorate, make worse]
名 impairment

0824
jeopardize
[dʒépərdàɪz]

を危険に陥れる
[= risk, imperil]
名 jeopardy

0825
mar
[mɑ:r]

を損なう
[= damage, disfigure, spoil, impair]

0826
mortify
[mɔ́:rtəfàɪ]

に恥をかかせる
[= embarrass]
形 mortifying 副 mortifyingly

0827
humiliate
[hjumílièɪt]

に恥をかかせる [= degrade, mortify]
名 humiliation
語源 humili (卑しい) + ate

0828
proclaim
[prəkléɪm]

を宣言する, を公表する
名 proclamation
語源 pro (公に) + claim (叫ぶ)

0829
profess
[prəfés]

(〜である)と自称する 〈to do〉
名 professor, profession 形 professional
語源 pro (公に) + fess (述べる)

Young writers should try not to **resent** constructive criticism.	若手作家は建設的な批評に腹を立てないようにすべきだ。
He had to **surmount** a number of legal problems before he could set up the new company.	彼は新しい会社を設立する前に，多くの法律上の問題を乗り越えなくてはならなかった。
The athlete finally **surpassed** the previous world record in 2009.	その運動選手は，ついに2009年樹立の過去の世界記録を上回った。
His hearing was **impaired** from years of playing in a rock band.	彼の聴力は長年のロック・バンドでの演奏活動によって損なわれた。
The whole agreement was **jeopardized** by his failure to produce the promised documents in time.	彼が約束していた書類を時間までに仕上げられなかったために，契約全体が危うくなった。
The Olympic Games were **marred** by a lethal bomb explosion.	そのオリンピックは殺害目的の爆弾の爆発で台無しになった。
My mother was sometimes **mortified** by the behavior of her children in public.	私の母は人前での子どもたちの行動によって時々恥をかかされた。
His father **humiliated** him by telling him off in front of his friends.	友人の目の前で叱り飛ばして，父親は彼に恥をかかせた。
After making a speech, the mayor **proclaimed** the sports meet open.	スピーチをした後で，市長はスポーツ大会の開催を宣言した。
I don't **profess** to be an expert in economics, but I enjoy reading about the subject.	私は経済学の専門家を自称することはないが，経済学に関するものを読むのは楽しい。

surmount (0821) のsurは (上に) を意味します。surrenderはsur (上に) +render (与える) なので「降伏する」とイメージできるでしょう。

0830 scatter [skǽṭɚr]	散り散りになる [= disperse], をまき散らす [= sprinkle, spread]
0831 congregate [kά(:)ŋgrɪgèɪt]	集まる [= gather, assemble] 名 congregation(集会) 語源 con(共に) + gregate(群がる)
0832 allocate [ǽləkèɪt]	を(~に)配分する [= allot] ⟨to⟩ 名 allocation 語源 al(~へ) + locate(置く)
0833 synthesize [sínθəsàɪz]	を統合する(⇔ analyze を分解する) 名 synthesis 形 synthetic
0834 pledge [pledʒ]	を誓約する [= promise solemnly]
0835 waive [weɪv]	(権利など)を放棄する [= relinquish, forgo] 名 waiver(権利放棄)
0836 assimilate [əsíməlèɪt]	(~に)同化する ⟨into⟩, を吸収する [= absorb] 名 assimilation
0837 merge [mə:rdʒ]	合併する, を合併する [= unite, combine] 名 merger ▶ merge A with B (AをBと合併する)
0838 censure [sénʃɚr]	を(~のことで)非難する [= criticize, blame] ⟨for⟩ 名 censure
0839 supplant [səplǽnt]	の地位を奪い取る [= replace, supersede]

The crowd of students **scattered** before the oncoming tanks.	学生の群れは近づいて来る戦車を前にして，散り散りになった。
The principal told the children to **congregate** in front of the school at 8 a.m.	校長先生は子どもたちに，午前8時に学校前に集合するようにと言った。
He sat at the desk **allocated** to him and began to take the test.	彼はあてがわれた机に座り，テストを受け始めた。
The book **synthesized** the research of many different experts.	その本は多くのさまざまな専門家の研究を統合していた。
A medieval knight was required to **pledge** allegiance to his lord.	中世の騎士は，領主に忠誠を誓うことを要求された。
He agreed to **waive** some of his rights in return for a reduced sentence.	彼は減刑判決の交換条件として，自分の権利のいくつかを放棄することに同意した。
Immigrant workers sometimes found it difficult to **assimilate** into society.	移民労働者たちは時々社会に同化することが難しいと感じた。
When the two companies **merged**, they became the largest conglomerate in the chemical industry.	両社が合併したことで，化学工業界で最大の複合企業が誕生した。
After he was publicly **censured** by the President, he resigned from office.	大統領に公然と譴責された後，彼は辞職した。
The prime minister suspected the man of trying to **supplant** him.	首相は，その男性が自分の地位を奪い取ろうとしているのだと疑った。

0840
stabilize
[stéɪbəlàɪz]

を安定させる
- 名 stability 形 stable
- ▶ stabilize the economy（経済を安定させる）

0841
intrigue
[ɪntríːg]

(〜と)共謀する〈with〉,
陰謀を企てる [= conspire]
- 形 intriguing（魅力的な）

0842
penetrate
[pénətrèɪt]

に侵入する, を貫通する
- 名 penetration 形 penetrable
- 語源 penetr（奥に）+ ate

0843
probe
[proub]

を厳密に調査する [= investigate],
を精査する [= explore thoroughly]
- 名 probe

0844
abuse
[əbjúːz]

を悪用する [= misuse], 濫用する
- ▶ abuse drugs（薬物を濫用する）

0845
poach
[poutʃ]

を密猟する, を侵害する [= intrude into]
- 名 poacher（密猟者）
- ▶ poach on *one's* preserves（〜の領域を侵す）

0846
cease
[siːs]

を終える,
終わる [= come to an end]

0847
circulate
[sə́ːrkjulèɪt]

広がる [= spread]
- 名 circulation（循環, 流布）

0848
claim
[kleɪm]

を主張する
- ▶ claim responsibility for 〜
  （〜に対して責任があると主張する）

0849
ratify
[rǽṭəfàɪ]

を批准する
- 形 ratifiable

The government introduced measures to **stabilize** the price of oil, which had been fluctuating wildly.	激しく変動していた石油価格を安定させる政策を政府は導入した。
The supermarkets were accused of **intriguing** with each other to fix prices.	複数のスーパーマーケットが互いに共謀して価格設定を行ったため,告発された。
The government offices admitted that their computers had been **penetrated** by hackers.	コンピューターがハッカーたちによって侵入されたことを,政府は認めた。
The Justice Department has **probed** allegations of presidential wrongdoing.	司法省は大統領の不正行為の申し立てを厳密に調査した。
The accountant had **abused** his position to enrich himself.	その公認会計士は,私腹を肥やすために自分の地位を悪用した。
In the past, **poaching** animals from the royal forests was punishable by death.	昔は,王家の森で動物を密猟することは,死をもって罰せられていた。
The moment he **ceased** speaking, the audience burst into applause.	彼が話し終えるとすぐに観客からどっと拍手が沸いた。
Rumors about the mayor began to **circulate** through the town.	市長についてのうわさが,町中に広がり始めた。
The arrested man **claimed** the police had mistreated him.	逮捕された男性は,警察が虐待したと主張した。
Congress will often not **ratify** bills proposed by the President.	議会は大統領が提出した法案を批准しないことがよくある。

0850
forfeit [fɔ́ːrfət]
を失う，を没収される
图 forfeit, forfeiture

0851
implicate [ímplɪkèɪt]
を(犯罪などに)巻き込む [= involve], を意味する [= imply]
图 implication (暗示)

0852
perpetrate [pə́ːrpətrèɪt]
(犯罪・過失など)を犯す [= commit]
图 perpetration

0853
monopolize [mənɑ́(ː)pəlàɪz]
を独占する [= dominate]
▶ monopolize the industry (産業を独占する)

0854
smuggle [smʌ́gl]
を密輸する [= carry illicitly]
▶ smuggle arms into America (武器をアメリカに密輸する)

0855
expire [ɪkspáɪər]
満期になる，終了する [= terminate], 死ぬ [= pass away]
图 expiration

0856
compile [kəmpáɪl]
(書物など)を編集する [= edit]
图 compilation, compiler

0857
hatch [hǽtʃ]
卵が孵化する [= incubate]
▶ hatch eggs (卵を孵化させる)

0858
hibernate [háɪbərnèɪt]
冬眠する
图 hibernation

0859
metabolize [mətǽbəlàɪz]
を新陳代謝する
图 metabolism (新陳代謝)

If we cannot afford to complete the deal now, we may **forfeit** our investment.	もし，今取引を完了することができなければ，我々は投資金を失うかもしれない。
The statement he gave to the police **implicated** many important businessmen.	警察での彼の供述は，多くの有力な実業家を巻き込むこととなった。
The crooked businessman was found guilty of **perpetrating** fraud.	その悪徳業者は詐欺行為を犯して有罪判決を受けた。
The tennis courts tended to be **monopolized** by the older students.	テニスコートは先輩の学生たちに独占されがちである。
Some tribes of Myanmar successfully **smuggled** drugs into Thailand.	ミャンマーの一部の部族がタイに首尾よく麻薬を密輸した。
The lease on my apartment will **expire** in two years.	私のアパートの賃貸契約は2年後に期限が切れる。
The scholar worked for years **compiling** a dictionary of the Basque language.	その学者はバスク語の辞書の編纂に長年取り組んだ。
The mother bird sits on the eggs until they **hatch** a week later.	親鳥は，ヒナがかえるまで1週間，卵を抱く。
Before the bears **hibernate**, they eat as much food as possible.	熊は冬眠する前に可能な限り大量に食べる。
Usually, the substance is **metabolized** by the liver and does no harm.	通常，その物質は肝臓で新陳代謝されるので害にならない。

0860 reap [riːp]
を刈り取る [= harvest]
▶ You reap what you sow.
(自分のまいた種子は自分で刈り取る；自業自得である)

0861 saturate [sǽtʃərèɪt]
を飽和状態にする，を完全に浸す
图 saturation (充満，飽和状態)

0862 inoculate [ɪnɑ́(ː)kjulèɪt]
に(〜の)予防接種をする
[= vaccinate] ⟨against⟩
图 inoculation

0863 evolve [ɪvɑ́(ː)lv]
(〜から)進化する [= develop] ⟨from⟩
图 evolution

0864 inject [ɪndʒékt]
を(〜に)注射する，を(〜に)注入する ⟨into⟩
图 injection
語源 in (中に) + ject (投げる)

0865 erupt [ɪrʌ́pt]
噴火する，
(感情が)爆発する [= blow up, explode]，
(戦争が)勃発する [= break out]

0866 wriggle [rígl]
体をくねらせる
▶ wriggle *oneself* through the hole
(体をくねらせ穴を通り抜ける)

0867 guzzle [gʌ́zl]
をがぶがぶ飲む，
をがつがつ食べる [= devour]
图 guzzler (ガソリンを食う(大型)車)

0868 nudge [nʌdʒ]
を(肘で)そっとつつく
▶ nudge *one's* way through 〜
(〜を押し分けて進む)

0869 sprawl [sprɔːl]
手足を伸ばして寝そべる
[= stretch out]

The local farmers helped each other to **reap** the wheat.	地元の農業者たちはお互いに助け合い小麦を刈り取った。
The market for television sets is completely **saturated** in some countries.	テレビの市場が完全に飽和状態になっている国もある。
All children should be **inoculated** against certain childhood diseases.	すべての子どもは、ある種の幼児期の病気の予防接種を受けるべきだ。
Darwin believed that humans **evolved** from less developed species of primates.	ダーウィンは、人間は低い発達段階の霊長類から進化したと信じていた。
The doctor **injected** the vaccine into the patient's arm.	医師は患者の腕にワクチンを注射した。
Government scientists said that there were fears that the volcano might **erupt** at any time.	その火山はいつ何時にも噴火する恐れがあると、政府系科学者は述べた。
The little girl began to **wriggle** uncomfortably on her chair.	少女はいすの上で落ち着きなくもじもじし始めた。
The little boy **guzzled** his lemonade and ran out to meet his friends.	男の子はレモネードをがぶがぶ飲んでから、友達に会いに外に走って行った。
When the meeting opened, my colleague **nudged** me to be quiet.	会議が始まった時、同僚は静かにするよう私を肘でそっとつついた。
He turned on the television and **sprawled** on the sofa.	彼はテレビをつけ、ソファーに手足を伸ばして寝そべった。

#	単語	意味
0870	**jiggle** [dʒígl]	を小刻みに動かす [= shake]
0871	**dangle** [dǽŋgl]	を(～の前に)ぶら下げる ⟨before, in front of⟩
0872	**invert** [ɪnvə́ːrt]	を逆さにする [= turn over] 图 inversion 語源 in(中に) + vert(向ける)
0873	**fumble** [fʌ́mbl]	手探りする ▶fumble in *one's* pocket for a coin (ポケットの中の小銭を手探りで捜す)
0874	**quiver** [kwívər]	震える [= tremble, quake, shiver] ▶quiver with rage(激しい怒りで震える)
0875	**assault** [əsɔ́(ː)lt]	に暴行する [= abuse, molest], を攻撃する [= attack, assail]
0876	**bombard** [bɑ(ː)mbɑ́ːrd]	に(質問などを)浴びせる ⟨with⟩
0877	**incapacitate** [ìnkəpǽsɪtèɪt]	を無力化する 图 incapacitation
0878	**devastate** [dévəstèɪt]	を破壊する [= destroy] ▶be devastated by grief(悲しみに打ちのめされる)
0879	**excel** [ɪksél]	(～において)優れている, (～において)に勝る [= surpass] ⟨in⟩ 图 excellence

He **jiggled** the power switch a few times but nothing happened.	彼は電源スイッチを数回動かしたが，何も起こらなかった。
The boss persuaded him to cooperate by **dangling** the prospect of promotion before him.	目の前に昇進の可能性をぶら下げることで，上司は協力するよう彼を説得した。
Even when we **inverted** the position of the painting it looked the same.	我々が絵の位置を上下逆にしてみても，それは同じに見えた。
The woman **fumbled** in her bag for the key to the front door.	その女性は玄関のドアのカギをかばんの中を手探りして捜した。
When we found the lost puppy, it was **quivering** in fear.	迷子になった子犬を見つけた時，子犬は不安げに震えていた。
The prisoner was punished for **assaulting** one of the guards.	囚人は看守の1人に暴行したために罰せられた。
Reporters **bombarded** the film star with questions about her health.	レポーターたちは，その映画スターに彼女の健康に関する質問を浴びせた。
The guerillas planned to use grenades to **incapacitate** the army's tanks.	ゲリラは戦車を無力化するために手榴弾を使う計画を立てた。
The whole region was **devastated** by floods.	地域全体が，洪水によって破壊された。
Asian Americans often **excel** in school at all levels of education.	すべての教育段階において，アジア系アメリカ人は学校の成績が優れていることが多い。

0880 esteem
[ɪstíːm]
を尊敬する、を高く評価する
[= respect, adore, venerate, worship]

0881 overrun
[òuvərrʌ́n]
にはびこる、にあふれる、を侵略する
[= infest]

0882 simulate
[símjulèɪt]
を模擬実験する、のふりをする [= counterfeit, feign, pretend]
名 simulation

0883 collaborate
[kəlǽbərèɪt]
(〜と)協力する〈with〉

0884 commence
[kəméns]
始まる [= begin, start]
名 commencement

0885 provoke
[prəvóuk]
を挑発する [= incite, stimulate]、
をいらだたせる [= irritate, annoy, anger]
語源 pro(前へ) + voke(呼ぶ)

0886 evaporate
[ɪvǽpərèɪt]
消滅する [= disappear, vanish]、蒸発する
名 evaporation
語源 e(外へ) + vapor(蒸気) + ate

0887 amplify
[ǽmplɪfàɪ]
を詳述する、を増幅する
形 ample(十分以上の)

0888 scrutinize
[skrúːtənàɪz]
を綿密に調べる [= examine minutely]
名 scrutiny

0889 submerge
[səbmə́ːrdʒ]
潜水する、を水中に沈める
▶ submerge *oneself* in (〜に夢中になる)
語源 sub(下へ) + merge(沈む)

The woman is highly <u>esteemed</u>, even by her political opponents.	政敵たちにさえも、その女性は大いに<u>尊敬</u>されている。
The city was completely <u>overrun</u> by crime.	その市では犯罪がすっかり<u>はびこっ</u>ていた。
At the Army training camp, the soldiers must <u>simulate</u> a battle operation.	陸軍の訓練キャンプで兵士たちは戦闘<u>の模擬演習をし</u>なければならない。
Those who had <u>collaborated</u> with the enemy were later punished.	敵に<u>協力した</u>人たちは、後に処罰された。
The term had not yet <u>commenced</u> and the campus was empty.	学期はまだ<u>始まっ</u>ていなかったので、大学構内に人がいなかった。
The drunk man tried to <u>provoke</u> the other customer into fighting him.	酔っぱらいは、もう1人の客<u>を挑発して</u>自分とけんかさせようとした。
His wife's enthusiasm for the idea <u>evaporated</u> when she heard how much the new car would cost.	新車の金額を聞いて、彼の妻の買おうという情熱は<u>消え失せた</u>。
The expert was asked to write a report <u>amplifying</u> his reservations about the project.	その専門家は、プロジェクトに留保条件を付けている訳<u>を詳述する</u>報告書を書くように求められた。
I had to <u>scrutinize</u> the students' papers before I could pass them.	学生たちを及第させる前に、私は彼らの答案<u>を精査し</u>なければならなかった。
The submarine <u>submerged</u> as soon as enemy ships approached.	敵艦が近づくやいなや、潜水艦は<u>水中に潜った</u>。

commence (0884)「始まる」の名詞形commencementには「学位授与式」という意味があります。ですので、commencement ceremonyは「開会式」などではなく、「卒業式」です。

0890	**permeate** [pə́ːrmièit]	に広まる [= pervade, spread through], に浸透する [= penetrate] 語源 per(〜を通して) + meate(行く)
0891	**affix** [əfíks]	を(〜に)取り付ける, を(〜に)添付する, を(〜に)書き添える [= attach] ⟨to⟩ 語源 af(〜へ) + fix(固定する)
0892	**discern** [dɪsə́ːrn]	(…ということ)がわかる ⟨that⟩, を見分ける
0893	**coax** [kouks]	をなだめて〜させる [= persuade, entice] ⟨into⟩ ▶coax *one* into good temper(なだめて機嫌を直させる)
0894	**denote** [dɪnóut]	(記号などが)を示す [= indicate, mark] 图 denotation(言葉の明示的意味) (⇔ connote ほのめかす)
0895	**exemplify** [ɪgzémplɪfàɪ]	を例証する [= illustrate]
0896	**harness** [háːrnɪs]	(自然の力)を利用する, (馬)に馬具を付ける 图 harness(馬具)
0897	**chafe** [tʃeɪf]	(〜に)いらだつ [= irritate] ⟨at, under⟩, を擦りむく [= scrape]
0898	**loom** [luːm]	ぼんやり現れる [= appear dimly] ▶loom large((危険などが)不気味に迫る)
0899	**rumble** [rʌ́mbl]	ごろごろと鳴る

Anxiety about the future had **permeated** every part of the company.	将来への不安が会社中に広まっていた。
He **affixed** some Christmas lights to the roof of his house.	彼は自宅の屋根にいくつかクリスマス用の照明を取り付けた。
The teacher was able to **discern** that her student was deeply troubled.	教師は，自分の生徒が深く悩んでいることがわかった。
The police officer tried to **coax** the old lady's cat into coming down from the tree.	警官はそのおばあさんが飼っているネコをなだめすかして木から降りて来させようとした。
In many cultures, black clothes **denote** a state of mourning.	多くの文化において，黒い衣服は喪に服していることを示す。
His paintings are considered to **exemplify** the style known as abstract expressionism.	彼の絵画は抽象表現主義として知られる様式を例証するものと目されている。
Scientists are finding better ways to **harness** the limitless energy of the sun.	科学者たちは太陽の持つ無限のエネルギーを利用する，より優れた方法を模索している。
The students were **chafing** under the strict rules introduced by the new principal.	新任の校長が導入した厳しい規則に学生たちはいらだっていた。
In spite of the good weather forecast, a dark cloud **loomed** on the horizon.	天気予報では晴天のはずだったのに，黒雲が地平線上の空にぼんやりと現れた。
As we headed home, thunder **rumbled** in the western sky.	家に向かう途中，西の空で雷がごろごろと鳴った。

0900	**snare** [sneər]	をわなに掛ける [= trap, wile] ▶ snare a mouse（ネズミをわなに掛ける）
0901	**steer** [stɪər]	を導く, の舵を取る [= direct, guide] ▶ steer the boat（ボートの舵を取る）
0902	**evoke** [ɪvóuk]	を呼び起こす [= draw forth, conjure up] 图 evocation
0903	**dub** [dʌb]	(いくつかの録音)を合成する, (音・映像)を複製する, を(別の言語に)吹き替える
0904	**grapple** [grǽpl]	(〜と)真剣に取り組む [= struggle] 〈with〉
0905	**exert** [ɪgzə́:rt]	を行使する, を働かせる [= exercise] 图 exertion ▶ exert all *one's* strength（全力を出し切る）
0906	**grumble** [grʌ́mbl]	文句を言う [= complain] 〈about〉
0907	**hover** [hʌ́vər]	空中に停止する [= float]
0908	**precede** [prɪsí:d]	に先んじる [= come before] (⇔follow), より重要な位置にいる
0909	**reside** [rɪzáɪd]	住む [= live in] 图 residence

When I was young, an uncle taught me how to **snare** rabbits.	子どもの頃，おじがウサギをわなで捕まえる方法を教えてくれた。
My parents always tried to **steer** me in the right direction.	両親はいつも正しい方向に私を導こうとした。
The film I just saw **evoked** memories of my childhood in the Midwest.	私がたった今見た映画は，中西部での子ども時代の記憶を呼び起こした。
We tried to **dub** additional voices onto the old soundtrack.	我々は元のサウンド・トラックに追加の音声を合成することを試みた。
Junior colleges around Japan must **grapple** with lower future enrollments.	日本中の短大はこれから続く入学生数の減少に取り組まねばならない。
Few of the employees have **exerted** their right to paternity leave.	父親育児休暇の権利を行使する従業員はほとんどいない。
His son **grumbled** but agreed to do what he was asked.	彼の息子は文句を言ったが，頼まれたことをすることには同意した。
The helicopter **hovered** for a few minutes before landing.	そのヘリコプターは，着陸する前に数分間，空中に停止していた。
Many famous scientists had **preceded** him in the post.	多くの有名な科学者が彼の前任者としていた。
After the couple retired, they **resided** in a small seaside town.	その夫婦は引退した後，小さな海辺の町に住んだ。

0910 **specify** [spésəfàɪ]	を具体的に述べる [= state] 图 specification
0911 **topple** [tá(:)pl]	バランスが崩れて倒れる [= overbalance]
0912 **usher** [ʌ́ʃər]	を(〜へ)案内する [= escort] 〈to〉
0913 **withhold** [wɪðhóʊld]	を与えない，抑える，差し控える [= keep back] ▶withhold payment（支払いを差し控える）
0914 **shatter** [ʃǽṭər]	を粉砕する [= break into pieces]， (健康など)を害する
0915 **dice** [daɪs]	をさいの目に切る
0916 **garble** [gáːrbl]	を文字化けさせる
0917 **flourish** [fláːrɪʃ]	栄える [= thrive]
0918 **dart** [dɑːrt]	突進する 图 dart（ダーツ）
0919 **diversify** [dəvə́ːrsɪfàɪ]	を多様化する

The inspector **specified** a number of improvements that were necessary.	その検査員は改良が必要な点をいくつも具体的に述べた。
The tall pile of books **toppled** and fell across his desk.	高く積まれた本の山のバランスが崩れて倒れ，彼の机に落ちた。
A waiter **ushered** the group of guests to a private room.	ウエーターは個室に客のグループを案内した。
The government was accused of **withholding** information about the disease.	政府はその病気についての情報を公開しないことを責められた。
The baseball **shattered** the huge picture window of a nearby house.	野球のボールが近くの家の大きな見晴らし窓を粉々に砕いた。
She **diced** the carrots and then put them on to boil.	彼女はニンジンをさいの目に切り，ゆでた。
When he opened the file, the letters were completely **garbled**.	彼がファイルを開けた時，完全に文字化けしていた。
The small company **flourished** under the guiding hand of the innovative entrepreneur.	その小さな会社は革新的な起業家の手腕によって栄えた。
Trying to evade the dog which was chasing it, the squirrel **darted** across the street.	追いかけてくる犬から逃れようとして，リスは素早く通りを駆け抜けた。
Many farmers **diversify** crops to hedge against unpredictable weather and climate.	多くの農民が予期できない天気と気候から防衛するために穀物の種類を多様化する。

でる度 B 覚えておきたい単語

名詞 258語

🎧 0920 ~ 0928

0920 **rationale** [rǽʃənæl]	理論的根拠 動 rationalize (を合理化する) 名 rationality (合理性)　形 rational
0921 **restraint** [rɪstréɪnt]	抑制 [= constraint]，遠慮 動 restrain
0922 **stem** [stem]	茎 [= stalk]，幹 [= trunk]， 船首 (⇔ stern) 動 stem (の流れを止める)
0923 **gorge** [gɔːrdʒ]	(渓流の流れる)渓谷，小峡谷
0924 **zest** [zest]	熱意，興味， 痛快味 [= relish, gusto, piquancy] 形 zestful
0925 **complex** [kɑ́(ː)mplèks]	集合体，強迫観念 ▶ apartment complex (団地)
0926 **artifact** [ɑ́ːrtɪfæ̀kt]	工芸品 [= craftwork]
0927 **reversal** [rɪvə́ːrsəl]	逆転，転換 [= turnaround, turnover] ▶ reversal of roles (役割変更)
0928 **altruism** [ǽltruɪzm]	利他主義，利他心 [= regard for others] 形 altruistic

The finance minister explained the **rationale** behind the tax reforms.	財務大臣は，税制改革の背後にある<u>理論的根拠</u>を説明した。
The crowd showed great **restraint**, waiting patiently for hours to get their tickets.	集まった人々は大いに<u>我慢</u>して，チケットを手に入れるために何時間も辛抱強く待っていた。
The flowers in my garden died because parasites attacked their **stems**.	寄生植物が<u>茎</u>に取り付いたので，庭の花が枯れてしまった。
They peered over the edge of the **gorge** and looked at the stream far below.	彼らは<u>峡谷</u>のへり越しにのぞき込み，そして，はるか下にある小川を眺めた。
The girl does everything with such **zest** that it is hard not to admire her spirit.	その少女は，何でも<u>熱心</u>にやるので，その心意気を称賛しないではいられない。
The institute was housed in a **complex** of old buildings.	その機関は古い建物の<u>集合体</u>の中にあった。
Various primitive **artifacts** were discovered by the archeologists.	多種多様な原始時代の<u>工芸品</u>が考古学者によって発見された。
In a dramatic **reversal** of policy, the refugees were accepted by the country.	方針が大きく<u>逆転</u>されて，難民たちはその国に受け入れられた。
He was renowned all over the world for his **altruism**.	彼は<u>利他主義</u>で世界中に知られていた。

#	見出し	意味
0929	**mimicry** [mímɪkri]	物まね [= imitation]
0930	**coincidence** [kouínsɪdəns]	偶然の一致 [= concurrence] 動 coincide ▶by coincidence（偶然の一致で）
0931	**oversight** [óuvərsàit]	見落とし, 監督, 管理 [= supervision] 動 oversee（監督する）
0932	**privilege** [prívəlɪdʒ]	特典, 特権 形 privileged
0933	**liaison** [líːəzɑ̀(ː)n]	連絡 [= connection, contact], 連絡係, 密通 [= illicit love affair] 動 liaise
0934	**assessment** [əsésmənt]	査定, 評価 [= appraisal, rating] 動 assess ▶environmental assessment（環境影響評価）
0935	**bias** [báɪəs]	えこひいき [= partiality], 先入観 [= prejudice], 傾向 [= tendency]
0936	**incidence** [ínsɪdəns]	発生率 [= degree of occurrence], 影響の範囲 [= extent of influence]
0937	**amity** [ǽməti]	友好 [= friendship]（⇔ enmity 敵意） ▶a treaty of amity（友好条約）
0938	**pageant** [pǽdʒənt]	華麗な行列 [= splendid procession], 山車（だし）

The little boy's brilliant **mimicry** of the teacher made the others laugh.	少年の見事な先生の物まねを見て，ほかの人たちは笑った。
Meeting her on the street after so many years was quite a **coincidence**.	何年ぶりかで街で彼女に出会ったのは，全くの偶然だった。
By an **oversight**, he failed to grade one of the students' essays.	見落としで，彼は生徒の作文の成績を1人分つけ損なった。
Railway employees have the **privilege** of being allowed to travel on any train for free.	鉄道会社の社員は，どんな電車にも無料で乗れるという特典を持っている。
They formed a **liaison** between two countries.	彼らは2つの国の間の連絡をした。
The school is now undergoing a formal **assessment** for accreditation.	その学校は今，認可のための公的査定を受けている。
The judge was accused of showing a **bias** towards the defendant.	判事は被告人寄りの姿勢を示したことで非難された。
Authorities were concerned about the increasing **incidence** of violent crime.	暴力犯罪の発生率が増加していることを当局は憂慮していた。
The festival was intended to promote **amity** between the nations.	その祭りは国家間の友好の促進を目的としていた。
Every year, a **pageant** is held to celebrate the town's history.	毎年，その町の歴史を祝うために華麗な行列が開催される。

日本語で「リエゾン」というと「音の連結」という意味ですが，liaison (0933) は「連絡，密通」という意味もあります。

0939
paragon
[pǽrəgɑ̀(:)n]

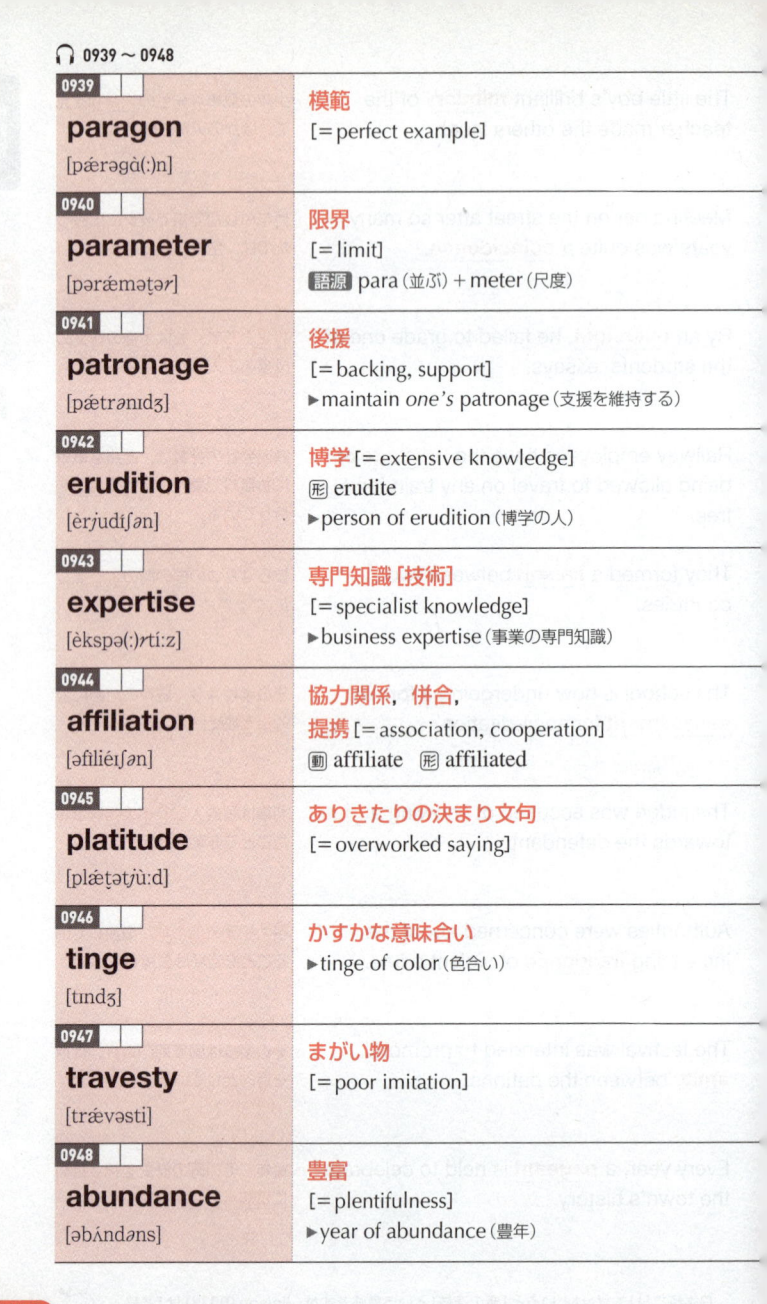

模範
[= perfect example]

0940
parameter
[pərǽmətər]

限界
[= limit]
語源 para (並ぶ) + meter (尺度)

0941
patronage
[pǽtrənɪdʒ]

後援
[= backing, support]
▶ maintain *one's* patronage (支援を維持する)

0942
erudition
[èrjudíʃən]

博学 [= extensive knowledge]
形 erudite
▶ person of erudition (博学の人)

0943
expertise
[èkspə(:)rtíːz]

専門知識 [技術]
[= specialist knowledge]
▶ business expertise (事業の専門知識)

0944
affiliation
[əfìliéɪʃən]

協力関係, 併合, 提携 [= association, cooperation]
動 affiliate 形 affiliated

0945
platitude
[plǽtətjùːd]

ありきたりの決まり文句
[= overworked saying]

0946
tinge
[tɪndʒ]

かすかな意味合い
▶ tinge of color (色合い)

0947
travesty
[trǽvəsti]

まがい物
[= poor imitation]

0948
abundance
[əbʌ́ndəns]

豊富
[= plentifulness]
▶ year of abundance (豊年)

The old couple saw their granddaughter as a **paragon** of virtue.	老夫婦は自分の孫娘を美徳の模範と見なした。
The budget imposed strict **parameters** on their spending.	予算は支出に厳しい限界を課した。
The promising scientist enjoyed the **patronage** of a powerful professor.	その有望な科学者は権力のある教授の後援を受けた。
The book showed the **erudition** typical of its author.	本はその著者特有の博学を示していた。
The ad said the company needed someone with computer **expertise**.	広告には、その会社がコンピューターの専門知識を持つ人を求めていると書かれていた。
The lawsuit certainly terminated his **affiliation** with that institution.	訴訟によって、その機関と彼との協力関係が終息したことは間違いない。
The ambassador's speech was full of **platitudes** about the need for peace.	その大使のスピーチは、平和の必要性についてありきたりの決まり文句が並べられていた。
Her comments about the company contained a **tinge** of resentment.	会社に対する彼女のコメントには、怒りのかすかな意味合いが含まれていた。
Critics denounced the production as a **travesty** of Shakespeare's play.	評論家たちはその作品をシェークスピア劇のまがい物だとして非難した。
Today's **abundance** of food is very unusual in historical terms.	今日、食料が豊富であることは歴史的に言うと極めてまれである。

0949 metaphor
[métəfɔ̀(:)r]
隠喩 [= application of a different term to a thing] (⇔ simile 直喩)

0950 infirmity
[infə́:rməti]
病気 [= sickness], 欠点
形 infirm (衰弱した)
語源 in (でない) + firm (固い) + ity

0951 deficiency
[difíʃənsi]
不足 [= shortage], 不完全(性) [= incompleteness]
形 deficient

0952 hygiene
[háɪdʒi:n]
衛生管理, 清潔 [= cleanliness]
形 hygienic
▶public hygiene (公衆衛生)

0953 antibiotic
[æ̀ntibaɪá(:)tɪk]
抗生物質 [= chemical substances that are used in treating infectious diseases]
語源 anti (反) + bio (生命) + tic

0954 tantrum
[tǽntrəm]
かんしゃく, 不機嫌
▶throw a tantrum (かんしゃくを起こす)

0955 cramp
[kræmp]
(筋肉の)痙攣, 生理痛
▶get a cramp in one's left leg (左足がひきつる)

0956 spasm
[spæzm]
(筋肉の)ひきつり
[= cramp]
▶muscle spasm (筋肉痙攣)

0957 tumor
[tjú:mər]
腫瘍
▶benign [malignant] tumor (良性[悪性]腫瘍)
▶brain tumor (脳腫瘍)

0958 diagnosis
[dàɪəgnóusɪs]
診断
▶make a wrong diagnosis (誤った診断をする)

The study of **metaphor** is a fascinating look into a special aspect of language use.	隠喩の研究は，言語使用の特別な一面を興味深く注視することである。
He suffered from an **infirmity** that made it difficult to breathe.	彼は呼吸困難になる病気を患っていた。
In this century, the world may face a severe energy **deficiency**.	今世紀中に，世界は深刻なエネルギー不足に直面することになるかもしれない。
Some children learn proper **hygiene** only in school since it is not taught to them at home.	一部の子どもたちは，適切な衛生管理を家庭で教わらないので，学校で学ぶだけだ。
Doctors fear that the overuse of **antibiotics** will lead to increasing resistance to them.	医師たちは，抗生物質の過剰投与は，危険な耐性を生み出すのではないかと心配する。
The mother was embarrassed when her child threw a **tantrum** at the party.	その母親は，子どもがパーティーでかんしゃくを起こして，恥ずかしい思いをした。
A **cramp** forced the star player out of the game at a crucial moment.	筋肉の痙攣のため，スター選手は大事な時に試合を降りなければならなかった。
As he bent over, he felt a **spasm** of pain in his back.	彼は腰を曲げた時，背中にひきつりによる痛みを感じた。
The doctors were trying hard to determine the extent of their patient's **tumors**.	医師たちは，その患者の腫瘍の広がりを見極めようと一生懸命だった。
Accurate **diagnosis** of the condition is not easy for doctors.	病気の正確な診断は医師にとって簡単なことではない。

0959
qualm [kwɑːm]

(〜に対する)良心の呵責(かしゃく) [= compunction], (〜に対する)不安 [= misgiving, uneasiness] 〈about〉

0960
enzyme [énzaɪm]

酵素 [= chemical ferment]
▶enzyme action(酵素作用)

0961
graft [græft]

移植 [= transplant]
▶graft cell(移植細胞)

0962
mutation [mjutéɪʃən]

変異型 [= transformation]
▶mutation gene(突然変異遺伝子)

0963
microbe [máɪkroʊb]

病原菌 [= germ], 微生物 [= microorganism]

0964
epicenter [épɪsèntər]

震源地, 核心

0965
coma [kóʊmə]

昏睡 [= trance]
▶be in a coma(昏睡状態にある)
▶come out of a coma(昏睡状態から覚める)

0966
paralysis [pəræləsɪs]

麻痺
▶cerebral paralysis(脳性麻痺)

0967
parasite [pærəsàɪt]

寄生生物, 居候 [= sponger]
形 parasitic

0968
autopsy [ɔ́ːtɑ̀(ː)psi]

検死 [= postmortem]
▶perform an autopsy on 〜(〜の死体解剖をする)

He had no **qualms** about telling a lie to his mother.	彼は母親に嘘をつくことに一切の良心の呵責を感じなかった。
Enzymes are catalysts for many significant biochemical reactions.	酵素は多くの重要な生化学上の反応の触媒である。
The bomb victims needed extensive skin **grafts** for their burns.	被爆者は火傷跡に広範囲な皮膚の移植を必要とした。
The new flu was said to be a **mutation** of an earlier virus.	新型インフルエンザは,以前に発生したウイルスの変異型だと言われている。
Many diseases are caused by **microbes** that are invisible to the naked eye.	多くの病気は,肉眼では見えない病原菌によって引き起こされる。
Seismologists are trying to locate the probable **epicenters** for future earthquakes.	地震学者たちは将来の地震の可能性が高い震源地を特定しようとしている。
The pilot was in a **coma** for a week in a hospital.	パイロットは1週間,病院で昏睡状態だった。
Following the stroke, he suffered **paralysis** of his left arm.	脳卒中の後で,彼は左腕の麻痺に苦しんだ。
Doctors finally identified the **parasite** that had caused the epidemic.	医師たちは,ついに流行病の原因となっていた寄生生物を突き止めた。
An **autopsy** showed that the murdered woman had been poisoned by someone.	検死によって,殺害された女性は誰かに毒を盛られていたことがわかった。

enzyme (0960) は「酵素」ですが,前にco (一緒に) がつくとcoenzyme「補酵素」を意味します。

0969
incubator
[íŋkjubèɪṭər]

保育器, 起業支援者
動 incubate 名 incubation (抱卵)

0970
hypnosis
[hɪpnóʊsɪs]

催眠術 [= mesmerism]
語源 hypno (催眠) + sis
▶under hypnosis (催眠状態で)

0971
limb
[lɪm]

手足
[= arm, leg]
▶out on a limb (孤立して, 危険な立場で)

0972
delusion
[dɪlúːʒən]

妄想 [= mistaken belief], 錯覚
形 delusive ▶be under the delusion that
(間違って…と思い込んでいる)

0973
deprivation
[dèprɪvéɪʃən]

(必需品の) 欠如 [= poverty, destitution],
(特権などの) 剥奪
動 deprive

0974
disposal
[dɪspóʊzəl]

処分
[= discarding]
▶at one's disposal ((人の) 意のままになって)

0975
dissolution
[dìsəlúːʃən]

解体, 分解 [= disintegration],
(議会などの) 解散
動 dissolve

0976
disgust
[dɪsɡʌ́st]

嫌悪
[= revulsion]
▶to one's disgust (うんざりしたことに)

0977
deference
[défərəns]

敬意 [= respect], 服従 [= obedience]
動 defer ▶pay deference to one's superiors
(目上の人に敬意を払う)

0978
diversion
[dəvə́ːrʒən]

迂回路 [= detour], 転換
動 divert (をそらす)

The baby was kept in an **incubator** for a few days after she was born.	その赤ちゃんは，生後数日間は保育器の中に入れられていた。
Some doctors have tried using **hypnosis** to treat the condition.	病気を治療するのに催眠術を使うことを試みた医師もいる。
Some of the veterans had lost eyes or **limbs** in the conflict.	退役軍人の中にはその紛争で視力や手足をなくした人もいた。
The man suffered from the **delusion** that he was from another planet.	その男性は，自分が別の惑星からやって来たという妄想に取り付かれていた。
His childhood **deprivation** caused him to save money all his life.	彼は幼少期の貧困ゆえに，生涯，金を節約するようになった。
The official was responsible for the **disposal** of unwanted files.	その職員は不要なファイルの処分を担当していた。
The issue of slavery once threatened the **dissolution** of the United States.	奴隷問題のために，合衆国はかつて分裂の危機に直面した。
The crime filled many people with a sense of **disgust**.	その犯罪は多くの人に嫌悪感を抱かせた。
In Asia particularly, one is expected to treat the elderly with **deference**.	特にアジアでは，高齢者を敬意をもって遇するよう期待されている。
There was a **diversion** to another route because of the roadwork.	道路工事のために別のルートへの迂回路があった。

0979 detour
[díːtùər]

回り道，迂回
▶take a detour（回り道をする）

0980 thesis
[θíːsɪs]

論文 [= dissertation],
論題 [= proposition]
▶master's thesis（修士論文）

0981 discourse
[dískɔːrs]

講演 [= lecture],
論文 [= treatise, dissertation],
会話 [= conversation]

0982 dissertation
[dìsərtéɪʃən]

論文 [= thesis]
▶doctoral dissertation（博士論文）

0983 inception
[ɪnsépʃən]

初め，開始
[= start, commencement]
▶at the inception of ~（~の初めに）

0984 advent
[ædvènt]

出現，到来
[= arrival, coming]
語源 ad（~へ）+ vent（来る）

0985 yardstick
[jáːrdstik]

基準，尺度
[= criterion, standard]
▶yardstick of success（成功の基準）

0986 criterion
[kraɪtíəriən]

基準，標準
[= standard, yardstick]
▶criterion evaluation（基準評価）

0987 expenditure
[ɪkspéndɪtʃər]

支出，消費
動 expend 名 expense（費用） 形 expensive

0988 proceeds
[próʊsiːdz]

収益 [= profits],
収入 [= income]
語源 pro（前に）+ ceeds（行く）

They took a **detour** on the way so that he could see the university.	彼が大学を見られるように，彼らは回り道をした。
My students are working hard to finish their graduation **thesis** before the deadline.	私が担当する学生たちは，頑張って期限までに卒業論文を終えようとしている。
The visiting professor's **discourse** was both erudite and lucid.	客員教授の講演は学究的かつ明快だった。
The scholar spent years writing his doctoral **dissertation**.	学者は博士論文を書くのに何年も費やした。
January 1st represents the **inception** of the New Year and symbolizes renewal.	元日は新年の初めを表しており，刷新を象徴している。
The **advent** of television changed forever the way news was reported.	テレビの出現はニュースの報道方法を決定的に変えた。
The book was hailed as a new **yardstick** for the field.	その本は，その分野の新しい基準として大いに認められた。
We had trouble deciding on the primary **criterion** for a promotion decision.	我々は昇進決定のための第一基準を決めるのに苦労した。
The new administration announced an increase in **expenditure** on health.	新政府は，保健に対する支出の増額を発表した。
The **proceeds** of the concert were used to help third-world children.	コンサートの収益金は第三世界の子どもたちを助けるために使われた。

0989 premium
[príːmiəm]

報奨金 [= reward],
保険料 [= payment for insurance]

0990 utility
[juːtíləti]

(電気・ガス・水道などの)公益事業,
有用性　動 utilize
▶of utility (役に立つ)

0991 balance
[bǽləns]

残高
[= remainder]
▶balance at a bank (銀行残高)

0992 dividend
[dívɪdènd]

(株の)配当金
動 divide

0993 surplus
[sə́ːrplʌs]

黒字 [= favorable balance] (⇔ deficit)
cf. be in the black (黒字である)
語源 sur (上に) + plus (プラス)

0994 deficit
[défəsɪt]

赤字
[= unfavorable balance] (⇔ surplus)
cf. be in the red (赤字である)

0995 deduction
[dɪdʌ́kʃən]

控除(額), 差し引き [= recoupment],
推論 [= reasoning],
演繹法 (⇔ induction 帰納法)

0996 dues
[djuːz]

会費
[= fee]

0997 insinuation
[ɪnsìnjuéɪʃən]

ほのめかし [= hint], 当てこすり
動 insinuate
▶by insinuation (遠回しに)

0998 innuendo
[ìnjuéndou]

暗示
[= insinuation, implication]
▶make innuendoes (当てこすりを言う)

He earned a handsome **premium** as payment for his services.	彼は尽力に対する支払いとして、かなりの額の報奨金をもらった。
The cost of **utilities** in Tokyo is higher than that of most American cities.	東京の公共サービスの料金は、ほとんどのアメリカの都市のそれと比べて高い。
The group decided to use the **balance** of the money on an excursion.	そのグループはお金の残額を小旅行に使うことに決めた。
We waited anxiously for the payment of our **dividends** at the end of the year.	我々は年末の配当金の支払いを気をもみながら待った。
The EU's representative expressed dissatisfaction with China's growing trade **surplus** with Europe.	EU（欧州連合）の代表は、中国の対欧貿易黒字の増大に対する不満を表明した。
The nation had to take steps to reduce the national **deficit**.	その国は赤字を減らす対策を講じなければならなかった。
Citizens with school-age children receive a **deduction** from their tax liability.	就学年齢の子どもがいる市民は、納税義務から一定額の控除を受けられる。
Many members had not paid their annual **dues** to the society.	多くの会員はクラブに年会費を支払っていなかった。
The students resented the **insinuation** that they were lazy.	学生たちは、自分たちが怠け者だとほのめかされて腹を立てた。
He resented the **innuendo** that he owed his success to his father.	彼の成功は父親のおかげだと言うほのめかしに彼は怒った。

0999	**connotation** [kà(:)nətéɪʃən]	言外の意味 [= hidden meaning]
1000	**craze** [kreɪz]	熱狂的な流行 [= vogue] 形 crazed ▶have a craze for 〜（〜に夢中である）
1001	**fad** [fæd]	一時的流行 [= temporary fashion] ▶fad words（流行語）
1002	**infusion** [ɪnfjúːʒən]	注入 ▶infusion of money（資金投入）
1003	**intake** [íntèɪk]	入学者数, 摂取
1004	**archaeologist** [àːrkiá(:)lədʒɪst]	考古学者 名 archaeology 形 archaic（古風な）
1005	**counterfeiter** [káʊntərfìtər]	偽造者 動 counterfeit
1006	**mediator** [míːdièɪtər]	仲裁者 [= intercessor, advocate] ▶financial mediator（金融仲介）
1007	**debtor** [détər]	債務者 [= borrower]（⇔ creditor） ▶joint debtor（連帯債務者）
1008	**outcast** [áʊtkæst]	追放された人, 浮浪者

Understanding the <u>connotations</u> of foreign words can be difficult.	外国語の言外の意味を理解するのは難しいことがある。
There was a <u>craze</u> among young people for flying kites.	若者の間で凧揚げが熱狂的な流行だった。
For a couple of years, there was a <u>fad</u> for studying philosophy.	2, 3年の間, 哲学の勉強が一時的に流行した。
The banks requested an <u>infusion</u> of capital from the government.	銀行は政府からの資金注入を要請した。
That year's <u>intake</u> of students was the best they had ever had.	その年の生徒の入学者数は今までの中で一番多かった。
We owe most of our knowledge of ancient civilizations to <u>archaeologists</u>.	私たちは, 古代文明に関する知識の大部分を, 考古学者に負っている。
The false banknotes were traced to a <u>counterfeiter</u> working abroad.	偽の紙幣は海外の偽造者によるものだと突き止められた。
A respected churchman offered to act as a <u>mediator</u> in the dispute.	尊敬されている聖職者が, 争いの仲裁者の役割をすることを申し出た。
Many <u>debtors</u> are forced to borrow even more money to pay interest.	多くの債務者は, 利子を支払うためにさらにお金を借りることを強いられる。
The village treated him as an <u>outcast</u> and refused to talk to him.	その村は彼をのけ者扱いして, 話しかけようともしなかった。

#	単語	意味
1009	**upstart** [ʌ́pstɑ̀ːrt]	成り上がり者, 成金 [= parvenu]
1010	**bigot** [bíɡət]	排他的な人
1011	**proprietor** [prəpráiətər]	所有者 [= owner] ▶sole proprietor（個人事業主）
1012	**beneficiary** [bènɪfíʃièri]	恩恵を受ける人 [= one who receives benefit] ▶beneficiary's agreement（受給者の同意）
1013	**warden** [wɔ́ːrdən]	監督者 [= superintendent] ▶wildlife warden（野生動物監視人）
1014	**matrimony** [mǽtrəmòuni]	結婚 [= marriage] (⇔divorce)
1015	**spouse** [spaus]	配偶者 [= partner in life, one joined in wedlock] ▶spouse allowance（配偶者手当）
1016	**naturalization** [nætʃərəlaɪzéɪʃən]	帰化すること [= acquiring citizenship] ▶naturalization of marriage（結婚による帰化）
1017	**infancy** [ínfənsi]	初期段階 [= early stage], 幼児期 ▶in *one's* infancy（子どもの頃に）
1018	**lineage** [líniidʒ]	家系 [= house], 血統 [= ancestry] ▶person of good lineage（家柄の良い人）

The king's favorite was considered a mere **upstart** by the other courtiers.	その王の寵臣は、ほかの廷臣たちからはただの成り上がり者と見なされていた。
The student said that only **bigots** opposed further immigration.	その学生は、排他的な人だけがさらなる移住に反対していると言った。
My grandfather was the **proprietor** of a small general store for many years.	私の祖父は長い間、小さな雑貨店の所有者だった。
On my life insurance policy, I listed my wife and children as **beneficiaries**.	私は自分の生命保険証券に、妻と子どもの名を受取人として載せた。
The math teacher was also **warden** of the student dorm.	数学の教師は学生寮の監督者でもあった。
The magistrate had the power to join people in **matrimony**.	その判事には人を結婚させる権限があった。
I was asked to fill in a form which included questions about my **spouse**.	私は、配偶者についての質問を含んだ書類に記入するように求められた。
It was not easy for a foreigner to receive **naturalization**.	外国人にとって帰化することは簡単ではなかった。
The subject of genetic research was still in its **infancy**.	遺伝子研究の問題は、まだ初期段階にあった。
He was enormously proud of the distinguished **lineage** of his family.	彼は自分の高貴な家系をとても誇りに思っていた。

1019 condolence
[kəndóuləns]

お悔やみ, 弔辞 [= funeral oration], 哀悼
▶condolence leave（忌引休暇）

1020 leftover
[léftòuvər]

（食事の）残り物
[= remainder, uneaten food]

1021 amenity
[əmíːnəṭi]

快適さ [= pleasantness], 生活を快適にするもの

1022 keepsake
[kíːpseɪk]

記念品
[= memento]

1023 thrift
[θrɪft]

倹約
[= economy]
形 thrifty

1024 subsistence
[səbsístəns]

生計 [= livelihood], 生存 [= existence, being], （最低必要な）生活手段
動 subsist

1025 habitat
[hǽbɪtæt]

生息環境, 居住地
名 habitation（居住）

1026 inhabitant
[ɪnhǽbəṭənt]

住民
[= resident]

1027 foliage
[fóuliɪdʒ]

木の葉
[= leafage]

1028 fertility
[fə(ː)rtíləṭi]

豊かさ [= richness], 肥沃 [= fecundity], 出生率
▶fertility of land（土地の肥沃度）

I sent a card to my friend offering my **condolences** over his recent loss.	友人の最近の不幸に対し，私は**お悔やみ**を述べたカードを送った。
After the party, the maid collected the **leftovers** to take home.	パーティー終了後，メイドは家に持って帰るために**料理の残り物**を集めた。
After working hard all his life, he wanted to enjoy the **amenity** of living in a cabin by the lake.	生涯働きづめだったので，彼は退職後，湖のほとりの小屋で暮らす**快適さ**を味わいたかった。
The family presented her with the picture as a **keepsake** of her visit.	その家族は彼女に訪問してくれた**記念品**として絵をプレゼントした。
She knew that it had been her parents' **thrift** that had sent her through college.	彼女は，自分が大学に行けたのは両親の**倹約**のおかげだとわかっていた。
He ensures his **subsistence** only by selling hot sweet potatoes on street corners in Tokyo.	彼は東京の街角で焼き芋を売るだけで**生計**を確保している。
Destruction of their **habitat** had dramatically reduced the animal's numbers.	**生息環境**が破壊されたせいで，その動物の個体数が劇的に減っていた。
The **inhabitants** of nearby villages were told to evacuate.	隣接している村の**住民**は避難するように指示された。
He sat drinking tea and admiring the colors of the autumn **foliage**.	彼は座ってお茶を飲みながら，秋の**木の葉**の色に感じ入っていた。
The SF writer was known for the **fertility** of his imagination.	その SF 作家は想像力の**豊かさ**で知られていた。

#	見出し	意味
1029	**ebb** [eb]	衰退, 減退, 引き潮 ▶the ebb and flow of ~ (～の干満)
1030	**primate** [práɪmeɪt]	霊長類 [= highest class of animals, including man, apes and monkeys]
1031	**pesticide** [péstɪsàɪd]	殺虫剤 [= chemical substance to kill insects] *cf.* herbicide (除草剤) 語源 pest(害虫) + cide(切る)
1032	**famine** [fǽmɪn]	飢饉 [= hunger, food shortage]
1033	**irrigation** [ìrɪɡéɪʃən]	灌漑, 水を引くこと 動 irrigate ▶irrigation canal (灌漑用水路)
1034	**palate** [pǽlət]	味覚 [= sense of taste], 好み [= liking] 形 palatable (口に合う)
1035	**guise** [gaɪz]	見せかけ, 外見 *cf.* disguise (を変装させる) ▶in [under] the guise of ~ (～を装って)
1036	**pretense** [príːtens]	ふり [= guise]
1037	**morsel** [mɔ́ːrsəl]	一口 [= mouthful], わずか
1038	**ratio** [réɪʃiòu]	割合 [= proportion] ▶in the ratio of five to two (5対2の比で)

There was an **ebb** in the company's fortunes as new rivals appeared.	新たな競合相手が出現してから、その企業の勢いに<u>かげり</u>が見られた。
Observation of human children reveals behavioral similarities to other **primates**.	人間の子どもたちを観察すると、ほかの<u>霊長類</u>と行動が似ていることが明らかになる。
Many people blamed **pesticides** for the disappearance of the bees.	多くの人が、ミツバチがいなくなった原因を<u>殺虫剤</u>のせいにした。
Global warming is leading to an increased occurrence of **famine**.	地球温暖化が<u>飢饉</u>の発生が増加する原因となっている。
Extensive **irrigation** of the desert had made it fertile farming land.	砂漠に広範に施された<u>灌漑施設</u>のおかげで、砂漠は肥沃な農地になった。
Some wine tasters have actually gone to school to train their **palates**.	ワイン鑑定人の中には、<u>味覚</u>を訓練するために実際に学校へ通った人もいる。
The terrorist entered the politician's hotel in the **guise** of a reporter.	そのテロリストは、政治家のいるホテルに記者の<u>ふり</u>をして潜入した。
The child soon gave up any **pretense** of doing his homework.	その子どもは宿題をしている<u>ふり</u>をすぐにやめた。
The model ate a **morsel** of cake and declared herself full.	そのモデルはケーキを<u>一口</u>食べて、満腹だとはっきり言った。
The **ratio** of applicants to those who were accepted began to drop.	募集人員に対する応募者数の<u>割合</u>は低下し始めた。

1039 modicum
[má(:)dɪkəm]

少量
[= bit, small quantity]
▶ a modicum of ~（少量の~）

1040 intervention
[ìntərvénʃən]

介入
[= intercession]
▶ government intervention（政府の介入）

1041 collision
[kəlíʒən]

衝突
[= crash]
▶ collision between two buses（2台のバスの衝突）

1042 agenda
[ədʒéndə]

協議事項（リスト） [= a list of things to be dealt with at a meeting]

1043 elevation
[èlɪvéɪʃən]

昇進 [= promotion]，**高度**
▶ at an elevation of 500 meters
（高度500メートルで）

1044 entrepreneur
[à:ntrəprəné:r]

起業家

1045 luminary
[lú:mənèri]

権威者 [= authority]，
天体

1046 monopoly
[məná(:)pəli]

独占（権），専売（権）
動 monopolize
▶ make a monopoly of ~（~を専売する）

1047 stake
[steɪk]

株 [= stock]，**投資，利害関係**
▶ at stake（危うくなって）

1048 coverage
[kʌ́vərɪdʒ]

報道，取材範囲
動 cover（を報道する）

It's my hope that she would still have at least a **modicum** of sympathy for him.	彼女が彼に対し，少なくともほんの少しの同情をまだ持っていたらというのが，私の願いだ。
But for the **intervention** of the police, there could have been a riot.	警察の介入がなければ，暴動が起こっていただろう。
An official investigation into the **collision** of the aircraft was announced.	航空機の衝突に関する公の調査が発表された。
The President had drawn up an impressive **agenda** of issues to discuss.	大統領は議論すべき問題の見事な協議事項リストを作成した。
People were surprised by the young man's **elevation** to the post.	人々は若者のそのポストへの昇進に驚いた。
In capitalist societies, **entrepreneurs** play a very important role.	資本主義社会において起業家はとても重要な役割を果たす。
At the society, various scientific **luminaries** met and exchanged views.	さまざまな科学の分野の権威者たちが協会で会って，意見を交換した。
The company has recently been accused of forming a **monopoly**.	その会社は，最近，独占を行ったとして告発されている。
He made a large profit when he sold his **stake** in the IT company to a bank.	彼はその IT 企業の株を銀行に売却して，多額の利益を得た。
The newspaper was criticized for its biased **coverage** of political issues.	その新聞は政治問題に対する偏った報道で非難された。

1049 hallmark
[hɔ́:lmà:rk]

特質 [= feature], 品質証明 [= authenticity]

1050 remuneration
[rɪmjù:nəréɪʃən]

報酬 [= reward, recompense, compensation], 給料 [= pay, salary]
動 remunerate

1051 confiscation
[kà(:)nfɪskéɪʃən]

没収 [= forfeit, expropriation]
動 confiscate

1052 conspiracy
[kənspírəsi]

共謀 [= collusion], 陰謀 [= plot]
動 conspire 名 conspirator (共謀者)

1053 asset
[ǽsèt]

資産 [= resources], 長所 [= strong point]
▶ cultural asset (文化遺産)

1054 commitment
[kəmítmənt]

責任 [= responsibility], 献身 [= devotion]

1055 inauguration
[ɪnɔ̀:gjəréɪʃən]

就任(式), 開始 [= commencement]
動 inaugurate 形 inaugural

1056 bankruptcy
[bǽŋkrʌptsi]

倒産

1057 embargo
[ɪmbá:rgoʊ]

輸出入禁止, 出入港禁止命令, 禁止 [= prohibition]
▶ gold embargo (金の通商禁止)

1058 rundown
[rʌ́ndàʊn]

概要(報告) [= summary, briefing, synopsis], 漸減

Curiosity about everything is the **hallmark** of the true scientist.	すべてのことに好奇心を持つことは，真の科学者の特質である。
The job was so difficult that no one would agree to do it without generous **remuneration**.	その仕事はとても大変だったので，十分な報酬なしには誰も引き受けようとしなかった。
A new American law permits the **confiscation** of any convicted drug dealer's property.	新しいアメリカの法律では，有罪となった麻薬取引業者の財産の没収を認めている。
The dissident was accused of organizing a **conspiracy** against the government.	政府への共同謀議を計画したことで反体制派は告発された。
The company's most important **asset** was its loyal workforce.	その会社の一番大切な資産は，その忠実な全従業員である。
Some men find marriage too big a **commitment** to make.	結婚は約束するには大きすぎる責任だと思う男性もいる。
Thousands of well-wishers attended the new president's **inauguration**.	何千人もの支持者が新しい大統領の就任式に出席した。
A series of rash investments brought the company to **bankruptcy**.	軽率な投資が続いたために会社は倒産した。
The United Nations imposed a trade **embargo** on the nation.	国連はその国に対して，禁輸措置を科した。
At the meeting, he began by giving a brief **rundown** of the company's recent performance.	会議で彼はまず，会社の最近の業績に関する手短な概要報告を行った。

embargo (1057) のbarは〈妨害する〉を意味します。p.190のembark「乗り出す」と間違わないようにしましょう。

#		
1059 **debit** [débət]	(銀行口座の)引き落とし，(帳簿の)借方　動 debit (を借り方に記入する)	
1060 **bribery** [bráibəri]	贈収賄　動名 bribe　▶commit bribery (贈賄する)	
1061 **transaction** [trænsǽkʃən]	取引　[= deal]	
1062 **imposition** [ìmpəzíʃən]	課税 [= levy]，負担 [= burden]	
1063 **loophole** [lúːphòul]	(法律などの)抜け穴	
1064 **bibliography** [bìbliá(ː)grəfi]	参考文献，出版目録　語源 biblio (本) + graph (書く) + y	
1065 **caricature** [kǽrɪkətʃʊər]	(人物の)風刺漫画　[= sarcastic cartoon]　動 caricature (を風刺漫画的に描く)	
1066 **chronicle** [krá(ː)nɪkl]	年代記，物語　[= narrative]	
1067 **specter** [spéktər]	恐怖，幽霊 [= ghost]	
1068 **apparition** [æpəríʃən]	幽霊 [= specter, ghost]，突然の出現	

He noticed a number of **debits** on his bank statement that he had not made.	彼は銀行の取引明細書に，覚えのない多数の引き落としがあることに気づいた。
In some countries, **bribery** of officials is an accepted part of doing business.	国によっては，官僚に対する贈賄は，ビジネスの一部として容認されている。
The **transaction** turned out to be very profitable for the company.	その取引は会社にとって大いに利益をもたらす結果となった。
The sudden **imposition** of the new tax was widely resented.	突然の新税の課税は多くの人の怒りを買った。
He used a **loophole** in the law to avoid paying tax.	彼は税金を払うのを回避するために法律の抜け穴を利用した。
The teacher told the students to include in their **bibliographies** all the books they use.	先生は学生たちに対して，利用するすべての書名を参考文献目録に載せるように言った。
In America, it is very common to see **caricatures**, even of the President.	アメリカでは，大統領さえ風刺漫画の対象になることがよくある。
A historian often relies on ancient **chronicles** to reconstruct history.	歴史家は歴史を再構築するために，しばしば古い年代記に頼る。
The **specter** of mass unemployment hung over the whole country.	大量失業の恐怖は国中に漂っていた。
Local people claimed to have witnessed **apparitions** at the old house.	地元の人たちは古い家で幽霊を見たと言い張った。

1069 stowage
[stóuɪdʒ]

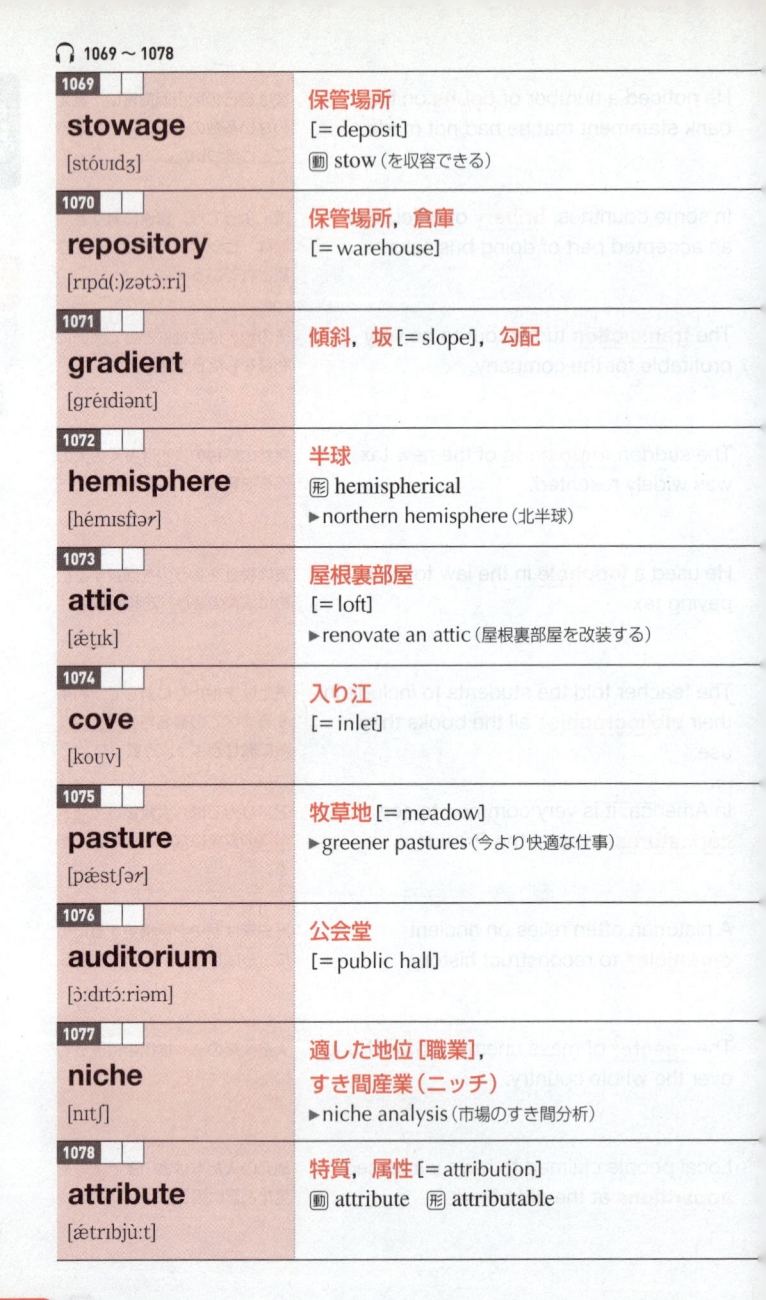

保管場所
[= deposit]
動 stow (を収容できる)

1070 repository
[rɪpá(:)zət(ò:)ri]

保管場所, 倉庫
[= warehouse]

1071 gradient
[gréɪdiənt]

傾斜, 坂 [= slope], **勾配**

1072 hemisphere
[hémɪsfìər]

半球
形 hemispherical
▶ northern hemisphere (北半球)

1073 attic
[ǽt̬ɪk]

屋根裏部屋
[= loft]
▶ renovate an attic (屋根裏部屋を改装する)

1074 cove
[kouv]

入り江
[= inlet]

1075 pasture
[pǽstʃər]

牧草地 [= meadow]
▶ greener pastures (今より快適な仕事)

1076 auditorium
[ɔ̀:dɪtɔ́:riəm]

公会堂
[= public hall]

1077 niche
[nɪtʃ]

適した地位[職業], すき間産業(ニッチ)
▶ niche analysis (市場のすき間分析)

1078 attribute
[ǽtrɪbjù:t]

特質, 属性 [= attribution]
動 attribute 形 attributable

There was not sufficient **stowage** to take the whole cargo.	すべての積荷を受け入れる十分な保管場所がなかった。
This bank is the **repository** of much of the country's gold reserves.	この銀行はこの国の金保有高の多くの保管所である。
As the **gradient** became steeper, some of the cyclists gave up.	傾斜が急になってきたので、自転車に乗るのをやめるサイクリストもいた。
In general, the world's wealthier economies are in the northern **hemisphere**.	概して、裕福な経済大国は北半球に位置する。
The artist lived in an **attic** in a poor part of Paris.	その芸術家はパリの貧しい地域の屋根裏部屋で暮らしていた。
The fishing village was situated on a **cove** in the peninsula.	その漁村は半島の入り江に位置していた。
The green hills provided excellent **pasture** for local cattle.	緑の丘はその土地の畜牛の素晴らしい牧草地となった。
The **auditorium** was packed with fans waiting for the concert.	公会堂はコンサートを待つファンで一杯だった。
Eventually the journalist found his **niche** as the newspaper's film critic.	そのジャーナリストは最終的に、新聞の映画評論家という適所を得た。
Does your pet dog have any special **attributes** by which it can be recognized?	あなたの飼い犬は、何か識別可能なはっきりとした特質を備えていますか。

hemisphere (1072) のhemiは (半分) を意味し、semiも同じです。semicircleは「半円」、semifinalは「準決勝」を意味することを確認しましょう。

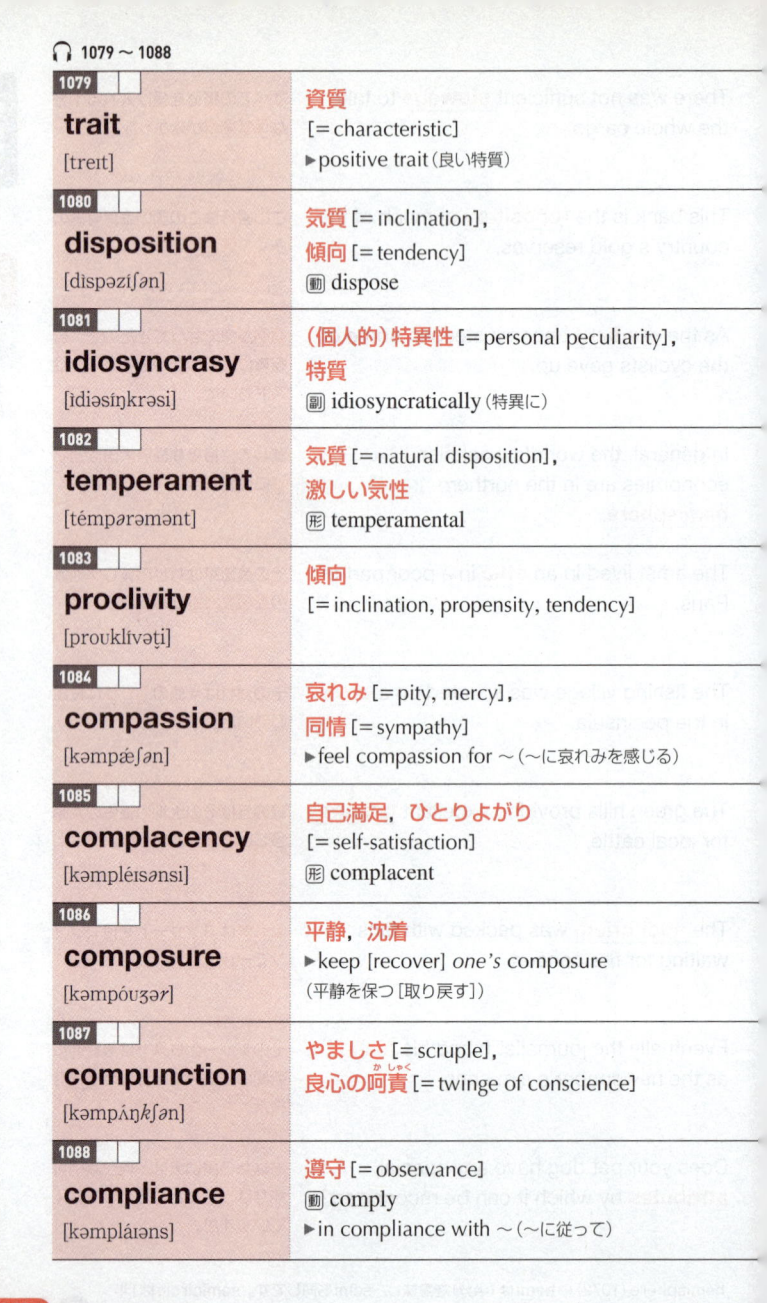

1079 **trait** [treɪt]	資質 [= characteristic] ▶positive trait（良い特質）
1080 **disposition** [dìspəzíʃən]	気質 [= inclination], 傾向 [= tendency] 動 dispose
1081 **idiosyncrasy** [ìdiəsíŋkrəsi]	(個人的)特異性 [= personal peculiarity], 特質 副 idiosyncratically（特異に）
1082 **temperament** [témpərəmənt]	気質 [= natural disposition], 激しい気性 形 temperamental
1083 **proclivity** [prouklívəti]	傾向 [= inclination, propensity, tendency]
1084 **compassion** [kəmpǽʃən]	哀れみ [= pity, mercy], 同情 [= sympathy] ▶feel compassion for ~（~に哀れみを感じる）
1085 **complacency** [kəmpléɪsənsi]	自己満足，ひとりよがり [= self-satisfaction] 形 complacent
1086 **composure** [kəmpóʊʒər]	平静，沈着 ▶keep [recover] one's composure （平静を保つ[取り戻す]）
1087 **compunction** [kəmpʌ́ŋkʃən]	やましさ [= scruple], 良心の呵責(かしゃく) [= twinge of conscience]
1088 **compliance** [kəmpláɪəns]	遵守 [= observance] 動 comply ▶in compliance with ~（~に従って）

The little boy had all the **traits** of a mathematical genius.	少年は数学の天才のあらゆる資質を備え持っていた。
We could never tell his **disposition** from the expression on his face.	私たちは顔の表情からは、彼の気質はわからなかった。
We could all tolerate his **idiosyncrasies** as long as he contributed to our work.	彼が我々の仕事に寄与しさえすれば、彼の特異性も許せるのだが。
His **temperament** is so gentle and quiet that it surprised us to see him angry.	彼の気質は非常に優しく物静かなので、彼が怒っているのを見て私たちは驚いた。
His parents were concerned by his **proclivity** for taking risks with his money.	彼の両親は、金を投機に使いがちな彼の傾向を心配していた。
Christ and Buddha both showed great **compassion** for human suffering.	キリスト、仏陀のどちらも、人間の苦悩に対して大いなる慈悲を示した。
He found the company's **complacency** that it was superior to its rivals irritating.	自分の会社が競合他社より優れているという自己満足が、彼にはいらだたしかった。
No matter how tense things get, she always seems to keep her **composure**.	いかに事態が緊迫しても、彼女はいつも平静を保っているようだ。
He was badly treated and felt no **compunction** about quitting the job.	彼はひどい待遇を受けたので、仕事を辞めることに何の後ろめたさも感じなかった。
The judge demanded the company's immediate **compliance** with his decision.	裁判官は彼の下した判決を会社が直ちに遵守することを要求した。

#	単語	意味
1089	**ambivalence** [æmbívələns]	ためらう気持ち [= hesitation], 相反する感情 [= dilemma] 語源 ambi (両方の) + valence (価値)
1090	**obscurity** [əbskjúərəṭi]	世に知られていないこと ▶ rise from obscurity to renown (無名から身を起こして有名になる)
1091	**boon** [bu:n]	恩恵 [= benefit, blessing, favor]
1092	**bounty** [báunṭi]	恵み深さ, 寛大 [= generosity, liberality], 助成金 形 bountiful
1093	**perseverance** [pə̀:rsəvíərəns]	不屈（の努力）, 忍耐 [= patience] 動 persevere
1094	**affability** [æfəbíləṭi]	愛想の良さ [= friendliness] 形 affable
1095	**magnetism** [mǽgnəṭɪzm]	人を引き付ける力 [= attractiveness] 形 magnetic
1096	**lure** [ljúər]	おとり [= decoy], ルアー, 魅力 [= enticement]
1097	**enticement** [ɪntáɪsmənt]	誘惑するもの [= allurement], 魅力 [= attraction] 動 entice 副 enticingly
1098	**captivation** [kæptɪvéɪʃən]	魅力, 魅惑 [= charm, fascination, enchantment] 動 captivate

Her **ambivalence** towards the plan was clear to everyone.	その計画についての彼女の<u>ためらいの気持ち</u>は，誰の目にも明らかだった。
The criminal's **obscurity** allowed him to disguise himself and escape.	その犯罪者は<u>世に知られていない</u>ため，変装して逃亡することができた。
We considered the splendid harvest a great **boon** to our fortunes.	素晴らしい収穫が我々の成功にとって大いなる<u>恵み</u>であると，我々は考えた。
Every year on Thanksgiving Day, Americans celebrate God's **bounty**.	毎年感謝祭には，アメリカ人は神の<u>恵み深さ</u>を祝う。
His success came more from **perseverance** than talent.	彼の成功は才能よりも<u>努力</u>の賜物だった。
His charm and **affability** made him popular with the students.	彼は魅力的で<u>愛想が良かった</u>ので，生徒に人気があった。
She had a **magnetism** that made her popular with her colleagues.	彼女には<u>人を引き付ける力</u>があったので，同僚の間で人気があった。
The undercover agent used the money as a **lure** to attract possible traitors.	工作員は，裏切り者を引き付けるための<u>おとり</u>として金を利用した。
Easy loans were an **enticement** to people to buy bigger houses.	簡単なローンはより大きな家を購入する人にとって<u>魅力</u>だった。
It was easy to see the **captivation** the children had for the clown.	その子どもたちがピエロに<u>魅了</u>されていたことは容易に見て取れた。

1099
hunch [hʌntʃ]

直感, 予感
▶have a hunch that ... (…という予感がする)

1100
whim [hwɪm]

思いつき
[= caprice, fancy]
形 whimsical

1101
credulity [krədjúːləti]

だまされやすいこと
[= gullibility]
形 credulous

1102
alacrity [əlǽkrəti]

敏活さ, 活発さ
[= briskness, agility]
▶with alacrity (てきぱきと, きびきびと)

1103
intoxication [ɪntɑ̀(ː)ksɪkéɪʃən]

酩酊(めいてい) [= drunkenness],
夢中 [= rapture]
動 intoxicate

1104
preoccupation [priɑ̀(ː)kjupéɪʃən]

没頭
[= engrossment]

1105
introvert [íntrəvə̀ːrt]

内向的な人
(⇔ extrovert)
語源 intro (中へ) + vert (向ける)

1106
clemency [klémənsi]

寛大さ [= leniency], **慈悲** [= mercy]
形 clement
▶lack of clemency (無慈悲であること)

1107
condescension [kɑ̀(ː)ndɪsénʃən]

恩着せがましさ, 丁寧
動 condescend

1108
drawback [drɔ́ːbæ̀k]

欠点 [= shortcomings],
不利な点 [= disadvantage]
▶drawback to success (成功を妨げるもの)

The detective had a **hunch** that the man was guilty but he lacked any hard evidence.	刑事はその男が犯罪者であるという直感があったが，確たる証拠を欠いていた。
He acts almost completely at **whim**.	彼はほとんどいつも思いつきで行動する。
Her **credulity** can only be explained by her sheltered childhood.	彼女のだまされやすさは，子どもの頃，箱入り娘で育てられたからとしか説明がつかない。
He marched ahead with such **alacrity** that we could scarcely keep up.	彼があまりにきびきびと先に進むので，私たちはほとんどついて行けなかった。
Many automobile road deaths are caused by the **intoxication** of drivers.	自動車による路上での死者の多くは，運転者の酔っ払いが原因だ。
His **preoccupation** with his career led him to neglect his family.	彼は仕事に没頭したために家族をなおざりにしてしまった。
An **introvert** is someone who regularly avoids social contact with others.	内向的な人とは，他人との社会的接触を通常避ける人を言う。
The convicted murderer begged the governor for **clemency**.	有罪となった殺人犯は，長官に情状酌量を請い求めた。
I could tolerate his sharp disagreements but not his **condescension**.	彼が激しく反対するのは我慢できたが，恩着せがましさは許せなかった。
One of his **drawbacks** as an administrator is his reluctance to make decisions.	管理者としての彼の欠点の1つは，決定を渋ることだ。

1109 oblivion
[əblíviən]

忘却 [= forgetting]
形 oblivious
▶ sink into oblivion (忘れられる)

1110 quirk
[kwə:rk]

奇癖
[= strange habit]

1111 malice
[mǽlɪs]

悪意 [= spite], 敵意
形 malicious

1112 abomination
[əbà(:)mɪnéɪʃən]

嫌悪感を起こすもの, 嫌悪 [= detestation, loathing]
動 abominate

1113 integrity
[ɪntégrəṭi]

誠実, 正直 [= honesty], 完全 [= completeness]

1114 ingenuity
[ìndʒənjú:əṭi]

独創性 [= inventiveness]
形 ingenious ▶ show remarkable ingenuity (素晴らしい才能を発揮する)

1115 conceit
[kənsí:t]

うぬぼれ
[= vanity, self-esteem]
動 conceit 形 conceited

1116 impartiality
[ɪmpà:rʃiǽləṭi]

公平
[= equity, fairness]
形 impartial

1117 absurdity
[əbsə́:rdəṭi]

不合理, 不条理, ばかばかしさ
形 absurd

1118 apathy
[ǽpəθi]

無関心 [= indifference, unconcern], 無感動
形 apathetic
語源 a (〜のない) + pathy (感情)

Eventually, all memory of the earlier culture fell into **oblivion**.	結局のところ，初期の知的活動のあらゆる記憶は忘却の淵に沈んだ。
One of his **quirks** was to read student essays in the bath.	彼の奇癖の1つは風呂の中で学生のエッセイを読むことだった。
He attacked the man with **malice**.	彼は悪意を持ってその男を攻撃した。
The expert denounced the conditions in the prison as an **abomination**.	専門家はその牢獄の状況を嫌悪感を起こさせるものであるとして糾弾した。
Everyone admired the **integrity** and honesty of the judge.	判事の誠実さと公正さを誰もが褒めたたえた。
Everyone praised the **ingenuity** of the new car's design.	皆が新車のデザインの独創性を褒めた。
His **conceit** led him to overestimate his importance to the company.	彼はうぬぼれが過ぎて，社内での自分の地位を過大評価していた。
She disagreed with her boss, but his **impartiality** was never in question.	彼女は上司と意見が合わなかったが，上司の公平さには疑問の余地はなかった。
He described the policy of paying farmers not to grow crops as a bureaucratic **absurdity**.	農家に作物を作らせないために金を払うという政策は，官僚的な不合理だと，彼は言った。
While I often enjoy students' arguing with me, I can't tolerate their **apathy**.	私は学生とちょくちょく議論するのが好きだが，彼らの無関心さは我慢できない。

1119 tedium
[tíːdiəm]

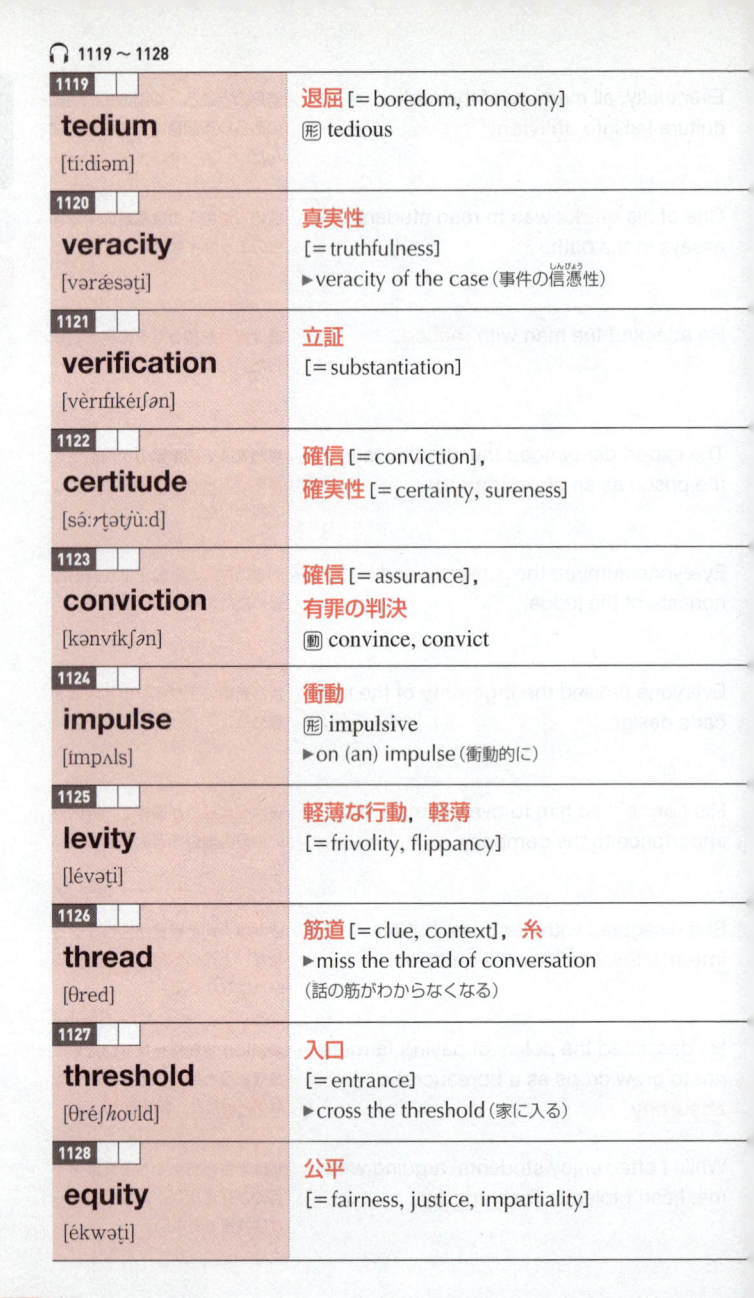

退屈 [= boredom, monotony]
形 tedious

1120 veracity
[vəræsəti]

真実性
[= truthfulness]
▶veracity of the case（事件の信憑性）

1121 verification
[vèrɪfɪkéɪʃən]

立証
[= substantiation]

1122 certitude
[sə́ːrtətjùːd]

確信 [= conviction],
確実性 [= certainty, sureness]

1123 conviction
[kənvíkʃən]

確信 [= assurance],
有罪の判決
動 convince, convict

1124 impulse
[ímpʌls]

衝動
形 impulsive
▶on (an) impulse（衝動的に）

1125 levity
[lévəti]

軽率な行動, 軽薄
[= frivolity, flippancy]

1126 thread
[θred]

筋道 [= clue, context], 糸
▶miss the thread of conversation
（話の筋がわからなくなる）

1127 threshold
[θréʃhould]

入口
[= entrance]
▶cross the threshold（家に入る）

1128 equity
[ékwəti]

公平
[= fairness, justice, impartiality]

While waiting in the airplane, we lessened the **tedium** by playing cards.	機内で待機している間，私たちはトランプをして退屈を紛らした。
The lawyer threw doubt on the **veracity** of the witness's account.	弁護士は目撃者の発言の真実性に疑問を投げかけた。
It was hard to provide convincing **verification** of the theory.	理論に対して納得のいく立証をすることは難しかった。
The **certitude** of his religious convictions never failed to astonish me.	彼の宗教上の信念の固さはいつも私を驚かすものだった。
He defended his position with absolute **conviction**.	彼は絶対的確信を持って自分の立場を守った。
On an **impulse**, he accepted the job even though he could not speak Chinese.	彼は中国語をしゃべれないのに，衝動的にその仕事を引き受けた。
The **levity** of the occasion led to an argument among the party guests.	その場の軽薄な行動の結果，パーティーの客の間で口論となった。
In the middle of the speech, he lost the **thread** of his argument.	スピーチの中ほどで，彼は論拠の筋道がわからなくなった。
The scientist said she was on the **threshold** of a major discovery.	その科学者は大きな発見の入口にいると語った。
The American ideal of **equity** for all is far from being realized in reality.	アメリカ人の理想であるすべての人にとっての公平は，実際には全く実現されていない。

veracity (1120) や verification (1121) のように veri は (真実) を意味します。verdict は「判決」，verify は「証明する」を意味することも覚えましょう。

1129	**constellation** [kà(:)nstəléɪʃən]	星座，(有名人などの)一団 語源 con (共に) + stell (星のある) + ation
1130	**deity** [díːəti]	神 [= god]
1131	**fragility** [frədʒíləti]	壊れやすさ [= frailty] 形 fragile
1132	**multitude** [mʌ́ltɪtjùːd]	群衆 [= crowd]， 多数 [= large number]
1133	**tactics** [tǽktɪks]	戦術 [= strategy] ▶ defensive tactics (防衛戦術)
1134	**precedence** [présɪdəns]	(〜に対する)優先 [= priority] ⟨over⟩ 動 precede (に先立つ)　名 precedent (先例)
1135	**effigy** [éfɪdʒi]	像，肖像 [= image]
1136	**mirage** [mərɑ́ːʒ]	幻影 [= illusion]， 蜃気楼
1137	**pendulum** [péndʒələm]	(時計の)振り子
1138	**culmination** [kʌ̀lmɪnéɪʃən]	絶頂 [= height, zenith, climax, acme] 動 culminate

One of his favorite **constellations** is Orion, named after a mythical Greek hunter.	彼が大好きな<u>星座</u>の1つはオリオン座で、それはギリシャ神話の狩人にちなんで名付けられている。
The building was a shrine to a **deity** of the local people.	その建物は土地の人々の<u>神様</u>の神社だった。
Due to their **fragility**, the old vases were kept in a locked case.	古い花びんは<u>壊れやすい</u>ので、カギのかかったケースに入れて保管されている。
The prince addressed the **multitude** of well-wishers from the balcony.	王子はバルコニーから<u>大勢</u>の支援者に話しかけた。
The workers used various **tactics** to resist the new rules.	労働者たちは新しい規則に反対するためにさまざまな<u>戦術</u>を使った。
At small liberal-arts colleges in the U.S., teaching usually takes **precedence** over research.	アメリカの小規模な教養系の大学では、たいてい研究活動よりも教育を<u>優先</u>する。
They found **effigies** of the ancient gods in the cave.	彼らは洞窟で古代の神々の<u>像</u>を発見した。
The huge profits he anticipated turned out to be a **mirage** and he ended up broke.	彼が期待していた莫大な利益は<u>幻</u>となり、ついに彼は破産した。
With nothing to do, I could only watch the grandfather clock's **pendulum** swing to and fro.	することがなくて、私は箱形大時計の<u>振り子</u>が揺れ動くのを眺めているしかなかった。
His lifework reached its **culmination** when he won the Nobel Prize.	彼の生涯の仕事は、ノーベル賞を獲得した時、<u>頂点</u>に達した。

1139 exhortation
[ègzɔːrtéɪʃən]

訓戒，（熱心な）勧告 [= counsel]
動 exhort
▶make an exhortation（勧告する）

1140 confinement
[kənfáɪnmənt]

監禁 [= imprisonment]，制限 [= limitation, restriction]
動 confine

1141 sobriety
[soubráɪəti]

禁酒 [= temperance]，落ち着き [= calmness]
形 sober（しらふの）
▶sobriety test（ドライバーに対する飲酒テスト）

1142 heritage
[hérətɪdʒ]

遺産 [= asset, legacy]
cf. inherit（相続する），inheritance（相続）
▶cultural heritage（文化遺産）

1143 impetus
[ímpətəs]

(〜に対する) 勢い 〈for〉，起動力，推進力
▶give an impetus to 〜（〜にはずみをつける）

1144 tribute
[tríbjuːt]

敬意，賛辞 [= praise]
▶pay tribute to 〜（〜に敬意を表する）

1145 novelty
[ná(ː)vəlti]

目新しさ，目新しいもの
形 novel

1146 courier
[kə́ːriər]

急送便業者
[= delivery service]

1147 windfall
[wíndfɔːl]

意外な授かりもの，風で落ちた果物
▶windfall profits（偶発利益）

1148 alienation
[èɪliənéɪʃən]

疎外，遠ざけること
動 alienate

All the **exhortations** in the world are useless if they are not followed by action.	行動が伴わなければ，世の中の訓戒などすべて無駄だ。
After only a week of solitary **confinement**, even strong men can become weak.	独房での監禁が1週間続くだけで，屈強な男も衰弱しうる。
In some religious sects, **sobriety** is mandated as a basic rule of behavior.	ある宗派では，禁酒が行動の基本原則として義務づけられている。
The country was proud of its cultural **heritage** and had many good museums.	その国は自国の文化遺産を誇りとしており，多くの優れた博物館を有していた。
The success of the operation may provide an **impetus** for further medical advances in the field.	その手術の成功は，この分野における医学の進歩に勢いをつけるかもしれない。
Many famous actors paid **tribute** to the Hollywood veteran.	多くの有名な俳優たちが，そのハリウッドのベテラン俳優に敬意を表した。
The visitor's **novelty** wore off and the children went back to their games.	客の目新しさは徐々に薄れ，子どもたちはいつもの遊びに戻っていった。
He worked as a **courier** carrying messages between companies thirty years ago.	30年前，彼は会社間のメッセージを運ぶ急送便業者で働いていた。
The woman had an unexpected **windfall** when an aunt left her some money in her will.	おばが遺言でいくばくかの金を残してくれたのは，その女性にとって思わぬ授かりものだった。
An increasing number of teenagers today feel a certain kind of **alienation** from society.	今日，ますます多くの若者が社会からの疎外を感じている。

wind（風）でfall（落ちる）ものだから，windfall（1147）は「意外な授かりもの」というイメージで覚えましょう。

1149 tenet
[ténɪt]
信条 [= belief]

1150 respite
[réspət]
(〜の)一時的中断 ⟨from⟩, 休息(期間)
▶ without respite (休みなく)

1151 stigma
[stígmə]
汚点, 不名誉 [= disgrace]
🔸 stigmatize
▶ put a stigma on *one* (人に汚名を着せる)

1152 rendition
[rendíʃən]
演奏, 翻訳
🔸 render

1153 ballot
[bǽlət]
投票, 候補者名簿
▶ ballot box (投票箱)
▶ cast a ballot (投票する)

1154 brawl
[brɔːl]
騒動 [= commotion], 口げんか [= row]

1155 crux
[krʌks]
核心 [= the bottom line], 十字架
▶ the crux of the matter [problem] (問題の核心)

1156 contraption
[kəntrǽpʃən]
(機械の)仕掛け, 工夫 [= device]

1157 incense
[ínsens]
香, 香のかおり
🔸 incense
▶ incense stick (線香)

1158 alignment
[əláinmənt]
調整 [= adjustment], 一列にすること [= bring into alignment]
🔸 align

One of the **tenets** of liberalism is a belief in freedom of speech.	自由主義の信条の1つは言論の自由である。
Peace-keeping forces only provided a temporary **respite** from the violence.	平和維持軍は暴力の一時的中断をもたらしただけだ。
The **stigma** of failure early in childhood can affect someone throughout life.	幼い頃の失敗という汚点は、生涯にわたって人に影響を与えることがある。
The audience was thrilled by the singer's **renditions** of various old favorites.	歌手のさまざまな懐メロ演奏に、観客たちはワクワクした。
The union took a **ballot** of its members to decide whether to accept the management's offer.	労働組合は経営陣の申し出を受諾するか否かを決定するために、組合員の投票を行った。
The **brawl** at the soccer stadium left many wounded and five dead.	サッカースタジアムでの乱闘によって、大勢が負傷し、5名が死亡した。
The **crux** of the matter was that the government refused to fund any more research into the disease.	問題の核心は、政府がその病気の研究にこれ以上の資金援助を拒んでいることだった。
He invented a **contraption** for removing snails from their shells.	彼はカタツムリを殻から取り出す仕掛けを考え出した。
In the 1960s, many young people associated with the hippie movement liked to burn **incense**.	1960年代、ヒッピー運動に関係した多くの若者は香を焚くことを好んだ。
After the minor car accident, I needed to take my car in for a wheel **alignment**.	ちょっとした自動車事故の後、私は自分の車を車輪調整に出さなければならなかった。

1159
axis
[ǽksɪs]

軸，枢軸
▶the Axis of Evil（悪の枢軸）

1160
circumlocution
[sə:rkəmloʊkjú:ʃən]

回りくどい表現，遠回しな言い方 [= periphrasis]

1161
configuration
[kənfìgjəréɪʃən]

外形
[= contour, outline, external form]，
（コンピューターの）接続機器の設定

1162
dimension
[dəménʃən]

規模 [= size]，
（長さ・幅・高さの）寸法 [= measurements in length, width and height]

1163
gait
[geɪt]

歩き方
[= manner of walking]

1164
perimeter
[pərímətər]

周囲，周辺，（軍の）防御線地帯
語源 peri（回りの）+ meter（計測）

1165
plagiarism
[pléɪdʒərìzm]

盗用，盗作
[= copying, piracy]

1166
recourse
[rí:kɔ:rs]

頼みとするもの [人]
[= resort, means of help]

1167
status quo
[stèɪṱəs kwóʊ]

現状
[= existing state of affairs]
▶vote against the status quo（現状に不満を持つ票）

1168
combustion
[kəmbʌ́stʃən]

燃焼
[= burning]
動 combust（を燃焼させる）

The **axis** of the earth is tilted at an angle of 23.4 degrees.	地球の軸は，23.4度傾いている。
The professor's **circumlocutions** were always entertaining to students.	その教授の回りくどい表現は，学生にとっていつも愉快なものだった。
No matter what **configuration** we tried, our architectural design seemed flawed.	外形をいかに整えようとも，我々の建築デザインには欠陥があるようだった。
The **dimensions** of our farm's largest soybean field were almost a square mile.	我々の農場で最大の大豆畑の規模は，約1平方マイルだった。
He could be recognized from a great distance by his characteristic **gait**.	彼は歩き方に特徴があるので，かなり遠くからでもわかっただろう。
The **perimeter** of the base was regularly patrolled by guards.	基地の周囲は警備兵が定期的に巡回していた。
Many American universities are expelling students found guilty of **plagiarism**.	多くのアメリカの大学は，文章盗用が見つかった学生を退学させている。
We had no **recourse** except mortgaging the house to pay the medical bills.	私たちには医療費を払うのに家を抵当に入れるほか頼るべき手段がなかった。
It is no longer possible to merely maintain the **status quo**; changes must be made.	単に現状を維持することはもはや難しい。変化が必要だ。
A simple spark can initiate **combustion** of a highly volatile substance.	ちょっとした火花も，高い揮発性を持った物質の燃焼を引き起こすことがある。

1169
delineation
[dɪlíniéɪʃən]

描写
[= depiction, description]
動 delineate

1170
diameter
[daɪǽmətər]

直径
形 diametrical
cf. radius (半径)

1171
milestone
[máɪlstòʊn]

画期的な出来事
[= epoch-making event]
▶ reach a milestone (重要な段階に達する)

1172
vernacular
[vərnǽkjulər]

その土地の言葉, 自国語

1173
semblance
[sémbləns]

ふり [= pretense],
外観 [= appearance]
▶ in semblance (外見は)

1174
inducement
[ɪndjúːsmənt]

刺激, 誘因
[= motive, incentive]
動 induce

1175
contamination
[kəntæmɪnéɪʃən]

汚染 [= pollution],
汚すこと [= defilement]
動 contaminate

1176
patent
[pǽtənt]

特許(権), 専売特許, 特許品
▶ patent pending (特許出願中)

1177
commodity
[kəmá(ː)dəti]

商品 [= merchandise],
生活用品

The novelist is praised for her sensitive **delineation** of character.	その作家は，登場人物の繊細な描写で称賛されている。
He used some rope to measure the **diameter** of the artificial pond.	彼はロープを使ってその人工池の直径を測定した。
The development of the vaccine was a **milestone** in medical history.	ワクチンの開発は，医学史上の画期的な出来事だった。
His French was good but he could not follow the local **vernacular**.	彼のフランス語は上手だったがその土地独特の言葉を理解できなかった。
The philosopher Suzanne Langer claims that art is a **semblance** of life.	哲学者スザンヌ・ランガーは，芸術は人生の見せかけだと主張している。
The military offered an attractive bonus as an **inducement** for reenlisting.	軍は再入隊への動機づけとして結構な額の特別手当を出した。
The accident at the chemical plant caused massive environmental **contamination**.	その化学工場の事故は，大規模な環境汚染を引き起こした。
The inventor was famous for the number of **patents** he had taken out.	その発明家は，取得した特許の数で有名だった。
The most important **commodity** in this century will be information itself.	今世紀における最も重要な商品は，情報そのものであろう。

でる度 B 覚えておきたい単語
形容詞・副詞　223語

🎧 1178 ~ 1186

1178 **prone** [proun]	(~する)傾向がある [= liable, tending] ⟨to *do*⟩, うつ伏せの [= prostrate] (⇔supine)
1179 **communal** [kəmjú:nəl]	共同体の，共有の [= shared] 名 commune ▶communal property（共有財産）
1180 **diverse** [dəvə́:rs]	多様な [= various] 動 diversify　名 diversity
1181 **seamless** [sí:mləs]	一貫して，途切れのない 名 seamlessness
1182 **vicarious** [vɪkéəriəs]	代わりの [= delegated, substitute, deputy] ▶vicarious agent（代理人）
1183 **virtually** [və́:rtʃuəli]	事実上 [= in fact]，実質的には 形 virtual（実質上の，仮の）
1184 **mandatory** [mǽndətɔ̀:ri]	義務的な，強制の [= obligatory, compulsory], 命令の 動名 mandate
1185 **abruptly** [əbrʌ́ptli]	突然 [= suddenly]
1186 **potential** [pəténʃəl]	潜在的な [= latent] (⇔actual) ▶potential abilities（潜在能力）

I am afraid he is **prone** to change his mind without prior notice.	彼は予告なしに考えを変える<u>傾向がある</u>と思う。
Religious cults often experiment with **communal** living.	カルト宗教は，しばしば，<u>共同</u>生活をしてみようとする。
The student body was very **diverse** and included people from over fifty countries.	その学生団体は非常に<u>多様</u>で，50か国以上の人々を含んでいた。
The boy's account of what happened was **seamless** and so hard to disprove.	出来事についての少年の話は<u>一貫している</u>ので，反論するのは難しかった。
Unlike Christianity, Buddhism does not acknowledge **vicarious** atonement.	キリスト教と異なり，仏教は<u>代わりの</u>償いを認めない。
The DVD was so popular that it became **virtually** unobtainable for a time.	そのDVDは人気があり過ぎて，しばらくの間，<u>事実上</u>入手不可能になっていた。
In order to pass this course, attendance is **mandatory**.	この教科に合格するには，出席が<u>義務</u>である。
The performance was **abruptly** cancelled when the actor fell ill.	公演は俳優が病気になったので，<u>突然</u>中止になった。
The businessman found that the **potential** profits would be huge.	その実業家は<u>潜在的な</u>利益はとても大きいと気付いた。

1187
indispensable
[ìndɪspénsəbl]

必要不可欠な
[= essential]（⇔dispensable）

1188
contiguous
[kəntígjuəs]

連続した [= adjacent, near]，
接触する [= touching]
▶contiguous events（連続した出来事）

1189
crude
[kru:d]

天然のままの，
粗野な [= uncultured, immature]
▶crude oil（原油）

1190
confidential
[kà(:)nfɪdénʃəl]

極秘の，機密の [= classified]
图 confidentiality
▶confidential document（機密書類）

1191
spontaneous
[spɑ(:)ntéɪniəs]

自然発生的な，自発的な [= voluntary]
图 spontaneity

1192
circumstantial
[sə̀ːrkəmstǽnʃəl]

状況的な，付随的な [= collateral]
图 circumstance

1193
overdue
[òʊvərdjúː]

（予定の日時より）遅れた，
支払期限を過ぎた
▶overdue bill（支配期限を過ぎた請求書）

1194
conspicuous
[kənspíkjuəs]

人目につく
[= noticeable, easily seen]
▶cut a conspicuous figure（異彩を放つ）

1195
tentative
[téntətɪv]

仮の
[= not final, done by way of trial]
▶tentative plan（試作）

1196
demographic
[dèməgrǽfɪk]

人口統計の
图 demography
▶demographic transition（人口統計的遷移）

The chairman found his secretary so **indispensable** that he even took her with him on business trips.	会長は秘書が<u>必要不可欠</u>だと思っていたので,出張にさえも彼女を連れて行った。
Contiguous consonants rarely occur in Japanese.	<u>連続</u>子音は日本語ではめったに生じない。
This facility processes the **crude** materials before sending them to the manufacturing plant.	この施設は,製造工場へ送る前に<u>生の</u>原料を加工する。
What I am about to tell you is **confidential**, so please do not repeat it.	私がこれから君に言うことは<u>極秘</u>だから,決して他言しないように。
The college's chemistry lab caught fire due to **spontaneous** combustion.	大学の化学実験室は<u>自然</u>発火により出火した。
The police decided not to prosecute as they could only find **circumstantial** evidence against him.	警察は,彼に対する<u>状況</u>証拠を見つけただけなので,起訴しないことに決定した。
Activists said the change in the law was long **overdue** and should have been introduced earlier.	法律の変更は長く<u>遅滞して</u>おり,もっと早々に導入されるべきだったと,活動家は発言した。
His purple and pink tie certainly made him **conspicuous** in a crowd.	彼は紫色とピンク色のネクタイをしていたので,確かに人の中で<u>目立った</u>。
We could only reach a **tentative** agreement after months of negotiation.	何か月か交渉した後も,我々は<u>暫定的な</u>合意にしか到達できなかった。
The sociologist began by describing the **demographic** profile of the community he was studying.	その社会学者は,研究対象である地域の<u>人口統計</u>データの説明から始めた。

democracyのように,demには(人々)という意味があります。demographic(1196)はdemo(人々)+graphic(グラフを用いた)で「人口統計の」とイメージしましょう。

#	英語	日本語
1197	**exploratory** [ɪksplɔ́:rətɔ̀:ri]	探索的な [= investigative] 動 explore ▶exploratory operation（調査活動）
1198	**hypothetical** [hàɪpəθéṭɪkəl]	仮定した [= supposed, imagined] ▶hypothetical reasoning（仮説推論）
1199	**outright** [áʊtràɪt]	完全な [= complete], 紛れもない ▶outright refusal（完全な拒否）
1200	**medieval** [mì:dií:vəl]	中世の
1201	**contemporary** [kəntémpərèri]	現代の [= modern], 同時代の 名 contemporary（同世代の人） ▶contemporary writers（現代の作家）
1202	**stagnant** [stǽgnənt]	よどんだ [= not flowing], 停滞した, 不景気の [= sluggish] 名 stagnation
1203	**bleak** [bli:k]	（見通しなどが）暗い, 荒涼とした [= desolate, dreary]
1204	**sluggish** [slʌ́gɪʃ]	活気のない [= inactive, dull, slow-moving] 名 sluggishness ▶sluggish economy（停滞している経済）
1205	**bionic** [baɪɑ́(:)nɪk]	生体工学の, 超人的な 名 bionics
1206	**genetically** [dʒənéṭɪkəli]	遺伝的に 名 genetics（遺伝学） ▶genetically modified food（遺伝子組み換え食品）

An <u>exploratory</u> survey had found clear signs of the presence of oil.	<u>探索的</u>調査によって石油の存在が明らかになった。
They made plans for a <u>hypothetical</u> terrorist attack on the airport.	彼らは空港へのテロリストの攻撃を<u>仮定した</u>計画を立てた。
He said her claims were an <u>outright</u> invention with no basis in fact.	彼は彼女の主張を事実に基づかない<u>完全な</u>作り話だと言った。
The building looked <u>medieval</u>, but it was actually not that old.	それは<u>中世の</u>建物のように見えたが，実はそれほど古くはなかった。
<u>Contemporary</u> furniture often values interesting designs over comfort.	<u>現代の</u>家具は，しばしば，快適さよりも面白いデザインの方に重点を置く。
In tropical climates, <u>stagnant</u> water can be a breeding place for malaria.	熱帯性気候では，<u>よどんだ</u>水はマラリアの温床となり得る。
The recent economic signs indicate <u>bleak</u> prospects for the near future.	最近の経済兆候は，近い将来の<u>暗い</u>展望を示している。
The giant sloth is characterized by its unusually <u>sluggish</u> movements.	巨大なナマケモノは異常に<u>活気のない</u>動きが特徴だ。
Artificial hearts are one example of <u>bionic</u> medicine.	人工心臓は<u>生体工学</u>医療の一例である。
The ethnic group was <u>genetically</u> liable to certain allergies.	その民族集団は<u>遺伝的に</u>，ある種のアレルギーにかかりやすい。

1207	**hybrid** [háɪbrɪd]	交配した，雑種の [= composite] 图 hybrid (交配種)
1208	**extinct** [ɪkstíŋkt]	絶滅した [= extinguished], 死に絶えた 图 extinction
1209	**dormant** [dɔ́ːrmənt]	(火山などが)活動していない [= inactive], 休眠中の [= sleeping] ▶dormant volcano (休火山)
1210	**toxic** [tá(ː)ksɪk]	有毒な [= poisonous] ▶toxic action (毒性作用)
1211	**respiratory** [réspərətɔ̀ːri]	呼吸器に関する，呼吸の 動 respire 图 respiration
1212	**chronic** [krá(ː)nɪk]	慢性の [= lingering, confirmed] (⇔acute 急性の) ▶chronic disease (慢性病)
1213	**addictive** [ədíktɪv]	中毒性のある 图 addict, addiction 形 addicted (中毒になっている) ▶addictive behavior (常習行為)
1214	**perennial** [pəréniəl]	永遠の，永続する [= enduring, everlasting], 多年生の 图 perennial (多年生植物)
1215	**inevitable** [ɪnévətəbl	-évɪ-]	避けられない [= unavoidable] 副 inevitably
1216	**imperative** [ɪmpérətɪv]	絶対に必要な，緊急の [= urgent], 命令的な，強制的な [= peremptory]

My wife enjoys creating **hybrid** species of orchids in our greenhouse.	妻は温室でランの交配種を作り出すことを楽しんでいる。
Though far from **extinct**, sea turtles are seriously endangered.	絶滅には程遠いが、ウミガメは絶滅危惧種になっている。
The border dispute remained **dormant** for years before suddenly flaring up again.	その国境紛争は長年にわたって休止状態であったのに、突然再燃した。
The government is finally pressuring industry to reduce **toxic** wastes.	政府は、有毒廃棄物を減らすよう、ようやく産業界に圧力をかけている。
Pollens at different times of the year can exacerbate **respiratory** problems.	1年のいろいろな時期の花粉が呼吸器系の症状を悪化させ得る。
John F. Kennedy suffered from **chronic** back pain.	ジョン・F・ケネディは慢性的な背痛を患っていた。
Once he started gambling, he found it **addictive** and was unable to stop.	彼は一度ギャンブルを始めると、それが病みつきになると気付いたものの、やめられなかった。
The Christmas pantomime of "Sleeping Beauty" is a **perennial** favorite with British children.	クリスマスの無言劇『眠れる森の美女』は、イギリスの子どもたちの永遠のお気に入りである。
We accepted the fact that our defeat was probably **inevitable**.	敗北はおそらく不可避であるという事実を我々は認めた。
Immediate action is **imperative** to prevent an AIDS epidemic in Asia.	アジアのエイズ蔓延を防ぐために、早急の行動をとることが絶対に必要だ。

1217	**ethical** [éθɪkəl]	道徳にかなった [= moral]
1218	**plausible** [plɔ́ːzəbl]	もっともらしい，まことしやかな ▶plausible argument（説得力のある議論）
1219	**psychologically** [sàɪkəlá(ː)dʒɪkəli]	心理的に
1220	**psychic** [sáɪkɪk]	霊的な，精神の [= mental] ▶psychic phenomena（心霊現象）
1221	**adolescent** [ædəlésənt]	思春期の [= pubescent]
1222	**dispirited** [dɪspírətɪd]	意気消沈した [= disheartened]
1223	**distressing** [dɪstrésɪŋ]	悲惨な 名 distress（苦悩）
1224	**empathic** [empǽθɪk]	共感を呼ぶ 名 empathy ▶empathic understanding（共感的理解）
1225	**emphatic** [ɪmfǽtɪk]	(…ということ)を強調する〈that〉，語気が強い，強調的な 動 emphasize
1226	**inanimate** [ɪnǽnɪmət]	生命のない [= lifeless] ▶inanimate eyes（生気のない目）

The group demanded the university adopt an **ethical** investment policy.	そのグループは，道徳にかなった投資計画を採用するように大学に要求した。
The theory is **plausible** but by no means proved.	その仮説はもっともらしいが，まったくもって証明されていない。
The defense lawyer said his client was **psychologically** unstable.	被告側弁護人が，依頼人は心理的に不安定だと言った。
Jeane Dixon was thought to have the **psychic** power to predict the future.	ジーン・ディクソンは未来を予測する霊的な能力を持っていると考えられた。
She suffered from the common **adolescent** worries about identity.	彼女は思春期特有のアイデンティティーの悩みに苦しんだ。
The team was **dispirited** by their failure to win even one game.	そのチームは1勝し損なっただけで意気消沈した。
The documentary told a **distressing** tale of cruelty and greed.	そのドキュメンタリーは残酷さと貪欲の悲惨な話を伝えていた。
The author published an **empathic** account of the accident's victims.	その著者は事故の被害者たちの共感を呼ぶ実話集を出版した。
In his statement, he was **emphatic** that he was innocent of the crime.	供述の中で彼はその犯罪に全く関与していないことを強調した。
The girl sat without moving, like an **inanimate** object.	その少女は生命のない物のようにじっと座っていた。

1227	**inane** [ínéɪn]	ばかげた [= foolish, silly], 空虚な [= empty, vacant] 图 inanity
1228	**innate** [ɪnéɪt]	生来の [= inborn, natural], 固有の [= native, inherent] ▶innate ability (生まれながらの能力)
1229	**incredulous** [ɪnkrédʒələs]	信じようとしない, 疑わしい [= dubious] ▶incredulous look (疑うような顔つき)
1230	**intolerant** [ɪntɑ́(ː)lərənt]	(狭量で) 我慢できない ▶be intolerant of ~ (~に我慢できない)
1231	**inhospitable** [ɪnhɑ(ː)spíṭəbl]	(土地などが) 寄せつけない [= uninviting]
1232	**intractable** [ɪntræktəbl]	手に負えない [= unmanageable] ▶intractable diseases (難病)
1233	**intrusive** [ɪntrúːsɪv]	押しつけがましい ▶intrusive behavior (押しつけがましい行動)
1234	**invalid** [ɪnvælɪd]	無効の [= void] 動 invalidate
1235	**intricate** [ɪ́ntrɪkət]	複雑な [= involved, entangled, knotty] ▶intricate puzzle (複雑なパズル)
1236	**invariably** [ɪnvéəriəbli]	いつも [= always] 形 invariable

His ideas were so **inane**, I didn't bother to refute them.	彼の考えはあまりにも**ばかげて**いたので，わざわざ異議を唱えることもしなかった。
Some birds have an **innate** tendency to mate for life.	鳥の中には，一生つがうという**生来の**性質を持つものもいる。
At first, people were **incredulous** but later they came to believe him.	最初，人々は彼を**信じようとしなかった**が，後に信じるようになった。
As he grew older, he became increasingly **intolerant** of outsiders.	彼は年を取るにしたがって，ますます部外者に対して**狭量**になった。
The icy desert terrain was highly **inhospitable** to travelers.	凍りついたような砂漠の地は旅行者を**寄せつけな**かった。
He found his accumulating debts an **intractable** problem.	彼は累積債務が**手に負えない**問題だと気づいた。
The woman objected strongly to the detective's **intrusive** questions.	その女性は探偵の**立ち入った**質問を強く拒絶した。
Relativity rendered some assumptions of classical physics **invalid**.	相対性原理は，古典物理学のいくつかの前提を**無効に**した。
The mystery novels of Arthur Conan Doyle are **intricate** puzzles.	アーサー・コナン・ドイルのミステリー小説は**複雑な**パズルそのものだ。
The absent-minded professor almost **invariably** forgot to attend staff meetings.	うっかり者の教授はほとんど**いつも**，教授会に出席するのを忘れた。

invalid (1234) は「無効の」だけでなく，「病気の，病人」の意味を持ちます。invalid ticket「無効のチケット」，invalid diets「病人向けの食事」のように使われます。

1237	**irrational** [ɪrǽʃənəl]	訳のわからない, 不合理な [= unreasonable] ▶ irrational decision making (非合理な意思決定)
1238	**irresolute** [ɪrézəlù:t]	優柔不断な [= indecisive]
1239	**irrelevant** [ɪréləvənt]	(〜にとって)不適切な, (〜にとって)関係のない [= not pertinent] 〈to〉
1240	**irate** [àɪréɪt]	怒った [= angry, wrathful, enraged, furious]
1241	**drastically** [drǽstɪkəli]	思い切って, 徹底的に 形 drastic (徹底的な, 深刻な)
1242	**overly** [óʊvərli]	過度に [= excessively]
1243	**obsolete** [à(:)bsəlí:t]	旧式の, 廃れた [= out-of-date]
1244	**stale** [steɪl]	鮮度の落ちた (⇔fresh), 陳腐な [= trite]
1245	**decrepit** [dɪkrépɪt]	老いぼれた [= senile], 使い古した [= worn-out] 名 decrepitude
1246	**gratified** [grǽtɪfàɪd]	(〜に)満足している 〈by〉

He had an **irrational** belief in his own invulnerability to harm.	彼は不死身であるという訳のわからない信念を持っていた。
The government's **irresolute** response to the economic crisis only made things worse.	その経済危機に対する政府の優柔不断な対応は事態を悪化させただけだった。
His point is valid, but **irrelevant** to the ongoing discussion.	彼の指摘は正当だが，今の議論には不適切だ。
When students slept in class, he would suddenly become very **irate**.	学生たちが授業中に眠ると，彼は突然怒り出すのだった。
Washington Automobiles **drastically** reduced the executives' expense allowances.	ワシントン自動車は幹部の交際費を思い切って削減した。
She did her best not to appear **overly** confident in the interview.	彼女は面接で自信過剰に見えないようにベストを尽くした。
The computer I bought last year is already **obsolete**.	昨年購入したコンピューターがもう旧式になっている。
After less than a week, bread is usually too **stale** to eat.	1週間もたたないうちにパンは普通堅くなって食べられなくなる。
A **decrepit** old man clung to the pole as the train lurched forward.	列車が突然前方へ揺れた時，1人のよぼよぼの老人が手すりにしがみついた。
The poet was highly **gratified** by the good reviews he received.	詩人は彼が受けた素晴らしい批評に大いに満足していた。

1247
blissful [blísfəl]

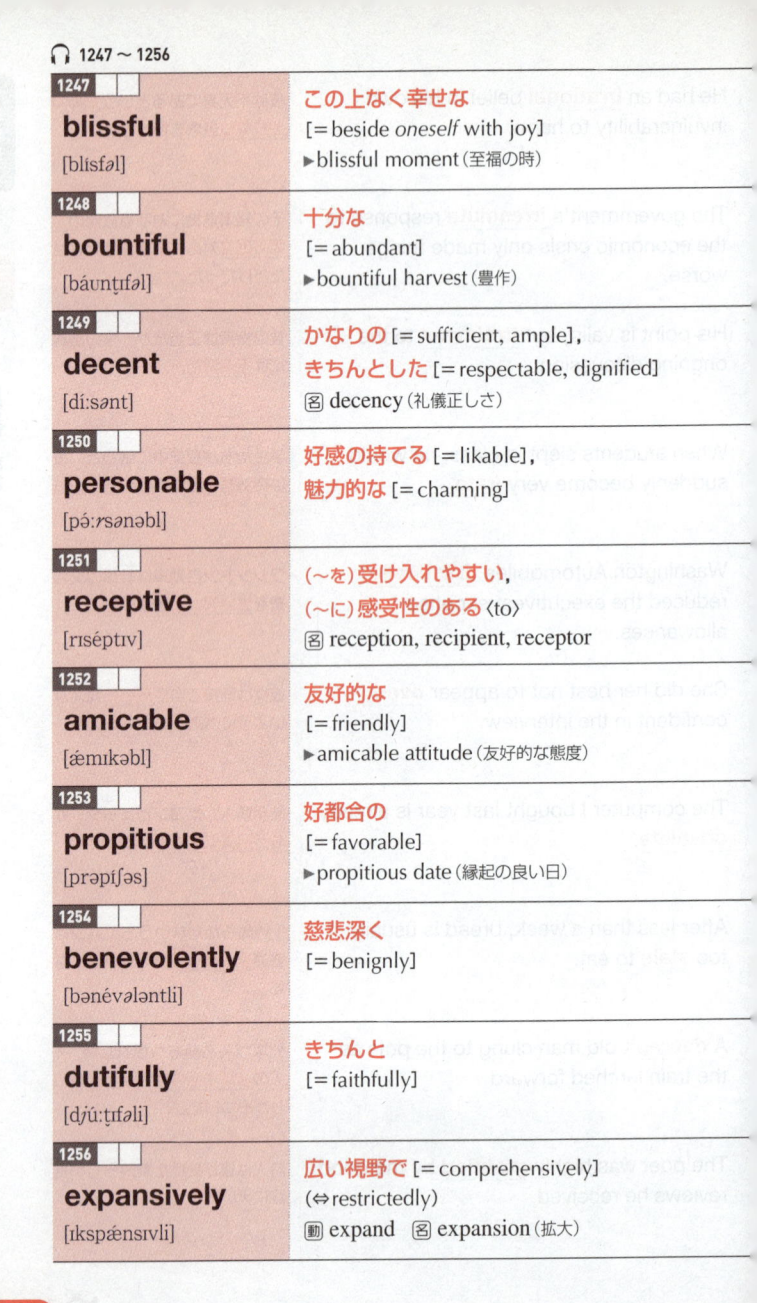

この上なく幸せな
[= beside *oneself* with joy]
▶blissful moment（至福の時）

1248
bountiful [báuntɪfəl]

十分な
[= abundant]
▶bountiful harvest（豊作）

1249
decent [díːsənt]

かなりの [= sufficient, ample],
きちんとした [= respectable, dignified]
图 decency（礼儀正しさ）

1250
personable [pə́ːrsənəbl]

好感の持てる [= likable],
魅力的な [= charming]

1251
receptive [rɪséptɪv]

(～を)受け入れやすい,
(～に)感受性のある ⟨to⟩
图 reception, recipient, receptor

1252
amicable [ǽmɪkəbl]

友好的な
[= friendly]
▶amicable attitude（友好的な態度）

1253
propitious [prəpíʃəs]

好都合の
[= favorable]
▶propitious date（縁起の良い日）

1254
benevolently [bənévələntli]

慈悲深く
[= benignly]

1255
dutifully [djúːtɪfəli]

きちんと
[= faithfully]

1256
expansively [ɪkspǽnsɪvli]

広い視野で [= comprehensively]
(⇔restrictedly)
動 expand 图 expansion（拡大）

Having won the race, the boy sat wearing a **blissful** expression.	レースに勝ったので,その少年はこの上なく幸せな表情をして座っていた。
The hotel provided its guests with a **bountiful** buffet breakfast.	そのホテルは客に十分なビュッフェ式の朝食を提供した。
His tutor told him the essay was a **decent** effort but not outstanding.	個人指導教員は彼の小論文にはかなりの努力の成果が見られるが,優れているわけではないと言った。
His assistant was a **personable** and intelligent young man.	彼のアシスタントは好感の持てる知的な若い男性だった。
The chairperson said that they would always be **receptive** to constructive proposals for improvement.	改善に向けての建設的提案はいつでも受け入れるつもりだと,議長は語った。
The divorced couple found it impossible to have an **amicable** conversation.	離婚した夫婦は友好的な会話をすることができなかった。
The weather was highly **propitious** for their journey across the sea.	彼らが航海するには大いに恵まれた天気だった。
The school was run **benevolently** by a gentle old lady.	その学校は優しい老婦人によって善意で運営されていた。
The boy did his homework **dutifully** but with little real pleasure.	少年はきちんと宿題をしたが,喜んでしたわけではなかった。
The man spoke **expansively** of his future plans for the company.	その男性は,会社に関する彼の将来の計画について広い視野から話した。

1257	**adequate** [ǽdɪkwət]	適切な [= appropriate], **十分な**
1258	**efficacious** [èfɪkéɪʃəs]	効果のある [= effective] ▶efficacious treatment（効果的な治療）
1259	**enormous** [ɪnɔ́ːrməs]	巨大な [= huge] ▶enormous capital（巨額資金）
1260	**invaluable** [ɪnvǽljuəbl]	非常に貴重な [= precious, priceless]（⇔valueless）
1261	**explicit** [ɪksplísɪt]	明白な [= clear, distinct, definite], あからさまな [= outspoken]（⇔implicit）
1262	**tranquil** [trǽŋkwɪl]	のどかな，穏やかな 图 tranquility, tranquilizer（精神安定剤） ▶tranquil life（平穏な生活）
1263	**virtuous** [vɚ́ːrtʃuəs]	高潔な（⇔vicious），**純粋な** [= pristine] 图 virtue（美徳）
1264	**urbane** [əːrbéɪn]	あか抜けた [= polished, refined] ▶urbane taste（あか抜けたセンス）
1265	**cozy** [kóʊzi]	居心地のよい [= comfortable, snug]
1266	**compatible** [kəmpǽtəbl]	相性がよい [= getting along well], 互換性のある（⇔incompatible） ▶compatible type（互換タイプ）

Even though the apartment was small, he found it **adequate** for himself.	アパートは狭かったが、彼にとっては十分な広さだった。
The new drug proved an **efficacious** remedy against the disease.	新薬はその病気に効果のある治療薬であることがわかった。
The millionaire lived in an **enormous** house on the edge of town.	大富豪は町の外れのとても大きな家に住んでいた。
The employee's ability to speak Chinese proved **invaluable** to the company.	中国語を話す従業員の能力は会社にとって非常に貴重であることがわかった。
The only response to my request was an **explicit** "no."	私の要求に対する唯一の反応は、明白な「ノー」であった。
Diana found the **tranquil** atmosphere of the little village soothing.	ダイアナは小さな村ののどかな雰囲気に癒やしを見いだした。
The young man led a **virtuous** life at college.	その若い男は大学で実直な生活を送った。
His **urbane** manners and classy dress contributed to his business success.	彼のあか抜けた態度と上等な服装は彼がビジネスで成功するのに役立った。
What a charming, **cozy** little house!	なんと魅力的で居心地のよいかわいい家だろう！
They divorced after only a year because they just weren't **compatible**.	彼らはただ相性がよくないという理由で、たった1年で離婚した。

1267	**genial** [dʒíːnjəl]	愛想のよい [= affable], (気候が)温暖な [= mild] 图 geniality
1268	**submissive** [səbmísɪv]	従順な [= obedient, docile] 動 submit 图 submission
1269	**amenable** [əmíːnəbl]	(~に)従順な [= obedient], (~に)従う義務がある ⟨to⟩ ▶be amenable to advice(忠告に快く従う)
1270	**feasible** [fíːzəbl]	実行可能な [= practicable, possible] ▶feasible goal(実行可能な目標)
1271	**copious** [kóʊpiəs]	多量の,豊富な [= abundant, plentiful, ample, rich]
1272	**discreet** [dɪskríːt]	思慮分別のある [= sensible, judicious] 图 discretion
1273	**hilarious** [hɪléəriəs]	浮かれ騒ぐ,陽気な [= jolly, mirthful] 图 hilarity
1274	**jubilant** [dʒúːbɪlənt]	大喜びの [= elated, shouting with joy] ▶jubilant look(喜びに満ちた面持ち)
1275	**pliable** [pláɪəbl]	柔軟な [= flexible, adaptable, easily bent]
1276	**assertive** [əsə́ːrtɪv]	積極的な [= strong-willed] (⇔submissive), 独断的な [= confident]

At first the man seemed quite **genial**, but then he became angry and aggressive.	その男は最初のうちはとても愛想がよく見えたが，やがて腹を立てて攻撃的になった。
Confronted by the larger dog, the puppy adopted the **submissive** pose of rolling onto its back.	自分よりも大きな犬に遭遇して，子犬はあお向けに寝転がり服従のポーズを示した。
He seems more **amenable** to compromise after today's meeting.	彼は今日の会議の後，妥協に一段と応じやすくなっているようだ。
Our new economic plan is both innovative and **feasible**.	私たちの新しい経済計画は革新的で実行可能だ。
We came to the party anticipating **copious** amounts of food and beverages.	我々は大量の食べ物や飲み物を期待してパーティーに来た。
I spoke to my friend about my problem because I know he is **discreet**.	私は友人を思慮分別があると知っているので，彼に自分の問題を相談した。
The character of Mr. Bean is a **hilarious** example of slap-stick comedy.	ミスター・ビーンの人物像は，どたばた喜劇の浮かれ騒ぐ一例である。
We all had a **jubilant** celebration at our high school reunion.	高校の同窓会で歓喜に満ちた祝賀会を皆で実施した。
Plastic is a valuable commodity because it is both **pliable** and strong.	プラスチックは柔軟かつ丈夫なので，価値ある物だ。
The girl took a course to learn how to be more **assertive**.	その女の子はもっと積極的になる方法を学ぶコースを取った。

1277	**devout** [dɪváʊt]	敬虔(けいけん)な [= religious, pious], 熱心な [= earnest]
1278	**intimate** [íntəmət]	詳細な, 親密な 名 intimacy ▶ intimate friend(親しい友人)
1279	**optimum** [á(:)ptɪməm]	最高の [= superlative], 最適の [= best, optimal] 名 optimum(最適条件)
1280	**placid** [plǽsɪd]	穏やかな [= calm, undisturbed, tranquil] ▶ in a placid voice(穏やかな声で)
1281	**assiduous** [əsídʒuəs]	勤勉な [= diligent, industrious, persevering] 名 assiduity
1282	**authoritative** [əθɔ́:rətèɪṭɪv]	信頼すべき, 当局の
1283	**full-fledged** [fùlflédʒd]	本格的な, 羽が生えそろった, 一人前の ▶ full-fledged painter(一人前の画家)
1284	**pertinent** [pə́:rtənənt]	適切な [= proper, fitting], 関連する [= relevant]
1285	**transcendent** [trænséndənt]	超越した [= supernatural]
1286	**crucial** [krú:ʃəl]	重大な [= critical], 決定的な [= decisive] ▶ crucial aspect(重要な側面)

My mother is a liberal but completely **devout** Roman Catholic.	母はリベラルだが，完全なまでに敬虔なローマ・カトリック教徒である。
She was furious that **intimate** details of her private life had been made public.	自分の私生活に関する詳しい細部が公にされて，彼女は激怒した。
The new car has an **optimum** speed of 140 miles per hour.	その新しい車は最高時速140マイルである。
The sea today is **placid** and the weather sunny and bright.	今日の海は穏やかで，天気は晴れて明るい。
She is the most **assiduous** and dedicated student in the class.	彼女はクラスで最も勤勉でひたむきな学生だ。
The book was an **authoritative** treatment of contemporary legal theory.	その本は，現代の法理論の権威ある論法の本だった。
The general decided to launch a **full-fledged** attack on the town.	将軍は市街地に本格的な攻撃を仕掛けることを決定した。
As the judge didn't think that the evidence was **pertinent**, he suppressed it.	判事はその証拠が適切でないと思ったので，それを認めなかった。
She felt as if she were being guided by a **transcendent** being.	彼女はあたかも超越した存在に導かれているような気がした。
The President is now facing the most **crucial** decision of his career.	大統領は，今，就任以来最も重大な決断に直面している。

1287 distinct
[dɪstíŋkt]

はっきりとわかる
[= unique]
動 distinguish

1288 legitimate
[lɪdʒítəmət]

道理にかなった [= reasonable],
合法の [= lawful]
名 legitimacy

1289 versatile
[vɚ́ːrsəṭəl]

多才な,用途の広い [= all-purpose]
名 versatility

1290 eligible
[élɪdʒəbl]

(〜に対して)資格がある
[= qualified] (⇔ ineligible) 〈for〉
名 eligibility

1291 ingenious
[ɪndʒíːniəs]

巧妙な [= inventive, resourceful],
器用な [= clever, skillfully made]
名 ingenuity

1292 judicious
[dʒudíʃəs]

思慮分別のある
[= reasonable, wise and careful]
cf. judicial (司法の, 裁判の)

1293 consummate
[kάːnsəmət]

完成された [= complete, perfect]
名 consummation
語源 con (共に) + sum (合わせる) + ate

1294 hostile
[hάː(ː)stəl]

敵意のある [= unfriendly, antagonistic],
敵の
名 hostility

1295 possessed
[pəzést]

取りつかれている
[= obsessed]

1296 vicious
[víʃəs]

残酷な [= brutal],
悪意のある [= malicious],
堕落した [= profligate, depraved]

He has a **distinct** Scottish accent that many found attractive.	彼には多くの人を引きつけるはっきりとわかるスコットランドのアクセントがあった。
Although not well articulated, the students' demands were **legitimate**.	十分に明確化されてはいなかったが,学生たちの要求は道理にかなっていた。
The footballer was a **versatile** player, equally good at attack and defense.	そのフットボール選手は多才なプレーヤーで,オフェンスにもディフェンスにも強かった。
The student was disappointed to discover that he was not **eligible** for a scholarship.	その学生は,自分に奨学金の資格があるわけではないと知って,がっかりした。
His inventions are **ingenious** solutions to practical problems.	彼の発明品は現実的な問題に対する巧妙な解決法である。
We considered the issue carefully to be sure of a **judicious** decision.	我々は,思慮分別のある決定だと確信できるように,その問題を注意深く考えた。
He has always been good, but now he has become a **consummate** violinist.	彼は今までも優れていたが,今では完璧(かんぺき)なバイオリニストになった。
The 1990s saw a larger number of **hostile** business takeovers.	1990年代は多くの敵対的な企業買収が見られた。
He studied like a **possessed** man for his examinations.	彼はまるで取りつかれているかのように試験勉強をした。
Police on the scene were appalled at the **vicious** nature of the crime.	現場の警察官たちは,その犯罪の残忍な内容にぞっとした。

consummate (1293) は動詞としてもよく使われます。consummate *one's* hope は「希望を実現する」を意味します。

#	単語	意味
1297	**frivolous** [frívələs]	軽薄な, ふまじめな [= flippant], くだらない [= trifling]
1298	**petulant** [pétʃələnt]	怒りっぽい [= peevish] 图 petulance
1299	**capricious** [kəpríʃəs]	気まぐれな [= changeable, whimsical] 图 caprice
1300	**deceptive** [dɪséptɪv]	欺瞞である [= delusive]
1301	**unruly** [ʌnrúːli]	手に負えない [= disorderly]
1302	**malevolent** [məlévələnt]	悪意のある [= spiteful, evil-minded, ill-disposed] 图 malevolence
1303	**crabby** [krǽbi]	気難しい [= crabbed, difficult] 图 crabbiness
1304	**haughty** [hɔ́ːti]	傲慢な [= arrogant, supercilious] ▶take a haughty attitude (傲慢な態度をとる)
1305	**obnoxious** [ɑ(ː)bnɑ́(ː)kʃəs]	鼻持ちならない, とてもいやな [= odious, snobbish, highly objectionable]
1306	**poignant** [pɔ́ɪnjənt]	心を打つ [= intense, moving], 痛切な [= keen, painful to the heart]

The lecturer said that he would not answer such a **frivolous** question.	そんな軽薄な質問には答えるつもりはないと，講師は言った。
His colleagues were surprised by his **petulant** display of bad temper.	彼の同僚たちは，彼の露呈された短気な性格に驚いた。
The young girl's **capricious** nature has baffled all her boyfriends.	その若い女の子の気まぐれな性格に，ボーイフレンドたちは皆当惑した。
The friendly behavior of the villagers turned out to be **deceptive**.	村人たちの友好的な振る舞いは欺瞞であることがわかった。
As the mob became more **unruly**, the police sent for help.	暴徒が手に負えなくなったので，警察は助けを呼び寄せた。
In Shakespeare's "Othello", Iago represents a totally **malevolent** force.	シェークスピアの『オセロ』では，イアーゴが完全なる悪意の力を表している。
The **crabby** old man was thoroughly disliked by his neighbors.	その気難しい老人は隣人たちにすっかり嫌われていた。
The society ladies were **haughty** and condescending toward the poor.	上流社会の女性たちは貧しい人々に対し横柄で，見下した態度をとっていた。
His **obnoxious** remarks made him unpopular with his colleagues.	彼は鼻持ちならないことを言うので，同僚の間で評判が悪かった。
"Romeo and Juliet" may be the world's most famous and **poignant** love story.	『ロミオとジュリエット』は世界中で最も有名で心を打つラブストーリーと言えよう。

1307
inert
[ɪnə́ːrt]

不活発な
[= inactive, sluggish, lifeless]
图 inertia (不活発, 慣性)

1308
vulgar
[vʌ́lgər]

下品な, 卑俗な
[= coarse, disgusting, filthy, indecent, nasty]
图 vulgarity

1309
trivial
[tríviəl]

取るに足らない
[= trifling, unimportant, insignificant]
▶trivial matter (ささいな問題)

1310
redundant
[rɪdʌ́ndənt]

冗長な [= verbose],
余分な [= excessive, superfluous]

1311
disorientated
[dɪsɔ́ːrientèɪtɪd]

頭が混乱した, 方向がわからなくなった
cf. orientation (方向づけ)

1312
arcane
[ɑːrkéɪn]

秘密の [= covert], 難解な
图 arcaneness

1313
fallible
[fǽləbl]

誤りやすい,
当てにならない [= fallacious] (⇔infallible)
图 fallacy (誤った考え)

1314
formidable
[fɔ́ːrmɪdəbl]

(敵などが) 手ごわい, (仕事などが) 大変な
[= daunting, frightening, intimidating]

1315
confrontational
[kɑ̀(ː)nfrʌntéɪʃənəl]

対決する覚悟の
[= defiant]
語源 con (共に) + front (前面) + ational

1316
corrosive
[kəróʊsɪv]

痛烈な [= biting],
腐食性の [= erosive]
图 corrosiveness

Drugs have rendered the virus **inert** but have failed to kill it completely.	薬品はそのウイルスを不活性にしたが，根絶はしていない。
Some of the audience felt embarrassed by the **vulgar** jokes he told.	聴衆の中には，彼が話した下品な冗談に当惑する者もいた。
The uproar over such a **trivial** problem is hard to understand.	そうした取るに足らない問題で騒ぐのは理解に苦しむ。
His ideas are good but his **redundant** writing style can be rather tedious.	彼のアイデアはいいが，冗長な文体はちょっとうんざりすることもある。
The released hostages looked tired and **disorientated** but happy to be free.	解放された人質たちは疲れていて混乱してはいるものの，自由になって喜んでいたようだった。
The sect's most **arcane** teachings were never written down.	その宗派の秘密の教義のほとんどは文書化されていなかった。
It was easy to forgive his error since everyone is **fallible**.	人は誰でも誤りを犯すものだから，彼の誤りを許すことはたやすかった。
The golfer was nervous because he knew that his opponent was a **formidable** player.	そのゴルファーは，対戦相手が手ごわいプレーヤーだと知っているので，神経質になっていた。
The politician's **confrontational** attitude in the debate lost him many supporters.	その政治家は討論会で挑戦的な態度をとったので，多くの支持者を失った。
The series of scandals had a **corrosive** effect on the government's support.	度重なるスキャンダルは，政府支援に痛烈な影響を及ぼした。

#	英語	日本語
1317	**lousy** [láuzi]	ひどく悪い [= awful, terrible] ▶lousy singer (下手な歌手)
1318	**menacingly** [ménəsɪŋli]	威嚇(いかく)するように [= intimidatingly] 動 menace
1319	**recklessly** [rékləsli]	向う見ずに [= daringly]
1320	**ruthless** [rúːθləs]	冷酷な [= cruel, merciless, unrelenting, relentless] ▶ruthless criminal (残酷な犯罪者)
1321	**rash** [ræʃ]	軽率な [= incautious, indiscreet], 無謀な [= foolhardy]
1322	**naive** [naíːv]	(軽蔑的に)単純な ▶naive person (世間知らずの人)
1323	**strenuous** [strénjuəs]	きつい,激しい,精力的な [= vigorous, energetic, zealous]
1324	**trite** [traɪt]	陳腐な [= hackneyed, stale, threadbare] 名 triteness
1325	**tedious** [tíːdiəs]	退屈な,つまらない [= boring, tiresome, wearisome]
1326	**stern** [stəːrn]	厳しい [= strict, severe, harsh]

The teenager said the food tasted **lousy** and he wouldn't eat it.	その10代の若者は食べ物がひどくまずいので,食べたくないと言った。
The dog growled **menacingly** as the man approached the front door.	男性が玄関に近づいた時,その犬は威嚇するようにうなった。
He drove so **recklessly** that the police stopped him for questioning.	彼があまりに向う見ずな運転をしたので,警察は尋問をするために彼を止めた。
The **ruthless** cuts in welfare expenditure made the prime minister unpopular.	福祉支出の非情な削減によってその首相の人気はなくなった。
In times of crisis, one must be swift but never be **rash**.	危機にあっては,人は敏速であらねばならないが,軽率であってはならない。
His views of the world are rather **naive**, probably due to his inexperience.	経験が浅いためだろうが,彼の世界観はかなり単純だ。
Rowing is said to be one of the most **strenuous** sporting activities.	ボートを漕ぐことは最も激しいスポーツの1つだと言われる。
The original novel was excellent, but the screenplay was a **trite** imitation.	その小説の原作は素晴らしかったのに,映画のシナリオは陳腐な模倣であった。
Although the work was **tedious**, the pay was very good.	その仕事は退屈なものだったが,給料はとても良かった。
We started to insist on our point when the boss gave us a **stern** look.	我々が自分の考えを主張し始めると上司が厳しい顔つきをした。

1327 **devoid** [dɪvɔ́ɪd]	(〜を)欠いている [= destitute, empty] 〈of〉
1328 **dreary** [dríəri]	陰うつな，わびしい，もの寂しい，退屈な ▶dreary work（退屈な仕事）
1329 **hectic** [héktɪk]	てんてこまいの，ひどく興奮した ▶hectic day（てんてこまいの1日）
1330 **dismal** [dízməl]	憂うつな [= gloomy, melancholic]，（成績などが）悲惨な ▶dismal performance（悲惨な演技）
1331 **frail** [freɪl]	弱々しい，壊れやすい 图 frailty ▶frail constitution（虚弱体質）
1332 **illicit** [ɪlísɪt]	不義の，不正な [= improper]，違法の [= unlawful, illegal]
1333 **bizarre** [bɪzɑ́ːr]	異様な，奇怪な [= odd, grotesque, eccentric] 图 bizarreness
1334 **coarse** [kɔːrs]	（きめ・粒などが）粗い [= rough, harsh, not fine]，下品な [= vulgar, indelicate, crude]
1335 **lax** [læks]	しまりのない，だらしない [= loose, flabby, slack]
1336 **pathetic** [pəθétɪk]	哀れな [= pitiable, wretched]，不十分な [= insufficient]

The novel was well written but **devoid** of any excitement.	その小説はよく書けてはいたが、刺激を全く欠いていた。
She was so happy that even the **dreary** weather could not depress her.	彼女はあまりにうれしかったので、どんよりとした天気でも憂うつにはならなかった。
Tokyo Station at rush hour is a **hectic** bustle of activity.	ラッシュアワー時の東京駅は、あわただしい雑踏そのものだ。
Despite the **dismal** rainy weather, they enjoyed their visit to London.	憂うつな雨天にもかかわらず、彼らはロンドンへの旅行を楽しんだ。
The old man was too **frail** to walk unaided.	その老人は手助けなしでは歩けないほどに衰弱していた。
Although highly competent, his company fired him for an **illicit** affair.	彼は極めて有能だったが、会社は不倫を理由に彼を解雇した。
He told me the most **bizarre** story I had ever heard.	彼は私に、これまでに聞いたうちで最も異様な話をした。
The shirt looked beautiful but its **coarse** fabric made it uncomfortable.	そのシャツは美しく見えたが、生地が粗いので着心地が悪かった。
The government inspectors criticized the **lax** discipline in the school.	政府の視察官たちは、その学校の緩い規律を批判した。
The abandoned cat looked so **pathetic** that he decided to rescue it and take it home.	その捨てネコがあまりにも哀れに見えたので、彼はそのネコを助けて家に連れ帰ることにした。

devoid (1327) の void は (空にする) ことを意味します。形容詞 void は「空の」、voidable は「無効にできる」を意味します。

#	単語	意味
1337	**lethal** [líːθəl]	致命的な [= mortal, deadly] ▶lethal injury (致命傷)
1338	**disheveled** [dɪʃévəld]	身なりのだらしない, (髪・服が) 乱れた [= untidy, tousled]
1339	**bedraggled** [bɪdrǽgld]	みすぼらしい
1340	**ambiguous** [æmbígjuəs]	曖昧(あいまい)な [= equivocal] (⇔explicit) ▶ambiguous shape (ぼんやりした輪郭)
1341	**equivocal** [ɪkwívəkəl]	曖昧な [= vague, ambiguous], 不確かな [= uncertain] ▶equivocal answer (曖昧な回答)
1342	**obscure** [əbskjúər]	曖昧な [= unclear], 無名の ▶obscure writer (無名の作家)
1343	**initially** [ɪníʃəli]	最初は [= firstly]
1344	**consequently** [kɑ́(ː)nsəkwèntli]	その結果として [= as a result]
1345	**ultimately** [ʌ́ltɪmətli]	最終的には [= eventually]
1346	**namely** [néɪmli]	具体的には [= specifically]

A person trained in martial arts can deliver <u>lethal</u> blows by hand.	格闘技訓練をした人は，素手で<u>致命的な</u>打撃を与えることができる。
After two weeks in the wilderness, we all looked rough and <u>disheveled</u>.	2週間荒野で生活したため，私たちはみんな，粗野で<u>だらしなく</u>見えた。
After the storm, the cat returned in a <u>bedraggled</u> state.	嵐が去った後，ネコは<u>みすぼらしい</u>状態で戻ってきた。
He made an <u>ambiguous</u> statement that could have signified an agreement.	彼は同意したと思わせるような<u>曖昧な</u>発言をした。
Her response to his marriage proposal was oddly <u>equivocal</u>.	彼の求婚に対する彼女の反応は，奇妙なほど<u>曖昧だっ</u>た。
His remarks were so <u>obscure</u> that few people understood them.	彼の意見はとても<u>曖昧だっ</u>たので，ほとんどの人は理解しなかった。
<u>Initially</u>, he enjoyed the class, but then it began to bore him.	<u>最初</u>，彼は授業を楽しんだが，次第に退屈し始めた。
Funds were low and, <u>consequently</u>, the annual picnic had to be cancelled.	資金が乏しかったので，<u>その結果として</u>，毎年恒例のピクニックは中止にしなければならなかった。
The woman said that she wanted <u>ultimately</u> to work as a lawyer.	女性は<u>最終的には</u>弁護士として働きたいと言った。
One problem faced the college, <u>namely</u>, a lack of students.	ある問題に大学は直面した，<u>具体的には</u>生徒不足だった。

1347	**nominally** [ná(:)mənəli]	名目上は [= in name only] (⇔really)
1348	**barren** [bǽrən]	味気ない [= dull, insipid], 不毛の [= sterile, unproductive] ▶barren soil (不毛の地)
1349	**sterile** [stérəl]	殺菌した [= germ-free], 不毛の [= barren] (⇔fertile), 無益な [= fruitless]
1350	**cardinal** [ká:rdɪnəl]	基本的な [= fundamental] ▶cardinal principles (基本的原理)
1351	**rudimentary** [rù:dɪméntəri]	基礎的な [= basic, elementary, fundamental], 原始的な ▶rudimentary knowledge (初歩知識)
1352	**static** [stǽṭɪk]	静的な [= stationary, inactive] (⇔dynamic)
1353	**stationary** [stéɪʃənèri]	静止した, 定住の ▶stationary population (変動しない人口)
1354	**countless** [káʊntləs]	無数の [= numerous] 副 countlessly
1355	**miscellaneous** [mìsəléɪniəs]	種々雑多の [= diversified, varied, mixed] 名 miscellany ▶miscellaneous expense (雑費)
1356	**dense** [dens]	密集した [= closely-packed], (霧・雲などが)濃い ▶dense fog (濃霧)

Although he was **nominally** in charge, the real decisions were made by others.	彼は<u>名目上は</u>責任者だったが，本当の決定はほかの人たちによってなされた。
The deserts of Arabia are vast, **barren** landscapes.	アラビアの砂漠は広大で<u>味気ない</u>眺めである。
It is extremely important to use **sterile** bandages when treating a wound.	けがを治療する時は<u>殺菌した</u>包帯を使うことが非常に重要である。
It was a **cardinal** rule of his to be always punctual.	いつも時間厳守することは，彼の<u>基礎的な</u>ルールだった。
My seven-year-old son is just learning the **rudimentary** principles of math.	私の7歳の息子は，ちょうど数学の<u>基本的な</u>公理を学んでいる。
I got a small shock from **static** electricity when I touched the door knob.	ドアの取っ手に触れた時，ちょっとした<u>静</u>電気のショックを感じた。
Please wait until the train is **stationary** before getting off.	電車が<u>停止して</u>から下車してください。
As he looked up at the **countless** stars, he felt very small indeed.	彼は<u>無数の</u>星を見上げた時，自分自身を本当に小さく感じた。
Anything we could not clearly classify belonged to a **miscellaneous** group.	明確に分類できないものはすべて<u>その他いろいろの</u>グループに属した。
It was difficult to get through the **dense** undergrowth.	低木の<u>密集した</u>場所を通り抜けるのは困難だった。

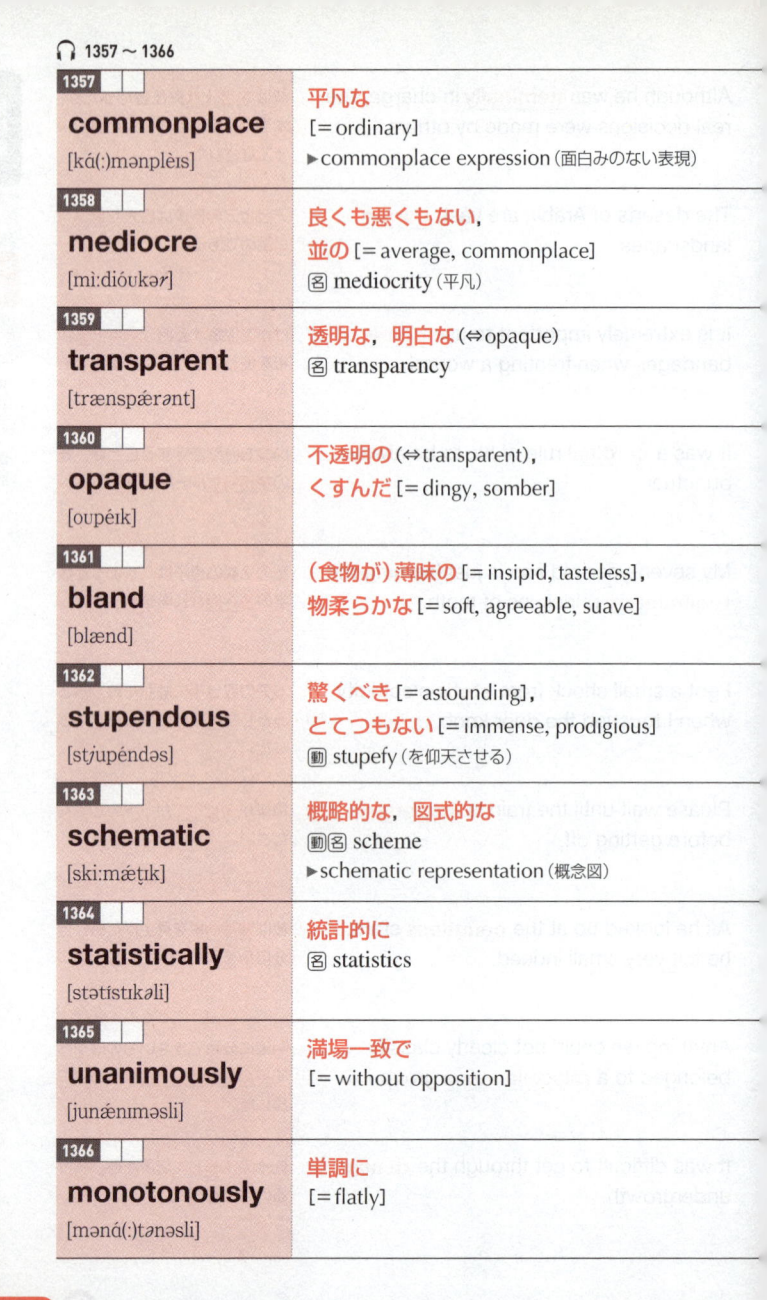

1357	**commonplace** [ká(:)mənplèɪs]	平凡な [= ordinary] ▶commonplace expression (面白みのない表現)
1358	**mediocre** [mì:dióukər]	良くも悪くもない, 並の [= average, commonplace] 图 mediocrity (平凡)
1359	**transparent** [trænspǽrənt]	透明な, 明白な (⇔opaque) 图 transparency
1360	**opaque** [oupéɪk]	不透明の (⇔transparent), くすんだ [= dingy, somber]
1361	**bland** [blænd]	(食物が)薄味の [= insipid, tasteless], 物柔らかな [= soft, agreeable, suave]
1362	**stupendous** [stjupéndəs]	驚くべき [= astounding], とてつもない [= immense, prodigious] 動 stupefy (を仰天させる)
1363	**schematic** [ski:mǽṭɪk]	概略的な, 図式的な 動图 scheme ▶schematic representation (概念図)
1364	**statistically** [stətístɪkəli]	統計的に 图 statistics
1365	**unanimously** [junǽnɪməsli]	満場一致で [= without opposition]
1366	**monotonously** [məná(:)tənəsli]	単調に [= flatly]

Although a brilliant researcher, he was a **commonplace** lecturer.	彼は優れた研究者だが、平凡な講演者だった。
His latest movie is **mediocre** at best.	彼の最新の映画はせいぜい可もなく不可もなくである。
We decided to protect our table top with a **transparent** plastic sheet.	私たちは透明なプラスチック・シートでテーブルの表面を保護することにした。
I knew the stone was not really an emerald because it was **opaque**.	その石は不透明だったので、私はそれが実はエメラルドでないことを知っていた。
She always prepares nutritious but **bland** meals for the family.	彼女は家族のために、いつも、栄養豊かだが薄味の食事を作る。
The pyramids have long been a **stupendous** sight for tourists.	ピラミッドは久しく観光客たちにとって驚くべき光景となっている。
His view of history was criticized as **schematic** and oversimplified.	彼の歴史観は、概略的で簡略化し過ぎていると批判された。
The social scientist demonstrated **statistically** the existence of discrimination.	その社会科学者は差別の存在を統計的に実証した。
The committee voted **unanimously** to fund the project.	委員会はプロジェクトに資金を提供することを満場一致で決定した。
The preacher spoke **monotonously**, with little expression in his voice.	牧師は声の調子をほとんど変えずに単調に話した。

unanimously (1365) の uni も monotonously (1366) の mono も 1 を意味します。unilateral は「一方通行の」, monopoly は「独占」を意味します。

1367 impulsive
[ɪmpʌ́lsɪv]

直情的な，衝動的な
- 名 impulse
- ▶impulsive remarks（衝動的な発言）

1368 reticent
[réṭəsənt]

無口な [= taciturn, reserved]
- 名 reticence

1369 habitual
[həbítʃuəl]

習慣化した，常習の [= customary]
- 名 habit 副 habitually
- ▶habitual bedtime（いつもの就寝時間）

1370 flabbergasted
[flǽbərgæstɪd]

（～に，～して）仰天した
[= astounding, very surprised] 〈at, to do〉

1371 destined
[déstɪnd]

運命である
[= fated]
- 名 destiny

1372 disciplinary
[dísəplənèri]

懲戒の，規則上の
- 名 discipline
- ▶disciplinary committee（懲罰委員会）

1373 divine
[dɪváɪn]

神の
- ▶divine blessing（神の祝福）

1374 jumbled
[dʒʌ́mbld]

ごちゃまぜになった
[= mixed-up]

1375 lanky
[lǽŋki]

背が高くて細い

1376 migratory
[máɪgrətɔ̀:ri]

移動する，移住する [= traveling]
- 動 migrate
- ▶migratory birds（渡り鳥）

She was a very **impulsive** person and often did things she regretted later.	彼女はとても<u>直情的な</u>人間で、後で悔やむようなことをよくやった。
Though usually **reticent**, he is sometimes quite talkative.	彼は普段は<u>無口</u>だが、時々とてもおしゃべりになる。
His health was eventually damaged by his **habitual** drinking.	彼の健康は、結局、<u>習慣化した</u>飲酒によって害された。
The man was **flabbergasted** when his wife left him.	男は妻が彼のもとを去った時<u>仰天した</u>。
The rocket launch seemed **destined** to fail from the start.	ロケットの打ち上げの失敗は最初から失敗するのが<u>運命だった</u>ように思われた。
The army decided to begin **disciplinary** proceedings against him.	軍は彼に対して<u>懲戒</u>手続きを始めることを決定した。
The man claimed to have received a **divine** revelation in a dream.	その男性は夢の中で<u>神の</u>啓示を受けたと言い張った。
The girl's clothes lay **jumbled** together in a heap on the floor.	女の子の服は床の上に<u>ごちゃまぜになって</u>積み重ねられていた。
Despite having been a small child, he was now a **lanky** teenager.	背の低い子どもだったのに、彼は今では<u>細くて背の高い</u>10代の若者になった。
The nomads had a **migratory** lifestyle, moving according to the season.	遊牧の民は季節に応じて<u>移動する</u>生活形式をとっていた。

#	語	意味
1377	**opposable** [əpóuzəbl]	向かい合わせにできる，抵抗できる 图 opposability
1378	**polytheistic** [pá(:)liθi:ɪstɪk]	多神教の 图 polytheism
1379	**succulent** [sʌ́kjulənt]	多汁質の [= juicy]
1380	**synonymous** [sɪná(:)nəməs]	同義語の (⇔ antonym)
1381	**adjacent** [ədʒéɪsnt]	隣接する [= neighboring] 图 adjacency ▶adjacent countries (近隣諸国)
1382	**paltry** [pɔ́:ltri]	ごくわずかな [= meager]，価値のない，卑劣な
1383	**bucolic** [bjukɑ́(:)lɪk]	牧歌的な [= pastoral]，田舎の [= rural, rustic]
1384	**celibate** [séləbət]	独身(主義)者の，独身を誓った ▶celibacy (独身生活)
1385	**pedestrian** [pədéstriən]	徒歩の [= going on foot]，単調な [= boring] 图 pedestrian (歩行者) ▶pedestrian mall (歩行者専用区域)
1386	**lunar** [lú:nər]	月の [= of the moon]，青白い [= pale, pallid] ▶lunar orbit (月の軌道)

One feature of primates is that they have **opposable** thumbs.	霊長類の特徴の1つは，ほかの4本の指と<u>対置できる</u>ようになった親指を持っていることだ。
The missionary tried to convert them from their **polytheistic** beliefs.	宣教師は彼らを<u>多神教の</u>信仰から改宗させようとした。
He plucked a **succulent** peach and began to eat it.	彼は<u>水気の多い</u>桃をもぎ取り，食べ始めた。
The famous old school was **synonymous** with high academic achievement.	その有名な伝統校は高い学業成績と<u>同義のよう</u>である。
The company bought an **adjacent** piece of land and turned it into the employee parking lot.	会社は<u>隣接する</u>土地を購入して，従業員用駐車場にした。
He felt insulted by the **paltry** sum he was paid for the translation.	彼は翻訳の代金として支払われた<u>はした</u>金に侮辱された気がした。
My mother enjoys buying paintings of **bucolic** scenes.	母は<u>牧歌的な</u>風景画を購入することを楽しんでいる。
Priests and nuns often vow to remain **celibate** throughout their lives.	僧や尼僧たちは，しばしば，一生<u>独身で</u>いることを誓う。
The residents petitioned their city government for a **pedestrian** walkway.	住民は市当局に<u>歩行者用</u>通路の設置を請願した。
In the early 1960s, John F. Kennedy inspired the first **lunar** landing.	1960年代の初めにジョン・F・ケネディは<u>月への</u>最初の着陸を鼓舞した。

synonymous (1380) のsyn は (似た) を意味します。
synergyは「相乗効果」，synchronizeは「同時に起きる」を意味します。

1387
simultaneous
[sàɪməltéɪniəs]

同時の [= concurrent]
图 simultaneity（同時性）
▶ simultaneous translation（同時通訳）

1388
lavish
[lǽvɪʃ]

ぜいたくな
[= extravagant]
▶ lavish praise（べたぼめ）

1389
quaint
[kweɪnt]

古風な，趣のある [= antique, archaic]，
風変わりで面白い [= oddly picturesque]

1390
conventional
[kənvénʃənəl]

従来の [= established]，
因習的な (⇔ unorthodox)
▶ conventional wisdom（一般通念）

1391
bewitched
[bɪwítʃt]

魅惑された
[= enchanted]
動 bewitch（に魔法をかける）

1392
comprehensive
[kà(:)mprɪhénsɪv]

総合的な [= all-inclusive]
▶ comprehensive insurance（総合保険）

1393
tremendous
[trəméndəs]

すさまじい
[= enormous]

1394
exponential
[èkspənénʃəl]

急激な，幾何級数的な
图 exponent（指数）

1395
idyllic
[aɪdílɪk]

牧歌的な，田園的な
[= pastoral, Arcadian]
▶ idyllic life（牧歌的な生活）

1396
pompous
[pá(:)mpəs]

尊大な
[= self-important, inflated]

She studied at a school for **simultaneous** translation.	彼女は<u>同時</u>通訳の学校で学んだ。
The foreign dignitaries were treated to a **lavish** banquet consisting of ten different courses.	各国高官は，10 種類のコース料理からなる<u>ぜいたくな</u>晩餐会でもてなされた。
England is known for the **quaint** cottages in its lush green countryside.	イングランドは緑豊かな田園地帯にある<u>古風な</u>小家屋で有名である。
All **conventional** approaches to the problem had failed to work.	その問題を解決するための<u>従来の</u>取り組みはすべて失敗に終わった。
The students sat completely still as if **bewitched** by the lecturer.	生徒たちは講演者に<u>魅惑されたか</u>のごとく，じっと座っていた。
The course included a **comprehensive** study on whales.	そのコースには，クジラについての<u>総合的な</u>研究が含まれていた。
There was the **tremendous** sound of an explosion nearby.	近隣で<u>すさまじい</u>爆発音がした。
Following five years of **exponential** growth, the country had huge reserves of foreign currency.	5年間の<u>急激な</u>成長の後，その国は膨大な外貨を蓄えた。
My siblings and I share an **idyllic** memory of our childhood on the farm.	私と私の兄弟姉妹は農場で過ごした子ども時代の<u>牧歌的な</u>思い出を共有している。
The late Shah of Iran angered his people with his **pompous**, lavish parties.	故イラン国王は<u>尊大ぶった</u>ぜいたくなパーティーを開き，国民を怒らせた。

1397 resonant
[rézənənt]

よく響く
[= resounding]
動 resonate 名 resonance

1398 rustic
[rʌ́stɪk]

田舎の [= rural],
素朴な [= plain, artless, unsophisticated]

1399 sparse
[spɑːrs]

まばらな
[= thin, thinly scattered or spread]
▶ sparse population (少ない人口)

1400 edible
[édəbl]

食用に適した [= eatable] (⇔ inedible)
cf. potable (飲料に適した)
▶ edible fish (食用の魚)

That baritone became a sensation for his versatile and **resonant** voice.	そのバリトン歌手は多彩で**よく響く**声で大評判になった。
I grew up in a **rustic** farm area of southern Indiana, in America.	私はアメリカ，インディアナ州南部の**田舎の**農業地帯で育った。
In semi-arid conditions, rainfall is too **sparse** for most crops.	半乾燥性の自然条件の中では，ほとんどの作物にとって降雨が**少なすぎる**。
He was poisoned by what he thought was an **edible** mushroom.	彼は**食用**だと思っていたキノコを食べて毒にあたった。

1分間 mini test

1 1分間

(1) His family still owns the land that the king (　　　) on them in the 17th century.

(2) Many farmers (　　　) crops to hedge against unpredictable weather and climate.

(3) He studied like a (　　　) man for his examinations.

(4) The military offered an attractive bonus as an (　　　) for reenlisting.

(5) She felt as if she were being guided by a (　　　) being.

(6) The deserts of Arabia are vast, (　　　) landscapes.

(7) The architect had to (　　　) the foundations of his latest building.

(8) The expert was asked to write a report (　　　) his reservations about the project.

(9) Some men find marriage too big a (　　　) to make.

(10) Scientists are finding better ways to (　　　) the limitless energy of the sun.

ここから選んでね。 ※選択肢はすべて原形で表示しています。

① diversify   ② transcendent   ③ harness
④ barren   ⑤ bestow   ⑥ reinforce
⑦ inducement   ⑧ commitment   ⑨ possessed
⑩ amplify

2 1分間

(11) The family presented her with the picture as a (　　) of her visit.

(12) The film I just saw (　　) memories of my childhood in the Midwest.

(13) The accident at the chemical plant caused massive environmental (　　).

(14) The crowd showed great (　　), waiting patiently for hours to get their tickets.

(15) The magistrate had the power to join people in (　　).

(16) That baritone became a sensation for his versatile and (　　) voice.

(17) The novelist is praised for her sensitive (　　) of character.

(18) His son (　　) but agreed to do what he was asked.

(19) The government inspectors criticized the (　　) discipline in the school.

(20) Please wait until the train is (　　) before getting off.

ここから選んでね。

① stationary　② grumble　③ delineation
④ matrimony　⑤ keepsake　⑥ resonant
⑦ lax　⑧ evoke　⑨ contamination
⑳ restraint

1分間 mini test 答え

1 P. 314

(1)	⑤	0716 bestow(bestowed)	(⇒p. 174)
(2)	①	0919 diversify	(⇒p. 214)
(3)	⑨	1295 possessed	(⇒p. 290)
(4)	⑦	1174 inducement	(⇒p. 266)
(5)	②	1285 transcendent	(⇒p. 288)
(6)	④	1348 barren	(⇒p. 302)
(7)	⑥	0735 reinforce	(⇒p. 178)
(8)	⑩	0887 amplify(amplifying)	(⇒p. 208)
(9)	⑧	1054 commitment	(⇒p. 242)
(10)	③	0896 harness	(⇒p. 210)

2 P. 315

(11)	⑮	1022 keepsake	(⇒p. 236)
(12)	⑱	0902 evoke(evoked)	(⇒p. 212)
(13)	⑲	1175 contamination	(⇒p. 266)
(14)	⑳	0921 restraint	(⇒p. 216)
(15)	⑭	1014 matrimony	(⇒p. 234)
(16)	⑯	1397 resonant	(⇒p. 312)
(17)	⑬	1169 delineation	(⇒p. 266)
(18)	⑫	0906 grumble(grumbled)	(⇒p. 212)
(19)	⑰	1335 lax	(⇒p. 298)
(20)	⑪	1353 stationary	(⇒p. 302)

でる度
A
B
C

単語編

力を伸ばす単語 700

動詞 (219語) ······ 318
名詞 (242語) ······ 362
形容詞・副詞 (239語) ······ 412
1分間 mini test ······ 460

でる度Cは，1級合格には必要となる単語です。ここに掲載されている700語を覚え，合格にさらに近づく語彙力をつけましょう。

	1周目	2周目
動	/	/
名	/	/
形・副	/	/

でる度 C 力を伸ばす単語

動詞

219語

🎧 1401 〜 1409

1401	**decipher** [dɪsáɪfər]	**(暗号など)を解読する** [= decode] (⇔encipher)
1402	**defy** [dɪfáɪ]	**に反抗する** [= disobey] 名 defiance 形 defiant
1403	**tackle** [tǽkl]	**に取り組む** [= handle, deal with] ▶tackle new challenges (新しい課題に取り組む)
1404	**antagonize** [æntǽgənàɪz]	**の反感を買う** [= arouse hostility]
1405	**precipitate** [prɪsípɪtèɪt]	**を引き起こす** 名 precipitation
1406	**capitulate** [kəpítʃəlèɪt]	**(〜に)(条件付きで)降伏する** [= yield, surrender] ⟨to⟩ 名 capitulation
1407	**vanquish** [vǽŋkwɪʃ]	**を打ち破る** [= conquer, defeat] ▶vanquish one's fears (不安に打ち勝つ)
1408	**brandish** [brǽndɪʃ]	**を振りかざす** [= swing, wave]
1409	**canvass** [kǽnvəs]	**(支持など)を求める** ▶canvass for votes (投票を頼んで回る)

During the war, his job was to **decipher** enemy codes.	戦時中の彼の仕事は敵の暗号を解読することだった。
She felt she could not **defy** her boss's direct order.	彼女は上司の直接の命令に反抗することができないと感じた。
A team was formed to **tackle** the problem of childhood obesity.	小児肥満の問題に取り組むため、チームが結成された。
Everything the new secretary did **antagonized** her employer.	新しい秘書のすることなすことすべてが雇用主の反感を買った。
In the end, the king's decision **precipitated** a civil war.	結局，国王の出した結論が内戦を引き起こした。
The official threatened retribution if they did not **capitulate** to his demands.	その役人は彼らが自分の要求に従わなければ報復があると言って脅した。
The boxer **vanquished** his opponent in the fourth round.	第4ラウンドでボクサーは対戦相手を打ち破った。
Brandishing a wad of bills, he ordered everyone drinks.	彼は札束を振りかざしながら，皆の酒を注文した。
The candidate visited local homes to **canvass** support in the election.	その候補者は選挙で支援を求めるために地元の家々を戸別訪問した。

precipitate (1405) のprecipitは (まっさかさまに) を意味し，「まっさかさまに落とす」から転じて，何かを「引き起こす」になります。precipitationは「降水量」です。

1410 contravene
[kà(:)ntrəvíːn]

に違反する [= infringe, violate]
▶contravene safety regulations
(安全基準に違反する)

1411 edify
[édɪfàɪ]

を啓発する
[= cultivate]
图 edification

1412 lobby
[lá(:)bi]

運動する，議員に働きかける
▶lobby against [for] ~
(〜に反対[賛成]の運動をする)

1413 matriculate
[mətríkjulèɪt]

大学に入学する，
入学を許可される
图 matriculation

1414 slump
[slʌmp]

急に落ち込む
[= fall steeply]

1415 augment
[ɔːgmént]

を増加させる [= increase]，
を大きくする [= enlarge]
图 augmentation

1416 blanch
[blæntʃ]

青ざめる [= turn pale]，
を漂白する

1417 consign
[kənsáɪn]

を託送する
[= send]
图 consignment

1418 delineate
[dɪlínièɪt]

をくわしく説明する
[= describe precisely]
图 delineation (描写)

1419 blurt
[bləːrt]

をうっかり口走る

He was warned to be careful not to **contravene** any of the conditions.	彼は条件のどれにも違反しないように注意するよう警告された。
The government tried to **edify** people about the dangers of the drug.	政府は薬物の危険性について人々を啓発しようとした。
The tobacco companies **lobbied** against the new regulations.	タバコ会社は新しい規則に反対運動をした。
He **matriculated** as a student of the college last year.	昨年，彼はその大学に入学した。
Following a rise in the value of the currency, exports **slumped** immediately.	通貨価値の上昇後，輸出はすぐに落ち込んだ。
In order to **augment** my income, I work several part-time jobs.	収入を増やすために，私はパートの仕事をいくつかしている。
The woman's face **blanched** when she heard the news.	そのニュースを聞いた時，女性の顔は青ざめた。
As soon as he arrived, he **consigned** the goods to the customer.	彼は到着するとすぐに顧客に商品を送った。
The committee asked her to **delineate** her plans for improvement.	委員会は彼女に改善計画をくわしく説明するように言った。
Without thinking, she **blurted** his name to the police.	何も考えずに，彼女は警察に彼の名前をうっかり口走った。

1420 deduce
[dɪdjúːs]

を推測する
[= infer]
語源 de(離れて) + duce(導く)

1421 impoverish
[ɪmpá(ː)vərɪʃ]

を貧しくする，(質)を低下させる
cf. poverty(貧乏)

1422 purvey
[pərvéɪ]

(情報)を提供する [= supply, provide], を調達する

1423 endow
[ɪndáʊ]

に(〜を)授ける [= endue],
に(〜を)寄贈する ⟨with⟩
图 endowment

1424 jostle
[dʒá(ː)sl]

押し合う
[= bump into]
▶ jostle *one's* way(押しのけて進む)

1425 levitate
[lévɪtèɪt]

空中を浮遊する
[= rise into the air]
图 levitation

1426 spawn
[spɔːn]

を生み出す [= produce, create],
(卵)を産む
▶ spawn eggs(産卵する)

1427 traffic
[træfɪk]

を密売買する
[= trade illegally]

1428 eschew
[ɪstʃúː]

(好ましくないことなど)を避ける
[= avoid]

1429 hedge
[hedʒ]

を(〜の)生け垣で囲む ⟨with⟩,
を未然に防ぐ
图 hedge

The journalist asked the detective what he had <u>deduced</u> so far.	ジャーナリストは，刑事に今のところ何を推測したか尋ねた。
Poor nations are worried that emission controls will <u>impoverish</u> them further.	貧しい国々は排ガス規制のために，もっと貧しくなることを懸念している。
The information had been <u>purveyed</u> to them by a concerned worker.	その情報は問題に関心のあるひとりの労働者によって彼らに提供された。
The American Constitution says that all men are <u>endowed</u> with certain rights.	合衆国憲法によれば，すべての人間は一定の権利が与えられている。
The fans <u>jostled</u> each other as they tried to get nearer to the stage.	ファンたちはステージに近づこうとして，互いに押し合った。
The magician claimed he could <u>levitate</u> two meters in the air.	その奇術師は2メートルの空中を浮遊することができると主張した。
The notorious novel <u>spawned</u> many similar works by other writers.	その悪名高い小説は，ほかの作家による多くの似たような作品を生み出した。
The teenager was caught <u>trafficking</u> drugs to local people.	その10代の若者は地元の人たちに薬物を密売しているところを捕まった。
The man did not <u>eschew</u> even blackmail to achieve his ends.	その男は目的を達成するためになら恐喝することさえいとわなかった。
The garden had been <u>hedged</u> with tall trees to break the wind.	その庭は風を遮るために高い木々の生け垣で囲まれていた。

hedge (1429) は「生垣で囲む」という安全なイメージをふくらませ，「(投機などで丸損)を未然に防ぐ」という意味も覚えましょう。「ヘッジファンド」は投資で使う言葉です。

1430 mount
[maunt]
を取り付ける
[= install]

1431 hypothesize
[haɪpá(:)θəsàɪz]
(…という)仮説を立てる〈that〉
形 hypothetical

1432 hypnotize
[hípnətàɪz]
に催眠術をかける [= send into a trance]
形 hypnotic

1433 consecrate
[ká(:)nsəkrèɪt]
を奉献する
名 consecration
語源 con(共に) + secrate(神聖にする)

1434 contrive
[kəntráɪv]
を考え出す,をたくらむ

1435 concede
[kənsí:d]
を(しかたなく正しいと)認める
[= acknowledge reluctantly]
名 concession

1436 concur
[kənkə́:r]
(~に)同意する [= agree],
(~に)一致する〈in, on, with〉
▶concur with one's views(~の考えに同意する)

1437 consolidate
[kənsá(:)lɪdèɪt]
を併合する,を強化する
名 consolidation

1438 acclaim
[əkléɪm]
を称賛する [= praise highly]
名 acclamation

1439 eulogize
[jú:lədʒàɪz]
を称賛する
[= praise, extol]
名 eulogy(追悼,賛辞)

The local council decided to **mount** security cameras in the area.	地方自治体がその地域に監視カメラを取り付けることを決定した。
The doctor **hypothesized** that the infection was carried by water.	その医師は，その伝染病は水が媒介しているという仮説を立てた。
The entertainer **hypnotized** the man into thinking he was a dog.	そのエンターテイナーは男性に催眠術をかけて犬だと思い込ませた。
The bishop performed a ceremony to **consecrate** the new church.	司教は新しい教会を奉献するための儀式を行った。
He **contrived** excuses to visit the shop and talk to the girl there.	彼は店を訪ねてそこの少女と話す口実を作った。
I must **concede** that I did not do as well as I should have in the competition.	私はその競技でベストを尽くさなかったことを認めざるを得ない。
Most members of the society **concurred** in the decision to expel him.	クラブのほとんどのメンバーは彼を除名する決定に同意した。
The company managed to **consolidate** its profits in the second quarter.	会社はどうにか第2四半期の利益を併合することができた。
His films were **acclaimed** for their honesty and realism.	彼の映画は，その誠実さと写実性ゆえに高く評価された。
After his death, many people **eulogized** him at the funeral.	彼の死後，葬儀の席で多くの人々が彼を称賛した。

concur (1436) の con は〈共に〉，cur は〈流れる〉を意味します。「一緒に流れる」ということから，concur は「同意する」や「一致する」になります。

1440 prosecute
[prá(:)sɪkjùːt]

を起訴する
[= take legal action against] (⇔ defend)
图 prosecution (告訴)

1441 adjudicate
[ədʒúːdɪkèɪt]

(事件を)裁く,
(人に)判決を下す

1442 anoint
[ənɔ́ɪnt]

を指名する [= ordain],
に軟膏を塗る [= smear with oil]

1443 arbitrate
[ɑ́ːrbɪtrèɪt]

を仲裁する
[= mediate]

1444 convict
[kənvíkt]

に(〜で)有罪判決を下す
[= pronounce guilty] ⟨of⟩

1445 litigate
[líṭəgèɪt]

訴訟を起こす
图 litigation (訴訟) 形 litigious (論争好きの)

1446 ameliorate
[əmíːliərèɪt]

を改善する
[= improve] (⇔ deteriorate)

1447 revamp
[riːvǽmp]

を改良する, を改訂する
▶ revamp a restaurant (レストランを改良する)

1448 reinstate
[rìːɪnstéɪt]

を復職させる [= return to a previous position],
をもとの状態に戻す

1449 resuscitate
[rɪsʌ́sɪtèɪt]

を生き返らせる, を復活させる
[= revive]
图 resuscitation

There was not enough evidence to **prosecute** the suspect.	容疑者を起訴するためには十分な証拠がなかった。
The murder case is supposed to be **adjudicated** in the High Court next month.	その殺人事件は，最高裁で来月判決が下されることになっている。
In a traditional ritual, the new king was **anointed** by a priest.	伝統的な儀式で，新国王が聖職者によって指名された。
An expert was called in to **arbitrate** the industrial dispute.	専門家が労働争議を仲裁するために呼ばれた。
After a lengthy trial, the businessman was **convicted** of fraud.	長期にわたる裁判の後，その実業家は詐欺罪で有罪判決を下された。
He decided not to **litigate** because of the expense it would involve.	彼はそれに伴う費用のことを考えて，訴訟を起こさないことに決めた。
The politician said he wanted to **ameliorate** conditions in the slums.	政治家はスラム街の現状を改善したいと言った。
The company employed a team of PR consultants to **revamp** its image.	その企業はイメージを改善するために PR コンサルタントチームを雇った。
The policeman was **reinstated** when the charges were shown to be false.	その警察官は嫌疑が晴れたので復職した。
The near-drowning victim was **resuscitated** by lifeguards.	そのおぼれそうになった人は救助員によって蘇生した。

1450 ambush
[ǽmbuʃ]
を待ち伏せする

1451 waylay
[wèiléi]
を待ち伏せする

1452 lurch
[ləːrtʃ]
千鳥足で歩く
[= stagger]

1453 lurk
[ləːrk]
潜む [= hide, stay hidden], 待ち伏せる [= lie in wait]

1454 astound
[əstáund]
をびっくり仰天させる
[= astonish, stun with surprise]
形 astounding

1455 baffle
[bǽfl]
を困惑させる
[= puzzle, confound]

1456 perturb
[pərtə́ːrb]
の心をかき乱す
[= upset, confuse]
語源 per (すっかり・完全に) + turb (混乱させる)

1457 rankle
[rǽŋkl]
をいらだたせる, を苦しめる

1458 agitate
[ǽdʒɪtèɪt]
を動揺させる [= perturb], を扇動する [= stir up]
名 agitation, agitator (扇動的な政治家)

1459 bemoan
[bɪmóun]
を嘆く
[= lament]
語源 be (〜にする) + moan (うめき声)

They were **ambushed** by a gang of bandits in the night.	夜に彼らは山賊に待ち伏せされた。
The fan managed to **waylay** the pop star in the corridor of his hotel.	そのファンはどうにかホテルの廊下で人気歌手を待ち伏せした。
The drunk suddenly **lurched** into a group of girls who were passing.	その酔っぱらいは，通りかかった一団の女の子の中に突然千鳥足で入っていった。
The young child was afraid of the monster that **lurked** under the bed.	小さな子どもはベッドの下に潜む怪物を恐れていた。
Many scientists were **astounded** at reports of primitive life on Mars.	多くの科学者が火星上の原始生命の報告を聞いてびっくり仰天した。
The students were totally **baffled** by the final examination questions.	学生たちは期末試験の問題にすっかり困惑させられた。
He was increasingly **perturbed** by the rumors of downsizing.	彼は人員削減のうわさにだんだん心配になってきた。
The fact that he had not been promoted **rankled** him.	彼が昇進しなかったという事実は彼をいらだたせた。
He was so **agitated** when his daughter failed to come home by 11 that he called the police.	娘が11時になっても帰宅しなかったので，彼は動揺して警察に電話した。
Although they **bemoaned** their lack of money, they did little about it.	彼らは，資金不足を嘆いてはいたが，それについて何の手も打たなかった。

ambush (1450) のamは (〜の中に) という意味です。bush「藪」の中で「待ち伏せをする」とイメージしましょう。

#		
1460 **lament** [ləmént]	を嘆き悲しむ [= mourn over, grieve at] 形 lamentable	
1461 **niggle** [nígl]	を悩ます [= annoy, bother]	
1462 **pester** [péstər]	を困らせる, を煩わせる [= badger, trouble] ▶ pester *one* with phone calls (電話で〜を悩ませる)	
1463 **debilitate** [dɪbílɪtèɪt]	を衰弱させる, を弱体化させる [= weaken, enervate] 名 debilitation	
1464 **demur** [dɪmə́:r]	反対する [= raise objections]	
1465 **abate** [əbéɪt]	衰える [= subside], を減らす [= diminish, lessen]	
1466 **pare** [peər]	を徐々に切り詰める [= reduce]	
1467 **prune** [pru:n]	を切り詰める [= cut back]	
1468 **truncate** [trʌ́ŋkeɪt]	を短くする [= shorten]	
1469 **obfuscate** [á(:)bfʌskèɪt]	をわかりにくくする [= obscure] 名 obfuscation	

People around the world <u>lamented</u> the death of Mother Theresa.	世界中の人々がマザー・テレサの死<u>を悼んだ</u>。
She felt <u>niggled</u> by the fact he had forgotten her birthday.	彼が彼女の誕生日を忘れてしまっていたので，彼女は<u>くよくよ悩んだ</u>。
She told her son not to <u>pester</u> his sister while she was doing her homework.	彼女は息子に，姉が宿題をしている間は<u>困らせる</u>なと言った。
The illness had <u>debilitated</u> him so much that he could no longer walk.	病気があまりにも彼の身体<u>を衰弱させた</u>ので，彼はもはや歩けなかった。
She did what he asked without <u>demurring</u> in the slightest.	彼女は少しも<u>異議を唱える</u>ことなく，彼に頼まれたことをした。
We hoped the storm would <u>abate</u> soon so we could go out.	外出できるように，嵐が間もなく<u>衰える</u>ことを我々は願った。
The couple did their best to <u>pare</u> their expenses to a minimum.	その夫婦は最小限まで経費<u>を少しずつ切り詰める</u>ために最善を尽くした。
He <u>pruned</u> all unnecessary personnel from the department.	彼はその部署からすべての不必要な人員<u>を削減した</u>。
In the end, he <u>truncated</u> the essay so as to meet the word limit.	結局，彼は語数制限に合わせるためにエッセイ<u>を短くした</u>。
He accused the scientist of trying to <u>obfuscate</u> his errors.	彼は科学者が自分自身の失敗<u>をわかりにくくし</u>ようとしていたので非難した。

#		
1470	**obliterate** [əblítərèit]	を消す [= erase] 語源 ob (逆に) + literate (文字を書く)
1471	**equivocate** [ɪkwívəkèit]	言葉を濁す 形 equivocal (曖昧な)
1472	**diffuse** [dɪfjúːz]	を広める [= spread, propagate, circulate] 語源 dif (別々に) + fuse (注ぐ)
1473	**proliferate** [prəlífərèit]	増殖する [= multiply], 蔓延する 名 proliferation 形 prolific (多作の)
1474	**promulgate** [prá(ː)məlgèit]	を普及させる [= spread, disseminate], を公表する [= proclaim, publish]
1475	**emanate** [émənèit]	(〜から)発する [= stem, issue] 〈from〉 名 emanation
1476	**emancipate** [ɪmǽnsɪpèit]	を解放する [= set free, release] 名 emancipation
1477	**embroil** [ɪmbrɔ́ɪl]	を(論争などに)巻き込む [= involve] 〈in〉 語源 em (〜の中へ) + broil (混ぜる)
1478	**encumber** [ɪnkʌ́mbər]	を妨げる [= obstruct] cf. cumbersome (厄介な) 語源 en (〜を与える) + cumber (妨害)
1479	**entrench** [ɪntréntʃ]	(〜 oneself で) (〜に)安全に身を隠す 〈in〉 cf. trench (塹壕)

The businessman did his best to **obliterate** all signs of his crime.	その実業家は，自分のすべての犯罪の跡を消すためにできる限りの手を尽くした。
When asked if he would resign, the minister **equivocated** on the issue.	大臣は辞任するかどうかを質問された時，その問題について言葉を濁した。
The society's aim was to **diffuse** their founder's ideas among the public.	その会の目的は創始者の考えを大衆に広めることだった。
Cancer is a disorder that causes affected cells to **proliferate** out of control.	がんとは，病変した細胞が増殖して，手がつけられなくなる疾病である。
The owner of the magazine used it to **promulgate** his environmentalist convictions.	その雑誌の社主は，その雑誌を自分の環境保護論者としての信念を広めるのに使っていた。
Modern algebra essentially **emanated** from Muslim culture in the Middle Ages.	現代の代数学は本質的には中世のイスラム文化から発祥した。
The American Civil War was fought in part to **emancipate** the slaves.	アメリカ南北戦争は，1つには奴隷を解放するために戦われた。
Through no fault of his own, he became **embroiled** in a scandal.	彼自身には何の過失もないのに，彼はスキャンダルに巻き込まれた。
Bad weather conditions **encumbered** the mountain climbers' efforts.	悪天候が登山者たちの努力を邪魔した。
During the Cold War, Soviet spies managed to **entrench** themselves in various Western security services.	冷戦中，ソビエトのスパイたちは西側各地の保安局の中にどうにか身を隠していた。

1480 enumerate
[ɪnjúːmərèɪt]

を列挙する
[= itemize]
語源 en (強意) + numer (数える) + ate

1481 preclude
[prɪklúːd]

を排除する [= exclude],
を妨げる [= impede, hinder]
名 preclusion

1482 prescribe
[prɪskráɪb]

を規定する [= set down as a direction],
を処方する
名 prescription (処方箋)

1483 prevaricate
[prɪværɪkèɪt]

言葉を濁す, 嘘をつく
名 prevarication (二枚舌)

1484 externalize
[ɪkstə́ːrnəlàɪz]

を言葉で表す, を具体化する
(⇔ internalize)

1485 exult
[ɪgzʌ́lt]

(〜に)大喜びする [= be jubilant] 〈over, at〉
名 exultation 形 exultant
語源 ex (強意) + ult (跳ぶ)

1486 expiate
[ékspièɪt]

を償う [= atone for]
名 expiation (罪滅ぼし)

1487 cogitate
[ká(ː)dʒɪtèɪt]

を熟考する
名 cogitation

1488 ponder
[pá(ː)ndər]

を熟考する
[= deliberate, consider carefully]

1489 banish
[bǽnɪʃ]

を(〜へ)追放する 〈to〉
名 banishment

334

He said it was impossible to **enumerate** all the problems they had faced.	彼らが直面したすべての問題を列挙することは不可能だと彼は言った。
His intransigent attitude does not completely **preclude** a final reconciliation.	彼の非妥協的な態度は，最終的な和解を完全に排除するものではない。
The rules for taking the exam were **prescribed** carefully in writing.	受験する際の規則は注意深く文書で規定されていた。
The police officer told him to stop **prevaricating** and to answer the question.	警官は彼に言葉を濁すのをやめて，質問に答えるように言った。
After the divorce, he found it hard to **externalize** his feelings.	離婚後，彼は自分の感情を言葉で表すことは難しいとわかった。
The fans **exulted** over their football team's first national championship.	ファンたちは，そのフットボール・チームの初の全国優勝に大喜びした。
He did his best to **expiate** his original mistake.	彼は自分の最初の失敗を償うために最善を尽くした。
He said he needed time to **cogitate** the problem before deciding.	彼は決定する前に問題を熟考する時間が必要だと言った。
Socrates was said to have gone into trances while he **pondered** enigmas.	ソクラテスは，不可解なものについて考え込むと，トランス状態に入ったと言われた。
The deposed leader was **banished** to a neighboring country.	退陣させられた指導者が隣国に追放された。

1490 debar
[dɪbáːr]

を(〜から)除外する ⟨from⟩
名 debarment

1491 harry
[hǽri]

を襲撃する
[= attack]

1492 infiltrate
[ínfɪltreɪt]

に潜入する
[= sneak into]
▶infiltrate an organization (組織に侵入する)

1493 assail
[əséɪl]

を襲撃する [= beset],
を悩ませる

1494 ravage
[rǽvɪdʒ]

(国など)を荒らす,
を略奪する

1495 plunder
[plʌ́ndər]

を略奪する
[= ransack, ravage, raven]
▶plunder a village (村を略奪する)

1496 loot
[luːt]

を略奪する
[= plunder]

1497 intercept
[ìntərsépt]

を迎撃する, を妨害する, を傍受する
語源 inter (〜の間) + cept (取る)

1498 impede
[ɪmpíːd]

を妨げる [= hinder, obstruct],
を遅らせる [= delay]
語源 im (中に) + pede (足)

1499 stunt
[stʌnt]

を妨げる
[= inhibit] (⇔ promote)
▶stunt the growth of 〜 (〜の成長を妨げる)

After the fight, he was **debarred** from the club permanently.	そのけんかの後、彼はそのクラブから永久に除名された。
The soldiers' job was to **harry** the advancing army.	その兵士たちの仕事は前進する軍を襲撃することだった。
Their spy managed to **infiltrate** the rival company and discover their plans.	彼らのスパイは、どうにかライバル会社に潜入し、彼らの計画を見つけ出すことができた。
He was about to sign the contract when he was suddenly **assailed** by doubts.	彼はその契約にまさに署名しようとした時、急に疑念に襲われた。
The area was **ravaged** by storms during the winter months.	その地域は冬の間に襲った嵐で荒廃していた。
Pirates would attack ships and **plunder** whatever of value they carried.	海賊たちは船を襲い、積荷のうち価値のある物は何でも略奪したものだった。
Some people took advantage of the hurricane to **loot** local stores.	ハリケーンを利用して地元の店を略奪した人たちがいた。
Anti-ballistic missiles are designed to **intercept** incoming missile attacks.	弾道弾迎撃ミサイルは、飛来するミサイル攻撃を迎撃することを目的として作られている。
The weather **impeded** our progress so much that we gave up work for the day.	(悪)天候が大幅に私たちの進捗を妨げたので、私たちはその日の仕事を断念した。
Years of poor management had **stunted** the company's profits.	何年にもわたるお粗末な経営が会社の利益を阻害した。

stunt (1499) と言うと日本語の「スタント」をぱっと思い浮かべるでしょう。名詞の「危険な離れ業」以外に動詞の「を防げる」という意味もあります。

1500〜1509

1500 persecute
[pə́ːrsɪkjùːt]

を迫害する
[= oppress]
語源 per(完全に) + secute(追跡する)

1501 stymie
[stáɪmi]

を妨害する，を阻止する
[= impede, thwart]

1502 annihilate
[ənáɪəlèɪt]

を完全に破壊する
名 annihilation (絶滅)
語源 an(強意) + nihil(ゼロ) + ate

1503 pulverize
[pʌ́lvəràɪz]

を粉砕する
[= crush]

1504 override
[òʊvərráɪd]

をくつがえす [= invalidate]，**より優位に立つ**
▶ override *one's* objections
(〜の反対をくつがえす)

1505 foil
[fɔɪl]

を挫折させる
[= frustrate, thwart]

1506 foist
[fɔɪst]

を(〜に)押し付ける
[= impose] 〈on, upon〉

1507 inhibit
[ɪnhíbət]

を抑制する [= restrain, check, repress]
名 inhibition
語源 in(中に) + hibit(所有する)

1508 recant
[rɪkǽnt]

を撤回する
[= take back]

1509 repudiate
[rɪpjúːdièɪt]

を拒絶する
[= reject, disclaim]
名 repudiation

The church had a bad record for **persecuting** rival faiths.	その教会は対抗する信仰を迫害した悪い記録を残していた。
Their boss did his best to **stymie** their project but he failed.	上司は彼らのプロジェクトを妨害しようと頑張ったが、できなかった。
The aim of the raid was to **annihilate** the enemy munitions factory.	襲撃の目的は敵の軍需工場を完全に破壊することだった。
The shells were **pulverized** in order to create a fine powder.	貝殻はきめ細かなパウダーを作るために細かく砕かれた。
The president **overrode** his subordinate's decision and restored the original plan.	社長は部下の決定をくつがえし当初の計画を復活させた。
It seemed like a miracle that the terrorists' plans were **foiled**.	テロリストたちの計画が挫折したのは奇跡に思えた。
Local people resented any attempt to **foist** foreign customs on them.	地元の人たちは外国の習慣を押し付けようとするどんな試みにも腹を立てた。
Some fear that environmental controls will **inhibit** material progress.	環境規制は物質的進歩を抑制すると危惧する人たちもいる。
The case collapsed after the chief witness **recanted** her evidence.	最重要証人が証言を撤回した時、その事件はなし崩しになった。
Later in life, he **repudiated** the radical ideas of his youth and became a leading conservative.	後年、彼は若い頃に持っていた急進的な思想を否定して、有数の保守主義者となった。

1510 revile
[riváil]
をののしる

1511 satirize
[sǽtəràiz]
を風刺する
[= squib]
形 satirical

1512 recede
[risíːd]
後退する (⇔ proceed 前進する)
名 recess (休み), recession (景気後退)

1513 relinquish
[rilíŋkwiʃ]
を放棄する
[= abandon, renounce, surrender, give up]
▶ relinquish *one's* position (地位を捨てる)

1514 reprieve
[ripríːv]
を一時的に救う [= relieve temporarily], の刑の執行を猶予する

1515 secede
[sisíːd]
(〜から) 脱退する [= withdraw] ⟨from⟩, 分離する
名 secession

1516 slash
[slæʃ]
をさっと切る [= slit],
を削減する [= reduce],
を酷評する [= criticize severely]

1517 snip
[snip]
(〜を) ちょきんと切り取る
[= cut off] ⟨off⟩

1518 snatch
[snætʃ]
をひったくる
[= steal]

1519 snitch
[snitʃ]
を盗む, ひったくる

The man was **reviled** for cooperating with the enemy.	その男性は敵陣と手を組んだことで**罵倒**された。
The comedian denied any intention to **satirize** the famous politician.	コメディアンはその有名な政治家**を風刺する**意図は少しもなかったと否定した。
As the war **receded** into the past, people began to analyze it more objectively.	戦争が過去に**遠ざかっていく**につれて、人々はそれを一層客観的に分析し始めた。
Although he had lived abroad for years, he never **relinquished** his citizenship.	彼は外国に何年も住んでいたのに、一度も市民権**を放棄し**なかった。
By a stroke of luck, the students were **reprieved** from taking the exam.	思いがけなく幸運なことに、学生たちはその試験**を一時的に猶予**された。
America's Civil War began when Southern states tried to **secede** from the Union.	アメリカの南北戦争は、南部諸州が米国から**脱退し**ようとして始まった。
A kitchen knife that could **slash** even through bone was advertised on television.	骨をも**切る**ことができる包丁がテレビで宣伝されていた。
He took some scissors and **snipped** off a lock of her hair.	彼ははさみを取り出し、彼女の髪の房**をちょきんと切り取った**。
A thief suddenly **snatched** her purse and ran out of the restaurant.	泥棒はいきなり彼女のハンドバッグ**をひったくり**、レストランから走り去った。
He was caught **snitching** some sweets from the supermarket.	彼はスーパーマーケットからお菓子**を盗む**ところを捕まえられた。

1520 pilfer
[pílfər]

を盗む [= filch], をくすねる

名 pilferage

1521 abrogate
[ǽbrəgèɪt]

を破棄する [= revoke, abolish]

名 abrogation

1522 absolve
[əbzá(:)lv]

を(義務・約束などから)解放する, を(義務などから)免除する [= acquit] ⟨of⟩

1523 rescind
[rɪsínd]

を撤回する, を無効にする [= annul, revoke, abrogate, repeal]

1524 decry
[dɪkráɪ]

を公然と非難する [= denounce, condemn]

1525 denigrate
[dénɪgrèɪt]

を中傷する [= slander], を見くびる [= belittle]

1526 detain
[dɪtéɪn]

を拘留する [= confine, keep in custody], を引き留める

名 detention

1527 disavow
[dìsəváʊ]

を否認する

名 disavowal

1528 disdain
[dɪsdéɪn]

(〜すること)を潔しとしない [= spurn, refuse] ⟨to do⟩, を軽蔑する [= scorn, despise]

1529 dissemble
[dɪsémbl]

(感情など)を隠す [= disguise], のふりをする [= pretend]

▶ dissemble one's feeling of fear (恐怖心を隠す)

It seemed that someone was **pilfering** small change from students' purses.	誰かが学生たちの財布から小銭を盗んでいるようだった。
The right to strike for workers is usually **abrogated** in wartime.	労働者のストライキ権は，普通，戦時中には破棄される。
The official inquiry **absolved** him of any responsibility for the accident.	公式調査はその事故に対するどんな責任からも彼を放免した。
The decision was **rescinded** because it was found unconstitutional.	その決定は憲法違反であることが判明したので撤回された。
Members of the public **decried** the corruption of their leaders.	国民は指導者たちの腐敗を非難した。
He told the young man to have more pride and to stop **denigrating** his own country.	彼はその若い男性に，もっと誇りを持ち，祖国を中傷するのをやめるように言った。
Immigration officials mistakenly **detained** me at the airport for five hours.	入国管理事務所の役人は，誤って空港に5時間私を拘留した。
When the scandal came to light, even his supporters began to **disavow** knowing him.	そのスキャンダルが明るみに出た時，彼の支持者でさえ彼と知り合いであることを否定した。
She said that she **disdained** to answer such an impertinent question.	そのような無作法な質問に答えることはお断りしますと，彼女は言った。
The spy said that he had grown tired of **dissembling** his true identity over the years.	何年も自分の正体を隠すことにうんざりした，とスパイは言った。

pilfer (1520) は「を盗む」の意味でも，「を横領する」の意味でも，少額，もしくは個数が少ないことを覚えましょう。

1530〜1539

1530 erode
[ɪróʊd]

損なわれる, を浸食する [= corrode, eat away]
图 erosion

1531 corrode
[kəróʊd]

を腐食する [= rust, erode, eat into], むしばむ [= canker]
图 corrosion

1532 molt
[moʊlt]

脱皮する

1533 mutate
[mjúː(ː)teɪt]

変化する [= metamorphose]
图 mutation
▶mutate into ～ (～に変化する)

1534 bereave
[bɪríːv]

から(～を)奪う [= deprive] ⟨of⟩
图 bereavement (死別)
▶the bereaved (遺族)

1535 exorcise
[éksɔːrsàɪz]

(悪霊・悪い考えなど)を取り除く
[= drive out]
图 exorcism

1536 exploit
[ɪksplɔ́ɪt]

を利用する [= take advantage of], を搾取する 图 exploitation
▶exploit one's workers (労働者を搾取する)

1537 expunge
[ɪkspʌ́ndʒ]

を(～から)抹消する
[= delete, efface, erase] ⟨from⟩

1538 extricate
[ékstrɪkèɪt]

を(～から)救い出す
[= relieve, rescue, liberate] ⟨from⟩

1539 extrapolate
[ɪkstræpəlèɪt]

(既知の事柄から)推定する ⟨from⟩
图 extrapolation

Public confidence in the economy has slowly been **eroding**.	経済に対する国民の信頼が徐々に損なわれてきている。
Acid will **corrode** even the toughest cast-iron structures.	酸は最も耐久性の高い鋳鉄構造物をも腐食する。
Some creatures **molt** at regular intervals.	一定の間隔で脱皮する生物がいる。
The flies were scientifically useful because they **mutated** so quickly.	ハエはとても速く変異するので科学的に役立った。
Having lost his father in early childhood, he was **bereaved** of his love and affection.	彼は幼い頃に父親を失い、父親の愛情や慈愛を奪われた。
The leader found it hard to **exorcise** the defeatism that gripped the party.	リーダーは、チームに蔓延した敗北主義を取り除くのは難しいと思った。
Human beings will need to increasingly **exploit** renewable energy sources in this century.	今世紀中には、人類はますます再生可能なエネルギー源を利用することが必要となるだろう。
People could not **expunge** the shocking incident from their memories.	人々は、記憶からその衝撃的な事件を消し去ることができなかった。
The bank found it difficult to **extricate** itself from the financial disaster.	その銀行は財政難から脱するのは困難だと気付いた。
By **extrapolating** from current statistics, we can predict the population level in 50 years' time.	現行統計から推測することによって、我々は50年後の人口水準を予測することができる。

1540 ~ 1549

1540 **extradite** [ékstrədàit]	(外国からの逃亡犯など)を(本国に)**引き渡す**, 送還する [= deport] 〈to〉 ▶extradite a suspect (容疑者を引き渡す)
1541 **execute** [éksɪkjùːt]	**を実行する** [= perform, carry out], **を死刑にする** 图 execution (処刑), executive (重役)
1542 **interrogate** [ɪntérəgèɪt]	**を尋問する** 图 interrogation 形 interrogative
1543 **legislate** [lédʒɪslèɪt]	**立法措置をとる** [= make laws] ▶legislate against [for, on] ~ (~を禁止する[を認める, に関する]立法措置をとる)
1544 **plead** [pliːd]	**を切に頼む** [= beg], **嘆願する** [= solicit] ▶plead for ~ (~を嘆願する)
1545 **solicit** [səlísət]	**を強く求める** [= beg, plead] 形 solicitous (心配して, 強く願って)
1546 **torture** [tɔ́ːrtʃər]	**を拷問する** [= inflict pain on] 語源 tort (ねじる) + ure
1547 **scavenge** [skǽvɪndʒ]	**(~を)あさる** [= rummage] 〈for〉 图 scavenger
1548 **scour** [skaʊər]	**(場所)を捜し回る**, (~を捜して)駆けめぐる 〈for〉
1549 **scrabble** [skrǽbl]	**(~を)手さぐりで捜す** [= grope] 〈for〉, なぐり書きする

The war criminal was **extradited** to Germany.	戦犯はドイツへ送還された。
As soon as they were given funding, they began to **execute** the plan.	彼らは資金を受領するとすぐに計画を実行し始めた。
Three detectives **interrogated** the suspect for hours, but he refused to betray his friends.	刑事3人が何時間にもわたって被疑者を尋問したが，被疑者は友人を売り渡すことを拒んだ。
There were calls for the government to **legislate** against such acts.	そのような行為を規制する立法措置をとるように，政府に対していくつかの要求があった。
The girl **pleaded** in vain to be allowed to attend the concert.	少女はそのコンサートに行きたいと切に頼んだが無駄だった。
The environmental activist was **soliciting** signatures for the petition from passers-by.	環境保護活動家が通行人たちに請願書への署名を求めていた。
The soldiers were convicted of **torturing** the terrorist suspects.	兵士たちはテロの容疑者を拷問したことで有罪の判決を受けた。
Stray dogs **scavenged** in the waste site for discarded food.	野良犬は廃棄物処理場で捨てられた食料をあさった。
They **scoured** the apartment looking for the missing earring but were unable to find it.	彼らはなくなったイヤリングを求めてアパート内を捜し回ったが，見つけられなかった。
The old man **scrabbled** on the floor for his spectacles.	老人は眼鏡を求めて床を手さぐりで捜した。

1550 ~ 1559

1550
vilify [vílɪfàɪ]
を中傷する，の悪口を言う
图 vilification

1551
wrangle [rǽŋgl]
言い争う
[= argue, dispute, quarrel]

1552
drawl [drɔːl]
(母音を伸ばして)ゆっくり話す
[= speak slowly, prolonging the vowels]

1553
elucidate [ɪlúːsɪdèɪt]
を説明する [= explain]，
を解明する [= make lucid]
图 elucidation

1554
percolate [pə́ːrkəlèɪt]
をこす，をろ過する
[= filter]

1555
pervade [pərvéɪd]
の隅々に広がる，
に蔓延(まんえん)する [= spread throughout]
图 pervasion 形 pervasive

1556
append [əpénd]
を(~に)つけ加える ⟨to⟩
語源 ap(~に) + pend(ぶらさがる)

1557
upend [ʌpénd]
を逆さまにする
▶ upend a bicycle(自転車をひっくり返す)

1558
dribble [drɪ́bl]
(よだれ)を垂らす
[= drool]

1559
gnaw [nɔː]
(~を)かじって穴をあける ⟨through⟩

However much the media **vilified** him, his popularity grew.	メディアがどれほど彼を中傷しようとも，彼の人気は上昇した。
He paid up because he hated **wrangling** with people over money.	彼はお金のことで人と争うのが嫌なので，借金を全額支払った。
Ex-President Jimmy Carter **drawled** in typical Georgian dialect when he spoke.	ジミー・カーター元大統領は，話す時，典型的なジョージア訛りで母音を伸ばしてゆっくり話した。
It took him numerous lectures to **elucidate** Saussure's linguistic theories.	ソシュールの言語学理論を説明するのに，彼は何度も講義をする必要があった。
They cleaned the water by **percolating** it through a layer of sand.	彼らは砂の層で水をこしてきれいにした。
Rumors of the illness **pervaded** a large section of the city.	その病気のうわさが市の大部分に広まった。
A file of relevant documents was **appended** to the report.	関連書類のファイルはレポートに添えられた。
The woman **upended** her bag and spilled the contents on the table.	その女性はバッグを逆さまにして，中にある物をテーブルの上にあけた。
Because he was teething, the baby **dribbled** saliva constantly.	歯が生え始めていたので，赤ん坊は絶えずよだれを垂らしていた。
They discovered that a rat had **gnawed** through the electricity cable.	彼らはネズミが電気のコードをかじって穴をあけたことを発見した。

1560〜1569

1560 regale
[rɪgéɪl]

に(食事などを)ごちそうする [= supply lavishly],
を(〜で)楽しませる ⟨with⟩

1561 swill
[swɪl]

をがぶ飲みする [= drink heavily]
▶ swill beer down (ビールをがぶ飲みする)

1562 snarl
[snɑːrl]

歯をむいてうなる [= growl]

1563 faze
[feɪz]

をひるませる
▶ be fazed by *one's* comment (〜の批評にひるむ)

1564 foment
[foumént]

を助長する [= encourage],
を扇動する [= instigate, incite, abet]

1565 straddle
[strǽdl]

にまたがる

1566 strut
[strʌt]

気取って歩く [= swagger]

1567 swarm
[swɔːrm]

殺到する,
群れをなして動く

1568 accrue
[əkrúː]

(当然の結果として)(利益などが)生じる,
(資本などが)増える

1569 chasten
[tʃéɪsən]

を懲らしめる [= subdue], 罰する

350

The millionaire loved to **regale** guests with expensive foods and wines.	その大金持ちは、客に高価な食べ物とワインを<u>ごちそうする</u>ことが大好きだった。
The students sat **swilling** tea and munching the homemade cookies.	生徒たちは座ってお茶<u>をがぶ飲みし</u>、手作りクッキーをむしゃむしゃ食べていた。
When the keeper approached the lion cubs, their mother **snarled** threateningly.	飼育係がライオンの子に近づいた時、母ライオンは威嚇的に<u>歯をむいてうなった</u>。
It seemed that nothing could **faze** his sense of self-confidence.	彼の自信<u>をひるませる</u>ものは何もないように思われた。
Her main objective seems to be to **foment** disharmony among staff members.	彼女の主な目的はスタッフメンバーの間に不和<u>を助長する</u>ことのようだ。
The boy **straddled** the branch and began to eat a banana.	その少年は木の枝<u>にまたがり</u>バナナを食べ始めた。
The coach **strutted** up and down, shouting at his team.	そのコーチは行ったり来たり<u>気取って歩き</u>ながら、彼の率いるチームに向かって怒鳴っていた。
As soon as the department store opened, shoppers **swarmed** in.	百貨店がオープンするとすぐに買い物客が<u>殺到した</u>。
All the profits that **accrued** were to be devoted to helping hungry children.	<u>発生した</u>利益のすべては、飢えた子どもたちの援助に充てられることになっていた。
Chastened by their scolding, the children sat quietly at their desks.	<u>叱</u>られて子どもたちはおとなしく、机に着席していた。

1570	**clump** [klʌmp]	群れをなす [= bunch, cluster] ▶clump together (グループでかたまる)
1571	**clutter** [klʌ́tər]	(〜を)散らかす [= jumble (up), put into disorder] ⟨up⟩
1572	**glean** [gliːn]	(情報)を少しずつ集める, (落ち穂など)を拾い集める ▶glean information (情報を少しずつ集める)
1573	**hobble** [hɑ́(ː)bl]	(〜で)両脚を縛る ⟨with⟩
1574	**huddle** [hʌ́dl]	体を寄せ合う [= gather] ▶huddle around the open fire (たき火の周りに集まる)
1575	**ignite** [ɪgnáɪt]	に火をつける [= kindle, set on fire], (感情など)を燃え立たせる 图 ignition ▶ignite resentment (憤りに火をつける)
1576	**incinerate** [ɪnsínərèɪt]	を灰と化す [= be reduced to ashes], を焼却する [= burn]
1577	**jilt** [dʒɪlt]	(恋人)を振る
1578	**prod** [prɑ(ː)d]	を(〜するように)駆り立てる [= urge, prompt] ⟨to do⟩
1579	**snub** [snʌb]	に冷たい態度をとる, (人)を鼻であしらう [= cold-shoulder] ▶snub *one* into silence (冷たくして〜を黙らせる)

He could see the bacteria **clumping** together under the microscope.	彼は顕微鏡でバクテリアが<u>群れをなしている</u>のを見ることができた。
Every day I seem to **clutter** up my office more with papers and books.	毎日，私は書類や本でますます自分のオフィス<u>を散らかし</u>ていくようだ。
He **gleaned** from his boss's expression that she did not agree with him.	彼は上司の表情から，自分に同意していないのだということ<u>を察した</u>。
To stop the prisoner escaping, his legs were **hobbled** with chains.	囚人が脱走しないように彼の足は鎖で<u>縛ら</u>れていた。
The children **huddled** together in their tent to keep warm.	子どもたちは暖を取るためにテントの中で互いに<u>体を寄せ合った</u>。
Fire experts determined that the fire had been **ignited** by an electric spark.	火災専門家は，その火事が電気の花花によって<u>引火した</u>ものと断定した。
All his research notes were **incinerated** in the fire at the lab.	彼のすべての研究記録は研究室の火事で<u>焼かれてしまった</u>。
Just before the wedding, she was suddenly **jilted** by her fiancé.	彼女は結婚を目前にして突然，婚約者<u>に振ら</u>れた。
He **prodded** me to continue walking even after I was exhausted.	私が疲れ果ててからも，彼は歩き続けるよう私<u>をせかした</u>。
She deliberately **snubbed** him at the party by refusing to dance with him.	彼女はパーティーで彼と踊ることを拒んで，わざと彼<u>に冷たい態度をとった</u>。

clump (1570) は名詞では「かたまり」を意味します。例としては clump of trees「木立」などがあります。

1580 sojourn
[sóudʒəːrn]

滞在する
[= stay]
► sojourn at one's aunt's (おばの家に一時滞在する)

1581 tangle
[tǽŋgl]

をもつれさせる
[= entwine]

1582 thrust
[θrʌst]

を(~に)押し付ける [= force, impose] ⟨upon⟩,
を強く押す [= push, shove]

1583 usurp
[jusə́ːrp]

を侵害する
語源 use(使用) + rp(強奪する)

1584 vacillate
[vǽsɪlèɪt]

変動する，(心・考えが)動揺する
[= fluctuate, oscillate, sway],
よろめく [= stagger, totter]

1585 accost
[əkɔ́(ː)st]

に声を掛ける，
に近寄る [= approach]

1586 attenuate
[əténjuèɪt]

を低くする [= reduce],
弱める [= weaken]

1587 beguile
[bɪɡáɪl]

をだます [= dupe, cheat, mislead, delude]

1588 clobber
[klá(ː)bər]

をひどく負かす，を酷評する

1589 cringe
[krɪndʒ]

(恐怖で)身を縮める [= cower]

During his trip, he **sojourned** for a few days on the tropical island.	旅行期間中，彼は数日間熱帯の島に滞在した。
His attempts to improve the situation only **tangled** it further.	状況を改善しようとする彼の試みは，さらに状況をもつれさせたにすぎなかった。
He didn't want the post, but the board of directors **thrust** it upon him.	彼はそのポストを望んではいなかったが，役員会が彼に押し付けた。
The subordinate was accused of **usurping** his superior's authority.	その部下は上司の権限を侵害していることを責められた。
Exchange rates over the past year have **vacillated** wildly, especially in Asia.	過去1年間の為替レートは，特にアジアにおいて激しく変動した。
As he walked past, a homeless man **accosted** him for money.	彼が横を通り過ぎた時，ホームレスの男が金をせびろうとして彼に話し掛けた。
Persistent inflation steadily **attenuated** the value of their wages.	持続的インフレは確実に賃金の価値を低下させた。
He was **beguiled** by the attractive saleswoman into buying a complete set of the encyclopedia.	彼は魅力的な女性販売員にだまされて百科事典一式を買わされた。
He picked up the ball and ran, but was immediately **clobbered** by the opposing team.	彼はボールを拾って走ったが，すぐに相手チームにやっつけられてしまった。
The frightened dog was **cringing** in the corner of the room.	おびえた犬は部屋の隅で身を縮めていた。

sojourn (1580) のjournには(一日を過ごす)の意味があります。ほかの例としてはjourney「一日の旅行」，journal「日々の記録」などがあります。

1590〜1599

1590 dissipate
[dísɪpèɪt]
散る [= disperse]，を浪費する
名 dissipation（放蕩）

1591 downplay
[dàʊnpléɪ]
を実際より控えめに話す
[= play down]

1592 frazzle
[fræzl]
をくたくたに疲れさせる
[= wear out]

1593 hoard
[hɔːrd]
を（ひそかに）蓄える
[= accumulate in a hidden place]

1594 impound
[ɪmpáʊnd]
を押収する，を囲い込む

1595 irk
[əːrk]
をうんざりさせる
[= annoy]
形 irksome

1596 mangle
[mǽŋgl]
を台無しにする [= spoil]
語源 mang（ずたずた切る）+ le（動作の反復）

1597 negate
[nɪgéɪt]
を否定する
[= deny, annul, nullify]
名 negation 形 negative

1598 parry
[pǽri]
（攻撃・質問など）をかわす

1599 procrastinate
[prəkrǽstɪnèɪt]
先延ばしにする
[= delay, put off]
名 procrastination

As the sun rose, the fog began to **dissipate**.	太陽が昇るにつれて、霧は散り始めた。
To prevent a panic, the expert **downplayed** the danger of the disease.	パニックを防ぐため、専門家はその病気の危険性を実際より控えめに話した。
She felt completely **frazzled** after looking after her grandchildren all day.	一日中孫の世話をして、彼女はすっかり疲れ果てた。
He **hoarded** money for many years, and eventually died wealthy, but miserable.	彼は長い間お金をこっそり蓄えて、最後には裕福だが惨めな死に方をした。
His car was **impounded** by the police after he left it illegally parked.	彼が違法駐車をした後、彼の車は警察に押収された。
He was **irked** by his colleague's critical remarks about his work.	彼は、自分の仕事に対する同僚の批判的発言にうんざりした。
The nervous young actor completely **mangled** his first speech.	若い俳優は緊張して、完全に初めてのスピーチを台無しにした。
His research **negated** the government's claims that it was uninvolved.	彼の調査は政府が関与していないという主張を否定した。
He cleverly **parried** the criticism by turning it back on his opponent.	彼は批判を相手にそのまま返して巧みに逃れた。
The students continued to **procrastinate** in completing their senior theses.	学生たちは卒業論文の完成を先延ばしにし続けた。

1600 quadruple
[kwɑ(:)drúːpl]
4倍になる

1601 reverberate
[rivə́ːrbərèit]
鳴り響く
名 reverberation

1602 shroud
[ʃraud]
を覆い隠す
[= cover, hide from view]
▶be shrouded in mystery(謎に包まれている)

1603 smear
[smɪər]
を塗りつける [= spread],
(名誉など)を汚す [= slander]

1604 spell
[spel]
(という結果)をもたらす
[= lead to]
▶spell trouble(厄介なことになる)

1605 splurge
[spləːrdʒ]
を(〜に)ぜいたくに使う〈on〉

1606 squint
[skwɪnt]
(目)を細める,
横目で見る [= look sidewise]

1607 streak
[striːk]
に(〜の)縞をつける〈with〉

1608 strive
[straɪv]
懸命に努力する, 頑張る
[= try hard]

1609 swerve
[swəːrv]
急に向きを変える
[= veer suddenly]
▶swerve from one's duty(本分からそれる)

The value of the IT company's shares **quadrupled** overnight.	そのIT会社の株価は一夜にして4倍になった。
The sound of the rifle **reverberated** across the empty field.	銃の発射音が人気のない野原に鳴り響いた。
The heavy mist **shrouded** Mt. Fuji from view.	濃い霧が富士山を包み隠した。
The man **smeared** butter, then honey on a chunk of bread.	男は厚切りパンにまずバターを、次にハチミツを塗った。
The closure of the factory **spelled** economic disaster for the community.	その工場の閉鎖は地域の経済破綻をもたらした。
He **splurged** most of the inheritance on an expensive holiday abroad.	彼は海外での豪華な休暇で遺産のほとんどをぜいたくに使った。
Since the photographer was looking into the sun, he **squinted** his eyes to see.	写真家は太陽を見ていたので、目を細めるようにして見た。
The artist's clothes were **streaked** with different colored paints.	芸術家の服には異なった色の絵の具で縞模様がついていた。
However hard they **strove**, they still fell into debt by the end of the month.	どんなに一生懸命努力しても、やはり彼らは月末には借金を負うことになってしまった。
The cyclist **swerved** to avoid the child and crashed into a wall.	サイクリストは子どもを避けようと急に向きを変えたので、壁に衝突してしまった。

quadruple (1600)「4倍になる」のpleは(倍)を意味します。ほかの例としてはtriple「3倍にする」などがあります。

1610 ~ 1619

1610
taunt
[tɔːnt]

をあざける [= mock, ridicule]，
をなじる

1611
throb
[θrɑ(ː)b]

ずきずきする
[= pulsate with pain]

1612
inundate
[ínʌndèɪt]

を水浸しにする [= deluge, flood]，殺到する
图 inundation (洪水，氾濫)
▶ be inundated with phone calls (電話が殺到する)

1613
resume
[rɪzjúːm]

再開する [= start again, take (up) again]
图 resumption

1614
lapse
[læps]

(以前の状態に) 逆戻りする，
(〜に) 陥る [= slip] ⟨into⟩

1615
wage
[weɪdʒ]

(戦争など)を行う [= engage in, carry on]
▶ wage a war on 〜 (〜と戦争する)

1616
confer
[kənfə́ːr]

(〜と) 相談する ⟨with⟩
图 conference (会議)

1617
malign
[məláɪn]

を中傷する [= slander]

1618
conjugate
[kɑ́(ː)ndʒʊgèɪt]

(動詞)を活用させる，
を共役させる，接合する

1619
decimate
[désəmèɪt]

を大量に減少させる

The other boys <u>taunted</u> him about the Valentine card he had received.	彼が受け取ったバレンタインカードのことで、ほかの男の子たちは彼をあざけった。
After drinking late the night before, his head <u>throbbed</u> with pain.	昨夜遅くまで酒を飲んだので、彼は頭がずきずきして痛かった。
The valley was <u>inundated</u> when a large dam sprung a major leak.	大きなダムが大規模な水漏れを起こし、水が谷に氾濫した。
About a week after New Year's, classes will <u>resume</u>.	新年に入って1週間ほどすると、授業が再開する。
At first, the students spoke English to each other, but after a while they <u>lapsed</u> into their native Chinese.	最初、学生たちはお互いに英語で話していたが、しばらくすると母語の中国語に戻った。
Irish nationalists <u>waged</u> a campaign against British occupation for decades.	アイルランドの民族主義者たちは、数十年にわたって、イギリスの占領に対する反対運動を行った。
After <u>conferring</u> with his client, the lawyer said that he had no more questions.	依頼人と協議した後、弁護士はこれ以上質問はないと言った。
He complained that he was being <u>maligned</u> for no reason.	彼は理由もなく中傷されていることに対して文句を言った。
Can you <u>conjugate</u> the verb "to go"?	「行く」という動詞を活用させることができますか。
The population had been <u>decimated</u> by warfare and hunger.	人口は戦争と飢餓のために大幅に減少した。

decimate (1619) のde は (10) を意味します。ほかの例としてdecade「10年」、decimal「10進法」があります。

でる度 C 力を伸ばす単語

名詞 242語

🎧 1620〜1628

1620 **custody** [kʌ́stədi]	養育権, 保管 [= keeping], 拘留 [= imprisonment]
1621 **faculty** [fǽkəlti]	才能 [= ability, talent], 機能, 教授陣
1622 **municipality** [mjuːnìsɪpǽləti]	地方自治体 [= borough]
1623 **nucleus** [njúːkliəs]	核 [= kernel], 中心, 核心 [= core]
1624 **paucity** [pɔ́ːsəti]	不足, 欠乏 [= scarcity, fewness, dearth, insufficiency, scantiness]
1625 **spur** [spəːr]	拍車, 刺激 [= stimulus]
1626 **proposition** [prɑ̀(ː)pəzíʃən]	提案, 計画 [= plan, scheme], 命題 動 propose 名 proposal
1627 **setback** [sétbæk]	妨げ, (景気の)後退, 挫折 ▶suffer a setback (挫折を味わう)
1628 **array** [əréɪ]	多数, 配列 [= arrangement] ▶an array of 〜 (多数の〜)

362

The divorcing couple waged a bitter court fight over **custody** of their children.	離婚する夫婦は，子どもの<u>養育権</u>をめぐって激しい法廷闘争を繰り広げた。
His intellectual **faculties** are still acute, despite his advanced age.	彼は年を取ったが，知的<u>能力</u>は依然として優れている。
Care of the local parks was the **municipality**'s responsibility.	地元の公園管理は<u>地方自治体</u>の責任だった。
The atom bomb was developed by splitting the **nucleus** of an atom.	原子爆弾は，原子<u>核</u>を分裂させることによって開発された。
I would like to travel after retirement, but I may be limited by a **paucity** of funds.	仕事を辞めたら旅をしたいが，資金<u>不足</u>で限界があるかもしれない。
The coach predicted that the loss would act as a **spur** to the team.	コーチは敗戦がチームにとって<u>拍車</u>をかけることになると強調した。
My friend said that he had a business **proposition** for me.	私に対する仕事の<u>提案</u>があるのだと，友人は言った。
The poor sales were a serious **setback** for the company.	売り上げの低迷は，その会社にとって深刻な<u>妨げ</u>となった。
The shop displayed an **array** of different kinds of cloth.	その店は<u>多く</u>のさまざまな種類の布を陳列していた。

#	英単語	意味
1629	**conscience** [kάː)nʃəns]	良心 ▶a matter of conscience（良心の問題）
1630	**dictum** [díktəm]	格言 [= maxim, adage, saying]
1631	**fervor** [fə́ːrvər]	熱意 [= passion] ▶with fervor（熱心に）
1632	**freight** [freɪt]	輸送 [= transportation]
1633	**mortgage** [mɔ́ːrɡɪdʒ]	住宅ローン，抵当 [= pledge, security]
1634	**inscription** [ɪnskrípʃən]	碑文，刻まれたもの 動 inscribe（(名前)を記入する）
1635	**latitude** [lǽtətjùːd]	緯度 (⇔ longitude 経度)
1636	**propriety** [prəpráɪəti]	礼儀正しいこと [= decorum], 妥当 [= suitability] 形 proper
1637	**rapport** [ræpɔ́ːr]	（調和した）関係 [= agreement, harmony] ▶develop a close rapport with *one* （〜と親密な関係を築く）
1638	**hypothesis** [haɪpάː)θəsɪs]	仮説 [= theory]

The leader said legislators should vote according to their **consciences**.	指導者は国会議員は**良心**に従って投票するべきだと述べた。
Socrates, like Confucius, is famous for his pithy **dictums**.	ソクラテスは孔子と同じように含蓄のある**格言**でよく知られている。
His initial **fervor** for studying philosophy began to wear off.	彼が哲学を勉強し始めた頃の最初の**熱意**は消え始めた。
Although the goods were cheap, the cost of the **freight** was too high.	商品は安かったが、**輸送**費が高すぎた。
The young couple managed to buy a house by accepting a 30-year **mortgage**.	若い夫婦は30年返済の**住宅ローン**を組んで、なんとか家を購入することができた。
The scholar was attempting to decipher the **inscription** on the tomb.	その学者は墓石に刻まれた**碑文**を判読しようと試みていた。
The animals could only survive above a certain **latitude**.	ある**緯度**を超えた地域でしか動物は生存できない。
Rules of **propriety** have changed a great deal over the past century.	**礼儀**の規範が過去1世紀で大きく変化した。
We hoped that our meeting would help us develop a trusting and fruitful **rapport**.	我々は会議が、信頼でき実りある**関係**を生む助けとなるよう願った。
For years, the man's theory remained nothing more than a **hypothesis**.	長年、その男性の学説は**仮説**でしかなかった。

1639	**icon** [áıkɑ(:)n]	崇拝の対象 [= idol], 図形, 記号
1640	**dispensation** [dìspənséıʃən]	配給 [= distribution], 施し 動 dispense (を分配する)
1641	**deferment** [dɪfə́ːrmənt]	延期 [= postponement] 動 defer
1642	**overture** [óʊvərtʃùər]	提案 [= proposal, offer], 序章, 序曲 [= introduction]
1643	**patriot** [péıtriət]	愛国者 形 patriotic *cf.* compatriot (同胞)
1644	**pollination** [pà(:)lənéıʃən]	授粉 動 pollinate ▶artificial pollination (人工授精)
1645	**alliance** [əláıəns]	同盟 [= association] 動 ally
1646	**consortium** [kənsɔ́ːrtiəm]	協会 [= association], 共同事業体 ▶industrial consortium (産業共同体)
1647	**delegation** [dèlıgéıʃən]	代表団, 委任 動 delegate
1648	**coalition** [kòʊəlíʃən]	連合, 合同, 連立 [= alliance, partnership, league] 語源 coali (合体する) + tion

His opposition to nuclear power made him an **icon** for environmentalists.	彼は原子力反対の姿勢をとったので、環境保護論者の間で崇拝の対象となった。
People queued up to receive their weekly **dispensation** of rations.	人々は、1週間の食料の配給を受け取るために列を作った。
During the Vietnam War, young men got a draft **deferment** for attending college.	ベトナム戦争中、若者たちは大学在学中を理由に、徴兵猶予を得ていた。
After their argument, he ignored all of his former friend's **overtures**.	いさかいの後、彼は旧友からの提案をすべて無視した。
John Paul Jones was a famous American **patriot** in the Revolutionary War.	ジョン・ポール・ジョーンズは、独立戦争時の有名なアメリカの愛国者だった。
Bees play an important role in the **pollination** of many fruit trees.	ミツバチは多くの果樹の授粉に重要な働きをする。
The countries formed a temporary **alliance** against their threatening neighbor.	諸国は脅威を与えてくる隣国に対して、一時的な同盟を結んだ。
I once worked for the Midwest University **Consortium** of International Affairs.	私はかつて、ミッドウェスト大学の国際情勢協会で働いていた。
The President sent a large **delegation** to represent his nation at the conference.	大統領は会議で国の代表を務める大勢の代表団を派遣した。
The prime minister was forced to call for new elections when his ruling **coalition** collapsed.	与党連合が崩壊した時、首相は新たな選挙を求めざるを得なかった。

#	見出し	意味
1649	**fraternity** [frətə́ːrnəṭi]	友愛会, 同業者仲間 [= association] 語源 fratern (兄弟愛) + ity
1650	**charade** [ʃəréɪd]	見え透いたごまかし [= false display] ▶political charade (政治的茶番)
1651	**charlatan** [ʃɑ́ːrlətən]	ぺてん師 [= quack], 大ほら吹き
1652	**catastrophe** [kətǽstrəfi]	大災害 [= calamity, great disaster], 破局 形 catastrophic
1653	**calamity** [kəlǽməṭi]	災難 [= disaster, cataclysm], 不運 [= misery, mishap, adversity]
1654	**expulsion** [ɪkspʌ́lʃən]	追放, 除名 動 expel 形 expulsive
1655	**extermination** [ɪkstə̀ːrmɪnéɪʃən]	駆除, 根絶 [= eradication] 動 exterminate
1656	**annihilation** [ənàɪəléɪʃən]	絶滅 [= obliteration, eradication, extermination, wiping out] 動 annihilate (を完全に破壊する)
1657	**outcry** [áʊtkràɪ]	激しい抗議, 叫び声 [= shout]
1658	**outrage** [áʊtrèɪdʒ]	激怒 [= fury, indignation] 形 outrageous

At university, the poet joined a **fraternity** that studied magic.	大学で，その詩人は手品を学ぶ友愛会に入った。
He denounced the investigation as a **charade** aimed at appeasing the public.	彼は，その調査が民衆をなだめるための見え透いたごまかしにすぎないと非難した。
The prince was revealed to be a **charlatan** unrelated to royalty.	その王子は王室には関係ないぺてん師であることが判明した。
The fire was a terrible **catastrophe** for the victims' families.	その火事は犠牲者の家族にとって大災害だった。
The typhoon was a major **calamity** to businesses in the area.	台風はその地域の企業にとって大きな災難だった。
His activities as a spy resulted in his **expulsion** from the country.	スパイとしての彼の活動は，祖国からの追放という結果となった。
They brought in specialists for the **extermination** of the rats that had infested the house.	彼らは，その家にはびこるネズミの駆除のために，専門家に来てもらった。
The world is threatened with **annihilation** from nuclear weapons.	世界は核兵器による絶滅の危険にさらされている。
A public **outcry** against the decision was soon raised.	その決定に反対する一般市民の激しい抗議がすぐに持ち上がった。
She could not suppress her **outrage** at the court's decision.	彼女は法廷の決定に対して怒りを抑えることができなかった。

1659 legislature
[lédʒəslèɪtʃər]

議会, 立法府

1660 juror
[dʒúərər]

陪審員
图 jury (陪審)

1661 jurisdiction
[dʒùərɪsdíkʃən]

管轄権, 支配(権) [= range of authority], 裁判権

1662 accusation
[ækjuzéɪʃən]

告訴 [= charge]
▶make an accusation of A against B
(AでBを告訴する)

1663 indictment
[ɪndáɪtmənt]

起訴
[= charge]
▶drop an indictment (起訴を取り下げる)

1664 litigation
[lìṭɪgéɪʃən]

訴訟
[= lawsuit]

1665 impeachment
[ɪmpíːtʃmənt]

弾劾, 告発
[= accusation, charge]
動 impeach

1666 legitimacy
[lɪdʒíṭəməsi]

正当性, 合法性
形 legitimate

1667 affidavit
[æfɪdéɪvɪt]

供述書,
宣誓供述書 [= written declaration upon oath]

1668 plaintiff
[pléɪnṭəf]

原告
(⇔ defendant 被告)

Opinion polls showed that the **legislature** was increasingly unpopular.	世論調査は議会がますます人気がなくなりつつあることを示した。
He had once served as a **juror** in a complicated murder trial.	彼はかつて，複雑な殺人事件の裁判で陪審員を務めたことがある。
The police could not make an arrest because they lacked legal **jurisdiction** in the area.	警察はその地域での法律上の管轄権を持たなかったため逮捕できなかった。
The **accusations** were dismissed because of a lack of evidence.	告訴は証拠不足のために却下された。
The articles led to the detective's **indictment** for corruption.	その記事が原因で，その刑事は汚職のかどで起訴された。
The company concluded that **litigation** was the only course available.	その会社は訴訟が唯一の有効な手段だという結論に達した。
When threatened with **impeachment**, Richard Nixon resigned from the American presidency.	弾劾される恐れが生じ，リチャード・ニクソンはアメリカ大統領職を辞任した。
Questions were raised concerning the **legitimacy** of the decision to attack.	攻撃決定への正当性に関して疑問の声が上がった。
The lawyer took my **affidavit** to use in court rather than insist that I appear in person.	弁護士は，私が自ら出頭することを主張せず，法廷で使うために私の供述を取った。
The **plaintiff** insisted that he had been the victim of a frame-up.	原告は偽証の被害者であると主張した。

#	語	意味
1669	**perpetrator** [pə́ːrpətrèɪtər]	加害者，犯罪者 [= criminal] 動 perpetrate（を犯す）
1670	**accomplice** [əká(ː)mpləs]	共犯者 [= partner in crime]
1671	**complicity** [kəmplísəti]	共犯 [= partnership in crime] ▶ complicity with terrorists（テロリストとの共犯関係）
1672	**plea** [pliː]	嘆願 [= appeal]，弁解 ▶ a plea for blood-donors（献血者を求める嘆願）
1673	**condemnation** [kà(ː)ndemnéɪʃən]	激しい非難 [= censure]，有罪宣告 [= conviction] 動 condemn
1674	**deliberation** [dɪlìbəréɪʃən]	審理 [= inquisition]，熟考 [= consideration]，慎重 動形 deliberate
1675	**acquittal** [əkwítəl]	無罪放免，（義務などの）免除 [= absolution]
1676	**bail** [beɪl]	保釈金 [= bailment, bond]，保釈 [= temporary release]
1677	**detention** [dɪténʃən]	拘置 [= confinement] 動 detain ▶ be kept in detention（拘留される）
1678	**infraction** [ɪnfrǽkʃən]	違反 [= breach] ▶ infraction of the rules（規則違反）

The <u>perpetrator</u> of the crime was betrayed by an informer.	その犯罪の<u>加害者</u>は密告者に裏切られた。
The detective said the criminal must have had an <u>accomplice</u> in the bank.	犯人は銀行に<u>共犯者</u>がいたに違いないとその刑事は言った。
Many of President Nixon's cabinet members were charged with <u>complicity</u> in the Watergate cover-up.	ニクソン政権の閣僚の多くが，ウォーターゲート事件隠蔽の<u>共犯</u>として起訴された。
The priest made a <u>plea</u> for both sides to stop fighting.	僧侶は争いをやめるよう双方に<u>嘆願</u>した。
The U.N. called for immediate <u>condemnation</u> of that nation's latest actions.	国連は，その国の最近の行動に対して，早急な<u>非難決議</u>を要請した。
The judge promised to take all the facts into account during his <u>deliberation</u>.	判事は，<u>審理</u>中にすべての事実を考慮に入れることを約束した。
New evidence led to the <u>acquittal</u> of all the defendants.	新しい証拠によってすべての被告は<u>無罪放免</u>となった。
The judge set <u>bail</u> at $30,000 for the robbery suspect.	判事は強盗の容疑者に3万ドルの<u>保釈金</u>を科した。
The judge ordered the boy to spend a week in a center for juvenile <u>detention</u>.	判事はその少年に少年<u>拘置</u>所で1週間過ごすよう命じた。
The acceptance of the gift was considered an <u>infraction</u> of the rules.	贈り物を受け取ったことはルール<u>違反</u>だと見なされた。

1679

fraud
[frɔːd]

詐欺
[= swindling]
▶ real-estate fraud（不動産詐欺）

1680

espionage
[éspiənàːʒ]

スパイ活動
[= practice of spying]
▶ industrial espionage（産業スパイ活動）

1681

larceny
[láːrsəni]

窃盗罪
[= theft]
形 larcenous

1682

perjury
[pə́ːrdʒəri]

偽証（罪）
[= giving false evidence]
▶ commit perjury（偽証罪を犯す）

1683

felony
[féləni]

重罪
名 felon（重罪犯人）　形 felonious
cf. misdemeanor（軽罪）

1684

commutation
[kà(ː)mjutéɪʃən]

減刑,
回数乗車券
動 commute

1685

impunity
[ɪmpjúːnəti]

刑罰［損害］を免れること
▶ with impunity（罰せられずに）

1686

indemnity
[ɪndémnəti]

賠償（金）
[= compensation]
語源 in（否定）+ demn（損失）+ ity

1687

aberration
[æbəréɪʃən]

常軌逸脱
[= anomaly]
形 aberrant（異常な）

1688

onus
[óunəs]

責任
[= responsibility]

The insurance scheme turned out to be a complex tax **fraud**.	この保険の企画は複雑な税金詐欺だということが判明した。
After twenty years of undercover **espionage**, he was finally discovered.	彼の潜入スパイ活動は、20年経過してようやく発覚した。
Eventually, the thief was found guilty of **larceny** and imprisoned.	結局, 泥棒は窃盗罪で有罪判決を受け, 刑務所に入れられた。
The witness who had lied was charged with **perjury** by the police.	嘘をついたその証人は偽証罪で警察に起訴された。
Anyone convicted of a **felony** in the United States may lose some of his rights as a citizen.	合衆国で重罪で有罪となった者は誰でも, 市民としての権利のいくつかを失う可能性がある。
The judge ordered the **commutation** of the man's death sentence to life imprisonment.	裁判官はその男性の死刑判決を終身刑へと減刑を命じた。
The man was so powerful that he could do virtually anything with **impunity**.	その男は強い権力を持ち, 事実上何をしても不問に付されることがあった。
The **indemnity** paid to the country was used to establish a university.	その国に支払われた賠償金は大学を設立するのに使われた。
The defendant said his behavior had been a temporary **aberration**.	被告は自分の行為を一時的な奇行だったと言った。
The lawyer said the **onus** to prove guilt lay with the prosecution.	弁護士は, 有罪を証明する責任は検察側にあると言った。

1689 amendment
[əméndmənt]

修正, 改正 [= revision]
動 amend
▶amendment bill (修正案)

1690 abstention
[əbsténʃən]

棄権 [= refusal to vote], 自制
▶abstention from drink (禁酒)

1691 annulment
[ənʌ́lmənt]

無効 [= invalidation, nullification]
動 annul

1692 suffrage
[sʌ́frɪdʒ]

参政権 [= franchise], 選挙権
▶universal suffrage (普通選挙権)

1693 constituency
[kənstítʃuənsi]

選挙区, 有権者

1694 ailment
[éɪlmənt]

病気 [= disease],
不快 [= indisposition]

1695 malady
[mǽlədi]

病気 [= disease, illness], 深刻な問題
語源 malad (病気の) + y

1696 migraine
[máɪgreɪn]

偏頭痛

1697 inflammation
[ɪnfləméɪʃən]

炎症, 赤くはれること
[= swelling]
形 inflammatory

1698 anatomy
[ənǽtəmi]

(動植物の) 構造, 解剖 (学),
(詳細な) 調査分析

I agreed to support their proposal if they would make minor **amendments**.	もし彼らが少し修正を加えていれば、私は彼らの提案を支持することに同意した。
In the vote on the appointment, there were three **abstentions**.	指名投票で棄権が3票あった。
The candidate requested the **annulment** of the election result.	その候補者は選挙結果の無効を申し入れた。
The playwright had been a strong supporter of women's **suffrage**.	その劇作家は女性参政権の強力な支持者だった。
The prime minister continued to be popular in his own **constituency**.	首相は彼自身の選挙区では依然として人気があった。
His mysterious **ailment** keeps him from working on a regular basis.	不可解な病気のため、彼は常勤の仕事ができないでいる。
She suffered from a mysterious **malady** that made her feel tired all the time.	彼女は、疲労感が常時続く原因不明の病気を患っていた。
Her severe **migraines** made it difficult for her to work properly.	彼女はひどい偏頭痛のためにきちんと働けなかった。
The tear gas caused severe **inflammation** of the eyes.	催涙ガスによって目にひどい炎症が起きた。
The fossil of the tail allowed the scientists to reconstruct the **anatomy** of the dinosaur.	その尾骨の化石のおかげで、科学者たちが恐竜の骨格構造を復元することが可能になった。

anatomy (1698) のtomは (切る) を意味します。ほかの例としてatomがあります。atomはa (否定) +tom (切る) なので「切ることができないもの」、つまり「原子」です。

1699	**anesthetic** [ænəsθétɪk]	麻酔剤, 麻酔薬 [= anesthesia] 形 anesthetic（無感覚の） ▶local anesthetic（局所麻酔）
1700	**panacea** [pæ̀nəsíːə]	万能薬 [= cure-all]
1701	**autism** [ɔ́ːtɪzm]	自閉症
1702	**neurologist** [njuərá(ː)lədʒɪst]	神経科医 形 neurological
1703	**orthodontist** [ɔ̀ːrθədá(ː)ntɪst]	歯列矯正医 cf. orthopedist（整形外科医）
1704	**embryo** [émbriòu]	胎児, 胚, (発達の)初期 cf. fetus（胎児） ▶in embryo（初期の段階で）
1705	**pinnacle** [pínəkl]	頂点 [= peak] ▶at the pinnacle of one's fame（名声を極めて）
1706	**pitfall** [pítfɔ̀ːl]	落とし穴, 思いがけぬ危険 [= peril]
1707	**pivot** [pívət]	中心軸 [= focal point]
1708	**precursor** [prɪkə́ːrsər]	先駆者 [= forerunner, harbinger], 前兆

He was given a complete **anesthetic** before the operation on his stomach.	彼は胃の手術を受ける前に，全身麻酔を打たれた。
Although the new treatment seemed very promising, doctors warned that it was not a **panacea**.	新治療法は極めて有望に思えたが，医者は万能薬ではないと注意した。
Experts are still divided as to the causes of **autism**.	専門家たちの自閉症の原因に関する見解は，いまだに分かれている。
Her doctor advised her to visit a **neurologist** as soon as possible.	主治医は彼女に，神経科医にできるだけ早く診てもらうよう助言した。
The little girl had her irregular teeth fixed by an **orthodontist**.	その小さな女の子は，歯並びの悪い歯を歯列矯正医に治してもらった。
Pro-abortionists make a distinction between a human **embryo** and human life.	人工妊娠中絶医は人間の胎児と人間の生命とを分けて考えている。
Then, at the **pinnacle** of his career, an injury forced the footballer to retire.	するとそのフットボール選手は，キャリアの絶頂期にけがのために引退せざるを得なくなった。
He fell into the common **pitfall** of becoming overconfident about his abilities.	彼は自分の能力について自信過剰になるという，ありがちな落とし穴にはまった。
The local church was the **pivot** of the community's social life.	地元の教会は地域社会の生活の中心軸の役割を果たしていた。
The ancient Greeks were **precursors** of modern science.	古代ギリシャ人は近代科学の先駆者であった。

#	英語	日本語
1709	**predator** [prédətər]	捕食動物, 略奪者
1710	**premonition** [prèmənίʃən]	(悪い)前兆 [= foreboding, presentiment, previous warning], 予告 [= forewarning]
1711	**prevalence** [prévələns]	普及 [= widespread presence]
1712	**precipitation** [prɪsìpɪtéɪʃən]	降水量, 落下 [= fall], 大慌て 動 precipitate 形 precipitous (絶壁の, 険しい)
1713	**preclusion** [prɪklú:ʒən]	排除
1714	**predilection** [prèdəlékʃən]	(〜への)特別な好み, (〜に対する)偏愛 [= preference, partiality] 〈for〉
1715	**prevarication** [prɪvæ̀rɪkéɪʃən]	言い逃れ [= evasion, parry] 動 prevaricate
1716	**posterity** [pɑ(:)stérəti]	後代, 子孫 [= descendants] (⇔ ancestry)
1717	**progeny** [prά(:)dʒəni]	子どもたち [= children], 子孫 [= descendant, offspring]
1718	**rebuttal** [rɪbʌ́t̬əl]	はん ばく 反駁 [= refutation] 動 rebut

The introduced species had few natural **predators** and spread rapidly.	外来種は天敵がほとんどいないため，急速に分布した。
There are now many dire **premonitions** about the end of the world.	世界の終末について，今や多くの不吉な前兆が存在する。
The **prevalence** of computers has both merits and demerits.	コンピューターの普及には長所と短所の両方がある。
Since **precipitation** is expected to be below normal this year, farmers fear a poor harvest.	今年は降水量が例年より少ないと予測されているので，農業者は不作を心配している。
The aim of the system was the **preclusion** of strangers from the campus.	この制度の目的は構内から部外者を排除することである。
I was unaware of his strong **predilection** for sweet cakes and hot tea.	私は彼が甘いケーキと熱いお茶が極めて好きだということには気付いていなかった。
After some **prevarication**, the clerk finally admitted losing the application.	いくつか言い逃れをした後で，その事務員はとうとう申込書を紛失したことを認めた。
The filmmaker decided to make a record of the event for **posterity**.	映画製作会社は後世のためにその大事件の記録を作ることを決定した。
Every man wants to do his best to protect and help his **progeny** succeed in life.	誰でも自分の子どもたちを守り，彼らが人生で成功する助けとなるよう最善を尽くしたいと思っている。
The prosecution's clever argument was countered by an even more convincing **rebuttal**.	検察側の巧みな論証に対して，さらに説得力のある反駁がなされた。

1719	**renunciation** [rɪnʌ́nsiéɪʃən]	放棄 [= relinquishment]
1720	**projection** [prədʒékʃən]	予測 [= forecast] ▶conservative projection（控え目な見積り）
1721	**prophecy** [prá(:)fəsi]	予言 動 prophesy 名 prophet（予言者） 形 prophetic
1722	**propagation** [prà(:)pəgéɪʃən]	普及 [= dissemination]
1723	**protagonist** [proʊtǽgənɪst]	主人公 [= central character]（⇔antagonist）
1724	**protrusion** [prətrúːʒən]	突出 [= bump] 動 protrude
1725	**reconciliation** [rèkənsɪliéɪʃən]	和解 [= restoration of harmony] 動 reconcile
1726	**referendum** [rèfəréndəm]	国民投票 [= plebiscite] ▶by referendum（国民投票で）
1727	**reparation** [rèpəréɪʃən]	償い [= amends]
1728	**restoration** [rèstəréɪʃən]	復旧，復興，修復 動 restore ▶restoration cost（復旧費）

Following his **renunciation** of the throne, the former king led a quiet life.	王座を放棄した後，前国王は静かな生活を送った。
The **projection** of future profits turned out to be too optimistic.	将来の利益の予測はあまりに楽観的なものとなった。
At the time, his **prophecy** of ecological catastrophe was ignored.	当時，生態系破壊が起こるという彼の予言は無視されていた。
He devoted himself to the **propagation** of his pacifist beliefs.	彼は平和思想の普及に専念した。
The **protagonist** of the play was seen as the author's self-portrait.	その劇の主人公は著者自身を描いたものと見なされた。
There was a large rocky **protrusion** on the side of the hill.	山腹には大きな岩の突起があった。
The couple finally agreed to a **reconciliation** after a long separation.	夫婦は長い間別居していたが，ようやく和解にこぎつけた。
A local **referendum** in California approved the use of marijuana for medicinal purposes.	カリフォルニアの住民投票は医薬用にマリファナを使用することを認めた。
As a **reparation** for being late, he offered to pay for the meal.	遅刻したことに対する償いとして，彼は食事代を支払うことを申し出た。
The **restoration** of the fire-damaged palace took over five years.	火事で損傷した宮殿の復旧には5年以上を要した。

1729 **resurgence** [rɪsə́ːrdʒəns]	回復 [= revival, comeback] 語源 re(再び) + surge(盛り上げる) + ence
1730 **resurrection** [rèzərékʃən]	復活 [= revival] 動 resurrect
1731 **turmoil** [tə́ːrmɔɪl]	騒ぎ [= tumult, disturbance, confusion, commotion]
1732 **treason** [tríːzən]	反逆 [= treachery] ▶ high treason (大逆罪)
1733 **retaliation** [rɪtæ̀liéɪʃən]	報復 [= revenge] 動 retaliate
1734 **plot** [plɑ(ː)t]	陰謀 [= conspiracy], 構想 [= scheme], 平面図
1735 **conscription** [kənskrípʃən]	徴兵 [= draft] 動 conscript
1736 **infighting** [ínfaɪtɪŋ]	内輪もめ [= interparty feud], 内紛
1737 **insurrection** [ìnsərékʃən]	暴動, 反乱 [= uprising] *cf.* insurgent (暴動の)
1738 **neutrality** [njuːtrǽləti]	中立性

The threat of war led to a **resurgence** of support for the President.	戦争の脅威が大統領支持の回復につながった。
Jesus' **resurrection** is a central tenet of orthodox Christian belief.	キリストの復活はキリスト教の正統的信仰における中心的教義である。
At the end of every term, the university always seems in great **turmoil**.	毎学期の終わりには、いつも大学は大騒ぎになるようだ。
After a secret trial, the military spy was executed for **treason**.	非公開裁判の後、軍事スパイは反逆罪で処刑された。
They guessed that the attack was a **retaliation** for their earlier raid.	彼らはその攻撃は先の襲撃に対する報復だと推測した。
Army leaders were involved in a **plot** to depose the country's President.	軍の指導者たちは、国の大統領を退陣させる陰謀に関与していた。
Conscription in the United States ended after the Vietnam War.	アメリカ合衆国の徴兵制度はベトナム戦争後に終わった。
The principal's problems were made worse by **infighting** among his staff.	校長の問題はスタッフ間の内輪もめで悪化した。
Troops were sent in to crush the **insurrection** in the province.	軍隊がその州の暴動を鎮圧するために送り込まれた。
Many people doubted the **neutrality** of the investigation.	多くの人々はその調査の中立性を疑った。

でる度B p.230に出てきたsurplus「黒字」のsurは（上がる）を意味します。
resurrection (1730)は再び「上がる」と考えればイメージしやすいでしょう。

#	見出し	意味
1739	**onrush** [á(:)nrʌʃ]	突撃, 突進
1740	**persecution** [pə̀ːrsɪkjúːʃn]	迫害 [= oppression]
1741	**bunker** [bʌ́ŋkər]	掩蔽壕（えんぺいごう）
1742	**debacle** [deɪbáːkl]	大失敗, 崩壊 [= collapse], 総崩れ [= downfall]
1743	**defector** [dɪféktər]	離反者 [= deserter], 脱党者
1744	**disarmament** [dɪsáːrməmənt]	軍縮 [= arms control], 武装解除 ▶nuclear disarmament（核軍縮）
1745	**mishap** [míshæp]	不幸な出来事 [= adversity, misfortune, calamity], 災害 ▶without mishap（無事に）
1746	**fatality** [feɪtǽləti]	不慮の死者, 死を招く災害 形 fatal（致命的な）
1747	**toll** [toʊl]	死傷者数 [= casualties], 通行料
1748	**rebellion** [rɪbéljən]	反乱 [= uprising] ▶rise in rebellion（暴動を起す）

The sudden **onrush** of the enemy took them by surprise.	敵の突然の突撃は彼らをとても驚かせた。
The spokesman denied that any **persecution** of dissidents had taken place.	スポークスマンは反体制派に対するいかなる迫害も否定した。
The prime minister directed operations from a secret **bunker**.	首相は秘密の掩蔽壕より軍事作戦を指揮した。
The attempt to rescue hostages in Iran turned into a **debacle**.	イランでの人質救出作戦は大失敗に終わった。
With time, the number of **defectors** from the regime increased.	時間がたつにつれて、政権からの離反者が増加した。
The scientists were powerful advocates of nuclear **disarmament**.	その科学者たちは核軍縮の有力な提唱者だった。
The factory should have taken proper measures to prevent such **mishaps**.	工場はそのような不幸な出来事を防ぐために適切な対策をとるべきだった。
The explosion caused a number of **fatalities** as well as widespread damage.	その爆発により、広範囲の被害とともに多数の死者が出た。
The death **toll** from the railway accident continued to climb.	鉄道事故での死者の人数は増え続けた。
After the defeat, a series of **rebellions** broke out around the country.	敗北後、国中で相次いで反乱が勃発した。

1749
schism
[skízm]

分裂

1750
maneuver
[mənú:vər]

策略
[= scheme, stratagem, artifice]
▶carry out large maneuvers（大演習を行う）

1751
massacre
[mǽsəkər]

大虐殺
[= slaughter]

1752
rapprochement
[ræprouʃmá:n]

(特に国家間の)和解, 国交樹立
[= establishing of friendly relations]

1753
surveillance
[sərvéiləns]

監視, 見張り
[= observation, scrutiny, guard]

1754
furlough
[fə́:rlou]

(軍人の)休暇
[= leave]

1755
inmate
[ínmèit]

(病院・老人ホーム・刑務所などの)収容者
[= person confined in a prison or institution]

1756
debris
[dəbrí:]

(破壊されたものの)瓦礫, 残骸, がらくた

1757
derelict
[dérəlìkt]

遺棄物 [= abandoned property], 社会的な落伍者 [= person rejected by society]

1758
fortification
[fɔ̀:rtəfikéiʃən]

要塞
[= rampart]

The dispute led to a **schism** in the opposition camp.	その論争が野党陣営の分裂へとつながった。
The company's clever **maneuver** in the market solidified its monopoly.	市場における会社の巧みな策略で独占が強化された。
Who carried out the **massacre** of the villagers remains a matter of dispute.	誰が村人の大虐殺を実行したかは，依然として論争の的である。
The recent **rapprochement** between India and the United States augurs well for peace in the region.	印米間の最近の和解は，地域の平和に向けての良い兆候である。
He did not know why, but he felt sure he was under police **surveillance**.	なぜかわからなかったが，彼は確かに警察の監視下にあることを感じていた。
The sailors were all headed home after getting a two-week **furlough**.	水兵たちは皆，2週間の休暇を得て故郷に向かった。
Inmates in a local prison rioted and took several guards hostage.	地元刑務所の囚人が暴動を起こし，数人の看守を人質に取った。
He spent the morning clearing up the **debris** left by the storm.	彼は午前中，嵐によって残された瓦礫を片付けて過ごした。
The city council voted to destroy an old **derelict** still afloat in the harbor.	市議会は，港に依然として漂う古い遺棄船を破壊することを決議した。
Remains of Roman **fortifications** were discovered near the town.	古代ローマの要塞の遺跡が町の近くで見つかった。

1759 ~ 1768

1759
fortress
[fɔ́ːrtrəs]

要塞
[= stronghold]

1760
fortitude
[fɔ́ːrtətjùːd]

不屈の精神, 忍耐 [= patience]

1761
inertia
[ɪnə́ːrʃə]

惰性, 不活発 [= inactivity]
形 inert
▶through inertia（惰性で）

1762
inhibition
[ìnhɪbíʃən]

抑制する気持ち
動 inhibit（を抑制する）

1763
atheist
[éɪθiɪst]

無神論者
語源 a（ない）+ the（神）+ ist

1764
heretic
[hérətɪk]

異端者

1765
benediction
[bènɪdíkʃən]

祝福 [= blessing],
神の恵み
語源 bene（良い）+ dict（言う）+ ion

1766
benefactor
[bénɪfæktər]

慈善 [恩恵] を施す人

1767
blasphemy
[blǽsfəmi]

（神への）冒涜 [= profanity],
不敬 [= irreverence, swearing, cursing]

1768
conversion
[kənvə́ːrʒən]

（～への）改宗 [= proselytizing],
（～への）転換〈to〉
動 convert

The <u>fortress</u> of a local warlord is rumored to be somewhere in the mountains.	地元の将軍の<u>要塞</u>は，山の中のどこかにあるとうわさされている。
Becoming a Zen monk often requires a great deal of zeal and <u>fortitude</u>.	禅僧になるには，しばしば大いなる情熱と<u>不屈の精神</u>が必要である。
Before we can make significant changes in society, we must overcome the <u>inertia</u> of the past.	社会に意義のある変化をもたらす前に，我々は過去の<u>惰性</u>を克服する必要がある。
After she left home, she threw off her <u>inhibitions</u> and enjoyed herself.	家を出てから，彼女は<u>抑制する気持ち</u>を振り捨てて楽しんだ。
He lost his religious faith and remained a confirmed <u>atheist</u> for the rest of his life.	彼は信仰を失い，残りの人生は確固たる<u>無神論者</u>で通した。
Eventually, the <u>heretics</u> were expelled, and they started their own church.	結局<u>異端者</u>は排斥され，彼らは自分たち自身の教会を作った。
The Pope himself offered <u>benedictions</u> at the groundbreaking for the new church.	新しい教会の起工式で，法王自身が<u>祝福</u>を与えた。
An anonymous <u>benefactor</u> had donated a large sum to the orphanage.	匿名の<u>慈善家</u>が多額の金を児童養護施設に寄付した。
During the inquisition in Europe, <u>blasphemy</u> was punishable by death.	ヨーロッパにおける異端審問では，<u>神への冒涜</u>は死刑に値した。
His <u>conversion</u> to Islam shocked many of his Christian friends.	彼のイスラム教への<u>改宗</u>は，キリスト教徒の多くの友人に衝撃を与えた。

inhibition (1762)のhibitは（持つ・保つ）を意味します。in（中に）と反対の接頭辞ex（外に）がついた，exhibit「を表す，を展示する」とセットで覚えましょう。

1769 consecration
[kà(:)nsəkréɪʃən]

聖職叙任(式)、神聖化 [= hallowing] (⇔desecration)
動 consecrate

1770 denomination
[dɪnà(:)mɪnéɪʃən]

名称 [= name]、
宗派 [= sect]、
(貨幣の)単位名称

1771 sanctuary
[sǽŋktʃuèri]

聖域 [= holy or sacred place]、
避難所 [= place of refuge]

1772 incarnation
[ìnkɑːrnéɪʃən]

肉体を持つこと
動形 incarnate

1773 discontent
[dìskəntént]

不満 [= dissatisfaction]

1774 dissonance
[dísənəns]

不調和 [= discord]、
不調和な音
形 dissonant

1775 divulgence
[dəvʌ́ldʒəns]

暴露 [= disclosure]
動 divulge

1776 destitution
[dèstɪtjúːʃən]

極貧(状態) [= abject poverty, indigence]
形 destitute

1777 demolition
[dèməlíʃən]

取り壊し、解体 [= destruction] (⇔construction)

1778 depletion
[dɪplíːʃən]

枯渇 [= exhaustion]、減少
動 deplete (を使い果たす)
▶ ozone depletion (オゾン減少)

The **consecration** of the new bishop was attended by many important dignitaries.	新司教の<u>聖職叙任式</u>には高位聖職者が多数出席した。
Although holding no political post, Christ was given the **denomination** of 'king.'	政治的地位はなかったが、キリストは「王」の<u>称号</u>を与えられた。
Tourists were strictly forbidden from entering the religious **sanctuary**.	観光客は、その宗教上の<u>聖域</u>に入ることを厳禁された。
The people believed that the boy was an **incarnation** of their god.	人々は、その少年が神の<u>受肉(肉体化)</u>だったと信じていた。
There was growing **discontent** with the cost-cutting policies.	コスト削減策に対する<u>不満</u>が高まっていた。
The growing **dissonance** between the two groups made cooperation difficult.	二派間の<u>不調和</u>が高じて、協力が難しくなった。
The **divulgence** of the secret agreement was a blow to the minister.	秘密協定の<u>暴露</u>は大臣にとって痛手だった。
The U.N. delegation was appalled at the **destitution** they saw in the war-torn country.	国連の代表団は戦禍を被った国の<u>窮乏</u>ぶりを見てがく然とした。
Many people protested against the **demolition** of the old courthouse.	多くの人が古い裁判所の<u>取り壊し</u>に抗議した。
Everyone is concerned about the rapid **depletion** of fossil fuels.	化石燃料の急速な<u>枯渇</u>をみんなが不安に思っている。

1779	**detriment** [détrɪmənt]	害になるもの，損失 [= loss, damage, harm] 形 detrimental (有害な) ▶to the detriment of ~ (~を犠牲にして)
1780	**deviation** [dìːviéɪʃən]	(~からの)逸脱 [= digression] 〈from〉，偏差 動形 deviate
1781	**solidarity** [sὰ(ː)lədǽrəṭi]	団結 [= unity] ▶solidarity among club members (クラブ員の団結)
1782	**sovereignty** [sá(ː)vrənti]	主権，統治権 [= supremacy]，独立国 形 sovereign ▶sovereignty dispute (主権論争)
1783	**conformist** [kənfɔ́ːrmɪst]	体制に従う人たち [= conventionalist] 動 conform (順応する)
1784	**deputy** [dépjuṭi]	代理(人) [= substitute, delegate]，副官 名 deputation (代表団) ▶a deputy chairman (副会長)
1785	**envoy** [énvɔɪ]	使者，外交官 [= diplomat]
1786	**monarch** [má(ː)nərk]	世襲的君主 [= king, queen]，独裁主権者 [= sole ruler] 名 monarchy (君主制)
1787	**laureate** [lɔ́(ː)riət]	受賞者 ▶Nobel laureate (ノーベル賞受賞者)
1788	**cortex** [kɔ́ːrteks]	(大脳)皮質

We viewed the Secretary of State's actions as a major **detriment** to world peace.	我々は国務長官の活動を世界平和にとって大きな害になるものと見なした。
The president of the university would tolerate no **deviation** from his regulations.	その大学の学長は、自分が作成した規則からの逸脱を一切許そうとしなかった。
In times of national crisis, the leaders often call for **solidarity**.	国家が危機の際は、指導者はよく団結を呼びかける。
America has fought several wars to protect its **sovereignty**.	アメリカは、自国の主権を守るため、いくつかの戦争をしてきた。
Most of the employees were **conformists**, unwilling to stand out.	従業員の大半は目立つのを嫌がる順応的な人たちだった。
The prime minister's **deputy** took control of the government in the crisis of power.	総理大臣の代理が、政権危機の際に政府を指揮した。
Neighboring countries were invited to send **envoys** to the talks.	近隣諸国は会談に使者を送るよう要請を受けた。
A **monarch** usually gains his or her power by virtue of his or her lineage.	君主は、たいてい家系のおかげで権力を得ている。
The **laureates** all arrived in Stockholm for the Nobel awards' ceremony.	受賞者がみんな、ノーベル賞授賞式に出席するため、ストックホルムに到着した。
He had suffered severe damage to the **cortex** of the brain.	彼は大脳皮質に深刻な損傷を受けた。

1789

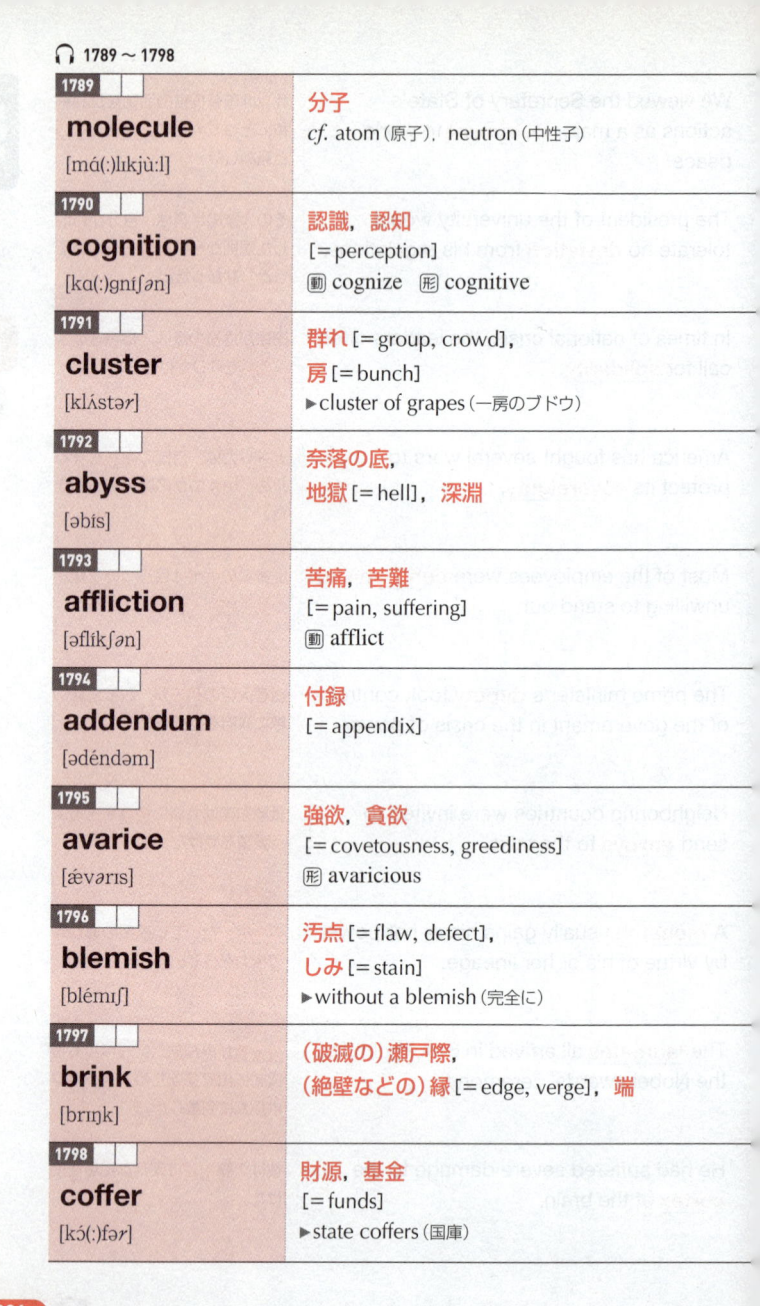

molecule
[má(:)ləkjùːl]

分子
cf. atom(原子), neutron(中性子)

1790

cognition
[kɑ(:)gníʃən]

認識, 認知
[= perception]
動 cognize 形 cognitive

1791

cluster
[klʌ́stər]

群れ [= group, crowd],
房 [= bunch]
▶ cluster of grapes (一房のブドウ)

1792

abyss
[əbís]

奈落の底,
地獄 [= hell], 深淵

1793

affliction
[əflíkʃən]

苦痛, 苦難
[= pain, suffering]
動 afflict

1794

addendum
[ədéndəm]

付録
[= appendix]

1795

avarice
[ǽvərɪs]

強欲, 貪欲
[= covetousness, greediness]
形 avaricious

1796

blemish
[blémɪʃ]

汚点 [= flaw, defect],
しみ [= stain]
▶ without a blemish (完全に)

1797

brink
[brɪŋk]

(破滅の)瀬戸際,
(絶壁などの)縁 [= edge, verge], 端

1798

coffer
[kɔ́(:)fər]

財源, 基金
[= funds]
▶ state coffers (国庫)

While atoms consist of sub-atomic particles, **molecules** consist of an arrangement of atoms.	原子は亜原子粒子から成り，分子は原子の配列から成る。
Language and **cognition** are important topics for psycholinguistic research.	言語と認識は，心理言語学研究の重要項目である。
The hillsides in spring are decorated with **clusters** of daffodils.	春の丘の斜面は，水仙の群落で飾られる。
In Milton's narrative poem "Paradise Lost", God threw Satan into the **abyss** of Hell.	ミルトンの物語詩『失楽園』の中で，神は悪魔を地獄の底に突き落とした。
Doctors tried as hard as they could to relieve his terrible **affliction**.	彼の大変な苦痛を和らげるために，医師たちはできる限りのことをした。
In an **addendum** to the book, he discussed the new findings.	本の付録の中で彼は新しい研究結果について論じた。
Motivated by **avarice**, the heirs to a family fortune reportedly committed murder.	強欲が動機で，一家の財産の相続人たちが殺人を犯したと言われている。
The only **blemish** on his record was a conviction for dangerous driving when he was a student.	彼の経歴における唯一の汚点は，学生時代に危険な運転をして有罪判決を受けたことであった。
The economy was hovering on the **brink** of a recession.	経済は不況寸前のところで低迷していた。
The new tax helped to swell the **coffers** of the government.	新税は国庫を潤す助けとなった。

1799	**constriction** [kənstríkʃən]	締めつけ [= tightening] ▶constriction in *one's* throat (のどを締めつけられる感じ)
1800	**dynasty** [dáinəsti]	王朝 [= family of sovereign rulers]
1801	**entreaty** [ɪntríːṭi]	懇願 [= plea] 動 entreat
1802	**epitaph** [épɪtæf]	碑文 [= inscription], 墓碑銘
1803	**foray** [fɔ́(ː)reɪ]	(新分野への)進出 [= challenge in the new field], 急襲 [= raid]
1804	**hermit** [hə́ːrmɪt]	隠遁者, 世捨て人 [= recluse, solitary] 形 hermitical
1805	**impurity** [ɪmpjúərəṭi]	不純, 不道徳 [= immorality], 堕落していること
1806	**insignia** [ɪnsígniə]	記章 [= badge]
1807	**jubilee** [dʒúːbɪliː]	特別な記念日 [= anniversary] ▶silver [golden, diamond] jubilee (25 [50, 60] 周年記念日)
1808	**ledger** [lédʒər]	台帳 [= account book] ▶general ledger (総勘定元帳)

He disliked the **constriction** that came from being a public official.	彼は役人であるがゆえの締めつけが嫌いだった。
The Romanov **dynasty** came to an end with the Russian communist revolution.	ロマノフ王朝はロシア共産革命で終焉を迎えた。
Despite his colleagues' **entreaties**, he insisted on resigning.	同僚たちの懇願にもかかわらず、彼は辞任すると言い張った。
Some of the **epitaphs** in the graveyard were surprisingly humorous.	墓地の碑文の中には思いのほかおどけたものもあった。
This was the author's first **foray** into non-fiction writing.	これはその著者のノンフィクション作品への初めての進出だった。
The old man lived the life of a **hermit** in the mountains for years.	その老人は山の中で、何年もの間隠遁者の生活を送った。
The obvious **impurity** of his motives laid him open to criticism.	彼の動機は明らかに不純だったので、彼は批判にさらされた。
She recognized the **insignia** of the military police on his uniform.	彼女は彼の制服に付けられた憲兵の記章に気付いた。
On the **jubilee** of the coronation, street parties were held everywhere.	戴冠記念日には、ストリートパーティーがあちこちで開催された。
She entered every detail of her expenditure in a large **ledger**.	彼女は大きな台帳に支出の詳細をすべて書き込んだ。

1809
malleability
[mæliəbíləti]

適応性，柔軟さ [= pliability]，素直さ

1810
repose
[rɪpóuz]

休むこと
語源 re（再び）+ pose（休止する）

1811
precinct
[príːsɪŋkt]

周辺，管轄区域
▶business precinct（商業地区）

1812
pseudoscience
[sjùːdousáɪəns]

疑似科学
語源 pseudo（見せかけの）+ science（科学）

1813
resonance
[rézənəns]

響き
▶have global resonance（世界的反響がある）

1814
sanctity
[sǽŋktəti]

高潔さ，神聖

1815
sanitation
[sæ̀nɪtéɪʃən]

公衆衛生
形 sanitary

1816
savvy
[sǽvi]

手腕，（実際的な）知識
[= skill]
▶political savvy（政治的手腕）

1817
servitude
[sə́ːrvətjùːd]

隷属，奴隷の境遇
[= slavery]
cf. servant（使用人）

1818
stealth
[stelθ]

こっそりした方法
▶by stealth（人目を忍んで）

The new teacher was surprised by the **malleability** of her students.	新任教師は生徒たちの適応性に驚いた。
He painted a picture of his wife in **repose** on a sofa.	彼は妻がソファーで休んでいるところの絵を描いた。
Each police **precinct** patrols its own neighborhood.	各警察管区はそれぞれの近隣をパトロールする。
He said that psychoanalysis was a mere **pseudoscience** like astrology.	彼は精神分析学は占星術のような単なる疑似科学だと言った。
The high-quality violin had a beautiful **resonance**.	その高品質のバイオリンは美しい響きを持っていた。
The priest was known for the **sanctity** of his private life.	その司祭は高潔な私生活で知られていた。
Improvements in **sanitation** contributed to the disease's eradication.	公衆衛生の改善がその病気の撲滅へとつながった。
Everyone admired the **savvy** with which the foreman solved problems.	皆が現場監督の問題解決の手腕を称賛した。
The slave dreamed of escaping from his **servitude** to his master.	その奴隷は、主人に隷属している状況から脱することを夢見ていた。
The guide emphasized the need for **stealth** so as not to frighten the deer.	ガイドは、シカを怖がらせないためにこっそりした方法が必要だと強調した。

1819	**swamp** [swɑ(:)mp]	沼地, 湿地 [= marsh, bog]
1820	**tyranny** [tírəni]	専制政治 [= despotism] ▶political tyranny（暴政）
1821	**velocity** [vəlá(:)səti]	速度, 高速 [= speed, swiftness, rapidity] ▶velocity of sound（音の速さ）
1822	**vestige** [véstɪdʒ]	名残 [= remnant]
1823	**volition** [voʊlíʃən]	意志 [= will] ▶of one's own volition（自分の意志で）
1824	**adulation** [ædʒuléɪʃən]	（極端な）賛美, お世辞 [= fawning, servile flattery], 追従 動 adulate
1825	**anachronism** [ənækrənɪzm]	時代錯誤 [= an error in chronology] 形 anachronistic
1826	**arrears** [əríərz]	滞納金 [= outstanding payment] ▶fall into arrears（支払いなどが遅滞する）
1827	**autonomy** [ɔːtá(:)nəmi]	自治(権) [= self-government], 自主性 [= independence] 形 autonomous
1828	**captive** [kæptɪv]	監禁された人, 捕虜

The Florida **swamps** are known as the 'Everglades.'	フロリダの沼地は「エバーグレーズ湿地」の名で知られている。
The students helped to overthrow the **tyranny** of the dictator.	学生たちは独裁者の専制政治を打倒するのに協力した。
Technical developments have increased the **velocity** of trains.	技術的進歩が電車の速度を高めた。
The judges' wigs were a **vestige** of the country's colonial period.	裁判官のかつらはその国の植民地時代の名残だった。
The man sold his car of his own **volition**.	男は自分自身の意志で車を売った。
Pop stars often receive tremendous **adulation** from their fans.	人気歌手たちは，しばしばファンから途方もない賛美を向けられる。
The humor of Mark Twain's "Connecticut Yankee" is based on **anachronisms**.	マーク・トウェインの『コネチカット・ヤンキー』のユーモアは，時代錯誤に基づいている。
The tenant still had not paid the **arrears** on his rent.	その借家人は家賃の滞納金をまだ支払っていなかった。
The organization has gained some **autonomy** from the government.	その組織は政府からいくらかの自治権を獲得した。
The man had kept his daughter a **captive** in her own home.	その男は自分の娘を，彼女自身の家に監禁していた。

anachronism (1825) のchronは（時間）を意味します。ほかの例としてはchronological「年代順の」，chronic「慢性の」などがあります。

1829 ~ 1838

1829
clamor
[klǽmər]

叫び声, わめき声
[= uproar, outcry]

1830
contrivance
[kəntráɪvəns]

計略 [= plot, artifice],
考案物 [= invention, device]
動 contrive

1831
decoy
[díːkɔɪ]

おとり
[= lure, bait]
▶ police decoy（警察のおとり）

1832
epiphany
[ɪpífəni]

ひらめき

1833
equilibrium
[ìːkwɪlíbriəm]

平衡 [= poise, balance],
釣り合い
語源 equi（等しい）+ librium（重さ）

1834
leeway
[líːwèɪ]

余裕
[= margin, extra time, money or space]

1835
leverage
[lévərɪdʒ]

影響力
[= influence]

1836
linkage
[líŋkɪdʒ]

関連性

1837
migration
[maɪgréɪʃən]

移住
[= relocation]
▶ migration of birds（鳥の渡り）

1838
periphery
[pərífəri]

周囲,
外縁（地域）[= outskirts, vicinity]

There was a huge public **clamor** over the recent political scandals.	最近の政治スキャンダルをめぐって，大衆は大いに<u>抗議の叫び</u>を上げた。
Although she tried by every **contrivance** to fool me, I didn't believe her.	彼女はあらゆる<u>計略</u>を練って私をだまそうとしたが，私は彼女を信じなかった。
The first brigade that advanced to the east was merely a **decoy** for the real attack.	東へ進軍した第1旅団は，本格攻撃に向けた単なる<u>おとり</u>だった。
The novelist had an **epiphany** while looking at the sea.	その小説家は海を眺めていて，突然<u>ひらめき</u>を得た。
Whenever he drinks more than one beer, he tends to lose his **equilibrium**.	彼はビールを2杯以上飲むといつでも<u>バランス</u>を失う傾向がある。
If he only had been given the **leeway** to look for other solutions, he might have solved the problem.	ほかの解法を探す<u>余裕</u>さえ与えられていたら，彼はその問題を解けていたかもしれない。
The man insisted that he had no **leverage** on the present administration.	その男性は自分が現政権に<u>影響力</u>を持たないと主張した。
The detective searched for evidence of some **linkage** between the two crimes.	刑事はその2つの犯罪を<u>関連</u>づける証拠を捜査した。
The **migration** of young people to the cities is a growing problem.	若者の都市への<u>移住</u>が問題となりつつある。
We posted guards on the **periphery** of the camp in case anyone tried to infiltrate in the night.	誰かが夜間に侵入するといけないので，我々は野営地の<u>周囲</u>に見張りを置いた。

1839

quantum
[kwá(:)nṭəm]

量 [= quantity, amount], 量子

1840

quorum
[kwɔ́:rəm]

定(足)数
▶have a quorum (定足数を満たす)

1841

rancor
[rǽŋkər]

恨み [= enmity, spite, malice, animosity], 敵意 [= animus, hostility]
形 rancorous

1842

ransom
[rǽnsəm]

身代金
▶pay ransom (身代金を払う)

1843

sabotage
[sǽbətɑ̀:ʒ]

(労働争議の際などの)破壊行為 [= willful damage by workers], 妨害

1844

scapegoat
[skéɪpgòʊt]

身代わり，他人の罪を負う者
▶make a scapegoat of ~ (~を身代わりにする)

1845

scheme
[ski:m]

計画 [= plan], 案
▶business scheme (事業計画)

1846

segregation
[sègrɪgéɪʃən]

隔離 [= separation], 人種差別 (⇔ integration)
動 segregate

1847

seismology
[saɪzmá(:)lədʒi]

地震学 [= science of earthquakes]

1848

shackle
[ʃǽkl]

手かせ [= manacle], 足かせ [= fetter], 拘束 [= restraint]

The serfs of the Middle Ages were given a specified **quantum** of grain in return for their labor.	中世の農奴は労働と引き換えに一定量の穀物が与えられた。
There wasn't a sufficient **quorum** for a legal vote at the meeting.	その会議では規定投票数を充足する定数に達していなかった。
He showed surprisingly little **rancor** towards those who had forced him to resign his position.	彼は自分を辞職に追いやった人々に対して、驚いたことにほとんど恨みを抱かなかった。
The kidnappers demanded an enormous **ransom** from the parents.	誘拐犯たちは親に莫大な身代金を要求した。
The recent crash of a 747 was first attributed to **sabotage**.	最近のボーイング747機の墜落は、当初は破壊工作が原因とされた。
The government prefers to find a **scapegoat** rather than acknowledge its own responsibility.	政府というものは自らの責任を認めるよりも、むしろ身代わりを見つけたがる。
The boys came up with a **scheme** to get revenge on the teacher.	少年たちは先生に報復するための計画を思いついた。
Racial **segregation** in the American South continued long after the Civil War.	アメリカ南部の人種隔離は南北戦争後も長く続いた。
Satellite photos of movements in the earth's surface have advanced the accuracy of **seismology**.	地球の表層の動きを撮影した衛星写真のおかげで地震学がより正確となった。
The unkempt prisoner appeared in court still in **shackles**.	髪がぼさぼさの囚人が、手錠をはめられたまま出廷した。

sabotage (1843) は日本語では「サボタージュ (=労働などをしないこと)」の意味で使われていますが、英語では「労働争議中に機械などに損傷を与えること」を意味します。

1849	**showdown** [ʃóudàun]	最後の対決 [= final confrontation], (持ち札の)公開
1850	**splinter** [splíntər]	とげ [= thorn], 破片, 分派 ▶break into splinters（粉々に割れる）
1851	**spree** [spri:]	浮かれ［ばか］騒ぎ ▶go on a spending spree（金を湯水のように使う）
1852	**stipend** [stáɪpend]	給付金 [= allowance, periodic payment], 奨学金 [= scholarship]
1853	**subsidence** [səbsáɪdəns]	地盤沈下 [= ground sinking]
1854	**sway** [sweɪ]	支配 [= influence], 統治 ▶under the sway of ~（～の支配下にある）
1855	**tariff** [tærɪf]	関税 [= customs]
1856	**testimonial** [tèstɪmóuniəl]	推薦状 [= reference, letter of recommendation]
1857	**triumph** [tráɪʌmf]	大勝利 [= victory] 形 triumphant ▶achieve a great triumph（大成功を収める）
1858	**upshot** [ʌ́pʃɑ(:)t]	結論 [= conclusion], 結果 [= outcome, result] ▶in the upshot（結局のところ）

The typical Western film ends with a **showdown** between the good guys and the bad guys.	西部劇はたいてい，善玉と悪玉の対決で終わる。
My son got a **splinter** in his hand from carrying the newly cut boards.	息子は切ったばかりの板を運んでいて，手にとげが刺さった。
His wife went on a shopping **spree** before Christmas and used all the money they had saved.	彼の妻はクリスマス前に買い物に浮かれて，ためていたお金を使い切ってしまった。
Even after retirement, the old man received an adequate **stipend** from his investments.	その老人は退職後でさえも，自分の投資先から十分な給付金を得ていた。
The earthquake had led to widespread **subsidence** in the area.	地震はその地域に広範囲な地盤沈下をもたらした。
He said that the Finance Ministry was still under the **sway** of outdated economic theories.	財務省はいまだに古臭い経済学説の支配下にあると，彼は言った。
To protect its own industry, the country placed a **tariff** on steel imports.	自国内の産業を保護するため，その国は輸入鉄鋼に関税をかけた。
The applicant had added a **testimonial** from his previous boss.	応募者は前の上司からの推薦状を添えた。
The fans were celebrating the **triumph** of their team in the championships.	ファンたちは自分たちのチームの決勝戦での大勝利を祝福していた。
The **upshot** of his confession was that he was responsible for the crime he had been accused of.	彼の告白の結論は，自分が告発されている犯罪に責任があるというものだった。

1859 ~ 1861

1859
verge
[və:rdʒ]

瀬戸際, 縁, へり
▶on the verge of ~(まさに~しようとして)

1860
simulation
[sìmjuléɪʃən]

シミュレーション, 模擬実験

1861
diatribe
[dáɪətràɪb]

(~への)痛烈な皮肉〈against〉

He was on the **verge** of losing his temper, but he managed to look calm.	彼はカッとなる瀬戸際だったが、どうにか平静を装っていた。
The army used a computer to produce a **simulation** of what would happen if the country was invaded.	陸軍はコンピューターを使って、国が侵略されたら何が起こるかのシミュレーションを作り出した。
The doctor delivered a **diatribe** against the evils of smoking.	その医者は、喫煙の弊害に関する痛烈な皮肉をまくし立てた。

でる度 C 力を伸ばす単語

形容詞・副詞 239語

🎧 1862〜1870

1862 **electoral** [ɪléktərəl]	選挙の ▶electoral system（選挙制度）
1863 **incumbent** [ɪnkʌ́mbənt]	現職の
1864 **aboveboard** [əbʌ́vbɔ̀ːrd]	公明正大な [= fair, impartial] (⇔underhand 秘密の)
1865 **fatally** [féɪṭəli]	致命的に，不運にも [= unfortunately]
1866 **neural** [njúərəl]	神経の ▶neural activity（神経作用）
1867 **ongoing** [á(ː)ŋgòʊɪŋ]	現在行っている [= in progress] ▶ongoing negotiation（継続中の交渉）
1868 **flawed** [flɔːd]	欠陥のある [= faulty] (⇔flawless) ▶flawed article（きず物）
1869 **imposing** [ɪmpóʊzɪŋ]	堂々たる [= stately, impressive]
1870 **mundane** [mʌndéɪn]	世俗的な [= worldly, earthly] (⇔heavenly, spiritual), ありきたりの

Electoral considerations led the government to delay the tax rise.	選挙への配慮のために政府は税金の引き上げを延期した。
The young candidate knew that it would be difficult to unseat the **incumbent** mayor.	その若手候補者は，現職の市長をその座から降ろすことは難しいだろうとわかっていた。
He insisted that the negotiations had been fair and **aboveboard**.	彼は交渉は公平で公明正大だったと主張した。
His answer in the interview **fatally** ruined his chances of getting the job.	面接での彼の応答が，仕事を得るチャンスを致命的に台無しにした。
The machine was used to measure **neural** activity in the brain.	その機械は脳の神経作用を測定するために使用された。
The police visit was part of an **ongoing** campaign against illegal drug use.	警察の訪問は，現在行っている不法薬物使用撲滅キャンペーンの一環だった。
The problem was finally traced to a **flawed** component in the engine.	問題はエンジンの欠陥部品にあることが，やっとわかった。
Although he was short in stature, Napoleon's bearing made him an **imposing** figure.	ナポレオンは背は低かったが，その態度で堂々とした姿に見えていた。
Most truly spiritual people help others with the **mundane** problems of life.	真に崇高な人たちのほとんどは世俗的な人生問題で他人を助ける。

---

aboveboard (1864) のboardは「ゲームをする台」のことです。above board「台の上で」は相手に隠さず「公明正大な」のでこの言葉が誕生しました。

1871 ~ 1880

1871 cohesive
[kouhíːsɪv]
結束した, 団結した, 密着した
名 cohesion, coherence 形 coherent

1872 daunting
[dɔ́ːntɪŋ]
人の気力をくじく
▶daunting problem（困難な問題）

1873 disproportionately
[dìsprəpɔ́ːrʃənətli]
過度に, 非常に
[= not appropriately]

1874 gallant
[gǽlənt]
勇敢な [= brave, daring],
堂々とした [= imposing, stately]
名 gallantry

1875 hefty
[héfti]
重い [= heavy]（⇔slight）,
頑丈な
▶hefty athlete（頑丈な競技選手）

1876 holistic
[hoʊlístɪk]
全体論的な

1877 interminable
[ɪntə́ːrmɪnəbl]
永遠に続く,
やむことのない [= endless, lasting]
▶interminable job（切りのない仕事）

1878 posthumously
[pá(ː)stʃəməsli]
死後に
[= after death]
形 posthumous

1879 sustainable
[səstéɪnəbl]
持続可能な,
地球にやさしい [= environmentally-friendly]
▶sustainable development（環境保全開発）

1880 obsessive
[əbsésɪv]
過度の, 頭から離れない
[= addictive]
▶obsessive fear（頭から離れない恐怖）

The immigrants formed a close **cohesive** community.	移民たちは，密接で<u>結束力のある</u>地域社会を形成した。
Sorting out all his father's papers was a **daunting** task for him.	父親の書類全部を仕分けすることは，彼にとって<u>くじけそうになる</u>仕事だった。
Many said the punishments were **disproportionately** severe.	多くの人は，それらの処罰は<u>過度に</u>厳しいと言った。
The knights of medieval times were supposed to be **gallant** and trustworthy.	中世の騎士は<u>勇敢で</u>信頼できるとされていた。
After eating a **hefty** lunch, he began to feel sleepy at his desk.	<u>ボリュームのある</u>昼食をとった後で，彼は机で眠くなってきた。
He said that such a complex problem needed a **holistic** solution.	彼は，このような複雑な問題は<u>全体論的な</u>解決方法が必要だと言った。
The movie was so long and boring it seemed **interminable**.	映画は長く退屈だったので<u>永遠に続く</u>かと思われた。
The scientist was awarded the prize for his achievements **posthumously**.	その科学者は<u>死後に</u>業績に対する賞を授与された。
Many scientists are looking for **sustainable** energy sources.	多くの科学者は<u>持続可能な</u>エネルギー源を求めている。
The boy's **obsessive** interest in guns began to worry his parents.	その少年の銃に対する<u>過度の</u>興味は両親を心配させ始めた。

1881
retentive
[rɪténtɪv]

記憶力がよい，保持力のある
▶be retentive of heat（熱を保つ）

1882
venerable
[vénərəbl]

由緒ある，敬うべき
[= respectable]
動 venerate

1883
idiosyncratic
[ìdiəsɪŋkrǽtɪk]

独特な，一風変わった [= eccentric]
名 idiosyncrasy

1884
condescending
[kà(:)ndɪséndɪŋ]

人を見下すような
[= supercilious]
▶condescending attitude（人を見下すような態度）

1885
clairvoyant
[kleərvɔ́ɪənt]

千里眼の，透視力を持つ [= keenly perceptive]
名 clairvoyance

1886
distractedly
[dɪstrǽktɪdli]

うわの空で
[= inattentively]

1887
chaotic
[keɪá(:)t̬ɪk]

無秩序の
[= disorderly]

1888
de facto
[deɪ fǽktoʊ]

事実上の
[= actual, virtual]
▶de facto government（事実上の政府）

1889
state-of-the-art
[stèɪt əv ði: á:rt]

最新鋭の
▶state-of-the-art factory（最新鋭の工場）

1890
logistically
[loʊdʒístɪkəli]

兵站上で，物資面で
名 logistics（物流管理）

The old secretary was famous for her **retentive** memory.	長く勤めているその秘書は記憶力がよいことで有名だった。
He believed that such a **venerable** tradition should not be cast aside lightly.	そのような由緒ある伝統は軽々しく放棄されるべきではないと彼は考えていた。
His **idiosyncratic** approach to teaching annoyed some of his colleagues.	彼の独特な教え方は同僚の何人かを悩ませた。
The children resented the **condescending** way the visitor spoke to them.	子どもたちはその訪問者の人を見下すような話し方に腹を立てた。
Since I am not **clairvoyant**, I cannot predict the future.	私は千里眼ではないから、将来のことは予測できない。
He answered her **distractedly**, as though he were thinking about something else.	彼はあたかも何かほかのことを考えているかのように、彼女にうわの空で答えた。
A **chaotic** mess of clothes and books lay on the floor.	衣服や本が床にめちゃくちゃな状態で散らかっていた。
The general became the **de facto** ruler of the country.	その将官はその国の事実上の統治者になった。
The rich man installed a **state-of-the-art** security system in his house.	その金持ちの男性は最新鋭のセキュリティーシステムを家に装備した。
The general said that the battle plan was **logistically** impossible.	将官はその戦術は兵站面で不可能だと言った。

1891
tribally
[tráɪbəli]
部族で

1892
cardiovascular
[kàːrdiouvǽskjulər]
心臓血管の

1893
carnivorous
[kɑːrnívərəs]
肉食の [= meat-eating]
▶carnivorous animal (肉食性動物)

1894
potent
[póʊtənt]
力のある [= strong, powerful],
有効な [= efficacious]
图 potency

1895
arrogant
[ǽrəgənt]
傲慢な
图 arrogance
▶arrogant attitude (横柄な態度)

1896
acute
[əkjúːt]
(痛みが) 激しい, 鋭い,
急性の (⇔chronic 慢性の), 深刻な
▶acute economic crisis (深刻な経済危機)

1897
astute
[əstjúːt]
鋭敏な [= acute],
洞察力のある [= insightful],
抜け目のない [= shrewd]

1898
preemptive
[priémptɪv]
先制の
[= forestalling]
▶preemptive attack (先制攻撃)

1899
prescient
[préʃənt]
予知の
副 presciently

1900
preferential
[prèfərénʃəl]
優遇の, 優先の
動 prefer 图 preference
形 preferable (好ましい)

Most of the people in the village worked in a **tribally** owned business.	その村のほとんどの人は部族で所有している仕事に携わっていた。
The Westernization of the diet led to increased **cardiovascular** problems.	食事の西洋化は心臓血管の問題を増やすことになった。
Carnivorous animals like cats need meat in their diet to survive.	ネコのような肉食の動物は、生きるためには食事に肉が必要だ。
Many were amazed by the **potent** display of military power in the Gulf War.	多くの人は湾岸戦争での軍事力の強大な展開に仰天した。
The principal's **arrogant** manner immediately annoyed the parents.	校長の傲慢な態度は、すぐに親たちをいらつかせた。
He went to the doctor because he was suffering **acute** pains in his stomach.	彼は胃の激しい痛みに苦しんでいたので、医者へ行った。
That film critic is famous for her **astute** but acerbic commentary.	その映画評論家は鋭敏だが辛辣な批評で有名である。
The air force was ordered to launch a **preemptive** strike on the site.	空軍はその場所に先制攻撃を開始するように命令された。
The scientist's warnings about the environmental dangers proved **prescient**.	環境危機に関するその科学者の警告から予知能力があることが判明した。
The employees complained about the **preferential** treatment given to other colleagues.	従業員たちはほかの同僚が受けていた優遇的な措置について不満を漏らした。

carnivorous (1893) のcarnは (肉) を意味します。ほかの例としてはcarnal「肉体の」、incarnation「化身」などがあります。

1901 ~ 1910

1901 prophetic
[prəfétɪk]

予言する [= predictive]
語源 pro(前もって) + phet(述べる) + ic

1902 provident
[prɑ́(ː)vɪdənt]

倹約な，将来に備えた

1903 prodigious
[prədídʒəs]

驚異的な，巨大な [= enormous]
图 prodigy (神童，驚異)
▶ prodigious ability (素晴らしい能力)

1904 profuse
[prəfjúːs]

惜しみのない [= lavish, generous]
图 profusion
語源 pro(前へ) + fuse(注ぐ)

1905 profane
[prəféɪn]

世俗的な，冒涜する

1906 promiscuous
[prəmískjuəs]

手当たりしだいの [= haphazard],
乱雑な [= indiscriminate]

1907 probationary
[proʊbéɪʃəneri]

見習い期間の
▶ probationary teacher (仮採用の先生)

1908 prolonged
[prəlɔ́(ː)ŋd]

長引く
▶ prolonged period (長期間)

1909 provincial
[prəvínʃəl]

偏狭な
[= narrow-minded, illiberal]
图 province (地方)

1910 provisional
[prəvíʒənəl]

暫定的な [= for temporary use],
条件付きの [= conditional]

His claims concerning the economy turned out to be **prophetic**.	彼の経済についての主張は先見的であることが判明した。
She had adopted the **provident** policy of saving for her old age.	彼女は老後のために倹約的な貯蓄方法を採り入れた。
Hercules is legendary for his **prodigious** strength and his twelve labors.	ヘラクレスは驚異的な大力と12の功業で伝説となっている。
The philanthropist made **profuse** donations to the needy.	その慈善家は貧しい人々に惜しみのない寄付をした。
It seemed unlikely that a priest would be interested in such a **profane** matter.	司教がこのような世俗的な事柄に興味があるとはありそうもないことだった。
Hollywood starlets are known to have a **promiscuous** nature.	ハリウッドの売り出し中の若手女優は見境のない気質を持っていることで知られている。
Eventually, they agreed to employ the girl on a **probationary** basis.	結局，彼らはその女の子を見習い扱いで雇うことに決めた。
After a **prolonged** pause, the lecturer began to speak again.	長い間の後，講師は再び話し始めた。
His decisions are often based on a somewhat **provincial** world view.	彼の決定は，しばしば，どちらかと言うと偏狭な世界観に基づいている。
The United Nations allocated **provisional** food supplies to the refugees.	国連は難民たちに暫定的な補給食糧を配分した。

1911～1920

1911	**extraterrestrial** [èkstrətəréstriəl]	地球外の ▶extraterrestrial life（地球外生物）
1912	**exempt** [ɪgzémpt]	(～を)免除された〈from〉 图 exemption
1913	**exorbitant** [ɪgzɔ́ːrbətənt]	法外な [= extravagant, immoderate]
1914	**extravagant** [ɪkstrǽvəgənt]	浪費する [= wasteful], 節度のない [= immoderate] 图 extravagance
1915	**fervent** [fə́ːrvənt]	熱烈な [= ardent, earnest, fervid, intense] ▶fervent believer（熱烈な信奉者）
1916	**vehement** [víːəmənt]	熱烈な [= fervent, passionate, ardent, zealous, impassioned] 图 vehemence
1917	**frantic** [frǽntɪk]	大急ぎの，取り乱した， 熱狂した [= frenzied, raving, frenetic]
1918	**fanatically** [fənǽtɪkəli]	熱狂的に [= eagerly]
1919	**coherent** [kouhíərənt]	統一のとれた，理路整然とした [= reasonable, legitimate] 图 cohesion 形 cohesive
1920	**constitutional** [kɑ̀(ː)nstətjúːʃənəl]	合憲である， 本質の

The movie was about a boy discovering an **extraterrestrial** life form.	その映画は地球外生物を見つけた少年の話だった。
Are you **exempt** from paying local taxes this year?	あなたは今年，地方税の支払いを免除されているのですか。
The food is delicious but the price is **exorbitant**.	その食品はおいしいが価格は法外だ。
Her **extravagant** spending has left her family virtually bankrupt.	彼女の浪費癖が原因で，家族は実質的に破産してしまった。
The letters of Abelard and Heloise were **fervent** proclamations of love.	アベラールとエロイーズの手紙は熱烈な愛の宣言だった。
His denial of all responsibility was **vehement** and sincere.	彼の全責任に対する拒絶は，熱烈で真剣なものだった。
Aimlessly **frantic** activity never leads to greater work efficiency.	目的もなしに慌ただしく動いても，仕事の効率は決して上がらない。
The environmentalists were **fanatically** devoted to their cause.	環境保護主義者は自分たちの大義のために熱狂的に献身した。
The researchers were asked to come up with a **coherent** energy policy.	研究者は統一のとれたエネルギー政策を考え出すことを求められた。
The high court ruled that the new law was **constitutional**.	最高裁判所は新法は合憲であるとの判決を下した。

exorbitant (1913) はorbit「軌道」のex（外に）出てしまうので，「法外な」とイメージしましょう。

1921
cognitive
[kɑ́(:)gnətɪv]

認知の
▶cognitive ability (認識能力)

1922
contradictory
[kɑ̀(:)ntrədíktəri]

矛盾している
[= conflicting]

1923
controversial
[kɑ̀(:)ntrəvə́:rʃəl]

問題の, 物議を醸す
▶controversial subject (物議を醸す問題)

1924
conciliatory
[kənsíliətɔ̀:ri]

和解の, 懐柔的な
[= propitiatory] (⇔ hostile)
動 conciliate (をなだめる)

1925
defamatory
[dɪfǽmətɔ̀:ri]

中傷的な [= libelous]
動 defame (の名誉を傷つける)   名 defamation
▶defamatory report (中傷的な報道)

1926
deferential
[dèfərénʃəl]

敬意を表する
[= respectful]
副 deferentially (うやうやしく)

1927
derisive
[dɪráɪsɪv]

嘲笑的な [= mocking, scoffing]
動 deride 名 derision
▶derisive term (ばかにした言葉)

1928
despondent
[dɪspɑ́(:)ndənt]

落胆した
[= dejected]
名 despondency

1929
despicable
[dɪspíkəbl]

卑劣な, いけ好かない
▶despicable criminal act (卑劣な犯罪行為)

1930
diabolic
[dàɪəbɑ́(:)lɪk]

悪魔の [= devilish]
名 diabolism (悪魔信仰)
▶diabolic plot (非道な策略)

The test was designed to measure a child's **cognitive** development.	そのテストは子どもの認知発達を判断する目的で作られた。
Many people pointed out how **contradictory** his arguments were.	多くの人は彼の主張がいかに矛盾しているかを指摘した。
The **controversial** new play was banned after three performances.	問題の新しい演劇は、3回公演をした後で上演禁止となった。
As a **conciliatory** gesture, he offered to take his wife to dinner.	和解の意思表示として彼は妻を夕食に連れて行くことを申し出た。
He had no choice but to respond to the **defamatory** articles.	彼は中傷記事に応える以外に選択の余地がなかった。
The younger scientist took a **deferential** attitude to the professor.	若手の科学者は教授に敬意を表する態度で接した。
The cartoonist usually depicts politicians in a **derisive**, cynical manner.	その漫画家は、たいてい、政治家たちを嘲笑的に皮肉っぽく描く。
Despondent and sullen, she finally realized she needed psychiatric help.	彼女は落胆してふさぎ込んでいたが、ようやく精神医学の助けが必要だと気付いた。
The judge said that no crime was more **despicable** than robbing old people.	高齢者から盗みを働く以上に卑劣な犯罪はないと、その裁判官は述べた。
Out of the corner of my eye, I could see his **diabolic** grin.	私は目の端で彼の悪魔のような笑みを見て取った。

1931
disconcerting
[dìskənsə́ːrtɪŋ]

当惑させるような, 厄介な
[= disturbing]

1932
dismissive
[dɪsmísɪv]

尊大な, 軽蔑的な
[= contemptuous, scornful] (⇔admiring)
動 dismiss 名 dismissal

1933
disparate
[díspərət]

全く異なる
[= dissimilar]
名 disparity

1934
dispensable
[dɪspénsəbl]

たいして重要でない, なくても困らない
[= disposable] (⇔indispensable)

1935
dissenting
[dɪséntɪŋ]

異議を唱える [= disagreeing]
名 dissent (不賛成)
▶dissenting opinion (反対意見)

1936
distraught
[dɪstrɔ́ːt]

取り乱した
[= perplexed, confused]
▶distraught with grief (悲しみに気持ちが動転した)

1937
diminutive
[dɪmínjʊtɪv]

小さい
[= tiny, very small]
動 diminish 名 diminution

1938
impalpable
[ɪmpǽlpəbl]

触知できない
[= intangible]

1939
imperious
[ɪmpíəriəs]

横柄な
[= high-handed]

1940
impermeable
[ɪmpə́ːrmiəbl]

通さない
▶a jacket impermeable to water
(水を通さないジャケット)

He found the student's questions **disconcerting** and hard to answer.	その生徒の質問は答えるのが難しく<u>当惑させる</u>ものだと彼は思った。
The professor's **dismissive** attitudes towards his students left him isolated.	学生たちに対する<u>尊大な</u>態度がその教授を孤立させた。
Japanese demonstrate widely **disparate** levels of English proficiency.	日本人の英語の習熟度は極めて<u>ばらつきがある</u>。
I was shocked when my boss said that the temporary workers were **dispensable**.	私は,上司が派遣社員は<u>たいして重要ではない</u>と言った時に衝撃を受けた。
Apart from a few **dissenting** voices, most people agreed with him.	何人かの<u>異議を唱える</u>声は別にして,ほとんどの人は彼に同意した。
I didn't understand how **distraught** she was until I saw her.	会って初めて,彼女がいかに<u>取り乱している</u>かがわかった。
Jockeys must be of **diminutive** size for their horses to compete.	騎手は馬が競争するために<u>小柄である</u>必要がある。
The symptoms had been **impalpable** at first, but later they were clearer.	最初,症状は<u>触知できない</u>ものだったが,後にはっきりしてきた。
The chief nurse spoke in an **imperious** way to her subordinates.	主任看護師は部下に<u>横柄な</u>態度で話した。
An **impermeable** layer of rubber kept the contents of the bag dry.	ゴムの<u>不浸透性の</u>おかげで,バッグの中の物は乾いたままだった。

imperious (1939) のimperiは (力強い, 命令する) を意味します。ほかの例としてはimperial「皇帝の」, imperialism「帝国主義」があります。

1941

implacable
[ímplǽkəbl]

なだめられない
图 implacability

1942

impregnable
[imprégnəbl]

難攻不落の
[= invincible, invulnerable]
▶impregnable position（揺るぎない地位）

1943

impersonal
[impə́ːrsənəl]

よそよそしい，
非人間的な
▶impersonal bureaucracy（非人間的な官僚主義）

1944

impudent
[ímpjʊdənt]

生意気な，ずうずうしい
[= impertinent]
图 impudence

1945

stalwart
[stɔ́ːlwərt]

確固とした，ぐらつかない，頑健な

1946

staunch
[stɔːntʃ]

筋金入りの，ゆるぎない
[= stalwart]
▶staunch supporter（忠実な支持者）

1947

stolid
[stɑ́(ː)ləd]

ぼんやりした
[= impassive]
图 stolidness

1948

suave
[swɑːv]

物腰の柔らかな
▶suave tone（柔らかな口調）

1949

incongruous
[inkɑ́(ː)ŋgruəs]

場違いである [= out of place]
(⇔ appropriate)
▶incongruous behavior（ふさわしくない行動）

1950

inconsequential
[inkɑ̀(ː)nsɪkwénʃəl]

取るに足らない [= trivial]，
重要でない [= insignificant]
▶inconsequential reason（取るに足らない理由）

The local people were **implacable** in their opposition to the plan.	地元の人たちのその計画に対する反対は<u>なだめられない</u>。
The castle's walls were **impregnable** against their primitive weapons.	城の外壁は彼らの原始的な武器に対して<u>難攻不落</u>だった。
He spoke in an **impersonal** way as if the problem did not concern him.	彼は，あたかもその問題とは無関係であるかのように<u>よそよそしい</u>そぶりで話した。
The teacher disliked the **impudent** way in which the boy answered him.	先生は，その男の子の<u>生意気な</u>返事の仕方が気に入らなかった。
He had been a **stalwart** supporter of the labor union for many years.	彼は長年，労働組合の<u>確固たる</u>支持者だった。
He was a **staunch** believer in the efficacy of herbal medicines.	彼は漢方薬の効能を<u>固く</u>信じていた。
She was a **stolid**, hardworking girl, who showed little emotion.	彼女は，<u>無表情で</u>勤勉な女の子で，ほとんど感情を表に出さない。
The **suave** young man turned out to be an insurance salesman.	<u>物腰の柔らかな</u>その男性は保険のセールスマンであることがわかった。
His remarks at the wedding struck many people as **incongruous**.	彼の結婚式での発言は多くの人に<u>場違いである</u>と感じさせた。
A few **inconsequential** changes were made to the contract for legal reasons.	<u>取るに足らない</u>数点の変更が法的な理由で規約に成された。

1951～1960

1951 indiscriminate
[ɪndɪskrímənət]

見境がない
[= undistinguishing]
▶indiscriminate reading（乱読）

1952 insidious
[ɪnsídiəs]

陰険な
(⇔ straightforward)

1953 insipid
[ɪnsípɪd]

退屈な [= dull, uninteresting],
味のない [= tasteless]
▶insipid life（退屈な生活）

1954 insolent
[ínsələnt]

傲慢な
[= arrogant]
▶insolent reply（無礼な返事）

1955 insubstantial
[ɪnsəbstǽnʃəl]

不十分な
[= inadequate]
▶insubstantial sum（わずかな金額）

1956 insurmountable
[ɪnsərmáʊntəbl]

克服不可能である
[= insuperable]

1957 intrepid
[ɪntrépɪd]

大胆不敵な
[= bold, fearless, dauntless]

1958 indelible
[ɪndéləbl]

消すことのできない
[= that cannot be erased]

1959 insolvent
[ɪnsá(:)lvənt]

破産した [= bankrupt],
支払い不能の [= unable to pay debts]
▶become insolvent（支払不能になる）

1960 wanton
[wá(:)ntən]

不当な
[= unreasonable]
▶wanton destruction（理不尽な破壊）

He was completely **indiscriminate** about who he invited to his parties.	彼は全く見境なくパーティーに招待する人を選んだ。
The speech was seen as an **insidious** attack on the new policy.	そのスピーチは新しい方針に対する陰険な攻撃のように思われた。
Most critics found his novel **insipid** and lifeless.	評論家の大半は，彼の小説は退屈で生気がないと感じていた。
In fact, he was fired for an **insolent** attitude toward the boss.	事実，彼は上司に不遜な態度をとったので解雇された。
After his rather **insubstantial** lunch, he soon began to feel hungry again.	量が十分でない昼食をとった後，彼はすぐに再び空腹になり始めた。
They had faced seemingly **insurmountable** problems at first.	彼らは最初，一見克服不可能であると思える問題に直面した。
The **intrepid** exploits of Superman exemplify a classic American hero.	スーパーマンの大胆な離れ技は古典的アメリカンヒーローを体現している。
Although the tragedy occurred in childhood, its effects were **indelible**.	その悲劇は子ども時代に起こったが，影響は消すことができなかった。
Just this week, another Japanese bank declared itself **insolvent**.	ほんの今週，また別の日本の銀行が自己破産を公表した。
The critic said the action showed a **wanton** disregard for human rights.	批評家は，その行動は人権の不当な無視を意味すると言った。

🎧 1961～1970

1961 abhorrent
[æbhɔ́ːrənt]

忌まわしい
[= abominable, hateful]

1962 abominable
[əbɑ́(ː)mɪnəbl]

極悪非道な，嫌悪すべき
[= loathsome]
▶abominable crime（極悪非道な犯罪）

1963 heinous
[héɪnəs]

極悪非道の
[= abhorrent, abominable, atrocious]
▶heinous crime（凶悪犯罪）

1964 incremental
[ìŋkrɪméntəl]

増加する
[= increasing]
▶incremental costs（膨れ上がるコスト）

1965 indebted
[ɪndétəd]

(～に)負うところがある〈to〉
cf. debt（借金），debtor（債務者）

1966 insurgent
[ɪnsə́ːrdʒənt]

反乱を起こした
[= rebellious]
名 insurgency（暴動，反乱）

1967 inflamed
[ɪnfléɪmd]

扇動されて激化した，炎症を起こした
▶inflamed area（炎症部分）

1968 indignant
[ɪndígnənt]

(～に)憤慨して
[= very angry]〈at〉
名 indignation

1969 incipient
[ɪnsípiənt]

初期の
[= initial, inceptive]
▶incipient stage（初期段階）

1970 unabashedly
[ʌ̀nəbǽʃɪdli]

臆面もなく
形 unabashed（厚かましい）

The atrocity was condemned as **abhorrent** to all civilized people.	その残虐行為はすべての文明人にとって忌まわしいものとして非難された。
The gang was accused of performing **abominable** acts for money.	その暴力団は金目当ての極悪非道な行為をしたことで告訴された。
The prosecutor called it a **heinous** crime and demanded the maximum sentence.	検事はその事件を凶悪犯罪と見なし，最高刑を求刑した。
He agreed to make **incremental** payments on the loan.	彼は段階的に増加するローンの支払いに同意した。
The novelist said that he was **indebted** to his wife for the idea for his latest book.	その小説家は，最新作の着想は妻に負っていると述べた。
Insurgent rebels launched another successful raid on government forces.	反乱軍が政府軍にさらなる急襲を仕掛け，成功した。
The man attempted to calm the **inflamed** feelings of the crowd.	男は群衆の激化した感情を抑えようとした。
He was still **indignant** at the rude way the bureaucrat had spoken to him.	彼はその官僚の彼に対する無礼な口の利き方に，いまだに憤慨していた。
He was still an **incipient** novelist at the time and had not yet become famous.	当時，彼はまだ駆け出しの小説家で，有名にはなっていなかった。
The new chairman adopted an **unabashedly** ruthless policy of job cuts.	新社長は臆面もなく無慈悲な雇用削減政策を打ち出した。

---

inflamed (1967) のinは「～の中に」，flameは「炎，情熱」を意味します。情熱をたきつける，つまり「扇動されて激化した」を意味します。

🎧 1971〜1980

1971 **untenable** [ʌnténəbl]	擁護[弁明]できない (⇔tenable)
1972 **precipitous** [prɪsípətəs]	絶壁の，険しい [= sheer, perpendicular] 動 precipitate 名 precipitation
1973 **predatory** [prédətɔ̀:ri]	捕食性の，略奪する [= plundering, pillaging] 名 predator (捕食動物) ▶predatory tactics (略奪戦術)
1974 **presumptuous** [prɪzʌ́mptʃuəs]	ずうずうしい [= impertinent] 動 presume 名 presumption
1975 **pretentious** [prɪténʃəs]	気取った [= affected]，うぬぼれた 動 pretend 名 pretentiousness
1976 **cagey** [kéɪdʒi]	(〜について)話したがらない [= tight-lipped, secretive] ⟨about⟩，秘密主義の ▶cagey reply (慎重な返事)
1977 **cryptic** [kríptɪk]	暗号を用いる，秘密の [= secret, hidden]，神秘的な [= mysterious]
1978 **furtive** [fə́:rtɪv]	人目を盗んでの [= stealthy, sly]，こそこそした [= surreptitious, sneaky]
1979 **adversarial** [ædvərséəriəl]	敵対的な [= hostile] ▶adversarial country (敵対国)
1980 **mutinous** [mjú:tənəs]	反抗的な [= rebellious]

434

It took the historian many years to admit that his theory was **untenable**.	彼の理論が擁護し難いものだと歴史家に認めさせるには，長い年月を要した。
The white cliffs of Dover are **precipitous** rock formations above the sea.	ドーバーの白い断崖は，海上に突き出た絶壁の岩の層からできている。
Anthropologists still argue over early man's **predatory** nature.	人類学者は初期人類の捕食性をめぐって今でも議論している。
It was **presumptuous** of him to make so many demands of a stranger.	見知らぬ人にそのように多くの要求をするなんて，彼はずうずうしかった。
Critics slammed the experimental new film as being **pretentious** and obscure.	批評家たちは，その実験的な新作映画は気取っていてわかりにくいと酷評した。
His **cagey** response immediately made the police suspicious of him.	彼が話したがらないので警察は直ちに彼を疑った。
She sent me a **cryptic** message that I had trouble understanding.	彼女が暗号で伝言を送ってきたので，私には解読困難だった。
His **furtive** glances at his colleagues led me to suspect a conspiracy.	彼が仲間を盗み見したため，私は共謀を疑った。
They successfully transformed their **adversarial** relationships into cooperative ones.	彼らは見事に敵対関係を協力関係に変えた。
He found it difficult to deal with a class of **mutinous** teenagers.	彼は反抗的な10代の生徒のクラスを相手にするのは難しいとわかった。

1981～1990

1981 averse
[əvə́ːrs]
反対して [= opposed], 気が進まない [= unwilling, reluctant]
图 aversion

1982 truculent
[trʌ́kjʊlənt]
攻撃的な
[= violent]

1983 abrasive
[əbréɪsɪv]
いらいらさせる
图 abrasive（研磨剤）

1984 irascible
[ɪrǽsəbl]
短気な
[= quick-tempered, irritable]
图 irascibility

1985 agrarian
[əgréəriən]
農地の, 農業の
[= agricultural]
▶ agrarian system（土地制度）

1986 forensic
[fərénsɪk]
犯罪科学の, 法廷の, 法医学の
▶ forensic evidence（法廷で用いられる証拠）

1987 ornithological
[ɔ̀ːrnəθɑ(ː)láʤɪkəl]
鳥類学の
图 ornithology（鳥類学）

1988 statutory
[stǽtʃʊtɔ̀ːri]
法定の
▶ statutory control（法定統制）

1989 empirically
[ɪmpírɪkəli]
実験結果に基づき

1990 erudite
[érjʊdàɪt]
学究的な [= scholarly], 博識の [= learned, deeply read]

I am not **averse** to further discussion, though I might not change my views.	私は自分の考えを変えないかもしれないが，議論を進めることに<u>反対している</u>わけではない。
As he spoke, the crowd began to grow increasingly **truculent**.	彼が話すにつれ，群衆はますます<u>攻撃的な</u>態度になった。
The philosopher's **abrasive** manner made him unpopular with students.	その哲学者は<u>癇にさわる</u>態度をとるので，学生に不人気だった。
Although he was known as **irascible**, his true nature was soft-hearted.	彼は<u>短気</u>だとして知られていたが，本質は穏和だった。
After the war, a number of important **agrarian** reforms were carried out.	戦後，多くの重要な<u>農地</u>改革が実施された。
Forensic investigations have become increasingly sophisticated.	<u>犯罪科学</u>捜査はますます最新技術になってきている。
The authorities consulted an **ornithological** expert about the eggs they had found.	当局は彼らが見つけた卵について，<u>鳥類学の</u>専門家に助言を求めた。
There were **statutory** penalties for breaking the regulations.	規則に違反したことに対する<u>法定</u>刑があった。
The hypothesis was later verified **empirically** by experiments.	その仮説は後に<u>実験結果に基づき</u>，実証された。
I just came across an impressively **erudite** study of pragmatism.	私は印象深い<u>学究的な</u>プラグマティズム研究にちょうど出くわした。

1991～2000

1991
esoteric
[èsətérɪk]

難解な [= recondite, abstruse]，
秘密の [= confidential, secret]，秘伝の
▶esoteric Buddhism（密教）

1992
perilous
[pérələs]

危険に満ちた [= dangerous, hazardous]
図 peril

1993
pernicious
[pərníʃəs]

有害な [= harmful, detrimental]，
破壊的な
▶pernicious disease（不治の病）

1994
intriguing
[ɪntríːgɪŋ]

興味をそそる [= fascinating]，
陰謀をたくらむ
▶intriguing festival（興味をそそる祭り）

1995
intuitive
[ɪntjúːətɪv]

直観的な
[= instinctive]
▶intuitive power（直観力）

1996
incisive
[ɪnsáɪsɪv]

辛辣な，痛烈な
[= acute]
▶incisive criticism（辛辣な批評）

1997
pungent
[pʌ́ndʒənt]

（においが）鼻につんとくる，
（批評などが）辛辣な [= scathing]
▶pungent sauce（香辛料のよく利いたソース）

1998
rampant
[rǽmpənt]

はびこる [= widespread, prevailing]，
荒々しい

1999
rapacious
[rəpéɪʃəs]

貪欲な
[= greedy]
▶rapacious disposition（強欲な性格）

2000
haggard
[hǽgərd]

やつれた
[= gaunt, drawn]

His book is interesting but full of difficult **esoteric** references.	彼の本は面白いが難解な論及でいっぱいだ。
He knew the journey across the winter mountains would be a **perilous** one.	冬山横断の旅が危険なものになるであろうことは，彼も知っていた。
Certain kinds of **pernicious** viruses thrive even in sanitary conditions.	ある種の有害なウイルスは衛生状態が良くても繁殖する。
He had bought the book because of its **intriguing** cover.	彼は興味をそそる表紙に引かれてその本を購入した。
The dog seemed to have an **intuitive** sense that they were going away.	その犬は彼らが去るということを直観する力を持っているようだった。
He was famous for his **incisive** reviews with their sharp observations.	彼は鋭い観察力で辛辣な評論を書くことで有名だった。
The moment he entered the house, he noticed a **pungent** smell of curry.	彼は家に入った瞬間に，カレーの刺激的なにおいを感じた。
Some say that bribery and distortion are **rampant** in post-communist Russia.	共産主義崩壊後のロシアでは，賄賂や事実の歪曲がはびこっているという話もある。
The Roman emperor Caligula's **rapacious** appetites helped destroy Rome.	ローマ皇帝カリグラの飽くことを知らない欲望がローマ破滅につながった。
Many people were shocked at the **haggard** faces of the survivors.	多くの人たちは生存者たちのやつれた顔を見てショックを受けた。

intriguing (1994) には「陰謀をたくらむ」の意味もあります。intriguing novel「興味をそそる小説」は，スパイ小説であることも多いです。

2001 ~ 2010

2001
harrowing
[hǽrouɪŋ]

痛ましい [= grievous, distressing]
動 harrow
▶harrowing tragedy (痛ましい悲劇)

2002
glib
[glɪb]

口達者な,口先だけの
▶glib speaker (口達者な話し手)

2003
verbose
[vəːrbóus]

回りくどい [= wordy, long-winded]
名 verbosity
▶verbose report (冗長なレポート)

2004
loquacious
[loukwéɪʃəs]

おしゃべりな
[= talkative, babbling]

2005
vociferous
[vousífərəs]

声高な
[= noisy]
▶be vociferous against ~ (~に猛反対する)

2006
taciturn
[tǽsɪtə̀ːrn]

口数の少ない [= quiet, reticent] (⇔talkative)
形 tacit (暗黙の)

2007
muffled
[mʌ́fld]

くぐもったような
[= indistinct]

2008
boisterous
[bɔ́ɪstərəs]

やかましい [= noisy, rowdy],
(天候などが) 荒れた [= stormy, turbulent]
▶a boisterous crowd (騒々しい群衆)

2009
rhetorically
[rɪtɔ́(ː)rɪkəli]

美辞麗句を並べて

2010
euphoric
[juːfɔ́ːrɪk]

幸福感にあふれた,
とてもうれしくなり陶酔する [= elated]
名 euphoria (幸福感)

She told her **harrowing** story to the press after her narrow escape.	彼女は命拾いをした後，報道関係者に対して痛ましい話をした。
Critics condemned the book as **glib** and insubstantial.	批評家たちは，その本を言葉巧みなだけで中身がないとしてこき下ろした。
I quickly tire of James Fenimore Cooper's **verbose** style.	私はジェームズ・フェニモア・クーパーのくどい文体にはすぐ飽きる。
Many traditional cultures claim that girls are more **loquacious** than boys.	多くの伝統的な文化は，女の子は男の子よりもおしゃべりだとしている。
When the teacher announced a test, there were **vociferous** protests from the class.	先生がテストの発表をした時，生徒の中から声高な抗議が上がった。
That child has always been **taciturn** but very perceptive of others.	その子どもはいつも口数が少なかったが，他人に対する洞察は鋭かった。
I could hear **muffled** voices next door, but couldn't make out any words.	隣家からくぐもったような声が聞こえたが，何の言葉も聞き取れなかった。
When the children became too **boisterous**, he took them outside so that they could run about.	子どもたちがやかましくなり過ぎたので，彼は子どもたちを外に連れ出して，走り回れるようにした。
The actor spoke **rhetorically** of the talents of his deceased colleague.	その俳優は他界した仲間の才能について美辞麗句を連ねて話した。
The townspeople became **euphoric** when the local team won.	町民は地元チームが勝利を収めたとき，幸福感でいっぱいになった。

2011 **expedient** [ɪkspíːdiənt]	好都合な [= proper, suited to the occasion] 图 expediency
2012 **felicitous** [fəlísətəs]	適切な [= appropriate, apt], 幸運な ▶felicitous remarks（適切な発言）
2013 **languid** [lǽŋgwɪd]	元気がない [= flagging, drooping], 物憂い [= listless, sluggish] 動 languish
2014 **sullen** [sʌ́lən]	不機嫌な, うっとうしい ▶a sullen look（不機嫌な顔つき）
2015 **jaded** [dʒéɪdɪd]	うんざりした, 疲れ果てた [= exhausted]
2016 **morose** [məróus]	気難しい, 不機嫌な ▶cast a morose glance at ~（~に気難しい視線を向ける）
2017 **fastidious** [fæstídiəs]	好みのうるさい [= fussy, particular], 気難しい [= squeamish], 神経質な
2018 **malignant** [məlíɡnənt]	悪意のある [= malicious], （病理学的に）悪性の [= malign] (⇔benign 良性の)
2019 **venomous** [vénəməs]	有毒な [= poisonous], 悪意のある [= spiteful, malicious] ▶venomous insect（有害な昆虫）
2020 **virulent** [vírjulənt]	悪性の, 悪意に満ちた ▶virulent attack（激しい攻撃）

His solution to the problem is the most **expedient** option.	彼のその問題に対する解決法が最も好都合な選択だ。
It took most of the night to reach a **felicitous** solution to our dilemma.	我々のジレンマの適切な解決法に到達するまで、ほぼ一晩かかった。
The boy seemed so **languid** we wondered if he was healthy.	その少年があまりに元気がなかったので、私たちは彼の健康をいぶかった。
The little girl stood with a **sullen** expression on her face.	その少女は不機嫌な表情を顔に浮かべて立っていた。
He felt **jaded** with a life of endless parties and expensive holidays.	彼は延々と続くパーティーと金のかかる休暇の暮らしにうんざりした。
His superior was a **morose**, pessimistic person with a bad temper.	彼の上司は気難しく悲観的で不機嫌な人だった。
Joe's **fastidious** attention to detail is often a waste of time.	ジョーは細かな点にこだわるが、時間の浪費であることが多い。
She had a **malignant** effect on the morale of the entire group.	彼女はグループ全体の士気に好ましくない影響を与えた。
India has many **venomous** species of snakes, such as cobras.	インドには毒を持つ種類の、コブラのようなヘビがたくさんいる。
A **virulent** disease began to rage through the refugee camp.	悪性の病気が難民キャンプで猛威を振るい始めた。

2021～2030

2021
penitent
[pénətnt]

悔い改めた，後悔している
[= remorseful]
图 penitence

2022
ascetic
[əsétɪk]

禁欲的な [= austere]，苦行の
图 asceticism（禁欲主義）

2023
juvenile
[dʒúːvənàɪl]

青少年の [= adolescent]（⇔ senile 老齢の）
▶ juvenile delinquency（少年犯罪，非行）

2024
adjunct
[ǽdʒʌŋkt]

非常勤の，補助の
▶ adjunct professor（非常勤教授）

2025
analogous
[ənǽləgəs]

(～に)似ている〈to〉
[= similar, comparable, corresponding]
图 analogy

2026
askew
[əskjúː]

不満そうに，斜めに，傾いて [= awry]

2027
ablaze
[əbléɪz]

輝いて

2028
agape
[əgéɪp]

口をぽかんと開けて

2029
agnostic
[æɡnɑ́(ː)stɪk]

懐疑的な [= skeptic, incredulous]，不可知論者の
图 agnosticism

2030
ambient
[ǽmbiənt]

周囲の
▶ ambient music（環境音楽）

Penitent pilgrims flock to that famous shrine every year.	毎年，悔い改めた巡礼者がその有名な神殿に集まる。
The founders of most major religions tended to lead **ascetic** lifestyles.	ほとんどの主要宗教の創始者たちは禁欲的な生活を送る傾向があった。
Juvenile delinquency is a social problem that seems to be getting worse.	青少年の非行は社会問題となっていて，悪化しつつあるように思われる。
He found a job as an **adjunct** professor but he wanted to become a permanent staff member.	彼は非常勤教授の職を見つけたが，終身職員になりたかった。
Fables are often **analogous** to moral dilemmas in real life.	寓話は，実生活の道徳的ジレンマに類似することが多い。
Despite their careful planning, the concert went **askew** from the beginning.	慎重に計画したにもかかわらず，コンサートは最初から不満な出来だった。
The whole street was **ablaze** with bright Christmas decorations.	通り全体が明るい色のクリスマスの飾りで輝いていた。
He watched her leave, his mouth **agape** with astonishment.	彼は驚いて口をぽかんと開けて，彼女が去るのを見ていた。
The scientist said that he remained **agnostic** about the new theory.	その科学者は，新理論に対して依然として懐疑的であると言った。
The hospital's **ambient** colors were designed to soothe the patients.	病院の周囲の色は患者を落ち着かせるためにデザインされた。

juvenile (2023) のjuveは (若い) を意味します。ほかの例としてはjunior「年下の」，rejuvenate「再活性化させる，若返らせる」などがあります。

#	単語	意味	補足
2031	**anemic** [əníːmɪk]	貧血(症)の, 元気のない	图 anemia ▶anemic condition (貧血状態)
2032	**attuned** [ətjúːnd]	合った	
2033	**burnished** [bə́ːrnɪʃt]	磨き上げられた	[= polished] ▶burnished silver (磨き上げられた銀)
2034	**bungling** [bʌ́ŋglɪŋ]	手際の悪い	[= amateurish, inexpert]
2035	**cavernous** [kǽvərnəs]	洞窟のような	▶cavernous entrance (洞窟のような入口)
2036	**inveterate** [ɪnvét̮ərət]	常習的な	[= chronic, habitual] ▶inveterate disease (持病)
2037	**cumulative** [kjúːmjʊlət̮ɪv]	累積する	[= accumulating] ▶a cumulative deficit (累積赤字)
2038	**fiendish** [fíːndɪʃ]	悪魔のような [= diabolical], 不快な	▶fiendish weather (ひどい天気)
2039	**fortuitously** [fɔːrtjúːət̮əsli]	偶然に	[= unexpectedly] 图 fortuity
2040	**grudgingly** [grʌ́dʒɪŋli]	しぶしぶ	[= unwillingly]

After her illness, she seemed to be recovering but was still **anemic**.	病気の後，彼女は回復しているように見えたが，まだ貧血気味だった。
The company wanted a designer **attuned** to the tastes of young people.	その会社は若者の好みに合ったデザイナーを求めていた。
The **burnished** metal statue shone brightly in the sunlight.	磨き上げられた金属像は太陽光線を浴びて光っていた。
His **bungling** attempts to fix the car had only made the problem worse.	彼の手際の悪い車を修理するやり方は，問題をさらに悪化させただけだった。
When they spoke, their voices echoed across the **cavernous** hall.	彼らが話した時，彼らの話し声は洞窟のような講堂に響き渡った。
Few believed his story because he was known to be an **inveterate** liar.	彼は常習的な嘘つきとして知られているので，彼の話を信じる人はほとんどいなかった。
The **cumulative** effect of the rainfall had been to weaken the soil.	降雨の蓄積作用で，土壌が弱くなってしまった。
Many people were horrified by the use of such **fiendish** weapons.	多くの人たちはそんな悪魔のような武器の使用に震えあがった。
He was beginning to feel lost when **fortuitously** he spotted a friend.	彼は偶然に友達を見つけた時，戸惑いを覚え始めていた。
His opponent **grudgingly** conceded defeat in the chess match.	チェスの試合で彼の対戦者はしぶしぶ敗北を認めた。

2041
ignominious
[ìgnəmíniəs]

不名誉な [= shameful]，屈辱的な
名 ignominy

2042
irrevocable
[ɪrévəkəbl]

取り消せない
[= unalterable]
▶irrevocable judgment（確定判決）

2043
illiberal
[ɪlíbərəl]

反自由主義の，
狭量な [= narrow-minded]

2044
subversive
[səbvə́ːrsɪv]

破壊的な [= destructive]
動 subvert
名 subversion, subversive（破壊分子）

2045
iridescent
[ìrɪdésənt]

玉虫色の，きらきら光る
[= shimmering, sparkling]
▶iridescent luster（虹色の光沢）

2046
kindred
[kíndrəd]

同種の，関連のある
▶kindred language（同族言語）

2047
superficial
[sùːpərfíʃəl]

表面的な
名 superficiality 副 superficially

2048
malleable
[mǽliəbl]

素直な，融通の利く [= pliable]，
可鍛性の
▶malleable casting（可鍛鋳物）

2049
microscopically
[màɪkrəskáː)pɪkəli]

極めて詳細に
[= in detail]

2050
murky
[mə́ːrki]

うさん臭い [= suspicious]，
暗い [= dark]
▶murky activities（うさん臭い活動）

His resignation was an **ignominious** end to a once promising career.	かつては前途有望なキャリアを期待されていたのに，彼の辞職は不名誉な結末だった。
The court declared that its ruling was **irrevocable**.	判決は確定であると，法廷は宣言した。
The newspaper was known for its **illiberal** views on immigration.	その新聞は外国からの移住に対して反自由主義の見解を示すことで知られていた。
So-called **subversive** elements in society are still being purged.	いわゆる社会の破壊分子は今でも追放されたままである。
He wore an **iridescent** suit made of some synthetic fabric.	彼は合成繊維でできた玉虫色のスーツを着ていた。
As the two schools had **kindred** problems, they decided to cooperate.	2校は同じような問題を抱えていたので協力し合うことにした。
The newspaper's report was criticized as **superficial** and misleading.	その新聞の報道は，表面的で誤解を招くものであるとして非難された。
She had the chance to shape the children's **malleable** minds.	彼女は子どもたちの素直な気質を形成する機会に恵まれた。
The committee examined the research proposal **microscopically** before approving it.	委員会は承認する前に調査企画書を極めて詳細に検討した。
The businessman was said to have a **murky** past in the construction business.	その実業家は建設業でうさん臭い過去があったと言われていた。

2051 nimble
[nímbl]
(動作・頭の)回転の速い [= quick-thinking]
▶nimble fingers(器用な手先)

2052 onerous
[óunərəs]
厄介な [= burdensome], 煩わしい, 骨の折れる

2053 pallid
[pǽlɪd]
(顔・肌などが)青白い [= pale, wan], つまらない
▶pallid performance(つまらない演技)

2054 phenomenal
[fəná(:)mɪnəl]
驚異的な [= outstanding], 自然現象に関する
▶phenomenal science(現象科学)

2055 reprehensible
[rèprɪhénsəbl]
非難されるべき
▶reprehensible behavior(非難すべき行動)

2056 sectarian
[sektéəriən]
派閥の, 分派の
▶sectarian violent(派閥の暴動)

2057 seditious
[sɪdíʃəs]
扇動を行う
▶seditious publication(扇動的な出版物)

2058 upscale
[ʌ̀pskéɪl]
高級な
(⇔downscale)
▶upscale residential area(高級住宅地)

2059 void
[vɔ́ɪd]
(〜の)ない〈of〉
▶null and void(法的に無効の)

2060 volatile
[vá(:)lətəl]
揮発性の, 気まぐれな, 変動しやすい
▶volatile stock and bonds market
(変動しやすい株式債券市場)

He was a **nimble** debater and it was hard to catch him in a contradiction.	彼は頭の回転が速い論客だったので，彼の矛盾点をつくのは難しかった。
He found dealing with students' parents an especially **onerous** duty.	彼は生徒たちの両親に応対することは特に骨の折れる仕事だということがわかった。
After months of severe dieting, her face looks drawn and **pallid**.	厳しいダイエットを数か月した結果，彼女の顔はげっそりとして青白く見える。
The little boy seemed to have a **phenomenal** knowledge of the city.	少年は都市について驚異的な知識を持っているようだった。
The judge said that such a **reprehensible** crime deserved a severe punishment.	裁判官はこのような非難されるべき犯罪は厳しい刑に値すると言った。
The revolutionary group was beset by a series of **sectarian** conflicts.	その革命グループは一連の派閥の闘争に悩まされた。
He was found to be in possession of a number of **seditious** pamphlets.	彼は多くの扇動的なビラを所有しているところを見つかった。
On their wedding anniversary, he took his wife to an **upscale** restaurant.	結婚記念日に彼は妻を高級レストランに連れて行った。
The area was **void** of houses for as far as he could see.	彼が見渡す限り，その地域に家はなかった。
The liquid in the tank is so **volatile** that it is necessary to seal it carefully.	タンクの中の液体は揮発性が高いので，注意深く密封する必要がある。

upscale (2058) は日本語的発想では「スケールの大きな」をイメージしてしまいそうになりますが「高級な」を意味することをしっかり覚えましょう。

2061
bent
[bent]

不正な [= corrupt, devious], 曲がった [= crooked]

2062
berserk
[bərsə́ːrk]

狂暴な [= wild]
▶ go [run] berserk（暴れ狂う）

2063
cerebral
[sérəbrəl]

理性的な, （大）脳の
图 cerebrum（大脳）
▶ cerebral action（脳の作用）

2064
contingent
[kəntíndʒənt]

(〜に) 依存する ⟨on⟩ [= dependent], 不測の
图 contingency（不慮の出来事）, contingent（代表団）　▶ contingent business（付帯業務）

2065
culpable
[kʌ́lpəbl]

有罪の [= guilty], 非難に値する [= blameworthy] (⇔inculpable)
▶ culpable negligence（有罪の過失）

2066
demure
[dɪmjúər]

内気な [= modest], おとなしい, 上品ぶった
图 demureness

2067
droll
[droʊl]

ひょうきんな [= funny] (⇔serious)
▶ droll actor（ひょうきんな俳優）

2068
frigid
[frídʒɪd]

酷寒の [= extremely cold], 冷淡な [= stiff and formal, lacking zeal]
▶ frigid day（とても寒い日）

2069
gaunt
[gɔːnt]

やせ衰えた [= emaciated]
▶ gaunt face（やせた顔）

2070
gluttonous
[glʌ́tənəs]

食いしん坊の
[= voracious]
图 glutton

He found a **bent** official and bribed him to give him a passport.	彼は不正な役人を見つけて，パスポートを発行してくれるようにと賄賂を贈った。
The man lost his temper and went **berserk**, attacking anyone in sight.	その男性は激怒して荒れ狂い，目に入る人を手当たり次第に攻撃した。
His approach to people is more **cerebral** than sympathetic.	彼の人々に接する態度は，感情に訴えるというより理性に訴えるものである。
My participation was **contingent** on your meeting specified conditions.	私の参加は，あなたが特定条件を満たしているかにかかっていた。
After a long trial, the jury determined that the defendant was **culpable**.	長い審理の後，被告は有罪であると陪審団は裁決した。
It was hard to believe that the **demure** young woman before them was on trial for murder.	彼らの前にいる若くて内気な女性が，殺人容疑で公判中だとは信じ難かった。
His **droll** sense of humor made him popular with everyone.	ひょうきんなユーモアで彼は皆に人気だった。
The winters in the northern American states are extremely **frigid**.	アメリカ北部の州の冬はひどく酷寒である。
I was concerned at his **gaunt** appearance after hearing of his long illness.	私は，長い間病気していたと聞いた後の彼のやせ衰えた姿を見て心配だった。
They spent a **gluttonous** week in Paris sampling local restaurants.	彼らはパリの地元のレストランで味見をしながら，食いしん坊な1週間を過ごした。

---

culpable (2065)「有罪の」のculpは〈過失〉を意味します。ほかの例としてはculprit「罪人」，inculpate「罪を負わせる」などがあります。

2071	**moot** [muːt]	意味を持たない, 議論の余地のある [= debatable]
2072	**munificent** [mjunífɪsənt]	気前のよい [= lavish, bounteous, liberal, generous] 名 munificence
2073	**narrowly** [nǽrouli]	かろうじて [= marginally]
2074	**notoriously** [noutɔ́ːriəsli]	札付きの, 悪名高く 形 notorious
2075	**oblique** [əblíːk]	遠回しの, 間接的な, 傾いた [= slanting]
2076	**obtrusive** [əbtrúːsɪv]	ひどく目立つ, 押しつけがましい 動 obtrude ▶obtrusive behavior（でしゃばった態度）
2077	**odious** [óudiəs]	嫌な [= hateful, repugnant, offensive] 名 odium（憎しみ）
2078	**ominous** [ɑ́(ː)mɪnəs]	不穏な, 不吉な [= sinister], 気味の悪い ▶ominous silence（気味の悪い沈黙）
2079	**opulent** [ɑ́(ː)pjulənt]	ぜいたくな, 裕福な, 豊富な 名 opulence
2080	**famished** [fǽmɪʃt]	飢えている [= very hungry]

He said it was a **moot** point whether he would actually attend the conference.	彼は，実際に会議に出席するか否かは<u>意味のない</u>問題だと言った。
We were astonished by the **munificent** gifts he had given us.	私たちは彼がくれた<u>気前のよい</u>贈り物にびっくりした。
The driver **narrowly** avoided running into the deer on the road.	運転手は道路上のシカに衝突するのを<u>かろうじて</u>避けた。
The previous chairman was a **notoriously** arrogant person.	前会長は<u>札付きの</u>傲慢(ごうまん)な人だった。
His comments on the painting were taken as an **oblique** criticism of its owner.	その絵画に対する彼の評論は，絵の所有者への<u>遠回しの</u>非難だと受け取られた。
An **obtrusive** poster warned students not to smoke on campus.	<u>ひどく目立つ</u>ポスターが，学生に構内でタバコを吸わないようにと警告していた。
The task was **odious** but necessary.	その仕事は<u>嫌な</u>ものだったが必要だった。
Recent economic signs in Southeast Asia have been becoming more and more **ominous**.	東南アジアの最近の経済状況はますます<u>不穏に</u>なってきた。
She was surprised when she saw his **opulent** home with its expensive furnishings.	高価な備え付け家具のそろった彼の<u>ぜいたくな</u>家を見て，彼女は驚嘆した。
After the rugby match, both teams felt thirsty and **famished**.	ラグビーの試合の後で，両チームはのどが渇いて<u>腹がペコペコだ</u>と感じた。

2081 recurrent
[rɪkə́:rənt]

再発性の
[= repeated]

2082 replete
[rɪplí:t]

(~が)豊富な〈with〉, いっぱいで
[= filled]
图 repletion

2083 senile
[sí:naɪl]

老齢による, 老人の (⇔ juvenile 若者の)
图 senility (老衰)
▶ senile dementia (老人性認知症)

2084 sheer
[ʃɪər]

全くの [= mere, utter, downright, absolute],
切り立った [= precipitous]

2085 sleek
[sli:k]

滑らかでつやつやした [= smooth and glossy],
人あたりが良い
▶ as sleek as a cat (人あたりが良い)

2086 snide
[snaɪd]

皮肉な [= sarcastic]

2087 sturdily
[stə́:rdili]

しっかりと [= persistently]

2088 sumptuous
[sʌ́mptʃuəs]

豪華な [= splendid, magnificent],
金をかけた [= costly]

2089 taut
[tɔ:t]

張り詰めた [= tense] (⇔ slack),
整然とした [= tidy, neat]

2090 tenuous
[ténjuəs]

希薄な [= rare, thin],
内容の乏しい [= flimsy, superficial]

For the rest of his life, he suffered from **recurrent** bouts of malaria.	彼は死ぬまで再発性のマラリアの発作に苦しんだ。
The American state of Indiana is **replete** with a variety of wild flowers.	アメリカのインディアナ州は、いろいろな野生の花が豊富だ。
His family realized that he was becoming **senile** when he forgot his own address.	彼が自分の住所を思い出せなくなった時、家族は彼が老いつつあるのだと気付いた。
I read his novel but thought it was **sheer** nonsense.	彼の小説を読んだが、全くのナンセンスだと思った。
He brushed the cat's fur until it looked **sleek** and tidy.	彼はネコの毛をつやつやしてこぎれいになるまでブラッシングした。
When the man promoted his own son, there were many **snide** comments.	男性が自分の息子を昇進させた時、多くの皮肉な意見が上がった。
The little boy answered the teacher's questions **sturdily**.	少年は先生の質問にしっかりと答えた。
We sat down to a **sumptuous** dinner with our guests.	私たちは客と一緒に、豪華な食卓に着いた。
A **taut** rope above the river allowed us to cross without getting wet.	川の上にぴんと張ったロープのおかげで私たちはぬれずに渡ることができた。
The student's essay indicated that he had only a **tenuous** understanding of the topic.	その学生の小論文は、彼がそのテーマに対して薄っぺらな理解しかしていないことを示していた。

2091 **terse** [tə:rs]	簡潔な [= condensed, compressed, laconic]
2092 **translucent** [trænslú:sənt]	半透明の cf. transparent (透明な) ▶translucent container (半透明の容器)
2093 **upstage** [ʌ́pstèɪdʒ]	舞台後方の (⇔ downstage 舞台前方の)
2094 **vigilant** [vídʒələnt]	慎重な, 油断のない [= watchful]
2095 **critical** [krítɪkəl]	(〜に)批判的な⟨of⟩, 重大な 動 criticize 名 critic (批評家), criticism (批評), critique (批評)
2096 **obtuse** [əbtjú:s]	鈍い, 鈍角の [= blunt, insensitive] (⇔ acute)
2097 **flawless** [flɔ́:ləs]	非の打ち所がない [= impeccable]
2098 **intact** [ɪntǽkt]	損なわれていない [= untouched, whole, unimpaired], 元のままの 語源 in (でない) + tact (触れる)
2099 **voluptuous** [vəlʌ́ptʃuəs]	肉感的な [= sensual, sexy, sultry]
2100 **identical** [aɪdéntɪkəl]	一卵性の, 同一の [= the same] 動 identify (を特定する) 名 identity (身元) ▶identical person (本人)

Proverbs are typically **terse** but wise expressions of traditional values.	諺は普通，伝統的な価値観の**簡潔だ**が賢明な表現である。
The box was made of a **translucent** green plastic material.	その箱は**半透明の**緑色のプラスチック素材でできていた。
He moved into an **upstage** position in order to deliver his speech.	彼はスピーチを行うために**舞台後方の**位置へ移動した。
The politician was known as a **vigilant** defender of human rights.	その政治家は人権の**慎重な**擁護者として知られていた。
Although he supported the proposal in public, he was known to be **critical** of it privately.	彼は表向きはその提案を支持したが，個人的にはその提案に**批判的である**と知られていた。
I couldn't believe how **obtuse** such an educated man could be.	それほど教育のある人がそんなに**鈍感に**なるなんて信じられなかった。
One critic said that the film was a **flawless** work of art, perfect in every way.	その映画は芸術作品として**非の打ち所がなく**，あらゆる点で完璧だと，ある評論家は語った。
No matter how difficult things got, he kept his integrity **intact**.	事態がどんなに厳しくなろうとも，彼は自分の誠実さを**損なわずに**保った。
Marilyn Monroe became an icon of **voluptuous** American beauty.	マリリン・モンローはアメリカの**肉感的な**美女の象徴となった。
Identical twins are siblings that originate from a single fertilized egg.	**一卵性**双生児は単一の受精卵から生まれる兄弟である。

translucent「半透明な」(2092)とtransparent「透明な」を間違えないようにしましょう。

1分間 mini test

1 1分間

(1) I couldn't believe how (   ) such an educated man could be.

(2) Everything the new secretary did (   ) her employer.

(3) As soon as he arrived, he (   ) the goods to the customer.

(4) One critic said that the film was a (   ) work of art, perfect in every way.

(5) The doctor (   ) that the infection was carried by water.

(6) Improvements in (   ) contributed to the disease's eradication.

(7) The man had kept his daughter a (   ) in her own home.

(8) We posted guards on the (   ) of the camp in case anyone tried to infiltrate in the night.

(9) For the rest of his life, he suffered from (   ) bouts of malaria.

(10) Proverbs are typically (   ) but wise expressions of traditional values.

ここから選んでね。 ※選択肢はすべて原形で表示しています。

① terse   ② antagonize   ③ periphery
④ flawless   ⑤ captive   ⑥ hypothesize
⑦ obtuse   ⑧ consign   ⑨ recurrent
⑩ sanitation

2 1分間

(11) He complained that he was being (　　　) for no reason.

(12) Racial (　　　) in the American South continued long after the Civil War.

(13) The driver (　　　) avoided running into the deer on the road.

(14) After (　　　) with his client, the lawyer said that he had no more questions.

(15) The task was (　　　) but necessary.

(16) He cleverly (　　　) the criticism by turning it back on his opponent.

(17) However hard they (　　　), they still fell into debt by the end of the month.

(18) He was on the (　　　) of losing his temper, but he managed to look calm.

(19) Becoming a Zen monk often requires a great deal of zeal and (　　　).

(20) After the rugby match, both teams felt thirsty and (　　　).

ここから選んでね。

- ⑪ fortitude
- ⑫ narrowly
- ⑬ verge
- ⑭ odious
- ⑮ segregation
- ⑯ parry
- ⑰ famished
- ⑱ strive
- ⑲ confer
- ⑳ malign

1分間 mini test 答え

1 P. 460

(1)	⑦	2096	obtuse	(⇒p. 458)
(2)	②	1404	antagonize(antagonized)	(⇒p. 318)
(3)	⑧	1417	consign(consigned)	(⇒p. 320)
(4)	④	2097	flawless	(⇒p. 458)
(5)	⑥	1431	hypothesize(hypothesized)	(⇒p. 324)
(6)	⑩	1815	sanitation	(⇒p. 400)
(7)	⑤	1828	captive	(⇒p. 402)
(8)	③	1838	periphery	(⇒p. 404)
(9)	⑨	2081	recurrent	(⇒p. 456)
(10)	①	2091	terse	(⇒p. 458)

2 P. 461

(11)	⑳	1617	malign(maligned)	(⇒p. 360)
(12)	⑮	1846	segregation	(⇒p. 406)
(13)	⑫	2073	narrowly	(⇒p. 454)
(14)	⑲	1616	confer(conferring)	(⇒p. 360)
(15)	⑭	2077	odious	(⇒p. 454)
(16)	⑯	1598	parry(parried)	(⇒p. 356)
(17)	⑱	1608	strive(strove)	(⇒p. 358)
(18)	⑬	1859	verge	(⇒p. 410)
(19)	⑪	1760	fortitude	(⇒p. 390)
(20)	⑰	2080	famished	(⇒p. 454)

熟語編

300

熟語(300語) ········· 464

熟語編では、1級の語彙問題でよく出題される句動詞を中心に取り上げました。まず、ここに掲載されている300語を確実に覚えましょう。

1周目	2周目
/	/

2101
abide by
(規則など)に従う [= live by]

The boy was warned that if he did not **abide by** the school rules, he would be expelled.
校則に**従わ**ないならば退学になると,その男の子は警告を受けた。

2102
act up
(興奮して)暴れる,(機械などが)異常に作動する [= go rampant]

At the banquet table, two drunken businessmen were **acting up**.
宴会では2人の酔っ払ったビジネスマンが**暴れて**いた。

2103
add up to
結局~になる [= amount to], **~につながる** [= lead to]

Bill's skill at the piano and Joanna's beautiful voice **added up to** a winning combination.
ビルのピアノの技量とジョアンナの美声は,必勝のコンビに**なった**。

2104
adhere to
~に従う,~に固執する [= cling to]

I must ask you to **adhere to** the terms of our agreement and not reveal any information to outsiders.
我々の合意の条件に**従って**いただき,情報は一切外部に漏らさないよう,お願いしたい。

2105
atone for
~を償う [= expiate]

The released prisoner said he had **atoned for** his crimes.
釈放された囚人は罪を**償った**と言った。

2106
attribute A to B
AはBに起因すると考える

The writer **attributed** his success **to** luck and good teachers.
その作家は自身の成功を運と良い先生たちの**おかげだと考えた**。

2107
bail out
(企業など)を救済する,~を保釈する

The central bank was criticized for **bailing out** companies that had made risky loans.
リスクの高い融資を受けてきた企業を**救済したこと**で,中央銀行は非難を浴びた。

2108
bank on
~を当てにする [= depend on]

The president always **banks on** the hard working nature of his employees.
社長は常に従業員たちのよく働く性格**を当てにしている**。

2109
barge into
~にどかどか入り込む [= thrust into], (会話など)に割り込む

Suddenly, a man **barged into** the room and began shouting.
突然，男性が部屋**にどかどか入り込み**，叫び始めた。

2110
bawl out
~を厳しく叱りとばす

His teacher **bawled** him **out** for missing the math test.
先生は彼が数学のテストを受けなかったので彼**を大声で非難した**。

2111
be bogged down in
~に行き詰まる

Sorry I couldn't call you last week; I **was bogged down in** work.
先週，電話をかけられなくてごめんなさい。仕事**に行き詰まって**いたんです。

2112
be cut out for
~に向いている [= have talent for]

I quit being a builder because I **wasn't cut out for** the physical labor.
私は肉体労働**に向いていなかった**ので建築作業員の仕事を辞めた。

2113
be geared up for
~の準備をする

Because the students **were** all **geared up for** the test, they were quite upset when it was suddenly postponed for a week.
学生たちはすっかり試験**の準備をしていた**ので，試験が急に1週間延期になった時，非常に動揺した。

2114
be keyed up
興奮している, 緊張している [= be strung up]

He **was** so **keyed up** about the forthcoming race that he could not settle down and relax at all.
彼はあまりにも次のレースのことで**興奮していた**ので，全く落ち着いてリラックスできなかった。

2115 bear down on
~に真剣に対処する

The minister promised that he would **bear down on** waste and inefficiency.
大臣は無駄と非効率に真剣に対処することを約束した。

2116 bear out
(仮説など)を証明する [= support, back up]

The recently discovered manuscript **bears out** the theory that Shakespeare spent part of his youth in France.
最近発見された原稿は、シェイクスピアは青年時代の一部をフランスで過ごしたという説を証明している。

2117 bear the brunt of
~の矢面に立つ

The soldiers at the front **bore the brunt of** the attack.
前線の兵士は攻撃の矢面に立った。

2118 beat up
~をさんざん殴る [= assault, attack]

The drug dealer was **beaten up** by members of a rival gang.
麻薬密売人は対立する暴力団員にさんざん殴られた。

2119 beef about
~のことで文句を言う [= complain about]

Jim often **beefs about** his salary.
ジムはよく給料のことで文句を言う。

2120 beef up
~を強化する [= strengthen]

The company headhunted a number of specialists in order to **beef up** its IT department.
その企業はIT部門を強化するために、大勢の専門家たちをヘッドハンティングした。

2121 belt out
~を大声で歌う [= sing out loud]

At the end of the ceremony, the students **belted out** the school song.
式典の最後に生徒たちは校歌を大声で歌った。

2122
black out
(発表など)を抑える [= suppress], 一時的に意識を失う [= faint]

The government attempted to **black out** any reference to the dissident.
政府は反対派のいかなる発言も公表を**抑え**ようとした。

2123
blare out
鳴り響く [= resonate]

Music **blared out** from the teenager's room day and night.
音楽がそのティーンエイジャーの部屋から四六時中，**鳴り響いた**。

2124
blot out
～を消し去る [= efface, erase]

The woman did her best to **blot out** all memory of the incident.
女性はその出来事のすべての記憶**を消し去る**ために最善を尽くした。

2125
blow over
(嵐・困難などが)過ぎ去る, (うわさが)忘れ去られる

I'm waiting for Europe's debt crisis to **blow over** before I invest.
私は投資する前にヨーロッパの債権危機が**過ぎ去る**のを待っている。

2126
boil down to
～に帰着する [= end up with]

The dispute between the two countries **boiled down to** the question of which was the rightful owner of the island.
2国間の紛争は，その島の正当な所有国はどちらかという問題**に帰着した**。

2127
botch up
～をしくじる [= mess up, foul up]

The police **botched up** the inquiry and the criminal was never brought to justice.
警察が捜査**をしくじった**ため，犯罪者は裁判にかけられることはなかった。

2128
bow out
辞任する

The retiring chairman said he intended to **bow out** gracefully.
退任の近い会長は潔く**辞任する**つもりだと言った。

2129
box up
~を箱詰めする

Her parents **boxed up** her belongings and sent them to her.
両親は彼女の持ち物を箱詰めし，彼女に送った。

2130
branch out into
~に事業を拡張する　[= extend *one's* business into]

As it grew, the company began to **branch out into** new areas of business.
会社は成長するにつれて，さまざまなビジネスの新しい分野に手を広げ始めた。

2131
break away from
~から脱却する　[= pull out of]

The company said it wanted to **break away from** its conservative image.
会社は保守的なイメージから脱却することを望んでいると言った。

2132
breeze into
~にすっと入ってくる

The boy **breezed into** the classroom twenty minutes late.
その少年は20分遅刻して，教室にすっと入ってきた。

2133
brim over with
~でみなぎる　[= be full of]

Her husband was **brimming over with** resentment at her.
彼女の夫は彼女に対する怒りでみなぎっていた。

2134
browse through
(本)を拾い読みする

The students **browsed through** newspapers and magazines to find topics for their speeches.
学生たちはスピーチの題材を探すために新聞や雑誌を拾い読みした。

2135
bubble over with
~で満ちあふれる

At the wedding, the bride **bubbled over with** happiness.
結婚式では，花嫁は幸福感に満ちあふれていた。

2136
buckle down to
〜に本腰を入れる

After he entered university, it took him a while to **buckle down to** his studies, but as soon as he did he began to get excellent grades.
大学入学後,勉強に**本腰を入れる**のにしばらく時間がかかったものの,本腰が入るやいなや,彼は素晴らしい成績を取り始めた。

2137
bundle up
〜を暖かく包み込む

She **bundled up** the baby in a blanket before taking him out.
彼女は外に連れ出す前に毛布で赤ん坊を**暖かくくるんだ**。

2138
bury *oneself* in
〜に没頭する
[= be engrossed in]

The boy **buried himself in** preparing for his final examinations.
その少年は期末試験の準備に**没頭した**。

2139
butt in
口を挟む
[= horn in, cut in]

As she explained the situation, her husband kept **butting in** and correcting her remarks.
彼女が状況について説明していると,夫が**口を挟んで**,彼女の発言を訂正し続けた。

2140
butter up
〜にごまをする
[= flatter, apple-polish]

I hate being **buttered up** by students who think that compliments will win them a good grade.
お世辞を言えば良い成績が取れると思っている学生に**ごまをすられる**のが,私は気に食わない。

2141
buy off
〜を買収する
[= bribe]

The crooked businessman tried to **buy off** the local police but he was arrested for bribery instead.
悪徳業者は地元警察を**買収**しようとしたが,反対に贈賄で逮捕された。

2142
cart A off to B
AをBへ連れ去る

Eventually, the police **carted** the men **off to** the station for questioning.
結局,警察は尋問するために男たちを署へ**連行した**。

2143 carve up
~を分割する [= divide]

The victorious nations **carved up** the territory into colonies.
戦勝国は領土を分割して植民地にした。

2144 cash in on
~に乗じる [= take advantage of, capitalize on]

In an attempt to **cash in on** the fashion for things Chinese, the TV channel decided to dramatize a classic Chinese novel.
中国ブームに乗じようとして，そのテレビ局は中国の古典小説のドラマ化を決定した。

2145 cast *one's* mind back to
(昔)のことを思い起こす

The speaker asked them to **cast their minds back to** their childhood.
話し手は彼らに子どもの頃のことを思い起こすよう頼んだ。

2146 cave in to
~に屈する [= give in]

After a few days of fighting, the rebels **caved in to** the government forces.
数日間の戦闘後，反逆者たちは政府軍に屈した。

2147 chalk up
~の記録を達成する [= record]

Matsui **chalked up** two more home runs.
松井はさらに2本のホームランを記録した。

2148 change over
交代する [= take turns]

On their journey, the two drivers **changed over** every few hours.
旅行中，2人の運転手が数時間ごとに交代した。

2149 chase up
~を探し出す [= ferret out]

Her boss asked her to **chase up** any documents concerning the case.
上司は彼女に事件に関するどんな書類でも探し出すようにと頼んだ。

2150
choke back
~をこらえる

Although he was angry, he **choked back** his complaints and remained silent.
彼は怒っていたが、文句を言うの**をこらえて**黙っていた。

2151
clam up
黙り込む
[= fall silent]

When the teacher questioned the boy, he **clammed up** immediately.
先生が少年に問いただすと、彼はすぐさま**黙り込んだ**。

2152
claw back
~を徐々に取り戻す

Japan Automobiles is trying to **claw back** market share.
ジャパンオートモビルズはマーケットシェア**を徐々に取り戻そう**としている。

2153
come in for
(非難など)を受ける
[= be subjected to]

After the riot, the police **came in for** a lot of criticism for their handling of the incident.
暴動の後、警察は事件の処理に関して多くの非難**を受けた**。

2154
cook up
~をでっち上げる
[= fabricate]

You are late again. Don't even think of **cooking up** an excuse this time.
君はまた遅刻だ。今度は言い訳**をでっち上げよう**なんて考えるんじゃないぞ。

2155
cop out of
~を回避する
[= skirt around]

He accused her of **copping out of** her duty as a mother.
彼は母親としての務め**を回避している**として彼女を責めた。

2156
cordon off
~を封鎖する
[= block off]

The police **cordoned off** the murder scene to prevent members of the public from entering.
警察は公衆の立ち入りを防ぐために殺人現場**を封鎖した**。

2157 crack down on ～を厳しく取り締まる

The principal warned that he was going to **crack down on** students copying their homework from each other.
学生たちが互いの宿題を複写し合っていること**を厳しく取り締まる**つもりだと、校長は警告した。

2158 crack up 精神的に参る、笑いこける

He **cracked up** under the pressure of his job and had to spend six months on leave to recover.
彼は仕事の重圧で**精神的に参って**しまい、回復するために6か月の休みを取らなければならなかった。

2159 crank out ～を機械的に量産する

The thriller writer **cranked out** a novel a year for ten years.
そのスリラー作家は10年間、年に1冊の割合で小説**を次々と量産した**。

2160 creep into ～にそっと忍び込む [= sneak into]

A suspicion that he was being cheated **crept into** his mind.
だまされているのではないかという疑念が、彼の心の中に**そっと忍び込んできた**。

2161 crop up （問題などが）急に持ち上がる [= come up]

The launch of the new car was delayed after a number of small problems **cropped up** at the last moment.
土壇場になっていくつもの小さな問題が**持ち上がった**ため、新車の発売は延期された。

2162 crouch down しゃがむ [= hunker down, squat down]

The children **crouched down** to watch the ants running about.
子どもたちはアリが走り回っているのを見るために**しゃがんだ**。

2163 dabble in ～に手を出す

She **dabbled in** the stock market and lost some money.
彼女は株取引に**手を出し**、いくらかの金を失った。

2164
dash off
～を一気に仕上げる

In the end, he **dashed off** the essay the night before it was due.
結局，彼は締め切りの前夜に小論を一気に書き上げた。

2165
deal out
～を分配する
[= share out]

The foreman **dealt out** the weekly wages to the gang of laborers.
作業長は週給を労働者の一団に分配した。

2166
delegate A to B
AをBに委ねる

Mr. Smith will **delegate** his authority **to** Mr. Garcia.
スミス氏は彼の権限をガルシア氏に委ねるつもりだ。

2167
descend on
～に押しかける，～を襲撃する

During the summer months, hordes of tourists **descended on** the little seaside resort.
夏の間に，観光客の大群が，その海辺の小さなリゾート地に押しかけた。

2168
dispense with
～なしで済ませる
[= do without]

The school decided to **dispense with** the services of the caretaker.
学校は管理人の業務なしで済ませることに決めた。

2169
distract A from B
AをBから気を散らす

She told her husband not to **distract** their son **from** his homework.
彼女は夫に息子が宿題から気を散らさないようにしてくれと言った。

2170
dote on
～を溺愛する

Both sets of grandparents **doted on** the new baby.
両家の祖父母が生まれたばかりの赤ん坊を溺愛した。

2171 drag off　　～を無理に連れていく

The security men **dragged off** the intruder for questioning.
警備員たちが尋問するために侵入者**を無理に連れていった**。

2172 drag on　　(会議などが)だらだら長引く
[= run on]

The lecture **dragged on** and the audience gradually became more and more restless.
講演が**だらだらと長引いて**，聴衆たちは次第に落ち着かなくなっていった。

2173 draw in　　～を勧誘する
[= introduce]

The man's job was to try and **draw in** new clients to the company.
男性の仕事は会社に新たな顧客**を勧誘**しようとすることだった。

2174 drift off to sleep　　うとうと眠る
[= fall asleep]

I was just **drifting off to sleep** when I was startled by a noise outside my window.
窓の外の音にはっとした時，私はちょうど**うとうと眠**っていた。

2175 drum up　　(支持・取引など)を懸命に得ようとする

He went from door to door trying to **drum up** support for his campaign against the new supermarket.
スーパーマーケット新設に反対する運動への支援**を得る**べく，彼は一軒一軒の家を回った。

2176 dwell on　　～を力説する，～を長々と話す

In his speech, the school principal **dwelt on** the need for students to prepare properly for classes.
校長はスピーチの中で，生徒たちが授業の準備を十分にすることの必要性**を力説した**。

2177 ease off　　(雨などが)小降りになる，和らぐ，緩む
[= calm down]

After a few hours, the typhoon began to **ease off**.
数時間後，台風が**静まり**始めた。

2178

ease out
〜を辞任に追い込む [= arrange the dismissal of]

The previous chairperson had been **eased out** after the bank was taken over by a rival.
銀行が競合相手に乗っ取られると、前会長は**辞任に追い込まれた**。

2179

egg ~ on
(人)にけしかける [= abet]

His friends **egged** him **on** to steal the money from her purse.
彼の友達は彼女の財布から金を盗むように彼に**けしかけた**。

2180

eke out
(生計)を何とかして立てる、〜の不足分を補う [= make up for]

For a few years he **eked out** a living doing odd jobs.
2、3年間、彼はアルバイトをして**生計を立てた**。

2181

face off
対決する [= take on]

The rival teams **faced off** in the championship finals.
決勝戦でライバルチーム同士が**対決した**。

2182

factor in
〜を考慮に入れる [= allow for, take ~ into consideration]

After **factoring in** all the expenses, they decided the plan would not make a profit.
すべての経費を**考慮に入れ**た後、彼らはその計画は利益が出ないとの結論に達した。

2183

fade in
〜を次第に明るくする

The movie began by **fading in** a scene of the couple on a beach.
その映画は、海辺のカップルのシーン**を次第に明るくする**ことから始まった。

2184

fall back on
(いざという時に)〜に頼る

Jim assured her that she could always **fall back on** him.
いつでも自分に**頼っ**ていいと、ジムは彼女を安心させた。

2185 fall flat
失敗となる [= get nowhere]

The advertising campaign **fell flat** when its star was arrested.
広告キャンペーンは，広告の人気スターが逮捕された時に**失敗となった**。

2186 fall out with
〜と仲たがいする [= disagree with]

They were good friends but they **fell out with** each other in an argument over a girl.
2人は仲の良い友達だったが，1人の女性をめぐって言い争いをして**仲たがいした**。

2187 fall through
失敗に終わる [= fail]

As long as the deal doesn't **fall through** at the last moment, the contract will be signed next Friday.
商談が最終段階で**失敗に終わら**ない限り，今度の金曜日に契約は締結されるだろう。

2188 fan out
四方八方に散らばる

Volunteers **fanned out** over the countryside in their search for the missing girl.
行方不明になった少女を捜して，ボランティアたちが田園地帯の**四方八方に散らばった**。

2189 farm out
〜を下請けに出す [= contract out]

When he was busy, the translator **farmed out** work to his students.
忙しい時，その翻訳家は自分の生徒に仕事を**下請けに出した**。

2190 fend for *oneself*
自力で生きていく [= stand up for *oneself*]

After her husband passed away, the widow had to **fend for herself**.
夫が亡くなった後，その未亡人は**自力で生きていか**なければならなかった。

2191 fend off
(質問)をかわす

The film star tried to **fend off** questions about his marriage by talking about his new movie.
その映画スターは自分の新しい映画について話すことで，結婚に関する質問**をかわそう**とした。

2192
ferret out
~を探し出す

They **ferreted out** a solution to sexism.
彼らは男女差別の解決法を探し出した。

2193
feud about
~をめぐって反目する

The two nations have been **feuding about** which of them owns the islands for decades.
両国は数十年にわたり，その島々の領有権をめぐって反目している。

2194
fill A in on B
AにBに関する情報を伝える

Susie **filled** us **in on** the details of the meeting.
スージーは私たちに会議について詳しく教えてくれた。

2195
firm up
~を確実なものにする
[= ensure]

They decided to **firm up** the arrangement by drawing up a contract.
彼らは契約書を作成することによって，協定を確実なものにしようと決めた。

2196
fizzle out
途中で失敗に終わる

The protest eventually **fizzled out** after it began to rain heavily.
反対運動は大雨が降り始めたので，結局のところ，途中で失敗に終わった。

2197
flare up (at)
(~に)むきになって怒る
[= fly into a temper]

Sometimes her boss **flared up at** her for no clear reason.
彼女の上司は，時折はっきりした理由もなく彼女に対してむきになって怒った。

2198
flash back to
~を急に思い出す

As he entered the campus, he **flashed back to** his own student days.
キャンパスに足を踏み入れると，彼は自分の学生時代を急に思い出した。

2199 flesh out
〜に肉付けする, 〜を具体化する [= embody]

His boss told him to **flesh out** his idea a bit and then bring it back for further consideration.
提案にもう少し**肉付けをして**から，さらなる検討に向けて再提出するように，と上司は彼に言った。

2200 flip out
かっとなる, ひどく興奮する

When he found out he was going to be fired, he **flipped out** completely.
彼は解雇されることがわかった時，**怒り狂った**。

2201 float around
広まる [= get about, gain ground]

The idea had been **floating around** for some time before it was discussed.
そのアイデアは，話し合われる前に，しばらくの間**広まって**いた。

2202 flood in
殺到する [= pour in]

Invitations for the singer to appear on stage **flooded in** from TV companies.
その歌手への出演依頼がテレビ局から**殺到した**。

2203 fly off the handle
かっとなる [= hit the roof]

Ms. Swain **flew off the handle** when Cal didn't behave.
キャルの態度が悪かったので，スウェイン先生は**かっとなった**。

2204 follow through
〜を最後までやり通す, 〜に最後まで従う

Unfortunately, he failed to **follow through** on his original offer.
残念ながら，彼は最初の提案**を最後までやり通す**ことができなかった。

2205 foreclose on
〜に担保権を行使する

When the couple fell behind with their payments, their bank **foreclosed on** the loan and seized their property.
その夫婦の支払いが滞った時，銀行は融資**に対する担保権を行使して**，夫婦の財産を差し押さえた。

2206
fork out
(大金)を支払う

He resented **forking out** money for his son's graduate studies.
彼は息子の大学院研究に多額の金**を支払う**ことを腹立たしく思った。

2207
freeze up
態度を固くする，(表情などが)こわばる

When he got up to speak, he suddenly **froze up** and stood there silently.
彼は話そうとして立ち上がった時，突然，**体がかちこちになってしまい**黙ったまま立ちすくんだ。

2208
fritter away
〜を無駄遣いする
[= waste, squander]

Diana got a part time job with the aim of saving money, but she **frittered away** most of her earnings on cosmetics and magazines.
ダイアナは貯金目的でパートの仕事に就いたが，化粧品や雑誌に稼ぎの大半を**無駄遣い**した。

2209
gain on
〜に追いつく
[= catch up with]

The new company rapidly began to **gain on** its rivals in the field.
新会社はその分野での競合会社**に**急速に**追いつき**始めた。

2210
gang up on
〜に集団で攻撃する

The girl complained that her classmates were always **ganging up on** her.
その少女は級友たちがいつも，少女**に集団で攻撃して**くることに文句を言った。

2211
get A across to B
AをBに理解させる

How can I **get** my point **across to** them?
自分の目的**を**どうやって彼ら**に理解させ**ればよいのだろうか。

2212
glance off
〜をかすめる

The bullet **glanced off** a rock and wounded him in the arm.
弾丸が岩**をかすめ**，彼の腕を負傷させた。

2213
gloss over 〜を取り繕う
You can't just **gloss over** his poor performance.
君は彼の能力不足**を取り繕う**なんてできないよ。

2214
grope for 〜を手さぐりで捜す
He **groped for** the appropriate words to use to tell her what he felt.
彼は自分の思いを彼女に伝えるための適切な言葉**を捜していた**。

2215
hail A as B AをBとして迎え入れる
Many people **hailed** the prime minister **as** the savior of the country.
多くの人が首相を国の救世主**として熱烈に支持した**。

2216
hammer out 〜を案出する
It took the diplomats months to **hammer out** the precise wording of the new treaty.
新条約の適切な言い回し**を案出する**のに、外交官たちは数か月を要した。

2217
hang out in 〜でぶらぶらして時を過ごす
The local youngsters would **hang out in** the café on weekends.
地元の若者たちは週末にはカフェ**でぶらぶらして時を過ごした**ものだった。

2218
harp on 〜について繰り返し話す
She hated the way her husband **harped on** money all the time.
彼女は夫が四六時中お金**についてくどくど話す**ことが大嫌いだった。

2219
have it out with 〜と議論して決着をつける
Peggy was not ready to **have it out with** Jim.
ペギーはジム**と議論して決着をつける**心構えができていなかった。

2220
head off
~を食い止める
[= prevent]

The company president said that he was confident they would be able to **head off** the threat from their new rivals.
新参の競合会社による脅威を**食い止める**自信はあると，社長は言った。

2221
hem in
~を囲む

After **hemming in** the enemy, the army attacked them at dawn.
敵陣を**囲んだ**後，軍隊は夜明けに彼らを攻撃した。

2222
hike up
~を引き上げる

The government decided to raise revenue by **hiking up** the tax on cigarettes.
政府はタバコ税**を引き上げる**ことで歳入を増加させることを決定した。

2223
hinge on
~次第である

The team's chance of victory **hinged on** the performance of its star players.
そのチームの勝利はスター選手の成績**次第である**。

2224
hit it off with
~と馬が合う
[= get along with]

Susie **hit it off** well **with** her mother-in-law.
スージーは義母ととても**馬が合った**。

2225
hit the roof
激怒する

When she told her father about the accident, he **hit the roof**.
彼女が事故について話した時，父親は**激怒した**。

2226
hold down
（職・地位など）に就いている

Charlie **held down** a good job at a high salary.
チャーリーは高収入のいい仕事**に就いていた**。

2227
hold out for
~を要求して譲らない

The workers decided to **hold out for** a better offer from management.
労働者たちは経営者側により良い提案を**あくまでも要求する**ことに決めた。

2228
hold over
~を延期する
[= carry over]

Because of the bad weather, the sports meet was **held over** for a week.
悪天候のため，スポーツ大会は1週間後に**延期された**。

2229
hole up
隠れる

The escaped convicts **holed up** in a remote farmhouse.
脱獄囚たちは人里離れた農家に**潜伏した**。

2230
horse around
ばか騒ぎをする

The teacher came in to find the students **horsing around**.
先生が入ってきて，生徒たちが**ばか騒ぎしている**のを見つけた。

2231
huddle with
~と相談する，~と密談する

During the break, the team **huddled with** their coach to discuss tactics.
小休止の間に，チームは戦略を検討すべくコーチと**話し合った**。

2232
hunker down
身を潜める

Most residents **hunkered down** in their homes until the storm passed.
ほとんどの住民は嵐が静まるまで家に**身を潜めた**。

2233
identify with
~に共感する
[= sympathize with]

Mary felt she could **identify with** the heroine of the novel as their experiences were so remarkably similar.
経験していることがあまりにもよく似ていたので，メアリーはその小説のヒロインに**共感する**ことができた。

2234
impose on
~を押しかける, つけ込む

I'm sorry to **impose on** you at home, but I really need to discuss tomorrow's meeting with you privately.
家まで押しかけてすみません。明日のミーティングについて, あなたと個人的に話し合う必要がどうしてもあったものですから。

2235
intercede with
~に取りなす

The group asked the politician to **intercede with** the government.
その団体は政治家に政府に取りなしてくれるよう頼んだ。

2236
interfere with
~を妨げる, ~に干渉する

The noise from the traffic outside **interfered with** his concentration, making it difficult for him to study.
往来の交通から届く騒音に集中力を妨げられて, 彼は勉強がしづらかった。

2237
iron out
~を解決する
[= solve, resolve]

The computer engineer spent the weekend **ironing out** various bugs in the new program.
そのコンピューター・エンジニアは, 週末を費やして, 新プログラムのいろいろな不具合を解決した。

2238
jack up
(価格)を引き上げる

Supermarkets took advantage of the paper shortage to **jack up** the prices of all paper products.
スーパーマーケットは紙不足につけ込んで, すべての紙製品の価格を引き上げた。

2239
keep after
~に催促し続ける

His wife **kept after** him until he finally agreed to fix the broken window.
彼の妻は彼が壊れた窓の修理を承知するまで, 彼にしつこく言い続けた。

2240
kick up
(騒ぎなど)を引き起こす, (ほこりなど)をけ立てる

The customer **kicked up** a fuss about his cutlery, saying that it had not been properly washed.
きちんと洗われていなかったと言って, その客は自分の食器のことで騒ぎを引き起こした。

2241 knuckle down — 真剣に取り組む
[= adopt a serious stance]

She told her daughter to **knuckle down** and write her science report.
彼女は娘に科学のレポート**に真剣に取り組み**，書くようにと言った。

2242 knuckle under — 屈服する
[= give in]

Finally, their lazy son **knuckled under** and got a job.
ついに彼らのぐうたらな息子**は降参し**，仕事に就いた。

2243 lag behind — ～に後れを取る

For most of the race, he was **lagging behind** the other competitors, but then in the last ten minutes, he made a supreme effort and came in first.
レース中ほとんどずっと，彼はほかの選手**に後れを取っていた**が，最後の10分で，彼は渾身の力を振り絞って，1位でゴールした。

2244 lash out at — ～を痛烈に非難する

The president **lashed out at** critics, saying they were in the pay of a foreign government.
彼らは外国政府の飼い犬だと，大統領は批判者たち**を痛烈に非難した**。

2245 launch into — ～を始める
[= start, begin]

Please don't ask him about work or he'll **launch into** a detailed description of all the problems the business is facing.
あの人に仕事のことを聞いちゃだめだよ。さもないと，彼は今仕事が直面しているすべての問題**を細々と説明し始める**から。

2246 lay it on thick — 大げさに言う

He **laid it on thick** when he told his excuse to his boss for being late.
彼は遅刻した理由を上司に話す時，**大げさに言った**。

2247 leaf through — ～をぱらぱらめくって目を通す

While she waited, she **leafed through** the magazines on the table.
彼女は待っている間，テーブルの上の雑誌**をぱらぱらめくって目を通した**。

2248 lean on
〜に圧力をかける
[= put pressure on]

The mayor was said to have **leaned on** the editor to shelve the story.
市長はその話を握りつぶすために編集者に**圧力をかけた**と言われた。

2249 let down
〜を失望させる
[= disappoint]

Everybody felt **let down** when their team failed to win the final.
チームが決勝戦で負けた時,皆**失望した**。

2250 level off
横ばいになる

Finally, the rise in the value of the dollar began to **level off**.
ついに,ドルの価値は**横ばいになり**始めた。

2251 level with
〜に対して率直に言う

I'll **level with** you. If your play doesn't improve, I'll take you off the team.
率直に言います。あなたのプレーが上達しないならば,チームから外れてもらいます。

2252 live down
(失敗)を人に忘れさせる,(悲しみなど)を忘れ去る

He never **lived down** his failure to secure the deal and eventually he left the company for another one.
彼は取引を確保できなかった失敗**を人々の記憶から消す**ことができないまま,結局,社を去って他社に移った。

2253 lop off
〜を切り取る
[= trim off]

He took out a knife and **lopped off** a bunch of bananas from the tree.
彼はナイフを取り出して,木からバナナの房**を切り取った**。

2254 make off with
〜を奪い去る
[= steal]

During the bomb scare at the museum, a thief **made off with** a valuable painting.
美術館が爆破予告による恐怖で揺れている間に,泥棒が貴重な絵画**を奪い去った**。

2255
mark down
〜を値下げする
[= lower the prices]

The store decided to **mark down** their prices by 50 percent.
その店は価格を50％値下げすることを決定した。

2256
mark out
〜を区画する

He **marked out** on a map the area they would patrol.
彼は地図上でパトロールする地域を区画した。

2257
mark up
〜を値上げする

Most shops make a profit by **marking up** the prices of goods they buy from wholesalers.
ほとんどの店は、問屋から仕入れた品物の値段を引き上げることで利益を得ている。

2258
measure out
〜を量り分ける

The chemist **measured out** a small amount of the new drug.
薬剤師は新薬を少量ずつ量り分けた。

2259
measure up to
（基準など）に達する

Jane was pleased that she had been promoted, but she was worried that she would not **measure up to** her new duties.
ジェーンは昇進してうれしくはあったものの、自分が新しい職務の水準に達していないのでは、と心配していた。

2260
mill about
〜を動き回る

Fans were **milling about** the festival site from the morning.
ファンたちは朝から祭りの会場を動き回っていた。

2261
mull over
〜を熟考する
[= chew over]

She asked for a few weeks to **mull over** the offer and to discuss it with her family.
その申し出についてよく考え家族と話し合うために、2、3週間の時間をもらえるよう彼女は頼んだ。

2262
muscle in on
〜に強引に入り込む

A neighboring gang tried to **muscle in on** their territory.
近隣の非行グループが彼らの縄張り**に強引に入り込も**うとした。

2263
nail down
（日取り）を確定する
[= determine]

He finally managed to **nail down** a meeting.
彼はようやく，何とか会議の日取り**を確定した**。

2264
narrow down
〜を絞り込む

The detective **narrowed down** the suspects to two men.
刑事は容疑者**を**2人の男に**絞り込ん**だ。

2265
nibble at
〜を少しずつかじる

He **nibbled at** some cheese while he worked at his desk.
彼はデスクで仕事中に，チーズ**をかじっていた**。

2266
nod off
うとうとして眠り込む
[= doze off]

It had been such a long day that he kept **nodding off** during the play.
その日はあまりにも長い1日だったので，彼は観劇中に**うとうとし**続けていた。

2267
nose around
〜を捜し回る

He hated it when his boss started **nosing around** his desk.
彼は上司が彼の机**を捜し回る**のが，とても嫌だった。

2268
nose out
〜に僅差で勝つ

He just managed to **nose out** his rivals and win the marathon.
彼はどうにかライバルたち**に僅差で勝って**，そのマラソン大会を制した。

2269 opt for　～を選ぶ
[= choose, select]

The students had the choice of taking an exam or writing an essay. Most **opted for** the latter.
学生たちには試験を受けるかレポートを書くかという選択肢があった。大半の学生は後者**を選んだ**。

2270 own up to　～を白状する
[= confess to]

After the teenager **owned up to** smoking in the backyard, his father gave him a lecture on the danger to his health.
その10代の若者が裏庭でタバコを吸っていたこと**を白状する**と，父親は彼に健康への危険性について説教した。

2271 pack off　～を送り出す
[= send]

In the end, they decided to **pack off** their children to a summer camp.
結局，彼らはサマーキャンプに子どもたち**を送り出す**ことに決めた。

2272 palm A off on B　AをBにだまして押し付ける

He accused the salesman of trying to **palm** a faulty computer **off on** him.
彼は，欠陥コンピューター**を彼にだまして押し付け**ようとしたセールスマンを訴えた。

2273 pan out　成功する
[= come off, come to the top]

When their plan did not **pan out**, they were forced to think again.
計画が**不成功**に終わると，彼らは再考を余儀なくされた。

2274 paper over　～を取り繕う
[= cover up]

Although they **papered over** the quarrel, they were never as friendly again.
彼らはもめ事**を取り繕った**が，決して再び仲よくなることはなかった。

2275 parcel out　～を分配する，～を分け与える
[= dish out]

The leader **parceled out** the remaining rations to his hungry men.
リーダーは腹をすかせた部下たちに残りの糧食**を分配した**。

2276 pass down
(後世に)～を伝える
[= hand down]

The jewelry had been **passed down** in his mother's family for generations.
その宝石は彼の母方の一族に代々**受け継がれて**いた。

2277 pass off A as B
AをBと偽る

The artist was caught trying to **pass off** one of his own works **as** a painting by Picasso.
その画家は，自分の作品の1枚をピカソの絵画**と偽ろう**として逮捕された。

2278 pass up
(機会など)を逃す

Don't **pass up** the pie; it's so good.
このパイ**を遠慮しないで**。おいしいから。

2279 patch up
～を急いでまとめる，
～に応急処置をする

The nations **patched up** a temporary peace for Christmas.
各国はクリスマスに向けて，一時停戦案**を急きょまとめた**。

2280 pay off
元が取れる，
(借金など)を完済する

He took a big risk buying the shares in the company, but it **paid off** and he was able to use the profit to start his own business.
彼は大きなリスクを負ってその会社の株を購入したが，**元が取れて**，彼はその利益を使って自分の事業を立ち上げることができた。

2281 pep up
～を盛り上げる
[= ginger up]

He always tried to **pep up** his classes with videos and games.
彼はいつもビデオやゲームを使って授業**を盛り上げ**ようとした。

2282 perk up
元気になる
[= cheer up]

After they had eaten, the children began to **perk up** again.
子どもたちは食事をした後に，再び**元気になり**始めた。

2283
peter out
次第に消滅する

After a while, the letters from their son **petered out** and they never heard from him again.
しばらくすると、息子からの手紙は**次第になくなり**、ついには息子の消息は途絶えた。

2284
phase out
〜を段階的に廃止する

The auto company gradually **phased out** production of the old model although it was still selling well.
旧型車の売り上げは依然として好調だったものの、自動車会社はその生産**を段階的に廃止した**。

2285
piece together
(事実・情報など)をつなぎ合わせる
[= put together]

When he had **pieced together** the evidence, he realized what had happened.
証拠**をつなぎ合わせた**時に、彼は何が起こったか納得がいった。

2286
pile up
たまる

The work kept **piling up** and he was forced to do overtime almost every day.
仕事が**たまり**続けたので、彼はほとんど毎日残業せざるを得なかった。

2287
pin down
〜を突き止める
[= run down]

He found it impossible to **pin down** the cause of the problem.
彼はその問題の原因**を突き止める**のは不可能だとわかった。

2288
pine for
〜を切望する
[= covet]

She had been **pining for** a chance to play on the school team.
彼女は学校のチームでプレーできる機会**を切望**していた。

2289
pipe down
静かにする
[= quiet down, belt up]

She shouted to the children to **pipe down** and go to sleep.
彼女は子どもたちに**静かにして**寝るようにと大声で言った。

2290
pitch in
協力する [= cooperate]

Paul thought that it would take ages to clean up after the party, but his friends all **pitched in** and the work was finished in no time.
パーティーの後片付けには長時間かかるだろうとポールは思っていたが、友達全員が**協力**してくれて、作業はあっという間に終わった。

2291
play down
〜をもみ消す [= rub out], **〜を軽視する** [= make light of]

The school did its best to **play down** the incident.
その学校は事件**をもみ消す**ために全力を尽くした。

2292
play off
(勝敗のつかなかった試合の)勝負をつける

As there was no score, the teams had to **play off** the following week.
0対0の引き分けだったので、両チームは次の週に**勝負をつけ**なければならなかった。

2293
pluck up
(勇気)を奮い起こす

I'm going to **pluck up** my courage and ask my boss to give me a raise.
勇気**を奮い起こし**て、上司に給料を上げてくれるよう頼んでみるよ。

2294
plug away at
〜にこつこつ励む

He said he was still **plugging away at** writing novels in his spare time.
彼は、今も空き時間に小説を書くことに**こつこつと励ん**でいると言った。

2295
plunge into
〜に飛び込む [= dive into], **〜をし始める**

The young man ran down the beach and **plunged into** the sea.
その若者はビーチを駆け下りて、海**に飛び込ん**だ。

2296
poke around
探し回る、引っかき回す

The professor loves **poking around** in second-hand bookshops, looking for works by his favorite authors.
教授は、古書店を**のぞき回っ**て、お気に入りの作家の作品を探すことが大好きだ。

2297
pore over
~を熟読する, ~を熟考する

He knew that his mother **pored over** his letters, reading them again and again until she had nearly memorized them.
彼は母親が自分の書いた手紙を熟読し，何度も何度も読み返して，ほとんど暗記するまでになっていることを知っていた。

2298
pull off
~をやってのける

Make up your mind to **pull off** something great.
何か偉大なことを成し遂げる決心をしなさい。

2299
pull through
(危機など)を乗り切る

The patient had a life-threatening disease, but thanks to the new drug, he was able to **pull through** and recover.
患者は命にかかわる病気にかかっていたが，新薬のおかげで乗り切って回復することができた。

2300
put down A on B
AをBの頭金として払う

The couple **put down** all their savings **on** the house and borrowed the rest of the money they needed from a bank.
その夫婦は家の購入の頭金として貯金全額を払い，必要な残額は銀行から借りた。

2301
put down A to B
AをBのせいにする　[= attribute A to B]

Some cynics **put down** the actress's success **to** her father's extensive connections in the movie business.
その女優の成功を，父親が映画業界に持つ強大なコネのおかげだと冷笑する人々もいた。

2302
puzzle over
~に頭を悩ませる　[= rack *one's* brain over]

He sat **puzzling over** the math problem for at least an hour.
彼は，少なくとも1時間，数学の問題に頭を悩ませて座っていた。

2303
rack up
~を獲得する　[= win]

After **racking up** his first million dollars, he decided to retire.
初めての100万ドルを獲得してから，彼は引退することにした。

2304
rail against
〜を激しく非難する [= lash out]

The union leader **railed against** the government's economic policies.
労働組合の幹部は政府の経済政策**を激しく非難した**。

2305
rake off
〜の分け前を(不正に)取る [= misappropriate]

He was accused of illegally **raking off** money from the pension fund.
彼は年金基金から不正に**ピンはねした**ことで訴えられた。

2306
rally around
結集する [= gather round], **〜の味方につく** [= take sides with]

When one of the villagers fell ill, the others would **rally around** to help.
村人の1人が病気になった時、村人たちは助けるために**結集した**ものだった。

2307
rattle off
〜をすらすらと言う[書く, 行う]

Although her son got poor grades at school, he could **rattle off** the names of all the players in the football league.
彼女の息子は、学校での成績は悲惨なものだったが、フットボールリーグの選手全員の名前**をすらすら言う**ことができた。

2308
rifle through
〜をくまなく探す

He caught his colleague **rifling through** the drawers of his desk.
彼は同僚が彼の机の引き出し**をくまなく調べている**ところを見つけた。

2309
rip through
〜を突き抜けて進む [= hit directly]

A powerful tornado **ripped through** the area, destroying homes.
強力な竜巻がその地域**を直撃し**、家屋を破壊した。

2310
root for
〜を応援する [= cheer for]

One of the presidential candidates, Bill Jones, was from the town so naturally, everyone there was **rooting for** him in the election.
大統領候補者の1人であるビル・ジョーンズはその町の出身だったので、当然のことながら地元のみんなが選挙で彼**を応援していた**。

2311
rope in
~を駆り出す

On Sunday, he found himself **roped in** to help with the spring cleaning.
日曜日に,彼はいつの間にか春の大掃除の手伝いに**駆り出**されていた。

2312
rub off on
~に良い影響を与える

The teacher made him sit next to the most serious boy in the class in the hope that some of his attitude would **rub off on** him.
先生が彼をクラスで一番まじめな子の隣に座らせたのは,その子の態度のいくらかが彼に**良い影響を与える**ことを願ってのことだった。

2313
ruminate over
~について思いめぐらす

The idea came to him suddenly one evening when he was sitting **ruminating over** what he should do after college.
その考えが彼に突然浮かんだのは,ある夜,大学を卒業したら何をしようか**と思いめぐら**しながら座っていた時のことだった。

2314
run off with
~を持ち逃げする

The stranger **ran off with** all the shop's earnings for the month.
見知らぬ人物がその店の1か月の売上金**を持ち逃げ**した。

2315
run up
(借金など)を重ねる
[= pile up, accumulate]

Before the man went back to his country, he **ran up** large debts at various banks.
男は国に帰る前に,あちこちの銀行で多額の借金**を重ね**た。

2316
rustle up
~を急いで準備する

The late guests asked the landlady to **rustle up** some supper for them.
遅く来た客が宿屋の女主人に夕食**を急いで準備してくれる**ように頼んだ。

2317
scrape by on
~で何とか暮らしていく
[= live from hand to mouth on]

While he was at college, he managed to **scrape by on** the allowance that his parents gave him.
彼は大学時代,両親がくれる小遣い**で何とか暮らし**ていた。

2318
scrape together
~を苦労してかき集める

Her parents managed to **scrape together** the money for her to go to college.
彼女の両親は彼女が大学に行けるようお金**を苦労してかき集めた**。

2319
scratch out
（生計）をどうにかこうにか立てる
[= scrape by]

After they married, they **scratched out** a living on his meager wages.
彼らは結婚後，彼のわずかな給料で生計**をどうにかこうにかして立てた**。

2320
scrub up
徹底的に洗浄する

The doctor and nurses began to **scrub up** in preparation for the operation.
医師と看護師たちは手術の準備をするために手や腕**を徹底的に洗浄し**始めた。

2321
scuffle with
~と乱闘する

Several demonstrators **scuffled with** the police and were arrested.
数人のデモ参加者が警察**と乱闘し**，逮捕された。

2322
set forth
~を説明する
[= account for]

He **set forth** his plans for reform to the board of directors.
彼は重役会に改革の計画**を説明した**。

2323
settle on
~を決める
[= decide on]

After much discussion, they finally **settled on** a day for the wedding.
十分に話し合った後，彼らはやっと挙式の日取り**を決めた**。

2324
shell out
（金額）をしぶしぶ支払う
[= fork out]

How much did you **shell out** for your uniform?
制服にいくら**支払ったの**？

2325

shove around
~をこき使う [= walk over]

The school bully was always **shoving around** the smaller boys.
学校のいじめっ子は、いつも自分より小さな少年たち**をこき使って**いた。

2326

show out
~を送り出す

He stood at the front door and **showed** the guests **out** one by one.
彼は玄関に立って1人ずつ客**を見送った**。

2327

shrug off
~を気にしない [= not care]

Whatever failures he suffered, he always **shrugged** them **off** and began again.
どのような失敗を経験しても、彼はいつもそれを**気にせず**再び始めた。

2328

shy away from
~を避ける、~を敬遠する

Those present at the party **shied away from** Susie.
パーティーの出席者たちは、スージー**を避けた**。

2329

simmer down
気持ちを静める [= calm down]

He lost his temper and resigned on the spot, but later, after he had **simmered down**, he began to regret what he had done.
彼はカッとなってその場で辞職してしまったが、後になって**落ち着いて**みると、自分のしでかしたことを後悔し始めた。

2330

sink in to
~に十分に理解される [= be deeply understood]

When will it **sink in to** you that the only way to pass exams is by studying for them?
試験に受かる唯一の方法は勉強することだってことが、君には一体いつになったら**わかってもらえる**んだい?

2331

siphon off
(資金など)を流用する、~を吸い上げる

The official was arrested for **siphoning off** money intended for the relief of the earthquake victims.
地震の被災者救済のための資金**を流用して**いたために、その公務員は逮捕された。

2332
skim off
(金)を横領する

It was discovered that the bank manager had been **skimming off** money from his customers' accounts for years.
銀行の支店長が長年にわたって顧客たちの口座から資金**を横領**していたことが明らかになった。

2333
slip by
(時などが)いつの間にか過ぎていく

Their time together on weekends always **slipped by** quickly.
彼らが週末に一緒にいる時間は、いつも**あっという間に過ぎ**ていった。

2334
smooth down
〜をなだめる
[= calm down]

She did her best to **smooth down** her parents' irritation.
彼女は両親のいらだち**をなだめる**ために最善を尽くした。

2335
smooth over
〜を取り繕う, 〜を和らげる

He tried to **smooth over** the mistake but it was quickly noticed.
彼はミス**を取り繕う**としたが、すぐに見つかってしまった。

2336
snap off
〜をぽきっと折る

The boys **snapped off** the long icicles and used them as swords.
少年たちは長いつらら**をぽきっと折り**、刀として使った。

2337
snap up
〜を先を争って買う

Demand for housing was so strong that any new properties that came on the market were **snapped up** immediately.
住宅への需要は非常に強かったので、市場に出てきた新しい物件はどんなものであれ、たちまち**先を争って買**われた。

2338
soak up
(雰囲気など)を楽しむ, (知識など)を吸収する

For a few days, he just **soaked up** the local atmosphere in the town.
数日間、彼はただ町の地元風な雰囲気**を楽しん**だ。

2339 sort out ～を整理する
[= organize]

Her first job was to **sort out** all the papers left by her predecessor.
彼女の最初の仕事は、前任者が残したすべての書類を整理することだった。

2340 sound A out on B BについてAの意向を打診する

Sound him **out on** whether he's interested in coming.
来る気があるかどうか、彼に打診してみてください。

2341 sound off まくし立てる

At dinner his father began **sounding off** again about politics and what he would do if he were president.
夕食の席で、また彼の父親は政治について、自分が大統領だったらどうするか、まくし立て始めた。

2342 spin off ～を副産物として生み出す、(会社・資産など)を分離独立させる

The popular police drama has already **spun off** two other series based on characters from the show.
その人気刑事ドラマはすでに、番組の登場人物を使った2つの別シリーズを副産物として生み出している。

2343 spoil for ～をしきりに求める

The opposition had been **spoiling for** a fight with the government for months and the scandal was the perfect opportunity.
野党は数か月にわたって政府とやり合いたくてうずうずしていたので、そのスキャンダルは絶好の機会だった。

2344 sponge off (親のすね)をかじる、スポンジでふき取る

The student said he hated people who just **sponged off** their parents.
その生徒は、ただ親のすねをかじっているだけの人が嫌いだと言った。

2345 spring up 急に起こる、現れる

In no time at all, new factories began to **spring up** in the town.
あっという間に、街に新しい工場群が誕生し始めた。

2346
spur on
〜を奮い立たせる
[= motivate, encourage]

He did not enjoy studying law, but he was **spurred on** by the thought of the money he could make once he qualified as a lawyer.
法律学の勉強は彼には楽しくなかったが，ひとたび弁護士の資格を得たら手に入るであろう収入のことを考えると，彼は**奮い立った**。

2347
square up
支払いを済ませる
[= pay]

After **squaring up** with the cashier, the couple left the restaurant.
レジ係のところで**支払いを済ませて**，カップルはレストランを出た。

2348
squeeze in
〜を（スケジュールに）割り込ませる

The dentist promised to **squeeze** her **in** in-between appointments.
歯科医はほかの予約の間に彼女を**割り込ませる**ことを約束した。

2349
stamp out
〜を撲滅する
[= eradicate, eliminate]

The principal swore to **stamp out** any smoking in his school.
校長は学校での喫煙を**撲滅する**ことを誓った。

2350
stand in for
〜の代役を務める
[= step in for]

The old man fell ill so his son had to **stand in for** him at the ceremony.
その老人は病気になったので，彼の息子が式典で彼の**代役を務め**なければならなかった。

2351
stand out
目立つ
[= be conspicuous]

Her height and bright red hair meant that she always **stood out** in a crowd.
彼女は背が高い上に，明るい赤毛をしていたので，いつも人込みの中で**目立った**。

2352
stand up for
〜を守る [= defend], **〜を支持する** [= support]

At the memorial service, his friend said that John Robinson had always **stood up for** his beliefs, even when it had made him unpopular.
ジョン・ロビンソンはたとえ自分が嫌われても，常に自分の信念を**守って**いたと，告別式で彼の友人は述べた。

2353 stick around
近くで待つ, 辺りをぶらぶらする

George told me to **stick around** so we could play catch.
キャッチボールをするので**近くにいて**，とジョージは僕に言った。

2354 stick up for
〜を弁護する

James **stuck up for** his friend and defended him against their classmates.
ジェームズは友達**をかばって**，同級生たちから彼を守った。

2355 stir up
(感情など)をかき立てる, (騒ぎなど)を引き起こす

The union leader was accused of trying to **stir up** discontent among the workers.
労働組合の幹部は労働者たちの不満**をかき立て**ようとしたとして非難された。

2356 store up
〜を蓄える
[= lay 〜 in stock]

The villagers began to **store up** vegetables to last them through the winter.
村人たちは冬越しの野菜**を蓄え**始めた。

2357 strike off
〜を除名する
[= disaffiliate]

After he was caught cheating, his name was **struck off** the club's membership.
彼はカンニングしているところを見つかったので，クラブ会員から名前が**削除**された。

2358 strike up
(関係)を取り結ぶ, 演奏を始める

The two new employees **struck up** a friendship that was to last the rest of their lives.
2人の新入社員の間に，生涯続くことになる友情**が芽生えた**。

2359 stumble upon
〜を偶然見つける, 〜に思いがけず出くわす

Late one night, the scientist **stumbled upon** a solution to the problem.
ある晩遅くに，科学者はその問題に対する解決方法**を偶然発見した**。

2360
suck up to
〜の機嫌をとる [= butter up]

His superior told him to stop **sucking up to** him all the time.
彼の上司は，しょっちゅう自分の**ご機嫌をとること**をやめるよう彼に言った。

2361
sweat it out
はらはらして待つ，最後まで頑張り通す

I have to **sweat it out** until I get my test result back.
私はテスト結果が戻ってくるまで，**はらはらして待た**なければならない。

2362
tack on
〜を付加する [= add 〜 to]

He found that the hotel had **tacked on** some extra charges.
彼はホテルが請求書に追加料金**を付加した**ことに気付いた。

2363
take in
〜をだます [= deceive]，〜を理解する [= understand]

She had been completely **taken in** by her friend's lie, so she was shocked to discover it was not true.
彼女はすっかり友達の嘘に**だまされていた**ので，それが真実でないとわかってショックを受けた。

2364
take it out on
〜に当たり散らす [= take *one's* anger out on]

Mother **takes it out on** me when she feels frustrated.
母はむしゃくしゃすると私**に当たり散らす**。

2365
take off
軌道に乗る，（売り上げが）急に伸びる

At first, the new product looked as though it might not **take off**, but then in March, sales began to soar.
その新製品は最初は**軌道に乗らない**ように思われたが，3月になって売り上げが急に伸び始めた。

2366
take on
（性質など）を帯びる [= assume]，（仕事など）を引き受ける

The leaves are **taking on** their brilliant hues.
木々の葉が素晴らしい色合い**を帯びて**きている。

2367
take to
~を好きになる [= fall for]

Although they had not met before, the child immediately **took to** him.
彼らはこれまで会ったことはなかったが、その子どもはすぐに彼のこと**を好きになった**。

2368
talk down
~を言い負かす、~を論破する [= argue *one* down]

At the meeting, he managed to **talk down** those opposing the plan.
ミーティングで、彼はその計画に反対する者たちを何とか**言い負かす**ことができた。

2369
tap into
~に進出する [= enter]、~を利用する

The clothing store decided to launch a new youth brand in order to **tap into** the expanding teenage market.
その衣料品店は拡大中のティーン市場に**進出す**べく、新しい若者向けブランドを立ち上げることにした。

2370
taper off
先細りになる

At first, sales grew steadily, but then they began to **taper off** as the economy weakened.
初めのうちは売り上げは着々と伸びていったが、不景気になると売り上げは**先細りになり**始めた。

2371
tear down
(建物など)を取り壊す [= demolish]

She was strongly opposed to the plan to **tear down** the old city hall and build a new one.
古い市役所**を取り壊し**て新しい市役所を建設する計画に対して、彼女は猛反対していた。

2372
thin out
~を減らす [= cut back]

The company decided to **thin out** the sales staff at their stores.
その会社は彼らの店の販売員**を減らす**ことを決定した。

2373
thrash out
~を徹底的に議論する [= discuss ~ fully]

We must hold a meeting to **thrash out** our marketing policy for next year.
会議を開いて、次年度のマーケティング方針**を徹底的に議論し**なければなりません。

2374
throw in — 〜を差し挟む

Every so often, the chairman **threw in** a comment of his own.
折を見つけては，議長は彼自身の意見**を差し挟んだ**。

2375
tide 〜 over — （人）に困難を乗り切らせる

He borrowed some money from the bank to **tide** him **over** until the new year.
新年まで**を乗り切る**ために，彼は銀行から借金をした。

2376
tie A in with B — AをBと結びつける
[= connect 〜 with]

They planned to **tie** the ceremony **in with** the opening of the new library.
彼らは式典を新図書館の開設**と結びつける**計画を立てた。

2377
tip off — 〜に密告する
[= give away]

One of the terrorists **tipped off** the local police about the bomb.
テロリストの1人が爆弾について地元の警察**に密告した**。

2378
tower over — 〜をはるかに超える

The scientist's achievements **towered over** those of his contemporaries.
その科学者の業績は彼と同時代の人の業績**をはるかに超えていた**。

2379
toy with — （考えなど）をいい加減に扱う

Actually, I'm **toying with** the idea of leaving my job, although I haven't completely made my mind up yet.
実はまだはっきり決めたわけではないんですが，仕事を辞めること**をなんとなく考えている**んです。

2380
trail off — 次第に小さくなる
[= tail off]

The boy began his recitation well but then he **trailed off** into silence.
少年は上手に暗唱を始めたが，声が**次第に小さくなり**黙った。

2381 trim down
〜を削減する [= cut back on, pare down]

All the executives were asked to **trim down** their expenses in the coming year.
重役は全員，来年度の経費を**削減する**ように求められた。

2382 trip over
転ぶ [= fall down]

He **tripped over** as he ran for the bus and broke his wrist.
彼はバスに間に合うように走った時，**転んで**しまい，手首を骨折した。

2383 trump up
〜を捏造する [cook up, fabricate, fake]

He said the police had **trumped up** the charges in order to punish him.
彼は警察が彼を罰するために罪を**捏造した**と言った。

2384 turn over a new leaf
心を入れ替える [= begin a new life]

After he got married, he **turned over a new leaf** and stopped drinking altogether.
結婚してから，彼は**心を入れ替えて**，酒をきっぱりやめた。

2385 vouch for
〜を保証する [= guarantee, endorse]

Is there anyone who can **vouch for** the truth of what you say?
君が言っていることの正当性を**保証する**ことのできる人は，誰かいるのかい？

2386 walk out on
(人)のもとを去る [= leave]

One day she just got up and **walked out on** her husband.
ある日彼女は起床すると，夫の**もとを去った**。

2387 wash out
(試合など)を(雨で)中止させる [= rain out], 〜を疲れさせる [= fatigue]

Persistent rain **washed out** the second day of the tennis tournament.
降りやまない雨のために，テニス大会の2日目が**雨天中止になった**。

2388 weed out 〜を排除する [= remove]

The background check was designed to **weed out** troublemakers from the organization.
その身元調査は，組織から厄介者**を排除する**ことが目的だった。

2389 weigh in 仲裁に入る [= intervene]，割り込む [= interpose]

In the middle of the argument, her brother **weighed in** to support her.
口論の最中に，彼女の兄が彼女を支持するために**仲裁に入った**。

2390 whip up (感情)をかき立てる，〜を手早くこしらえる [= cook up]

The politician was accused of **whipping up** anger against the immigrant community.
その政治家は移民グループに対する怒り**をかき立てている**として糾弾された。

2391 whisk away 〜を持ち去る

As soon as he showed them the painting, he **whisked** it **away** for safekeeping.
彼は彼らに絵画を見せるとすぐに，保管のためにそれ**をさっさと片付けた**。

2392 win over 〜を味方に入れる [= get someone on *one's* side]

The boy did his best to **win over** her father but to no avail.
少年は父親**を味方に引き入れる**ために最善を尽くしたが，無駄だった。

2393 wind down くつろぐ [= relax]，(ネジが)ゆるむ

After getting home, he usually **wound down** by having a drink and reading the newspaper.
彼は普段，帰宅後には，酒を飲みながら新聞を読んで**くつろいでいた**。

2394 wind up *doing* 〜する羽目になる [= end up *doing*]

The evening **wound up costing** him over a hundred dollars as he had to take a taxi home.
その晩，彼はタクシーで帰宅しなくてはならなかったので，結局100ドル以上も**使う羽目になった**。

2395

wipe out
~を撲滅する
[= eradicate]

Thanks to the vaccine, the disease has now been almost completely **wiped out** in Africa.
ワクチンのおかげで，その病気は今やアフリカではほとんど完全に**撲滅**されている。

2396

wolf down
~をがつがつ食べる
[= scarf down]

She told her son not to **wolf down** his food so quickly.
彼女は息子に，そんなに急いで食べ物**をがつがつ食べ**ないようにと言った。

2397

wrap up
~を終える
[= finish]

Let's **wrap up** the homework and hit the sack.
宿題**を終わらせ**て，床に就こう。

2398

wriggle out of
~をうまく切り抜ける
[= evade]

He had always managed to **wriggle out of** criminal charges before.
彼はこれまでのところ，いつも何とか刑事訴訟**からうまく切り抜け**てきた。

2399

wring A out of B
AをBから絞り出す
[= squeeze out]

She **wrung** the water **out of** her wet towel and hung it up to dry.
彼女はぬれたタオルの水**を絞り出し**，乾かすためにつるした。

2400

zero in on
~に照準を合わせる
[= home in on, focus on]

Scientists **zeroed in on** the cause of the epidemic.
科学者たちは伝染病の原因**に照準を合わせ**た。

さくいん

単語編

A

- abate 330
- abdicate 58
- aberration 374
- abhorrent 432
- abject 136
- ablaze 444
- abominable 432
- abomination 254
- abort 54
- aboveboard 412
- abrasive 436
- abridged 136
- abrogate 342
- abruptly 268
- abscond 58
- absolve 342
- abstention 376
- absurdity 254
- abundance 220
- abuse 200
- abyss 396
- accelerate 178
- accentuate 176
- acclaim 324
- accomplice 372
- accost 354
- accrue 350
- accusation 370
- acquittal 372
- acrimony 102
- acute 418
- adamant 132
- addendum 396
- addictive 274
- address 32
- adept 136
- adequate 284
- adherent 84
- adjacent 308
- adjourn 54
- adjudicate 326
- adjunct 444
- administer 32
- admonish 64
- adolescent 276
- adorn 188
- adroit 136
- adulation 402
- advent 228
- adversarial 434
- advocate 82
- aesthetically 126
- affability 250
- affable 148
- affidavit 370
- affiliation 220
- affinity 90
- affix 210
- affliction 396
- affluent 134
- affront 102
- agape 444
- agenda 240
- aggravate 56
- agility 86
- agitate 328
- agnostic 444
- agonize 68
- agrarian 436
- ailment 376
- alacrity 252
- alienate 64
- alienation 260
- alignment 262
- allay 44
- allegory 90
- alleviate 44
- alliance 366
- allocate 198
- allude 42
- allure 88
- aloof 138
- altruism 216
- altruistic 122
- ambient 444
- ambiguous 300
- ambivalence 250
- ambivalent 134
- ambush 328
- ameliorate 326
- amenable 286
- amend 36
- amendment 376
- amenity 236
- amicable 282
- amity 218
- amnesty 112
- amplify 208
- anachronism 402
- analogous 444
- anatomy 376
- anemic 446
- anesthetic 378
- animosity 100
- annihilate 338
- annihilation 368
- annotation 94
- annulment 376
- anoint 326
- anonymous 122
- antagonistic 138
- antagonize 318
- antibiotic 222
- antipathy 110
- apathetic 138
- apathy 254
- apex 90
- appalled 166
- apparition 244
- appease 44
- append 348
- apprehend 26
- aptitude 84
- arbitrary 138
- arbitrate 326
- arcane 294
- archaeologist 232
- archaic 164
- arduous 156
- array 362
- arrears 402
- arrogant 418
- artifact 216
- ascension 92
- ascetic 444
- askew 444
- assail 336
- assault 206
- assertive 286
- assessment 218
- asset 242
- assiduous 288
- assimilate 198
- astound 328
- astute 418
- asylum 96
- atheist 390
- atrocity 110
- attenuate 354
- attic 246
- attribute 246
- attuned 446
- audacity 90
- auditorium 246
- augment 320
- auspice 78
- auspicious 156
- austere 130
- authentic 122
- authoritative 288
- autism 378
- autonomy 402
- autopsy 224
- avarice 396
- averse 436
- aversion 100
- avert 46
- avid 138
- axis 264

B

- [ ] backlash 76
- [ ] backlog 96
- [ ] baffle 328
- [ ] bail 372
- [ ] balance 230
- [ ] balk 46
- [ ] ballot 262
- [ ] banal 160
- [ ] banish 334
- [ ] bankruptcy 242
- [ ] banter 100
- [ ] barrage 112
- [ ] barren 302
- [ ] bask 68
- [ ] beckon 62
- [ ] bedraggled 300
- [ ] beguile 354
- [ ] belittle 186
- [ ] bellicose 166
- [ ] belligerent 138
- [ ] bemoan 328
- [ ] benchmark 94
- [ ] benediction 390
- [ ] benefactor 390
- [ ] beneficiary 234
- [ ] benevolently 282
- [ ] benign 148
- [ ] bent 452
- [ ] berate 52
- [ ] bereave 344
- [ ] berserk 452
- [ ] bestow 174
- [ ] bewitched 310
- [ ] bias 218
- [ ] bibliography 244
- [ ] bigot 234
- [ ] bionic 272
- [ ] bizarre 298
- [ ] blanch 320
- [ ] bland 304
- [ ] blasphemy 390
- [ ] blatantly 138
- [ ] bleak 272
- [ ] blemish 396
- [ ] blissful 282
- [ ] blister 100
- [ ] bluff 60
- [ ] blunder 110
- [ ] bluntly 138
- [ ] blur 60
- [ ] blurt 320
- [ ] boisterous 440
- [ ] bolster 34
- [ ] bombard 206
- [ ] boon 250
- [ ] bountiful 282
- [ ] bounty 250
- [ ] bout 98
- [ ] brandish 318
- [ ] brawl 262
- [ ] breakthrough 74
- [ ] brevity 76
- [ ] bribery 244
- [ ] brink 396
- [ ] broach 60
- [ ] brunt 112
- [ ] bucolic 308
- [ ] buffer 78
- [ ] bungling 446
- [ ] bunker 386
- [ ] buoyant 148
- [ ] burgeon 38
- [ ] burnished 446

C

- [ ] cagey 434
- [ ] cajole 58
- [ ] calamity 368
- [ ] caliber 86
- [ ] camaraderie 80
- [ ] candid 132
- [ ] candor 88
- [ ] canvass 318
- [ ] capitulate 318
- [ ] capricious 292
- [ ] captivation 250
- [ ] captive 402
- [ ] cardinal 302
- [ ] cardiovascular 418
- [ ] caricature 244
- [ ] carnivorous 418
- [ ] catalyst 110
- [ ] catastrophe 368
- [ ] catastrophically 158
- [ ] caustic 130
- [ ] cavernous 446
- [ ] cease 200
- [ ] celibate 308
- [ ] censure 198
- [ ] cerebral 452
- [ ] certitude 256
- [ ] cessation 114
- [ ] chafe 210
- [ ] chaotic 416
- [ ] charade 368
- [ ] charlatan 368
- [ ] chasten 350
- [ ] chronic 274
- [ ] chronicle 244
- [ ] cinch 116
- [ ] cipher 114
- [ ] circulate 200
- [ ] circumlocution 264
- [ ] circumstantial 270
- [ ] circumvent 50
- [ ] claim 200
- [ ] clairvoyant 416
- [ ] clamor 404
- [ ] clandestine 128
- [ ] clarify 172
- [ ] classified 128
- [ ] clemency 252
- [ ] clench 62
- [ ] clique 120
- [ ] clobber 354
- [ ] clout 120
- [ ] clump 352
- [ ] clumsy 124
- [ ] cluster 396
- [ ] clutter 352
- [ ] coalition 366
- [ ] coarse 298
- [ ] coax 210
- [ ] coerce 36
- [ ] coffer 396
- [ ] cogitate 334
- [ ] cognition 396
- [ ] cognitive 424
- [ ] coherent 422
- [ ] cohesive 414
- [ ] coincidence 218
- [ ] collaborate 208
- [ ] collation 96
- [ ] collision 240
- [ ] coma 224
- [ ] combustion 264
- [ ] commence 208
- [ ] commensurate 126
- [ ] commiserate 28
- [ ] commitment 242
- [ ] commodity 266
- [ ] commonplace 304
- [ ] commotion 116
- [ ] communal 268
- [ ] commutation 374
- [ ] compassion 248
- [ ] compatible 284
- [ ] compile 202
- [ ] complacency 248
- [ ] complex 216
- [ ] compliance 248
- [ ] complicity 372
- [ ] composure 248
- [ ] comprehensive 310
- [ ] compunction 248
- [ ] concede 324
- [ ] conceit 254
- [ ] concession 116
- [ ] conciliatory 424
- [ ] concoct 68
- [ ] concur 324
- [ ] concussion 100
- [ ] condemnation 372
- [ ] condescending 416
- [ ] condescension 252
- [ ] condolence 236
- [ ] condone 28
- [ ] conducive 156

- ☐ confer 360
- ☐ confidential 270
- ☐ configuration 264
- ☐ confinement 260
- ☐ confiscate 26
- ☐ confiscation 242
- ☐ conflagration 106
- ☐ conformist 394
- ☐ confound 50
- ☐ confrontational 294
- ☐ conglomerate 92
- ☐ congregate 198
- ☐ conjecture 104
- ☐ conjugate 360
- ☐ connotation 232
- ☐ conscience 364
- ☐ conscription 384
- ☐ consecrate 324
- ☐ consecration 392
- ☐ consequently 300
- ☐ consign 320
- ☐ consignment 92
- ☐ consolidate 324
- ☐ consort 82
- ☐ consortium 366
- ☐ conspicuous 270
- ☐ conspiracy 242
- ☐ constellation 258
- ☐ constituency 376
- ☐ constitutional 422
- ☐ constriction 398
- ☐ consummate 290
- ☐ contagious 140
- ☐ contaminate 56
- ☐ contamination 266
- ☐ contemplate 188
- ☐ contemplative 140
- ☐ contemporary 272
- ☐ contend 186
- ☐ contentious 122
- ☐ contiguous 270
- ☐ contingency 98
- ☐ contingent 452
- ☐ contraband 94
- ☐ contradict 186
- ☐ contradictory 424
- ☐ contraption 262
- ☐ contravene 320
- ☐ contrivance 404
- ☐ contrive 324
- ☐ controversial 424
- ☐ conventional 310
- ☐ conversion 390
- ☐ conveyance 92
- ☐ convict 326
- ☐ conviction 256
- ☐ conviviality 86
- ☐ copious 286
- ☐ corroborate 42
- ☐ corrode 344

- ☐ corrosive 294
- ☐ cortex 394
- ☐ counterfeit 96
- ☐ counterfeiter 232
- ☐ counterpart 84
- ☐ countless 302
- ☐ courier 260
- ☐ cove 246
- ☐ coverage 240
- ☐ covert 128
- ☐ cozy 284
- ☐ crabby 292
- ☐ cramp 222
- ☐ craze 232
- ☐ credibility 76
- ☐ credulity 252
- ☐ creed 118
- ☐ cringe 354
- ☐ criterion 228
- ☐ critical 458
- ☐ crucial 288
- ☐ crude 270
- ☐ crunch 60
- ☐ crux 262
- ☐ cryptic 434
- ☐ culmination 258
- ☐ culpability 110
- ☐ culpable 452
- ☐ culprit 82
- ☐ cumulative 446
- ☐ curb 44
- ☐ curfew 116
- ☐ cursory 142
- ☐ curtail 48
- ☐ curtly 138
- ☐ custody 362

D

- ☐ dainty 156
- ☐ dangle 206
- ☐ dart 214
- ☐ daunting 414
- ☐ dawdle 60
- ☐ dazzle 38
- ☐ dearth 106
- ☐ debacle 386
- ☐ debar 336
- ☐ debase 48
- ☐ debilitate 330
- ☐ debit 244
- ☐ debris 388
- ☐ debtor 232
- ☐ debunk 38
- ☐ decadence 104
- ☐ decant 180
- ☐ decay 188
- ☐ deceased 154
- ☐ decent 282
- ☐ deceptive 292
- ☐ decimate 360

- ☐ decipher 318
- ☐ decorum 88
- ☐ decoy 404
- ☐ decree 104
- ☐ decrepit 280
- ☐ decry 342
- ☐ deduce 322
- ☐ deduction 230
- ☐ deface 188
- ☐ de facto 416
- ☐ defamatory 424
- ☐ defame 188
- ☐ defector 386
- ☐ deference 226
- ☐ deferential 424
- ☐ deferment 366
- ☐ defiance 102
- ☐ deficiency 222
- ☐ deficit 230
- ☐ deflect 190
- ☐ defraud 58
- ☐ defunct 124
- ☐ defuse 44
- ☐ defy 318
- ☐ deity 258
- ☐ delegation 366
- ☐ deliberation 372
- ☐ delineate 320
- ☐ delineation 266
- ☐ deluge 106
- ☐ delusion 226
- ☐ delve 68
- ☐ demean 48
- ☐ demeanor 86
- ☐ demise 98
- ☐ demographic 270
- ☐ demolition 392
- ☐ demoralized 142
- ☐ demur 330
- ☐ demure 452
- ☐ denigrate 342
- ☐ denomination 392
- ☐ denote 210
- ☐ denounce 52
- ☐ dense 302
- ☐ depiction 118
- ☐ deplete 72
- ☐ depletion 392
- ☐ deplorable 136
- ☐ deploy 62
- ☐ deportation 102
- ☐ deprecate 186
- ☐ deprivation 226
- ☐ deputy 394
- ☐ deregulate 180
- ☐ derelict 388
- ☐ deride 182
- ☐ derision 104
- ☐ derisive 424
- ☐ derive 26

Word	Page
derogatory	142
descendant	82
despicable	424
despondent	424
destined	306
destitute	144
destitution	392
detain	342
detect	38
detention	372
deter	46
deteriorate	188
detest	26
detonate	62
detour	228
detract	48
detriment	394
detrimental	142
devastate	206
devastation	112
deviate	48
deviation	394
devious	150
devoid	298
devout	288
dexterity	88
diabolic	424
diagnose	60
diagnosis	222
diameter	266
diatribe	410
dice	214
dictum	364
diffident	142
diffuse	332
dilapidated	144
dimension	264
diminish	48
diminutive	426
disarmament	386
disavow	342
disband	56
discard	186
discern	210
discernible	124
discharge	184
disciplinary	306
disconcerting	426
discontent	392
discourse	228
discreet	286
discrepancy	106
disdain	342
disgruntled	142
disguise	104
disgust	226
disheveled	300
dislodge	56
dismal	298
dismantle	184
dismiss	50
dismissive	426
disoriented	294
disparage	70
disparate	426
disparity	106
dispatch	62
dispel	184
dispensable	426
dispensation	366
disperse	56
dispirited	276
displace	184
disposal	226
disposition	248
disproportionately	414
dispute	110
disrupt	186
dissect	50
dissemble	342
disseminate	40
dissension	106
dissenting	426
dissertation	228
dissident	142
dissipate	356
dissolution	226
dissonance	392
dissuade	64
distend	184
distinct	290
distractedly	416
distraught	426
distressing	276
ditch	186
diverge	190
diverse	268
diversify	214
diversion	226
diversity	74
divert	188
dividend	230
divine	306
divulgence	392
docile	164
dogmatic	158
dormant	274
downplay	356
drab	150
drain	180
drastically	280
drawback	252
drawl	348
dreary	298
drench	180
dribble	348
droll	452
dub	212
dubious	134
dues	230
dupe	58
duplicate	32
duplicity	88
durability	92
duration	90
dutifully	282
dwindle	48
dynasty	398

E

Word	Page
ebb	238
ebullience	88
echelon	92
eclipse	48
ecstatic	134
edible	312
edify	320
eerie	150
efficacious	284
efficacy	98
effigy	258
elaborate	174
electoral	412
elevation	240
elicit	26
eligible	290
elimination	104
elocution	86
elongate	172
eloquent	156
elucidate	348
elude	50
elusive	162
emaciated	144
emanate	332
emancipate	332
embargo	242
embark	190
embedded	164
embezzle	190
emblazon	188
embody	190
embolden	190
embrace	190
embroil	332
embryo	378
emigrate	178
eminence	86
empathic	276
empathize	190
emphatic	276
empirically	436
empower	190
emulate	38
enact	32
encapsulate	182
encompass	62
encroach	46
encrypt	64
encumber	332

Word	Page
endemic	140
endorse	36
endow	322
endowment	74
enforce	194
enforcement	74
engender	194
engrossed	134
engulf	194
enhance	34
enlighten	30
enormous	284
enroll	194
ensue	194
entail	182
entice	38
enticement	250
entity	118
entreaty	398
entrench	332
entrepreneur	240
entrust	182
enumerate	334
enunciate	42
envoy	394
enzyme	224
epicenter	224
epidemic	140
epiphany	404
epitaph	398
epitomize	28
equilibrium	404
equity	256
equivalent	128
equivocal	300
equivocate	332
eradicate	56
erode	344
erratic	142
erroneous	142
erudite	436
erudition	220
erupt	204
eschew	322
esoteric	438
espionage	374
esteem	208
ethical	276
eulogize	324
eulogy	102
euphoric	440
evacuate	184
evade	68
evaporate	208
evict	184
evoke	212
evolve	204
exacerbate	56
exasperate	194
excavate	40
excel	206
exclusive	136
excruciatingly	162
execute	346
exemplary	126
exemplify	210
exempt	422
exert	212
exhilaration	88
exhort	36
exhortation	260
exodus	112
exonerate	64
exorbitant	422
exorcise	344
exorcism	104
expand	172
expansively	282
expedient	442
expedite	34
expel	184
expenditure	228
expertise	220
expiate	334
expire	202
explicit	284
exploit	344
exploratory	272
exponential	310
expulsion	368
expunge	344
exquisite	130
exterminate	180
extermination	368
externalize	334
extinct	274
extinction	74
extol	38
extort	180
extract	180
extradite	346
extrapolate	344
extraterrestrial	422
extravagant	422
extricate	344
extrinsic	128
exuberant	134
exult	334

F

Word	Page
fabricate	32
facade	80
facet	80
facetious	164
facilitate	34
faction	114
faculty	362
fad	232
fallacy	104
fallible	294
famine	238
famished	454
fanatically	422
farce	120
fastidious	442
fatality	386
fatally	412
faze	350
feasible	286
feat	78
feign	26
felicitous	442
felicity	118
felony	374
ferocious	144
fertility	236
fervent	422
fervor	364
fetter	64
feud	110
fiasco	110
fidelity	88
fiendish	446
filthy	144
fiscal	154
flabbergasted	306
flagrant	144
flamboyantly	152
flattery	102
flaunt	44
flawed	412
flawless	458
flimsy	158
flourish	214
fluctuate	28
foil	338
foist	338
foliage	236
foment	350
footage	92
foray	398
forebode	172
forensic	436
forfeit	202
forgery	96
forgo	28
formidable	294
fortification	388
fortify	34
fortitude	390
fortress	390
fortuitously	446
founder	72
fragility	258
frail	298
frantic	422
fraternity	368
fraud	374
fraudulent	162
fraught	158

Word	Page
☐ frazzle	356
☐ freight	364
☐ frenetic	134
☐ frigid	452
☐ frisk	28
☐ frivolous	292
☐ frugal	132
☐ fuel	172
☐ fugitive	82
☐ full-fledged	288
☐ fumble	206
☐ furlough	388
☐ furtive	434
☐ futile	124

G

Word	Page
☐ gadget	92
☐ gait	264
☐ gallant	414
☐ galvanize	34
☐ garble	214
☐ garner	40
☐ garnish	40
☐ gaudy	152
☐ gaunt	452
☐ genetically	272
☐ genial	286
☐ gimmick	120
☐ gist	76
☐ glean	352
☐ glib	440
☐ glitch	92
☐ gloat	64
☐ gluttonous	452
☐ gnaw	348
☐ gorge	216
☐ gradient	246
☐ graft	224
☐ grapple	212
☐ gratified	280
☐ gratuity	82
☐ gravity	78
☐ gregarious	154
☐ grievance	102
☐ grind	26
☐ grudge	90
☐ grudgingly	446
☐ grueling	144
☐ grumble	212
☐ guarantee	176
☐ guise	238
☐ gullible	152
☐ guzzle	204

H

Word	Page
☐ habitat	236
☐ habitual	306
☐ haggard	438
☐ haggle	64
☐ hallmark	242
☐ halt	172
☐ hamper	192
☐ haphazardly	152
☐ harbinger	80
☐ harness	210
☐ harrowing	440
☐ harry	336
☐ hassle	110
☐ hatch	202
☐ haughty	292
☐ haven	96
☐ havoc	112
☐ hazard	108
☐ heave	62
☐ hectic	298
☐ hedge	322
☐ heed	172
☐ heedless	152
☐ hefty	414
☐ heinous	432
☐ hemisphere	246
☐ hereditary	154
☐ heretic	390
☐ heritage	260
☐ hermit	398
☐ hibernate	202
☐ hilarious	286
☐ hinder	192
☐ hindrance	108
☐ hindsight	116
☐ hoard	356
☐ hoax	90
☐ hobble	352
☐ holistic	414
☐ homage	102
☐ homogeneous	154
☐ hostile	290
☐ hover	212
☐ hub	96
☐ huddle	352
☐ humiliate	196
☐ hunch	252
☐ hurtle	70
☐ hybrid	274
☐ hygiene	222
☐ hygienic	154
☐ hype	94
☐ hypnosis	226
☐ hypnotize	324
☐ hypothesis	364
☐ hypothesize	324
☐ hypothetical	272

I

Word	Page
☐ icon	366
☐ identical	458
☐ idiosyncrasy	248
☐ idiosyncratic	416
☐ idyllic	310
☐ ignite	352
☐ ignominious	448
☐ illiberal	448
☐ illicit	298
☐ illustrious	156
☐ immaculate	144
☐ imminent	132
☐ immunity	98
☐ impair	196
☐ impalpable	426
☐ impartiality	254
☐ impasse	108
☐ impeachment	370
☐ impeccable	146
☐ impede	336
☐ impediment	108
☐ impending	132
☐ imperative	274
☐ imperious	426
☐ impermeable	426
☐ impersonal	428
☐ impervious	132
☐ impetus	260
☐ implacable	428
☐ implant	30
☐ implement	32
☐ implicate	202
☐ implicit	166
☐ implore	36
☐ imposing	412
☐ imposition	244
☐ impound	356
☐ impoverish	322
☐ impregnable	428
☐ improvise	174
☐ imprudent	152
☐ impudent	428
☐ impulse	256
☐ impulsive	306
☐ impunity	374
☐ impurity	398
☐ inadvertently	152
☐ inane	278
☐ inanimate	276
☐ inaugurate	32
☐ inauguration	242
☐ incapacitate	206
☐ incarnation	392
☐ incense	262
☐ incentive	80
☐ inception	228
☐ incessant	146
☐ incidence	218
☐ incinerate	352
☐ incipient	432
☐ incisive	438
☐ incite	36
☐ inclement	164
☐ inclusive	136
☐ incoherent	146
☐ incongruous	428

☐ inconsequential	428	☐ insignia	398	**J K**	
☐ incredulous	278	☐ insinuation	230	☐ jaded	442
☐ incremental	432	☐ insipid	430	☐ jeer	182
☐ incriminate	194	☐ insolent	430	☐ jeopardize	196
☐ incubator	226	☐ insolvent	430	☐ jeopardy	108
☐ inculcate	30	☐ instigate	36	☐ jest	100
☐ incumbent	412	☐ instill	194	☐ jiggle	206
☐ incur	70	☐ insubstantial	430	☐ jilt	352
☐ indebted	432	☐ insular	158	☐ jinx	78
☐ indelible	430	☐ insulate	28	☐ jostle	322
☐ indemnity	374	☐ insurgent	432	☐ jubilant	286
☐ indicative	156	☐ insurmountable	430	☐ jubilee	398
☐ indictment	370	☐ insurrection	384	☐ judicious	290
☐ indigenous	126	☐ intact	458	☐ juggle	58
☐ indignant	432	☐ intake	232	☐ jumbled	306
☐ indiscretion	88	☐ intangible	146	☐ juncture	120
☐ indiscriminate	430	☐ integral	158	☐ jurisdiction	370
☐ indispensable	270	☐ integrate	182	☐ juror	370
☐ indoctrinate	30	☐ integration	94	☐ justify	72
☐ indolence	88	☐ integrity	254	☐ juvenile	444
☐ induce	182	☐ intercept	336	☐ keepsake	236
☐ inducement	266	☐ interject	68	☐ kindred	448
☐ inept	136	☐ interminable	414	☐ knack	78
☐ inert	294	☐ intermittently	146	**L**	
☐ inertia	390	☐ interrogate	346	☐ lackluster	162
☐ inevitable	274	☐ intervene	44	☐ lambaste	52
☐ infancy	234	☐ intervention	240	☐ lament	330
☐ infatuated	134	☐ intimate	288	☐ languid	442
☐ infectious	140	☐ intimidated	158	☐ languishing	160
☐ infer	40	☐ intolerant	278	☐ lanky	306
☐ infested	140	☐ intoxication	252	☐ lapse	360
☐ infighting	384	☐ intractable	278	☐ larceny	374
☐ infiltrate	336	☐ intrepid	430	☐ latent	126
☐ infirmity	222	☐ intricate	278	☐ latitude	364
☐ inflamed	432	☐ intrigue	200	☐ laudable	156
☐ inflammation	376	☐ intriguing	438	☐ laureate	394
☐ influx	76	☐ intrinsic	126	☐ lavish	310
☐ infraction	372	☐ introvert	252	☐ lax	298
☐ infringement	106	☐ intrusive	278	☐ ledger	398
☐ infusion	232	☐ intuitive	438	☐ leeway	404
☐ ingenious	290	☐ inundate	360	☐ leftover	236
☐ ingenuity	254	☐ invalid	278	☐ legislate	346
☐ ingratiate	182	☐ invaluable	284	☐ legislature	370
☐ inhabitant	236	☐ invariably	278	☐ legitimacy	370
☐ inherent	126	☐ invert	206	☐ legitimate	290
☐ inhibit	338	☐ inveterate	446	☐ lenient	150
☐ inhibition	390	☐ invigorate	34	☐ lethal	300
☐ inhospitable	278	☐ invincible	146	☐ lethargic	152
☐ initially	300	☐ invoke	60	☐ leverage	404
☐ inject	204	☐ irascible	436	☐ levitate	322
☐ inmate	388	☐ irate	280	☐ levity	256
☐ innate	278	☐ iridescent	448	☐ liability	94
☐ innocuous	156	☐ irk	356	☐ liaison	218
☐ innuendo	230	☐ irrational	280	☐ libel	94
☐ inoculate	204	☐ irrelevant	280	☐ liken	174
☐ inquisitive	148	☐ irreparably	162	☐ limb	226
☐ insatiable	148	☐ irresolute	280	☐ lineage	234
☐ inscription	364	☐ irrevocable	448	☐ linger	68
☐ inscrutable	124	☐ irrigation	238		
☐ insidious	430				

☐ linkage	404	☐ meticulous	142	☐ nimble	450
☐ liquidate	28	☐ microbe	224	☐ nominally	302
☐ litigate	326	☐ microscopically	448	☐ nonchalant	164
☐ litigation	370	☐ migraine	376	☐ notable	148
☐ lobby	320	☐ migrate	178	☐ notoriously	454
☐ logistically	416	☐ migration	404	☐ novelty	260
☐ longevity	98	☐ migratory	306	☐ novice	84
☐ loom	210	☐ milestone	266	☐ nucleus	362
☐ loophole	244	☐ mimicry	218	☐ nudge	204
☐ loot	336	☐ mirage	258	☐ nullify	54
☐ loquacious	440	☐ miscellaneous	302		
☐ lousy	296	☐ misgiving	102	**O**	
☐ lucrative	124	☐ mishap	386	☐ obfuscate	330
☐ luminary	240	☐ misnomer	120	☐ obligatory	166
☐ lunar	308	☐ mock	26	☐ oblique	454
☐ lurch	328	☐ modicum	240	☐ obliterate	332
☐ lure	250	☐ modulate	44	☐ oblivion	254
☐ lurid	162	☐ molecule	396	☐ oblivious	166
☐ lurk	328	☐ mollify	44	☐ obnoxious	292
		☐ molt	344	☐ obscure	300
M		☐ momentous	164	☐ obscurity	250
☐ magnetism	250	☐ momentum	76	☐ obsequious	160
☐ malady	376	☐ monarch	394	☐ obsessive	414
☐ malevolent	292	☐ monopolize	202	☐ obsolete	280
☐ malice	254	☐ monopoly	240	☐ obstinate	132
☐ malign	360	☐ monotonously	304	☐ obstruct	192
☐ malignant	442	☐ moot	454	☐ obtrusive	454
☐ malleability	400	☐ morale	80	☐ obtuse	458
☐ malleable	448	☐ morbid	150	☐ occidental	124
☐ mandatory	268	☐ morose	442	☐ odious	454
☐ maneuver	388	☐ morsel	238	☐ offshoot	92
☐ mangle	356	☐ mortality	98	☐ omen	78
☐ manifest	124	☐ mortgage	364	☐ ominous	454
☐ manipulate	32	☐ mortify	196	☐ omniscient	146
☐ mar	196	☐ mount	324	☐ onerous	450
☐ marginally	126	☐ muffled	440	☐ ongoing	412
☐ massacre	388	☐ multitude	258	☐ onrush	386
☐ materialize	190	☐ mundane	412	☐ onset	76
☐ matriculate	320	☐ municipality	362	☐ onslaught	112
☐ matrimony	234	☐ munificent	454	☐ onus	374
☐ maxim	116	☐ murky	448	☐ opaque	304
☐ mayhem	108	☐ muster	38	☐ opposable	308
☐ meager	130	☐ mutate	344	☐ oppress	46
☐ meander	28	☐ mutation	224	☐ optimum	288
☐ meddle	28	☐ mutinous	434	☐ opulent	454
☐ mediate	188	☐ mutter	58	☐ orchestrate	32
☐ mediator	232	☐ myriad	74	☐ ordeal	120
☐ medieval	272			☐ ordinance	104
☐ mediocre	304	**N**		☐ ornithological	436
☐ meditate	188	☐ naive	296	☐ orthodontist	378
☐ meekly	132	☐ namely	300	☐ ostensible	126
☐ memento	116	☐ narrowly	454	☐ ostracize	52
☐ menace	114	☐ naturalization	234	☐ oust	184
☐ menacingly	296	☐ negate	356	☐ outage	106
☐ menial	150	☐ negligent	150	☐ outcast	232
☐ mentor	84	☐ neural	412	☐ outcry	368
☐ merge	198	☐ neurologist	378	☐ outrage	368
☐ mesmerize	174	☐ neutrality	384	☐ outright	272
☐ metabolize	202	☐ niche	246	☐ overdue	270
☐ metaphor	222	☐ niggle	330	☐ overly	280

Word	Page
override	338
overrun	208
oversight	218
overture	366

P

Word	Page
pageant	218
palatable	154
palate	238
pallid	450
paltry	308
pamper	30
panacea	378
pandemic	140
pandemonium	108
paragon	220
paralysis	224
parameter	220
paramount	122
parasite	224
pare	330
parry	356
pasture	246
patent	266
paternity	76
pathetic	298
patriot	366
patronage	220
paucity	362
pawn	68
pedantic	146
pedestrian	308
peer	84
penchant	100
pendulum	258
penetrate	200
penitent	444
perceptible	148
perception	74
percolate	348
perennial	274
perfunctory	150
perilous	438
perimeter	264
periphery	404
perish	62
perjury	374
perk	94
permeate	210
pernicious	438
perpetrate	202
perpetrator	372
persecute	338
persecution	386
perseverance	250
persist	34
personable	282
perspective	74
pertinent	288
perturb	328

Word	Page
peruse	30
pervade	348
pervasive	140
pester	330
pesticide	238
petrified	160
petulant	292
phase	80
phenomenal	450
philanthropy	80
pilfer	342
pinnacle	378
pinpoint	156
pique	30
pitfall	378
pivot	378
placate	44
placid	288
plagiarism	264
plagiarize	30
plague	50
plaintiff	370
platitude	220
plausible	276
plea	372
plead	346
pledge	198
pliable	286
plight	108
plot	384
plummet	30
plunder	336
poach	200
poignant	292
polarization	120
pollination	366
polytheistic	308
pompous	310
ponder	334
ponderous	160
possessed	290
posterity	380
posthumously	414
posture	86
potent	418
potential	268
pragmatic	164
precarious	134
precede	212
precedence	258
precedent	80
precept	104
precinct	400
precipitate	318
precipitation	380
precipitous	434
preclude	334
preclusion	380
precursor	378
predator	380

Word	Page
predatory	434
predicament	108
predilection	380
predominate	174
preemptive	418
preferential	418
prelude	80
premises	118
premium	230
premonition	380
preoccupation	252
prerequisite	78
prerogative	120
prescient	418
prescribe	334
preservation	76
prestige	86
presumptuous	434
pretense	238
pretentious	434
pretext	118
prevail	40
prevalence	380
prevaricate	334
prevarication	380
primate	238
pristine	146
privilege	218
probationary	420
probe	200
proceeds	228
proclaim	196
proclivity	248
procrastinate	356
procure	70
prod	352
prodigious	420
prodigy	84
profane	420
profess	196
profound	122
profuse	420
progeny	380
prognosis	100
project	72
projection	382
proliferate	332
prolific	124
prolonged	420
promiscuous	420
promulgate	332
prone	268
propagate	40
propagation	382
propensity	100
prophecy	382
prophetic	420
propitious	282
proponent	82
proposition	362

Word	Page
proprietor	234
propriety	364
prosecute	326
prosecutor	82
prostrate	166
protagonist	382
protrusion	382
provident	420
provincial	420
provision	114
provisional	420
provoke	208
proximity	90
prudence	86
prune	330
pseudoscience	400
psychic	276
psychologically	276
pulverize	338
pundit	82
pungent	438
purge	52
purvey	322

Q

Word	Page
quadruple	358
quaint	310
qualm	224
quandary	118
quantum	406
quarantine	98
quell	48
quench	48
quirk	254
quiver	206
quorum	406
quota	94

R

Word	Page
ramification	120
rampage	114
rampant	438
rancor	406
rankle	328
ransack	62
ransom	406
rapacious	438
rapport	364
rapprochement	388
rash	296
ratify	200
ratio	238
rationale	216
ravage	336
reap	204
rebate	176
rebel	54
rebellion	386
rebuff	50
rebuke	52

Word	Page
rebut	52
rebuttal	380
recant	338
recapitulate	178
recede	340
receptive	282
recipient	82
reciprocate	176
recklessly	296
reclaim	70
recluse	84
reclusive	158
reconcile	176
reconciliation	382
recoup	40
recourse	264
rectify	36
recuperate	40
recur	70
recurrent	456
redeem	176
redress	178
redundant	294
referendum	382
refurbish	178
refute	50
regale	350
regime	112
rehash	30
reimburse	176
reinforce	178
reinstate	326
reiterate	42
rejuvenate	178
relegate	184
relentless	160
relinquish	340
remedy	98
reminisce	70
remit	176
remuneration	242
rendition	262
renege	54
renounce	54
renunciation	382
reparation	382
repatriate	52
repeal	114
repel	180
repercussion	114
replenish	70
replete	456
replicate	122
repose	400
repository	246
reprehensible	450
reprieve	340
reprimand	52
reprisal	114
repudiate	338

Word	Page
repulse	54
requisite	78
rescind	342
resent	196
reside	212
resonance	400
resonant	312
respiratory	274
respite	262
resplendent	148
restoration	382
restraint	216
resume	360
resurgence	384
resurrection	384
resuscitate	326
retain	174
retaliation	384
retard	46
retentive	416
reticent	306
retort	182
retribution	114
retrieve	172
retroactively	164
revamp	326
revel	54
reverberate	358
reversal	216
revert	176
revile	340
revise	178
revitalize	178
revoke	54
rhetorically	440
rife	140
rigorous	128
robust	148
roundabout	162
rout	56
rowdy	160
rubble	112
rudimentary	302
rumble	210
rundown	242
rustic	312
ruthless	296

S

Word	Page
sabotage	406
salient	164
sanctity	400
sanctuary	392
sanitation	400
satirize	340
saturate	204
savor	100
savvy	400
scapegoat	406
scarce	130

Word	Page	Word	Page	Word	Page
scatter	198	somber	160	strut	350
scavenge	346	sophisticated	130	stubborn	132
schematic	304	sovereignty	394	stump	50
scheme	406	sparse	312	stunt	336
schism	388	spasm	222	stupendous	304
scour	346	spawn	322	sturdily	456
scrabble	346	specify	214	stymie	338
scrawl	70	specimen	74	suave	428
scruple	102	specter	244	subdued	152
scrupulous	140	speculation	94	subjugate	46
scrutinize	208	spell	358	sublime	130
scuttle	68	spillage	106	submerge	208
seamless	268	splinter	408	submissive	286
secede	340	splurge	358	subordinate	66
seclude	52	spontaneous	270	subsequent	166
sectarian	450	sporadic	146	subsidence	408
sedentary	162	spouse	234	subsidize	36
seditious	450	sprawl	204	subsistence	236
segregation	406	spree	408	substantiate	42
seismology	406	sprout	38	subtle	130
semblance	266	spur	362	subversive	448
senile	456	spurious	150	subvert	46
serene	158	spurn	174	succinct	136
servitude	400	squabble	60	succulent	308
setback	362	squander	66	succumb	66
shackle	406	squeamish	160	suffocate	180
shatter	214	squint	358	suffrage	376
sheer	456	stabilize	200	sullen	442
showdown	408	stagger	194	sumptuous	456
shrewd	162	stagnant	272	superficial	448
shroud	358	stake	240	superfluous	134
shun	64	stale	280	supplant	198
simulate	208	stalemate	108	supplement	34
simulation	410	stalwart	428	suppress	46
simultaneous	310	stammer	58	surge	186
sinister	138	state-of-the-art	416	surmise	42
skeptical	122	static	302	surmount	196
skyrocket	186	stationary	302	surpass	196
slam	64	statistically	304	surplus	230
slash	340	status quo	264	surreptitiously	128
sleek	456	statutory	436	surrogate	84
sluggish	272	staunch	428	surveillance	388
slump	320	stealth	400	susceptible	130
smear	358	steer	212	suspend	54
smother	180	stem	216	sustain	34
smuggle	202	sterile	302	sustainable	414
snare	212	stern	296	swamp	402
snarl	350	stifle	46	swarm	350
snatch	340	stigma	262	sway	408
sneer	182	stimulate	172	swerve	358
snide	456	stipend	408	swill	350
snip	340	stipulate	176	swindle	58
snitch	340	stolid	428	synonymous	308
snub	352	stowage	246	synthesize	198
soar	186	straddle	350		
sobriety	260	stray	174	**T**	
sojourn	354	streak	358	taciturn	440
solace	118	strenuous	296	tackle	318
solicit	346	stringent	128	tactics	258
solidarity	394	strive	358	tally	66

Term	Page
tamper	58
tangle	354
tantamount	128
tantrum	222
tariff	408
tarnish	70
taunt	360
taut	456
tedious	296
tedium	256
teeming	166
teeter	66
temperament	248
tenacious	148
tenet	262
tentative	270
tenuous	456
tenure	90
tepid	152
terrestrial	154
terse	458
testimonial	408
thesis	228
thread	256
threshold	256
thrift	236
thrifty	132
thrive	26
throb	360
throng	84
thrust	354
thwart	56
tinge	220
toll	386
topple	214
torment	50
torrid	154
torture	346
tout	66
toxic	274
traffic	322
trait	248
trance	118
tranquil	284
transaction	244
transcend	192
transcendent	288
transfusion	98
transgression	106
transient	126
translucent	458
transmit	40
transparent	304
transpose	192
traumatic	154
traverse	66
travesty	220
treacherous	150
treason	384
tremendous	310
tribally	418
tribute	260
trigger	36
trite	296
triumph	408
trivial	294
truancy	116
truculent	436
truncate	330
tumor	222
turmoil	384
tyranny	402

U

Term	Page
ubiquitous	124
ulterior	128
ultimately	300
ultimatum	116
unabashedly	432
unanimously	304
uncouth	160
uncover	192
undergo	32
undermine	60
underscore	42
undertake	192
unearth	192
unfold	192
unprecedented	144
unravel	38
unruly	292
unscathed	144
unsettle	192
untenable	434
upend	348
upheaval	116
uphold	174
upscale	450
upshot	408
upstage	458
upstart	234
urbane	284
usher	214
usurp	354
utility	230

V

Term	Page
vacillate	354
valiant	158
validate	42
validity	96
vandalism	110
vanquish	318
veer	66
vehement	422
velocity	402
venerable	416
venomous	442
vent	118
venue	96
veracity	256
verbose	440
verdict	76
verge	410
verification	256
verify	42
vernacular	266
versatile	290
vestige	402
veto	66
viability	78
vibrant	166
vicarious	268
vicinity	96
vicious	290
vie	60
vigilant	458
vigorous	136
vilify	348
vindicate	42
virtually	268
virtuous	284
virulent	442
vociferous	440
void	450
volatile	450
volition	402
voluptuous	458
voraciously	162
vulgar	294
vulnerable	130

W Y Z

Term	Page
wage	360
waive	198
wanton	430
warden	234
waver	194
waylay	328
weather	66
whim	252
widespread	122
wince	68
windfall	260
withhold	214
wrangle	348
wreak	56
wreckage	112
wrench	62
wriggle	204
yardstick	228
zeal	86
zenith	90
zest	216

旺文社の英検対策書

試験まで

3ヶ月前なら

定番教材

出題傾向をしっかりつかめる英検対策の「王道」
英検過去6回全問題集
[過去問集] 1級～5級 ★別売CDあり

一次試験から面接まで英検のすべてがわかる！
英検総合対策教本
[参考書] 1級～5級 ★CD付

1ヶ月前なら

効率型

手っ取り早く「出た」問題を知る！
短期完成 英検3回過去問集
[過去問集] 準1級～5級 ★CD付

大問ごとに一次試験を短期集中攻略
DAILY英検集中ゼミ
[問題集+参考書] 1級～5級 ★CD付

二次試験まで完全収録！頻度順だからムダなく学習できる
英検でる順合格問題集
[問題集] 準1級～3級 ★CD付

7日前なら

速攻型

7日間でできる！一次試験対策のための模試タイプ問題集
7日間完成 英検予想問題ドリル
[模試] 1級～5級 ★CD付

単熟語

でる順だから早い・確実・使いやすい！
英検でる順パス単
1級～5級 ★無料音声ダウンロード付 ★別売「書き覚えノート」あり

単熟語

文章で／イラストで覚えるから記憶に残る！
英検 文で/絵で 覚える単熟語
1級～5級 ★CD付

二次試験

DVDで面接のすべてをつかむ！
英検二次試験・面接完全予想問題
1級～3級 ★CD・DVD付

このほかにも多数のラインナップを揃えております。

〒162-8680 東京都新宿区横寺町55　お客様相談窓口0120-326-615　**旺文社**
旺文社ホームページ http://www.obunsha.co.jp/

[英検1級 でる順パス単]　S6f005